634.0.2 ALD

FORESTRY COMMISSION BULLETIN 111

Forest Nursery Practice

Edited by
J. R. Aldhous and W. L. Mason

D1368273

LONDON: HMSO

ISBN 0 11 710323 3
FDC 232.32 : (410)

KEYWORDS:
Seed
Forest Nurseries
Forestry
Propagation

Enquiries relating to this publication
should be addressed to:
The Research Publications Officer,
The Forestry Authority, Research Division,
Alice Holt Lodge, Wrecclesham,
Farnham, Surrey GU10 4LH.

Front cover: Precision sowing into prepared beds
at Wykeham Nursery using a Summit precision
sower. *(39375)*

Contents

Appendices

Preface

This Bulletin is a revision of the first edition of Bulletin 43 *Nursery practice* published in 1972. That edition provided an introduction to nursery practice for managers, supervisors and students and had been in steady demand until it went out of print. The preparation of a second edition has provided the opportunity to bring its contents more into line with contemporary developments in forestry and nursery practice.

While the substantial programmes of upland afforestation of the 1970s and 80s have lessened in recent years, there has been an off-setting increased interest in planting at lower elevations and greater emphasis on planting stock for conservation of amenity and wildlife. At the same time, new developments in techniques – such as, for example, container-raised plant production – have widened the range of commercially viable production systems available to the nursery manager.

Possibly the most significant long-term development is the increasing availability of seed of superior performance potential, resulting from tree selection and breeding programmes. The large-scale vegetative propagation of plants raised from such seed marks the emergence of the forest nursery industry from being based solely on seed from wild populations to one where, increasingly, the products of genetic improvement will play an important part in forest composition.

Associated with increasing use of vegetatively propagated stock is the ability in the nursery to exercise greater control over the growing environment for plants, both through more sophisticated instrumentation, and through the ability of electronic data capture to provide information to managers in a way that had previously been thought totally impossible.

A development of a different sort is the recognition of the need to keep distinct the variety of seed sources of native Scots pine where these occur within the natural range of the species. Nevertheless, this and the increased use of vegetatively propagated plants from 'improved' seed have in common the need for high standards of nursery management and record keeping, to ensure plants are supplied true to name.

A further recent development has been a greater understanding of the physiological response of plants to handling in the critical period between lifting in the nursery and delivery to the forest.

A dilemma faced by the editors has been whether to mention proprietary products and firms. We concluded that it is more helpful to mention these where relevant, at the same time making it clear that no judgement is to be inferred where other similar products are available on the market. Mention in the text of the Bulletin does not imply endorsement of the particular product or company, nor does omission infer any criticism.

This second edition has been prepared along similar lines to the first edition, except that the authors of the individual chapters are named in the chapter headings. All contributors have been faced with the challenge of producing an informative introduction to their particular topic within the space contraints of a single volume. Where readers find they would like more detailed information, it is hoped that the references given will provide relevant sources.

Finally, most sincere thanks must be expressed to everyone who has contributed to the content of the revised Bulletin. This includes not only present staff in Forestry Commission and private nurseries, but also all those whose past work has provided the foundation of knowledge and practice on which present methods and understanding are based.

J. R. Aldhous
W. L. Mason

Forest Nursery Practice

Summary

This Bulletin, written by experts in their field, describes techniques involved in successful production of bare-rooted and cell- (small container-) grown stock of the tree species most widely planted in United Kingdom forestry. The subjects covered include: formation of new nurseries; maintenance of the fertility of existing nurseries; procurement of seed; production of seedlings and transplants; production of cell-grown planting stock; the role of mycorrhizas; vegetative propagation; irrigation; weed control; control of diseases and insect and other pests; plant storage and handling; legislation affecting nursery management. References are given to supplementary sources of information.

La Gestion des Pepinières Forestières

Résumé

Ce Bulletin, composé par des experts pertinents, décrit les techniques pour la production réussie des plants à racines nues et des plants en cellules (petits récipients) pour les espèces forestières plus plantées dans Le Royaume-Uni. Les sujets y compris sont: la formation des nouvelles pepinières; l'acquisition des graines; la production des semis et des plants repiqués; la production des plants en cellules (récipients); le rôle des mycorhizes; la propagation végétative; l'irrigation; le désherbage; la lutte contre des maladies, des insectes nuisibles et des autres déprédateurs; le stockage et la manutention des plants; et la législation à l'égard de la gestion des pepinières. Des références à des sources additionelles d'information sont pourvues.

Baumschulverfahren

Zusammenfassung

Dieses Bulletin, daß von Experten geschrieben wurde, beschreibt Techniken zur erfolgreichen Produktion von wurzelnackten und in Zellen (kleine Behälter) gezogenen Beständen der Baumart, die vorwiegend in UK Försten gepflanzt wird. Die behandelten Themen umfassen: Formierung neuer Baumschulen, Erhaltung der Ergiebigkeit bestehender Baumschulen, Beschaffung von Samen, Produktion von Sämlingen und Setzlingen, Produktion von in Zellen gezogenen Beständen, die Rolle von Mykorrhiza, vegetative Fortpflanzung, Unkrautkontrolle, Bekämpfung von Krankheiten, Insekten und anderen Schädlingen, Pflanzenlagerung und - handhabung, Gesetzgebung die den Baumschulbetrieb betrifft. Die Quellenangabe enthält weitere Informationsquellen.

List of Contributors

J. R. Aldhous

Former Head of Silviculture Division, The Forestry Commission. Author of Forestry Commission Bulletin 43 *Nursery practice* (1972).

W. L. Mason

Head of Silviculture (North) Branch, Research Division, The Forestry Authority.[1] (Previously Nursery Silviculturist[1])

P. G. Gosling

Head of Plant Production Branch, Research Division, The Forestry Authority.[2]

S. C. Gregory

Forest Pathologist, Research Division, The Forestry Authority.[1]

S. G. Heritage

Forest Entomologist, Research Division, The Forestry Authority.[1]

R. L. Jinks

Plant Production Branch, Research Division, The Forestry Authority.[2]

H. M. McKay

Plant Physiologist, Research Division, The Forestry Authority.[1]

A. C. Miller

Conservator, North Wales, The Forestry Authority; formerly, Manager, Delamere Nursery, Forest Enterprise.

J. L. Morgan

Silviculturist, Research Division, The Forestry Authority.[1]

M. F. Proe

Plants Division, Macaulay Land Use Research Institute, Craigiebuckler, Aberdeen.

D. G. Pyatt

Wildlife Ecology Branch, Research Division, The Forestry Authority.[1]

[1] Northern Research Station, Roslin, Midlothian, EH25 9SY.

[2] Alice Holt Lodge, Wrecclesham, Farnham, Surrey, GU10 4LH.

R. G. Strouts

Forest Pathologist, Research Division, The Forestry Authority.[2]

C. Walker

Head of Mycorrhizal Research Unit, Research Division, The Forestry Authority.[1]

C. T. Wheeler

Department of Botany, The University of Glasgow.

D. R. Williamson

Forest District Manager, South Downs Forest District, Forest Enterprise; formerly, Silviculturist, Research Division, The Forestry Authority.[2]

[1] Northern Research Station, Roslin, Midlothian, EH25 9SY.

[2] Alice Holt Lodge, Wrecclesham, Farnham, Surrey, GU10 4LH.

Chapter 1
Nursery policy and planning

J. R. Aldhous

Introduction

Forest nurseries are an essential part of forestry in Britain. Each year for the last 20 years, between 80 and 120 million plants have been sent from British forest nurseries to extend or restock privately and nationally owned forest. In addition, in many years considerable numbers of trees have been exported to other EEC countries.

In the immediate postwar period, afforestation of bare land dominated planting activities. In the last decade however, areas being restocked annually have increased substantially. In the 1990/91 planting season, restocking accounted for 49% of the demand for plants and is likely to continue to increase in scale. The ratio of broadleaves to conifers is likely to increase in the short term in response to availability of better quality land for planting, and increased public interest in woodland landscapes and wildlife habitat.

Forest nurseries are certain to continue to be the main source of new trees for future British woodland, for although natural regeneration is the recognised way of restocking in many parts of the world, in Britain, it cannot be relied on. Also, forest managers may wish to replant either with more productive species, or with strains of the same species of improved quality and vigour raised either in the open nursery, or by one of the more intensive methods described in Chapters 9 and 10. There is, in addition, increased interest in native species and in local seed sources of native species.

In the 1950s and 1960s an intensive programme of research resulted in the cost of planting stock falling from about 25% of plantation establishment costs to about 12½%; more recently, this cost relationship has been maintained for similar bare-rooted stock. However, stock resulting from tree-improvement programmes, especially where this has been bulked up by vegetative propagation, is more expensive to produce, this increased cost being justified commercially by expectations of enhanced growth rates and superior form in plantations (Gill, 1983; Lee, 1990).

Purpose of this Bulletin

This Bulletin is intended as a ready reference for the nursery owner or manager, giving guidance on most points of practice relating to the raising of young trees for planting in the forest, and describing some underlying principles on which practice is based.

It is written on the assumption that the policy of the nursery manager is to raise good quality plants at the lowest cost. Little allowance is made for the estate owner or the amenity group who want to raise plants on a small scale on ground that may not be well suited to the best growth of young trees. Such owners are advised to follow the recommendations in this Bulletin as far as they apply; the stocks raised will probably grow more slowly while in the nursery, but should be suitable for woodland or forest planting. They will probably have cost more to produce than in a large nursery, though not necessarily more than the purchase price from a reputable nursery manager. The owner will have had the convenience of having his plants available whenever he can lift them, and also the satisfaction of seeing them grow.

No attempt is made to describe practice in raising ornamental varieties of trees or the production of large trees for planting as specimens or for landscape work.

Throughout this Bulletin, quantities are given in metric units. A table of conversion factors to imperial measure is given in Appendix V.

1.1 Whether to start a nursery

1.1.1 Market prospects

Forest nurseries may be managed either to produce plants for sale on the open market, or to produce plants to meet a previously known commitment, whether a long-term planting programme or a contract. Many nurseries produce for both outlets, and thereby have the income and security from regular contract sales as well as the opportunity to increase these sales and profits by selling the rest of their stock on the open market.

However, careful research into market prospects and a rigorous investment appraisal must always be undertaken before deciding to open a nursery for commercial production.

Figure 1.1 shows the annual area planted by private woodland owners in Great Britain over the period 1971–92 using figures from Forestry Commission Annual Reports.

The demand in this period for plants for afforesting privately owned bare land reflects the fiscal provisions incorporated in Government budget legislation and the level of grant aid for planting. For example, fiscal changes in 1972 and in 1988 both led to a sharp drop in demand for plants for bare land afforestation, with a period between 1978 and 1988 of sustained increase in planting. More recently, incentives have been increased for planting on farm land through 'Better land' supplements (Forestry Commission, 1993).

The area of privately owned woodland restocked after felling has been much less each year than the annual area of new planting; also, it has fluctuated less over the same period. It has increased slowly during

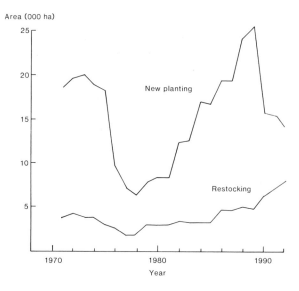

Figure 1.1 Private forestry new planting and restocking, 1971–1992.

the last decade and will continue to increase as forests planted during the last 50 years are cut and replanted, ultimately reaching at least twice the present annual rate.

1.1.2 The nursery site

The features of a good nursery site for producing bare-rooted stock are described at length in Chapters 2 and 3. If any of the more important of these are ignored, costs of production are likely to be higher and growth slower than on good sites.

Where production is to be exclusively of stock in containers, such as Japanese paper pots, 'rootrainers', plugs, etc., the main requirements are reduced to mains power, good quality water, a level site and ready access.

1.1.3 Size of nursery

The simplest guide to size in relation to output is that 1 ha of nursery area gross (i.e. including paths, fallow, etc), is required for every 180 000 to 250 000 forest planting stock to be produced. It is seldom economical to start a nursery for less than a regular annual production of 250 000 planting stock.

Seedbed area

For every unit of area cultivated, approximately 60% is sown; the remaining area is taken up by alleys between beds. The number of seedlings produced from fully stocked conifer seedbeds range from 400 to 1000 per square metre (nett sown area) according to species and season; columns (8) and (9) of Table 6.1 (in Chapter 6) 'Seed quality, sowing density and expected yields: major conifers' give average conifer stock in good nurseries, while Table 6.2 'Seed quality and seedling production: broadleaves' gives data for broadleaved species. NB: space for alleys between beds has to be added if using the figures in these tables to calculate gross areas for any sowing programme.

Transplant area

In most nurseries, transplanting is by machine, setting out five or six long lines of plants between alleys. This layout allows subsequent tractor-based operations such as pesticide applications, undercutting/wrenching and mechanical lifting. According to the initial spacing of plants, between 75 and 120 plants per square metre (*including alleys*) must be allowed when planning transplanting areas.

Hand lining out, using boards (e.g. the 2 m Paterson board) is still practised locally. This may either reproduce the pattern of lines similar to that from machine lining out or the boards may be set side by side to make breaks of plants the length of the board and many board-widths wide. In the latter case, the benefit of any more economical use of land has to be set against more costly hand work applying sprays during the season, and hand lifting at the end of the year.

The relationship of spacing of plants in and between rows is shown in Table 6.7. When planning nursery areas, it is advisable to plan for 70% usable plants in the lines.

Fallow land

Between a quarter and a third of the cultivated area should be planned to be under fallow or a green crop at the end of the sowing season. There are many calls on fallow land. These include: summer lining out of rising 2-year-old plants, plants from cold stores or from vegetative propagation houses; completion of a substantial proportion of the dormant season lining out programme before Christmas (some foresters try to complete half by this time); throwing up of seedbeds in the autumn or winter in preparation for the spring; holding over for another year surplus seedlings or transplants.

If it is anticipated that there will be regular and substantial calls on fallow ground for two or more of these reasons, the proportion of fallow land should be increased to 40% of the total cultivated area. When planning a nursery, it is far better to err on the generous side with the allowance of fallow land; the cost of maintaining surplus fallow is small and is a worthwhile insurance.

Uncultivated ground

The area occupied by permanent roads, buildings, hedges, dumps of materials, machine parks and other permanently uncultivated areas within the nursery perimeter, taken together, usually amount to between 20 and 30% of the total nursery area. Separate, specifically calculated, additional allowances should be made for access to plant cold stores and for safety zones around pesticide stores and fuel stores.

1.2 Planning production

Forest nursery work requires to be planned well in advance, by a person thoroughly experienced in *forest* nursery work. The benefits of such experience can be expected not only in any advance planning, but also in the execution of plans and in timing them in relation to the day-to-day conditions of the nursery.

Nursery planning, whether of the requirements of manpower and machines or of plants and materials, can be simplified if records are available from which can be estimated:

- the annual demand for planting stock, by species, provenance, age and size;

- the year-by-year saleable out-turn from seedbeds and lines, noting also wastage factors (percentage of plants that are culled as being below specification, diseased, etc.), and unsold plants;
- the cost, labour and time requirements of various operations.

Such records should assist the nursery manager to determine his future programme, give him some idea of what margins of error he should allow for seasonal variations in yield and provide the basis for identifying where he should give priority in any attempts to improve efficiency/reduce unit costs.

1.3 Records

Nursery records can be divided into those required by law and those optional records whose value lies in the insight they provide to the nursery manager about his operations.

The financial records necessary to prepare accounts so as to meet current company law, PAYE and VAT requirements are not discussed in this Bulletin.

Obligations under the 'Forest Reproductive Material Regulations' are set out in Chapter 15, section 15.1, and those relating to plant health in section 15.5. These include a requirement for nursery managers to keep reliable production records for all the species covered by the Regulations. By far the larger part of such records needs to be kept for the value of the information that is provided for nursery management, irrespective of FRM and plant health requirements.

1.3.1 Nursery management records

The first and most important preliminary is to decide why and how any given record is wanted, e.g. to provide a guide as to the financial and technical efficiency of the nursery, to provide the basis for stock control and sales or to meet statutory requirements for retention of records (e.g. VAT, Forest Reproductive Material, etc.). Records collected without a clear idea of their purpose are quite likely to have omitted vital points required in a later study.

Computer-based management and record-keeping systems are taking an increasingly important role in nursery management. They offer many possible aids to managers. There are several systems in use in horticultural nurseries. One which is specifically tailored to forest nursery production is produced by 'Growing Information Systems', Hyndland, Glasgow, G12 9JA. However, whatever system is installed, it must be readily adaptable to changing perceptions of need.

Management records whether manual or computer-based, can be divided up into:

- Plant production
  Details of seed origin/provenance; amount of seed sown; seedlings lifted; plants lined out; forest plants lifted; size, or proportions in size categories; cuttings inserted in vegetative propagation programmes; proportion rooted; proportion successfully repotted/transplanted to be suitable for forest planting; storage dates and conditions.
- Cash outgoings
  (a) *Recurring costs of materials:* fertilisers, seedbed cover, seed, fuel, pesticides, machinery maintenance and running costs, protective clothing, etc.
  (b) *Capital expenditure:* buildings, site improvements, equipment and machines with more than a 1 year life, etc.
  (c) *Manpower costs:* wages, salaries, contract payments for work done.
  (d) *Overheads:* rent/rates on premises, heating and lighting, insurance, interest on loans, etc., depreciation on capital items, VAT, etc.
- Operations
  (a) *Technical:* details of those operations and conditions in the nursery which may affect yields and help comparison of one year's results with another. These may best be kept in a diary; this should be divided by nursery sections so as to show readily the events during the season for each section.
  (b) *Legal:* details of applications of pesticides and similar operations, where records are required to be kept under pesticide legis-

lation. Records of stocks of species covered by the Forest Reproductive Material Regulations and for plant health obligations should be kept in such a way that the number and disposal of stock of each seed lot initially sown can be audited.

1.3.2 Stocktaking

This is a most important operation, normally falling due in late summer. For saleable plants, over-estimates of numbers can lead to over-selling and the need to buy in stock; under-estimates may lead to wastage. Both alternatives are likely to result in loss of profits.

Numbers of stock in the nursery not intended for sale in the current year are required for annual valuation/accounting purposes, as well as for showing whether the future production targets for the nursery are likely to be met.

In many cases, the nursery manager will know his stock very well and will know intuitively the average stocking in beds and lines; nevertheless, it is easy to misjudge. Objectively taken sample counts provide the basis for reliable short and long term records of production.

If time and effort are not to be wasted, any stocktaking system must be well designed statistically, in relation to the number and size of samples taken. Advice on sampling systems for stocktaking may be sought from the Forestry Authority, Northern Research Station, Roslin, Midlothian.

A perpetual problem is that nursery sale catalogues and stock forecasts often have to be prepared in mid-summer, at a time when many plants have still to put on a substantial part of their growth. The amount of this late growth is often critical in determining the size, grade or usability of the plants concerned.

Early assessments of potentially saleable stocks based on estimates of the percentage survival of the number of plants in the ground at the beginning of the growing season have subsequently to be reconciled with actual stocks shown from stocktaking.

Wherever computers with appropriate software are available, they can speed up the availability of stock estimates once the stocktaking counts have been made. When in doubt, nursery managers should enquire what is currently available for the computer system they have installed in the nursery.

1.3.3 Labelling in the nursery; nursery plans

Customers rely absolutely on the nursery manager to provide stock which is true to name; at the same time, nursery managers have a legal obligation to take all reasonable precautions to ensure that the stock offered is correctly described and stock sold is true to name. (See also Chapter 15, sections 15.1 and 15.8). It is strongly recommended that all blocks of plants growing in the nursery are both marked and mapped.

Labels, while essential, by themselves are not enough – there are many instances of these having been disturbed by passing machinery, visitors/vandals and, occasionally, animals and birds. Nursery section maps or plans should also be prepared, showing the position of each lot of seedlings or transplants, so that, should a label be lost or displaced, there is an indisputable record as to where any replacement label should go.

In transplant lines of similar species or different origins of the same species, it acts as a reminder to men lifting, if the change in identity is marked by a plant of a totally different genus. Lawson cypress makes a good marker plant.

All these efforts will be wasted if similar care is not exercised to maintain the identity of plants at all stages during handling and despatch.

1.4 Sale of plants

Plants may be offered for sale by advertising in any of the forestry and other journals reaching potential customers. At the same time, a price list or catalogue giving details of the available species, origins, sizes and prices of plants, must be ready by at least mid-summer. The list or catalogue has to be prepared, based on early season survival and growth as it appears in the nursery, on the assumption that plants will grow normally in the remainder of the season. Every encouragement should be given to prospective customers to see the growing stock in the nursery before placing orders.

1.4.1 Forestry Commission surplus plants

The Forestry Commission does not sell plants to private woodland owners; any surpluses from its production are offered to the forest nursery trade, to whom enquiries should be made.

1.4.2 Horticultural Trades Association

The Horticultural Trades Association has a Forestry Group currently with 32 forest nursery members, between them producing most of the UK forestry planting stock. The group regularly liaises with Government ministers and departments responsible for forestry policy, keeping to the fore, issues of concern to the forest nursery industry.

The group meets annually with the Forestry Commission and the Timber Growers Association to exchange information on current production and market trends. The group also prepares statistics of production by the private sector. At one time, the HTA acted as clearing house for surplus forestry plants but is no longer doing so.

Further details of the Forestry Group can be obtained from the Horticultural Trades Association, 19 High Street, Theale, Reading RG7 5AH.

1.4.3 Samples

Any enquirer wishing to purchase any substantial quantity of forest plants should ask for samples. The nursery manager should welcome requests for samples, and should take pains to include plants of the full range of the lot in question; if this is done, much unprofitable argument between the nursery manager and the purchaser about whether the plants sent were as advertised can be avoided. A sample of any lot should consist of at least 10 transplants, or 25 seedlings.

The purchaser should bed out sample plants so as to be able to compare them with the full consignment when received.

1.5 Quality of plants

Quality in the context of this Bulletin means the fitness of plants for planting in the forest or woodland, where the intensive after-planting care that can be provided in parks and gardens is not available.

Forest and woodland planting sites vary, both inherently in soil and climate, and through the scale and type of cultivation and pre-planting vegetation control. Foresters' demands may vary therefore, according to the circumstances of the site to be planted and to the season of the year. Within this range of demand, however, and given otherwise equal treatment, good quality plants have a better chance of becoming established and getting away to a good start than poor quality stock. Nursery managers' long-term reputation is based on their customers' perception of this quality of stock.

There are three main attributes of quality:

- inherent genetic quality;
- physical characteristics;
- physiological characteristics.

These result partly from the starting material (seed or cuttings), partly from the way plants are grown in the nursery and partly from the way plants are handled between commencement of lifting and final planting.

Much stock which was of good genetic and physical quality in the nursery has deteriorated to worthlessness through failure to ensure good treatment during lifting, storage and despatch (See Chapter 14).

Uniformity or otherwise of a batch of plants is an aspect of quality which can be improved by appropriate grading before despatch. See last paragraph of section 1.5.2 below.

1.5.1 Inherent genetic quality: seed origin and improved seed

Seed origins

Recommended seed origins for the species

most commonly planted in British woodlands are given in Forestry Commission Bulletin 66 *Choice of seed origins for the main forest species in Britain* (Lines, 1987).

Improved seed

Limited but increasing amounts of seed are becoming available from tested ('approved') and untested seed orchards, derived from selected superior ('plus') trees. Trees in tested orchards have undergone rigorous selection, breeding and field trial testing, so as to distinguish and retain trees whose quality derives principally from their superior heritable genetic make-up, discarding those whose quality derives from favourable local site conditions. For most 'untested' seed orchards, this process is still under way. See 'The choices and relative values of different seed sources', Chapter 2 in Forestry Commission Bulletin 83 *Seed manual for forest trees* (Faulkner, 1992); also further reading and references under Mason, W.L. *et al.*, and Rook, D., at the end of this chapter.

EEC legislation

Programmes of origin/provenance research, seed stand selection and tree improvement, when first started in Great Britain, were justified by their inherent potential value to national forestry. Subsequently, the same concepts have been adopted by the EEC and have been embodied in EEC legislation and national legislation described in Chapter 15 below.

The tree improvement programmes and legislation come together in that:

- the current register of seed stands and poplar stoolbeds;
- the current register of seed orchards; and
- the availability of small quantities of Sitka spruce seed from progeny-tested seed orchards for bulking by vegetative propagation;

all now operate within the framework of 'The Forest Reproductive Material Regulations, 1977'. The regulations apply both to bare-rooted stock and to container-grown stock used for forestry purposes.

What nursery managers have to do in response to the regulations is set out in Chapter 15, sections 15.1 to 15.3. See also the references at the end of that chapter.

1.5.2 Physical attributes of plant quality

These include:

- physical dimensions – height, root collar diameter and the ratio between them (i.e. sturdiness);
- morphology – stem form, branch habit, leader persistence, foliage condition, root development and shoot:root ratio; and
- nutrient status.

Height

Height of plants sent out for planting in the forest should exceed the minima given in Table 1.1. Height is here defined as the distance from the bud of the leading shoot to the root collar or, in the case of vegetatively propagated stock, from the leading bud to the point of root emergence nearest the leading bud.

Root collar diameter

The diameter of the stem at the root collar for plants of a given height depends primarily on the amount of growing space they have been given in the preceding growing season. However, the range of possible root collar diameters does differ from one species to another, and the commonly planted forest species can be grouped into four stem diameter classes shown in Table 1.1. Species in Class I are the most sturdy for a given height, while those in Class IV are slenderest.

For the species most commonly propagated vegetatively (Sitka spruce and hybrid larch), the stem diameter just above the point of root emergence nearest the leading bud should be substituted for root collar diameter.

Table 1.2 gives standards for minimum root collar diameters for various heights of trees when sent out bare-rooted for forest planting.

These standards agree closely with those satisfying the 'EEC standard' under the Forest Reproductive Material directive 71/161/EEC.

Table 1.1 Minimum height and stem diameter class of transplants for planting in the forest

Species	Minimum height (cm)	Stem diameter class*
Conifers		
Scots pine	15	I/II
Corsican pine	10	I
Lodgepole pine	15	II
European larch	20	III
Japanese larch	20	III
Hybrid larch	20	III
Douglas fir	20	II/III
Sitka spruce	15	III
Norway spruce	15	I/II
Noble fir	15	I
Grand fir	15	I
Western hemlock	20	IV
Western red cedar	20	II
Lawson cypress	20	III
Broadleaves		
Oak	20	I
Beech	20	II
Ash	25	I
Sycamore	25	II
Sweet chestnut	25	I
Birch	25	III
Alder spp.	20	II

* Where two classes are given, the first class should be applied to 'stocky' plants and the second to 'standard' plants. This also corresponds to the similar distinction in the EEC standards.

(NB: Table 1.2 includes species not covered by the FRM directive and *vice-versa*.) Appendix IV gives full details of EEC Plant Standards; see also section 15.1.7.

Plate 1 illustrates acceptable quality plants, based on visual standards.

Chapter 5, section 5.6 describes standards for seed.

Shoot development

Conifers when dormant should have a single main stem and (except for *Cupressus*, *Thuya* and allied genera) a single well formed terminal bud.

Broadleaves should similarly have a well formed central main stem and healthy buds.

Table 1.2 Standards of sturdiness (minimum stem diameters for given heights) for transplants sent for planting in the forest. Species grouped by classes shown in Table 1.1

Height (cm)	Minimum stem diameter at collar			
	Class I (mm)	Class II (mm)	Class III (mm)	Class IV (mm)
10	3.5			
11–15	4.5	3.5	3.0	
16–20	5.5	4.5	3.5	3.0
21–25	6.5	5.0	4.0	3.5
26–30	7.5	5.5	4.5	4.0
31–35	9.0	6.5	5.0	4.0
36–40	10.0	7.0	5.5	4.5
41–45	11.0	7.5	6.0	5.0
46–50	12.0	8.0	6.5	5.5
51–60	14.0	8.5	7.5	6.5

The leading shoot of otherwise vigorous species such as *Nothofagus procera* frequently die back to some extent but normally sprout from the uppermost live bud and do not lose apical dominance.

Vegetatively propagated stock showing strong plagiotropism, i.e. the tendency to grow like a side branch, should either be grown on for another year in the nursery or should be culled.

Branch growth should be normal for the species.

Foliage condition and nutrient status

During the growing season, plant foliage can exhibit transitory or long-lasting symptoms of disease, damage or deficiency. These can arise from:

- nutrient deficiency or excess,
- drought,
- damage by wind or frost,
- attack by pests.

See Chapters 4 and 13. Plants with poor, discoloured or damaged foliage at the time of lifting are normally culled out and discarded. Seasonal bronzing of species like western red cedar is not a defect.

Studies on the nutrient content of nursery

stock in British nurseries were carried out in the 1960s but remain valid (Benzian, 1965). Expected values of major and some micronutrients for conifer seedlings based on this work (which analyses needles rather than whole shoots or whole plants) are given in Table 4.8. Deficiency symptoms associated with low nutrient content in needles are given in Chapter 4, section 4.3. See also plates in Benzian, 1965.

Root morphology and shoot:root ratio

In spite of many attempts, it is not yet possible to find any simple objective non-destructive physical assessment of quality of root morphology and shoot:root ratio. Subjective criteria have to govern practice.

For all species, the ideal forest planting stock have well-branched root systems carrying many short fibrous roots, each capable of quickly regenerating new growing tips. However, there are substantial differences between species and it is easier, for example to generate fibrous rooting in spruces than pines.

Roots must not have been stripped of bark.

The bigger and better developed the main stem is, the larger and more fibrous should the root system be. A plant with a moderate size main stem and a good root system is more likely to become established quickly than a plant with a similar root system but larger top.

Shoot:root ratio

The current rule of thumb is that the ratio of shoot to root on a dry weight basis should not be more than 3:1.

Damage overwinter and during handling or storage

Plants must not have been subject to waterlogging in the winter before lifting as this may kill the roots without visibly affecting the foliage. Such waterlogged plants may start to flush shortly after planting out, but thereafter the tops soon die.

Plants must not have been allowed to dry out in the period between lifting and planting in the forest, nor become heated while in store or in transit (see also Chapter 14, section 14.2).

Uniformity of stock

Batches of plants can be made more homogeneous by grading. However, this can be overdone; it is preferable to achieve uniform stock by good nursery practice (Cannell, 1989; Ritchie, 1989.) Almost always, plants are graded by height categories; occasionally, they may also be graded by sturdiness.

Grading may be desirable to avoid early variation in plant size in young plantations leading to some requiring, for example, weeding and some not, or to subsequent uneven growth. South and Mason (1993) describe how in carefully measured studies of performance following planting, smaller plants never catch up and if anything fall behind as the plantation reaches canopy closure.

Cannell (1989) warns that in excessively uniform plantations, trees may not be able to assert dominance so that the woodland does not produce the larger dimension log sizes expected in a normal assortment; however, this danger is not great, given the inherent variation in most planting sites.

1.5.3 Physiological attributes

Physiological criteria are only slowly coming into practical use in British forest nursery practice. Until 1990, the physical attributes discussed above, together with a visual assessment of hardening-off/dormancy, have been taken as working substitutes for physiological tests, because of the lack of quick on-site tests for physiological condition. See also Chapter 14.

Hardening off and dormancy

Until the beginning of the 1980s, hardening off, i.e. the lignification of the current year's growth and the development of healthy winter resting buds, was taken as a visible physical manifestation of internal physiological changes, indicating that plants could be safely moved from nursery to forest. Currently, almost all bare-rooted plants are expected to be fully dormant when lifted, dormancy being maintained, where necessary, by cold storage (see also Chapter 14, section 14.3).

Root growth potential (RGP)

RGP assesses the ability of plants to grow new roots under controlled growth conditions; it has become an important criterion for defining both the planting season, the time for putting plants into and removal from winter cold-storage, and a potential index of the condition of plants after handling (Tabbush, 1985, 1986 a and b, 1987, 1988; Aldhous, 1989; also Plate 3).

Electrolyte leakage

This techique is being tested as a promising rapid and simple test of the extent that roots have suffered damage allowing leakage of the salts in the cell (McKay, 1992) (Chapter 14, section 14.3).

1.5.4 Quality criteria for other plant production systems

Alternatives to bare-rooted transplants for forest planting are coming into increasing use in British forestry practice. These include:

1. bare-rooted undercut and side-cut seedlings raised at low density in seedbeds following precision sowing (Chapter 8);

2. bare-rooted transplants of cuttings rooted in polyhouses, principally of genetically improved Sitka spruce and hybrid larch (Chapter 10, section 10.2);

3. container-grown stock, initially Corsican pine in Japanese paper pots, but with many other species now being reared in a wide range of containers.

The concepts outlined in sections 1.5.2 and 1.5.3 above for bare-rooted transplant stock raised from seed are likely to apply in principle to these other types of stock, and the sturdiness figures given in Table 1.2 provide a starting point for quality standards for undercut and vegetatively propagated stock. Nevertheless, the criteria and values have not been critically tested for such stock and must be applied with discretion. For example, some rooted cuttings of Sitka spruce have a poorer stem form than stock from transplanted seedlings. (Mason *et al*, 1989). This is an ephemeral effect of taking cuttings from side branches of the parent plant; after a few years in the forest, the inherent vigour and good form which justified the selection of the parent stock for vegetative propagation asserts itself.

Similarly, British Standard 3936, part 4 (BSI, 1984) gives some figures for container plants, but these are based largely on Japanese paper pot production and should not be related to plants from other containers.

The present grading standards have to be reassessed for this extended range of types of stock, and where necessary, adjusted for these and for plants from any other new plant production system.

1.6 Names and ages of plants

The names given in Appendix III are used throughout the Bulletin. Column 2 of the appendix gives current botanical names.

1.6.1 Types of plant

Definitions of types of plant commonly raised in nurseries in the UK are listed in the Glossary (Appendix II); they follow British Standard 3936, part 4 (BSI, 1984).

1.6.2 Age and type conventions

The length of time plants have spent in the nursery and the treatments they have been given follow a well-established convention.

For many years, the alternative techniques available when raising stock for forest planting were restricted, so that the convention remained simple; however, additional techniques introduced in the last decade have led to the need to extend the old convention to accommodate the new types of plants. Forestry Commission Research Information Note 135 (Samuel and Mason, 1988) sets out the framework for the extended convention now in use in the Forestry Commission.

Age

Age in years is indicated by the sum of figures describing the plant.

Type and duration of treatment

The approximate duration of treatment of plants is expressed as the time spent separately in the seedbed, cutting bed, transplant line or container. A numeral shows how long the plant spent undisturbed at each stage, '1' or '2' representing the corresponding number of growing seasons, parts of a season being given as '½'. Where plants are lined out very late in the growing season, it is a matter for local judgement whether these are better described as 1½+1½ or 2+1.

Letters and symbols representing treatment

Unless preceded by a letter, the first figure in any plant description is the time spent undisturbed in seedbeds.

Letters preceding the first figure indicate:

C plants raised from cuttings;
P container-grown stock.

Symbols following a figure indicate an operation after the period indicated by the figure:

+ transplanting
u undercutting
S stumping (applied to willows and poplars, usually in addition to transplanting)

Two-year-old seedbeds which have been undercut are normally described as '1u1'; however, the 'u' is not a reliable indication as to the undercutting prescription followed. See also Chapter 8.

Examples of age and type descriptions:

1-year-old stock: 1+0   C1+0   P1+0   ½+½
2-year-old stock: 1+1   1u1   1½+½ C1+S1
3-year-old stock: 2+1   1½+1½ 1+1+1
4-year-old stock: 2+2

Information on plant identity numbers is given in Chapter 5, section 5.2.

FURTHER READING

MASON, W.L., DEANS, J.D. and THOMPSON, S. (eds) (1989). Producing uniform conifer planting stock. (Proceedings of a workshop at York, UK, IUFRO working party S3.02–03, Nursery operations.) *Forestry* **62** (Supplement), 1–314.

MASON, W.L., and GILL, J.G.S. (1986). Vegetative propagation of conifers as a means of intensifying wood production in Britain. *Forestry* **59**, 155–172.

MASON, W.L., MANNARO, P.M. and WHITE, I.M.S. (1986). Growth and root development in cuttings and transplants of Sitka spruce 3 years after planting. *Scottish Forestry* **40** (4), 276–284.

ROOK, D.A. (1992). *Super Sitka for the 90s.* Forestry Commission Bulletin 103. HMSO, London.

REFERENCES

ALDHOUS, J.R. (1989). Standards for assessing plants for forestry in the United Kingdom. *Forestry* **62** (Supplement), 13–19.

BENZIAN, B. (1965). *Experiments on nutrition problems in forest nurseries.* Forestry Commission Bulletin 37. HMSO, London.

BRITISH STANDARDS INSTITUTION (1984). *Specification for nursery stock. Part 4: Forest trees.* B.S. 3936: Part 4: 1984. British Standards Institution, London.

CANNELL, M. (1989). Uniform nursery stock and plantation development. *Forestry* **62** (Supplement), 263–273.

FAULKNER, R. (1992). The choices and relative values of different seed sources. Chapter 2 in *Seed manual for forest trees,* ed. A.G. Gordon. Forestry Commission Bulletin 83. HMSO, London.

FORESTRY COMMISSION (1993). *Woodland Grant Scheme – applicant's pack.* Forestry Commission, Edinburgh.

GILL, J.G.S. (1983). Comparison of production costs and genetic benefits of transplants and rooted cuttings of Sitka spruce. *Forestry* **56** (1), 61–73.

LEE, S.J. (1990). *Potential gains from genetically improved Sitka spruce.* Research

Information Note 190. Forestry Commission, Edinburgh.

LINES, R. (1987). *Choice of seed origins for the main forest species in Britain.* Forestry Commission Bulletin 66. HMSO, London.

MASON, W.L., BIGGIN, P. and McCAVISH, W.L. (1989). *Early forest performance of Sitka spruce planting stock raised from cuttings.* Research Information Note 143. Forestry Commission, Edinburgh.

McKAY, H.M. (1992). *Electrolyte leakage: a rapid index of plant vitality.* Research Information Note 210. Forestry Commission, Edinburgh.

RITCHIE, G.A. (1989). Integrated growing schedules for achieving physiological uniformity in coniferous planting stock. *Forestry* **62** (Supplement), 213–226.

SAMUEL, C.J.A. and MASON, W.L. (1988). *Identity and nomenclature of vegetatively propagated conifers used for forestry purposes.* Research Information Note 135. Forestry Commission, Edinburgh.

SOUTH, D.B. and MASON, W.L. (1993). Influence of differences in planting stock size on the early height growth of Sitka spruce. *Forestry* **66**(1), 83–96.

TABBUSH, P.M. (1985). *The use of co-extruded polythene bags for the handling of plants.* Research Information Note 118/86/SILN. Forestry Commission, Edinburgh.

TABBUSH, P.M. (1986a). Plant handling. *Forestry Commission Report on Forest Research 1986,* 17. HMSO, London.

TABBUSH, P.M. (1986b). Rough handling, soil temperature and root development in outplanted Sitka spruce and Douglas fir. *Canadian Journal of Forest Research* **16,** 1385–1388.

TABBUSH, P.M. (1987). Effect of desiccation on water status and forest performance of bare-rooted Sitka spruce and Douglas fir transplants. *Forestry* **60**, 31–43.

TABBUSH, P.M. (1988). *Silvicultural principles for upland restocking.* Forestry Commission Bulletin 76. HMSO, London.

Chapter 2

Selection, layout and formation of a nursery for the production of bare-root plants

A. C. Miller and J. R. Aldhous

Introduction

Careful attention to the selection of a nursery site will amply repay all the effort involved. Failure to select a soil that is sufficiently acid inevitably results in costly and unsatisfactory production of many commonly planted conifer species, while selection of sites which are unsatisfactory in other respects, e.g. on a heavy soil, weedy, or in frost hollows, will sooner or later (and generally, sooner) add to the cost of one or more operations or lead to unnecessarily high losses.

2.1 Physical limits for nursery sites

The physical limits within which sites should be sought are given below.

2.1.1 Elevation

In England and Wales, nursery sites should be sought certainly below 300 m and preferably below 100 m above sea level; in Scotland, sites should be below 100 m. The higher the site, the colder it will be at all times of the year, the shorter the growing season and the greater the chance of the soil being frozen or covered with snow when plants are required or other work should be proceeding. While plants in nurseries at higher elevations will remain dormant later in the spring than those in lowland nurseries, this advantage is offset by the disadvantages previously mentioned.

2.1.2 Soil depth

There should be at least 25 cm of readily workable, well-draining soil; the subsoil must also be free-draining. Any pan or compacted layer must be able to be broken up to maintain good drainage.

Soils containing many large stones or much gravel should be avoided. Tractor-based sowing, undercutting and transplanting operations are becoming increasingly precise; while small numbers of stones can be cleared off with a stone-picker or modified potato lifter behind a tractor, sites with stones that are large enough to throw undercutters or transplanting machines out of alignment should be avoided.

2.1.3 Rainfall

The mean annual rainfall for the site should preferably be in the range 700–1000 mm. Sites with a mean rainfall value less than 700 mm should only be considered if irrigation will be available at all times. Sites with more than 1000 mm annual rainfall should only be selected if the soil drainage is excellent.

2.1.4 Previous land use

The previous use of land may influence its value as a potential nursery site because of the effect of some forms of husbandry on soil acidity and the amount of weed seed present. Young plantation or any other type of woodland should not be spurned as possible sites for a nursery, if the soil texture and acidity are right; see Chapter 3, section 3.1.1.

The sites most readily converted to successful forest nursery production in Great Britain since 1950 have been on acid, light-textured soils covered with bracken or heather.

Where the production of poplars is intended, soils classified by texture as sands should be avoided in favour of soils with a sandy loam texture.

Nurseries have sometimes been described according to the previous history of the site, as: 'heathland', 'woodland' or 'agricultural'. These terms have never coincided exactly with any particular soil characteristic and their names are seldom used in any context of nursery planning or management.

At one time it was thought that heathland nurseries would become exhausted and would need to be replaced after a few years, as the nutrients made available by the initial cultivation were used up. However, with attention to fertiliser prescriptions, maintenance of soil acidity and control of weeds, some nurseries of heathland origin remain productive after two or three decades of cropping. On the continent, nurseries of similar origin have been in cultivation for over 100 years.

2.2 Site selection

Within the physical limits given above, the factors to be taken into account when selecting a nursery are:

- soil acidity (Chapter 3, section 3.2);
- soil texture, workability and drainage;
- access and services;
- local topography in relation to frost hollows, exposure and aspect;
- freedom from weeds, and effective barriers against invasion by weeds (Chapter 12);
- labour supply;
- distance from trunk road network.

Of these, the first three are the most important, but none can be safely ignored.

2.2.1 Soil analysis

It is essential that tests be made on a repre-sentative series of samples from any potential nursery site. (See Chapter 3, section 3.3.6 for instructions on taking soil samples.) Samples should be tested for acidity, organic matter and nutrient status. A mechanical analysis is not normally required, except when there is doubt about the texture, drainage characteristics or workability of the soil when cultivated.

Sites found to have soils with a pH of 6.0–6.5 should normally be rejected unless there are special circumstances favouring the site and the soil can readily be acidified.

Sites with a soil pH over 6.5 should be rejected for the production of bare-rooted stock.

2.2.2 Soil texture, workability and drainage

Most forest nursery work involving soil movement takes place in the winter and early spring, whenever the weather is mild. The ideal forest nursery soil should therefore be quickly draining and free-working at this time of year. It should contain only a little clay and silt and not too much very fine sand because of its water-retaining properties. In the last 30 years, the large majority of new forest nurseries have been established on sandy or loamy sand soils with a maximum of 10% clay and 15% silt; indeed, the soils in many such nurseries have practically no clay at all. Such nurseries have often been most successful and productive, and while the light soils usually retain less soluble nutrients compared with heavy soils, they are usually acid and relatively weed-free.

Light soils quickly lose water from the surface 1–2 cm, especially if left loose after cultivation. However, crops' water needs can be ensured by judicious irrigation.

While the organic matter content of nursery soils is not crucial, a high content of fine organic matter assists retention of nutrients and water, and plentiful coarse organic matter (e.g. as from residues of a fibrous greencrop such as rye-grass) may improve the working qualities of loamy soils (but see also Chapter 4, section 4.4 on coarse organic matter and seedling germination). In most nurseries on sandy soils, there is at least 3% organic matter in the soil, and in many Scottish nurseries of this type, the organic matter content may be 10% or more. The organic matter content of loamy soils, especially those which are in warmer regions of the country and which have been in nursery or arable cultivation for some time, is usually less than 3% and often less than 2%.

A soil very low in organic matter is less able to retain and store plant nutrients, and may require a more intensive 'little and often' nutrient regime, compared with better provided sites.

If drainage is not satisfactory because of an iron-pan or other compacted layer impeding drainage, the possibilities should be investigated of initially breaking it up using a subsoiler with a winged tine. This configuration of tine is particularly effective in breaking indurated layers.

It is important to distinguish 'pans' and similar indurated layers of soil where less dense (and freely draining) soil is within reach of the bottom of the subsoiler, from more substantial layers of compact soil which continue below subsoiling depth so that the lower part remains a barrier to drainage even though the upper part is shattered.

Where surface water from adjacent land enters the potential nursery site, cut-off or other surface drains or ditches should prevent water entering the nursery. Other drains may be needed to lead away water accumulating in the nursery, especially from the permanent road system and hardstandings around buildings.

Any minor hollows where water might accumulate can be filled with soil from adjacent slightly higher ground leaving a gently domed surface so that water drains to the edges. However, it is vital always to leave at least 20 cm of topsoil over all ground that is to be cropped.

If it is necessary to reshape the landform of any section, the top 25–30 cm of topsoil must be moved to one side while the underlying subsoil is levelled. The lowest exposed subsoil surface should itself be ripped before any subsoil or topsoil is spread back over it. Care should be taken to ensure that the subsoil is not compacted by heavy machinery working when it is too wet. See also section 2.4.5 below.

Tile drains should not normally be necessary for a new nursery site. In normal nursery management, it is difficult to avoid compaction of sandy and sandy loam soils, and some subsoiling is likely to be necessary from time to time. If tiles are put in (for example if the lower subsoil drainage is impeded), the tiles must be at least 60 cm deep, and well below the depth of any subsoiler that may be used in the nursery. It is important that the drains are properly constructed with suitable porous backfill immediately above the drain. If tile drains exist from the previous land use, their position and depth should be mapped as far as possible, to minimise the risk of damaging them in subsequent operations.

2.2.3 Freedom from weeds

Ideally, the site of a new nursery should be free from annual and perennial weeds and weed seeds. With proper management, (i.e. continued vigilance and cultivation, application of herbicide or hand-weeding to remove any weeds before they set seed), such sites can be kept substantially weed-free for many years. The difference in the direct annual cost of weeding in a clean nursery compared with a weedy one is significant, though less now thanks to the weedkillers currently available, than formerly when hand-weeding played a dominant role in nursery weed control. See Chapter 12, for recommendations for weed control.

Steps should be taken to minimise the risk of weed invasion. If the nursery is reasonably clean, import of plants should be minimised, wherever possible transplanting only seedlings raised on the nursery.

Some weeds, e.g. groundsel, have developed strains which are resistant to some weedkillers. By raising and lining out only your own stock, import of resistant strains of weeds is avoided.

Where there is any serious risk of weed seeds blowing in from adjacent weedy land, and it is not possible to persuade the neighbour responsible to manage the land so as to prevent weeds from seeding, a boundary shelterbelt/hedge may act as a filter intercepting weed seed. Care has to be taken, however, to keep that ground clean, otherwise it could harbour more weeds than the neighbouring ground!

2.2.4 Frost hollows; slope; exposure; aspect

These are all features related to local topography.

Frost hollows

Avoidance of frost hollows is important to escape the worst consequences of late spring frosts. Frost hollows occur wherever cold air can accumulate – in the bottoms of valleys, large or small depressions, and where there are barriers to the drainage of cold air down a slope. Where trees and shrubs form such a barrier, a gap as least as wide as the trees are high, created at the point in the barrier furthest down the slope, will enable the cold air to drain off. Little can be done to remove cold air in natural frost hollows and nursery managers may have to resort to overnight irrigation or netting or slatting shelters to protect specially vulnerable stock; see also, Chapter 11, section 11.4.3 and Chapter 13, section 13.1.1.

Nurseries located near the coast may find the influence of the sea reduces the incidence of severe radiation frosts.

Slope

By choice, a nursery should lie on a gentle slope of 2–4°, with sufficient gradient to allow rain to run off, but without eroding the soil. Moderate slopes easily become eroded and are more difficult to work by machine, while completely flat land may be subject to poor natural drainage and frosts.

Exposure

Sites which are exposed to strong winds from any direction, but particularly from the east, should be avoided unless protection by means of internal hedges or shelterbelts can be provided.

Aspect

There are various opinions about the best aspect for a nursery, the only point of agreement being that an easterly aspect should be avoided. The reasons are, firstly, that the winds that most damage plants are the cold easterly winds of winter and early spring, and secondly, that if plants are caught by a late spring frost, the ill-effects are most acute if plants are thawed rapidly by the morning sun. Sites with a southern rather than a northern aspect should be chosen for poplar production because of their greater warmth.

2.2.5 Access and services

The nursery must be accessible to large commercial vehicles, so that plants and materials may be received and despatched and tractors and implements brought in when required. The entrance and access to the main buildings should be metalled and able to take traffic in all weathers. If the existing access is not adequate for expected needs, the highway authority should be consulted before any specification for a new or improved access is finalised.

An electricity supply will need to be three-phase if any substantial cold-storage facilities are envisaged, or if high capacity pumps are required for the irrigation system.

In addition to a water supply for drinking and sanitation, estimates of water requirements for irrigation must be included. These can be obtained from the calculations necessary when preparing plans for irrigation on open ground and for misting in propagation houses (Chapter 11, section 11.4). The availability of water and any restrictions to be observed in times of prolonged drought must be identified, so that plans and costings for the nursery can include provision for boreholes or a private reservoir to supply the nursery.

Early discussions should be sought with the

authority responsible locally for waste disposal; inevitably, there will be some washings and waste from pesticides applied as part of everyday nursery husbandry. Whether these can be sprayed on to the soil, processed through a small on-site treatment unit or held in a special tank for specialist off-site disposal will depend on the pesticides expected to be used, the geographical and geological circumstances of the nursery site, and the requirements of current legislation (Chapter 15, section 15.6).

2.2.6 Labour and supervision

No nursery can be run without a labour force. Their number and terms of employment depend on the degree of mechanisation envisaged and the availability of other work when the work force is not wanted in the nursery. In practice, the labour requirement ranges from $\frac{1}{2}$ to 1 man-year per hectare of nursery productive ground, exclusive of special requirements for vegetative propagation or other similar intensive production system.

While it has often proved possible to employ a substantial proportion of staff seasonally, some key personnel (e.g. tractor drivers) must be retained all the year round, amounting to 25–35% of the total annual labour requirement.

There should be one ganger or senior worker for every 8–12 workers, while a forester or other supervisor will be required full-time if the nursery exceeds 15 ha. The forester or nursery manager in charge of a nursery, whether full or part-time, should have had recent training or up-to-date experience in nursery work. Nursery management requires specialist knowledge and few untrained or inexperience staff do well in a nursery until they have gained that knowledge.

2.2.7 Access to markets

Nurseries producing the bulk of their plants for sale are best sited near the motorway and trunk road network. Geographical proximity to potential markets is less important than the time taken for delivery lorries to reach their market destination.

Substantial numbers of plants may be required for upland or moorland sites where spring is late; northerly nurseries have the advantage that their season is more closely synchronised to such sites than those in the south of England. However, cold stores and lorries or trailers with or without chilled storage make it practical for plants' dormancy to be maintained so that they can be distributed when required (Chapter 14, section 14.7.4). As a consequence, the more southerly nurseries can take advantage of warmer growing conditions to produce regularly, good quality planting stock in 2 years and, by late-winter cold storage, avoid premature loss of dormancy in the early part of the planting season.

2.3 Layout of nursery

2.3.1 Shape of nursery

The nursery should be as compact, i.e. as near square as possible, and regular in shape so as to minimise the length of boundary fence and to reduce the amount of time lost moving from one part of the nursery to another by both labour and supervisors.

2.3.2 Size and shape of sections

These should be related to the method of working, the scale of mechanisation, the need for hedges and the topography of the ground.

Sections should be not less than 0.5 ha in area, and if lining out is by transplanting machine or by plough, sections twice this size (i.e. 1 ha) are preferable so that machines can get a continuous run of between 100 and 150 m before they need to turn. If the nursery is exposed and hedges are required for local wind protection, they should be parallel to the line of machinery and irrigation runs, the location of which should be decided before hedges are planted.

Where permanent shelterbelts are to be planted or existing woodland retained as shelterbelts, these should be outside the nursery boundary fences.

Some nursery managers arrange the size of sections so that in the direction of lining out, the number of plants filling a full line across the section is a multiple of 1000; this eases control of piecework payments and lining out programmes and subsequent stocktaking.

2.3.3 Buildings*

Nursery buildings should be located in the nursery where most convenient for efficient management, within constraints imposed by any planning approval or building bye-law consent and the need for security of premises and their contents.

Buildings should provide the following facilities:

1. Offices for the nursery manager and his support staff, conforming to the requirements of the current regulations made under the Offices, Shops and Railway Premises Act, 1963, and Health and Safety at Work Act, 1974, in respect of cleanliness, ventilation, temperature, lighting, sanitation, storage of clothing, etc. (HSE, 1989).

2. Stores for:
   - *Machinery and tools* – some items in this category are costly and are attractive to thieves. There must at least be part of any machinery or tool store able to withstand casual attempts at forced entry. If any machinery maintenance is anticipated, the floor should be concreted and the store appropriately equipped as a work area.
   - *Petrol and other machine fuels and lubricants* – such a store must conform with the Petroleum Spirit (Motor Vehicles etc.) Regulations, 1929 (SR&O 1929/ 952).
   - *Pesticides* – this must be dry, secure and conform with the requirements of current pesticide legislation. If only small quantities of pesticides are ever held in the nursery, a secure 'vault' store may suffice; see Chapter 15, section 15.6.5.

   - *Fertilisers* – while fertilisers packed in polythene bags can be stored out of doors under a waterproof sheet, there is less risk of theft or vandalism if they are under cover.
   - *Plants* – if large numbers of lifted, bare-root plants are to be held while awaiting grading, packing or despatch, some sort of plant storage is necessary.

   A cool, very well ventilated shed or shaded storage area, capable of holding a substantial number of plants in co-extruded black and white polythene bags would meet this need; plants have often been kept under the shelter of a dense canopy in conifer plantations. However, while this last is often well-suited to short-term storage in upland plantations, it is not recommended as the sole means of storage for any forest nursery.

   If plants have to be kept dormant beyond the time of bud-break, a refrigerated store will be needed, enabling plants to be lifted while fully dormant in December/January and kept in that condition until required 3–4 months later; see Chapter 14, section 14.7.
   - *Seed* – the need for a separate seed store will be determined by the scale and choice of species to be raised in the nursery. All seed must be kept cool; in addition, any seed requiring moist prechilling treatment will need refrigerated storage where the temperature can be closely controlled.

   Where there is a coldstore for plants on the nursery, it will also usually be suitable for storage of dry seed and seed being prechilled. For main-stream conifer and similar small seeds, there should be sufficient space even in the busiest years. If, however, large quantities of bulky seeded broadleaved species are expected to be grown, more careful planning and management will be required to ensure that space is available in a plant coldstore when needed.

   If no suitable plant store is available, a refrigerator will have to be purchased, or coldstore space hired for this purpose.

---

*The Acts of Parliament, Regulations etc. quoted here were in force in summer 1993. There is no guarantee that this list is comprehensive or that it will remain up to date.

3. Working rooms or working space for:
   - *Seed preparation* – including separating, cleaning and drying any locally collected seed, soaking prior to prechilling, stratification, hot and cold treatment to induce germination, etc.
   - *Receipt, grading, packing and despatch of plants* – this area must be cool and sheltered; see also Chapter 14, sections 14.5 and 14.6;
   - *Application of insecticide* – by dipping or by electrodyn treatment before despatch of plants, if specified by the customer (see Chapter 14, section 14.8).

4. *Mess room, washing and separate lavatory facilities* for men and women staff. These should be up to the standards prescribed under the Agriculture (Safety, Health and Welfare Provisions) Act, 1956, plus any supplementary facilities required for staff who have been handling pesticides such as separate storage room for clean and potentially contaminated clothes.

5. *Readily accessible first aid equipment,* meeting the requirements of the Health and Safety (First Aid) Regulations, 1981 (SI 1981/917) and the current code of practice issued by the Health and Safety Commission (HSC, 1991).

Some of the above can be combined in one building if convenient. On private estate or company sites where forest nursery production is combined with other rural land-based businesses, some of these facilities will form part of the overall provision for the site.

2.3.4 Roads, paths and alleys

The buildings should be served by an all-weather metalled road connecting to the nearest public road. Permanent roads to nursery sections need only be sufficiently well surfaced to carry a tractor and trailer. Often, the natural soil, when compacted by traffic, is adequate for this purpose, but in nurseries on stony soil, any stones collected from the sections should be thrown on to the most heavily used roads to reinforce them.

Where possible, a road should also be made round the perimeter of the nursery. This will ensure that machines can get in from both ends of all sections unless baulked by ditches or hedges, and will also provide a barrier against weeds encroaching from outside the nursery fence. Permanent roads should not be allowed to be covered with weeds. See Chapter 12 for means of keeping them clean.

Roads, together with the associated headlands, should always be wide enough for tractors and implements to be able to turn without damaging plants. The actual dimensions depend on the equipment in use on the particular nursery. However, for the longer items, an overall width of 10 m should be allowed for road plus headland.

On sloping ground, the layout of roads has to take account of the permanent open drains and the risk of scour and/or soil erosion. Where possible, roads should cross the tops and bottoms of sections so that loads can always be taken downhill; this will reduce the risk of compaction of soil or bogging under wet conditions where tractors are used, and will be less fatiguing for staff moving plants, etc., by hand.

Paths and alleys within or between sections and unmetalled roads, should always be considered temporary and should be cultivated whenever necessary. Alleys between seedbeds or beds of transplants should be 45–50 cm wide to allow tractor wheels to pass easily. Wider paths, up to twice this width, will be needed where hand barrows and trolleys are to be used regularly, or where stock is undercut/wrenched several times in a season.

2.3.5 Hedges and windbreaks

Hedges and shelterbelts have three distinct, though often combined, roles: security, visual screening and a means of reducing wind-flow.

Traditionally, hedges have been grown to provide security against incursions by livestock. Such hedges are managed so as to maintain dense live foliage throughout, but especially at the bottom of the hedge.

Hedges providing visual screening are often taller than stock hedges; nevertheless, dense lower foliage is desirable if the screen is to remain effective.

The aim in designing windbreaks and shelterbelts is to reduce windspeed without generating additional turbulence. Such belts do not provide the security that a dense stock-proof hedge will provide; a dense hedge provides good shelter in its immediate lee but is ineffective after a short distance because of the turbulence generated as the wind passes over it.

Within a nursery, there may be need for hedges for security or as windbreaks, or both. However, hedges also have disadvantages. They impede the work of machines and take up space, they can harbour weeds, pests and diseases, they can root out into sections, competing for water and nutrients and, if wrongly sited, can create frost pockets.

Security hedges

Where security hedges are required, good quality plants should be put in at 50 cm spacing along ground that has been trenched, dressed with fertiliser as for transplants, plus a liberal application of hop-waste or other bulky organic manure, if used in the nursery. The following species make good hedges:

- Lawson cypress,
- western hemlock,
- tamarisk (for areas near the coast in the south of England),
- holly.

Unsuitable species include:

- beech (may harbour aphis),
- western red cedar (may become infected with 'Keithia' (*Didymascella thujina*)),
- Monterey cypress (may be killed in severe winters and may become infected with *Seiridium cardinale,* (Phillips and Burdekin, 1992)),
- Leyland cypress (grows very vigorously, requires heavy regular cutting to keep it under control, and may also be affected by *Seiridium*),
- hawthorn (because of risk of fireblight (*Erwinia amylovora*)), similarly,

- *Cotoneaster* spp.,
- Scots pine (may harbour pine needle diseases),
- *Prunus* spp. in plum growing areas (plum pox virus (Buczacki and Harris, 1981)).

See also, Chapter 13, last paragraph of introductory section.

Windbreaks

For best effect, hedges intended as windbreaks should be 50% permeable to the wind. Denser barriers increase the turbulence of the air-stream crossing the windbreak and the benefit to crops is less (Baxter, 1985; Garner, 1988; NSCA, 1985).

Hedge maintenance

Hedges should be cut, preferably not with vertical sides but tapering towards the top. This will give branches at the base a better chance of remaining alive, so that the hedge will not go thin at the bottom. Hedges should not be allowed to intrude into the nursery. They are more effective as permeable barriers if kept narrow.

Roots of hedge plants may enter cropped areas and compete with plants nearest the hedge. In addition to cutting the hedge to keep it properly shaped, periodic deep ripping or hand trenching, parallel and close to the hedge should be undertaken, to check lateral spread of roots, taking care not to disturb drains, cables or other services.

2.4 Breaking-in a new nursery

2.4.1 Sequence and timing of operations

Much the same sequence of operations is required whether the site is covered with trees, with heather and bracken or with grass, except that for grass and heather sites, the earlier operations are unnecessary. The best sequence is:

- removal of trees and scrub;
- removal of aerial parts of woody weeds;
- ploughing;

- cleaning (i.e. removal of woody roots);
- subsoiling;
- incorporation of initial application of nutrients;
- final cultivation.

If possible, the nursery fence should not be erected until the cultivations are completed, so as to give the greatest degree of freedom of manoeuvre to mechanical equipment for as long as possible. However, if the site is heavily infested with rabbits, it may be necessary to fence and commence control operations before the final cultivations. Temporary fencing may be required where other operations, e.g. road or major building construction, are not scheduled to be complete before the site has been broken in.

Ideally, trees should be felled, and stump and scrub removal completed during the summer, so that cleaning can go on in suitable weather until the beginning of the nursery season when the ground is to be cropped. Stones collected during initial cultivations may be suitable for metalling the main nursery road.

In all the initial operations, as little subsoil as possible should be brought to the surface. Undesirable compaction of the soil can be minimised if every opportunity is taken to clear and prepare the site in dry conditions.

2.4.2 Removal of vegetation

Trees and woody weeds

In all clearing operations, tractors extracting timber and machinery preparing the site should *not* run over brash/lop and top. This will avoid it being pressed into the soil, and made more difficult to lift from the site. This is the opposite of what many timber harvesters may expect, so that they must be specifically instructed on this point. The soil types selected for nurseries are likely to be fully capable of supporting harvesting equipment without a brash mat except for any wet depressions on the site.

Where trees and scrub have to be cleared rather than being sold as timber or firewood, a bulldozer fitted with a toothed grubber blade should be used to push out stumps and scrub. A toothed blade is preferable to a standard dozer blade; it does not disturb the soil more than is necessary and removes less soil with the roots, so making burning easier. Where trees are of any size, their crown and stems should be felled before the bulldozing starts, leaving stumps 70 cm to 1 m high, so as to give the bulldozer good leverage on the root system.

Where there are only low stumps, stumps can be picked out by excavator using a bucket attachment. Two shallow trenches are made one either side of the stump, severing lateral roots, after which the stump can usually be lifted out from the front with minimal soil disturbance.

Alternatively, trees can be winched down while still standing, either by tractor fitted with a winch or by hand winch. Within reason, the higher the winch cable can be attached up the tree to be removed, the easier the tree comes down.

All stumps, roots, brash/lop and top should be removed from the cleared site, using a forwarder, or loader and dumper trucks. If such material is to be burned, the fires must be outside the nursery cultivated area otherwise the fungus *Rhizina inflata* may colonise the site and, in later years, may kill newly planted stock (Phillips and Burdekin, 1992).

If care is taken to pick up and cart off the large bulk of the roots, stumps and brash, and the brash has not been forced into the soil by harvesting equipment, the soil can be rotovated to 25 cm and subsequently a stone picker behind a tractor will clear the remaining woody material.

Herbaceous vegetation, heather, bracken, etc.

Low woody vegetation such as heather, bracken, bramble and gorse should be cut by tractor-mounted swipe or rotary cutter, the loose vegetation raked up and taken off the site. Alternatively, if there is only a light cover of woody vegetation, it may be reduced to a mulch by a rotary chopper.

On heathland and non-woodland sites, the surface mat of roots, grass and residues of herbaceous weeds and heather must be broken up. The best means of doing this is to plough to a depth of between 10 and 15 cm. Alternatively a very heavy rotovator may be used, followed by a stone picker, as for woodland sites.

Grassland

Any grassland should be ploughed to a depth of 20 cm and should not be rotovated, nor should the turf be removed from the site. The grass should be first ploughed as early in the summer as possible to give it time to break down thoroughly. Spraying with herbicide (glyphosate or paraquat) a week or two before ploughing may hasten its breakdown and reduce the unevenness of the first crop grown subsequently.

Any patch of couch or similar deep-rooted creeping weed-grass should be treated chemically, about 2 weeks before ploughing; see Chapter 12, sections 12.2 and 12.3.

2.4.3 Cleaning cultivations

The soils should next be worked repeatedly, alternately ploughing to about 15 cm and harrowing or cultivating with spring tines until all the coarse woody remnants of stumps, stems and roots have been removed. Alternatively, a stone-picker (e.g. Kverneland) can be used to screen out and remove woody material.

Once the initial cultivations have been completed, a careful watch should be kept for any patches of creeping perennial weeds, e.g. couch, sorrel, which may have survived. If these appear, appropriate steps must be taken to kill them by spraying and cultivation before the first crops are sown or transplanted.

2.4.4 Levelling and grading

Sections should slope evenly or, if on a flat site, should be slightly domed. During the cleaning cultivations, a skilful ploughman can move soil across a section to level out very minor humps and hollows. However, large-scale transfer of top soil must be avoided as denuded areas will produce poorer plants for several years afterwards.

If it is necessary to level the ground involving more than a few centimetres change of depth of soil, the top 25 cm of soil should be carefully removed from the whole of the area affected (i.e. both the ground to be lowered and the ground to be raised). The whole area should then be ripped with a winged tine, levelled, ripped again and the topsoil then spread back into place.

Sections disturbed in this way should in addition to the initial application of mineral nutrients prescribed following soil analysis, be given either a heavy application of bulky organics immediately after replacement of the top-soil, or, preferably, be put under a ryegrass green crop for a growing season.

2.4.5 Deep subsoiling/ripping

If there is an iron-pan or other hard layer of soil within 0.4–0.5 m of the soil surface which may impede drainage or rooting, this may be broken up by deep subsoiling with a tine at intervals of 1.2 m across the nursery. After running in one direction, a second series of runs should be made at right angles to the first.

The first operation in a nursery should be undertaken using a winged tine ripper. This requires a greater drawbar pull than is available from the tractors standard in forest nurseries, and an 80–100 hp tractor will be required. For best effect, the soil must be dry when any subsoiling is carried out.

Winged tines are able to lift a greater volume of soil and be more effective in disturbing the lower layers of the soil if deep tining is preceded by cultivation or shallow tining. Both operations can be carried out at the same time if the shallow tines are placed well forward of the deep tine on the trailor toolbar. See Davies, 1982.

2.4.6 Incorporation of nutrients

If a soil analysis indicates that the soil is too acid or is unduly low in phosphorus or magnesium, this can be adjusted by an initial application of lime (for excessively acid soils), ground mineral phosphate (for soils low in phosphorus), kieserite or calcified magnesite (for soils low in magnesium), dolomitic limestone (excessively acid soils low in magnesium) or sulphur for local patches of excessively high pH. The amounts of each to be applied should be determined on the basis on soil analysis; see Chapter 3, section 3.3.

These additions may be made at any time in the winter preceding the first crop, once the ground has been levelled. Materials should be spread evenly and incorporated by ploughing followed by rotovation.

2.4.7 Final cultivation

The nursery site should finally be cultivated either by plough to a depth of 20 cm, or by spading machine or vertical rotovator to a depth of 15 cm. If any nutrients have been added, a rotovator incorporates these more thoroughly in the soil, but it may be more difficult to firm the soil sufficiently, if seedbeds are to be thrown up shortly after rotovation.

2.4.8 Fencing

Only one nursery in a hundred can safely be run without a rabbit fence, but only a small proportion need a deer fence. See *Forest fencing,* Forestry Commission Bulletin 102, pages 6–7 (Pepper, 1992) for fence specifications.

2.5 Costs of formation

Recent direct costs (1991) of breaking in new ground for a nursery have been of the order of £1100 per hectare for green field sites and £5000 per hectare for woodland, exclusive of overheads and the cost of the ground. Rabbit-proof fencing is £2–3 per metre run additional to this.

Irrigation for a large site costs between £1000 and £1500 per hectare.

Industrial buildings are in the range £150–250 per square metre floor area, while the capital cost of cold-storage facilities is of the order £50 per cubic metre of store volume.

The facilities recommended for vegetative propagation of Sitka spruce cuttings from improved seed orchard seed are described in Chapter 10. The initial capital costs of such facilities are additional to those given above

for setting up open nursery production. They are also much more dependent on the successfulness of the techniques being followed, and in particular the yield of well-rooted cuttings from stock plants. Nevertheless, preliminary indications are that direct costs in setting up for vegetative propagation are of the order of £100 000 for a production unit aiming to produce 500 000 saleable rooted cuttings annually.

No costs can sensibly be given for access roads as these depend so much on the particular circumstances of the nursery location.

2.6 Site requirements for nurseries producing other types of forest planting stock

2.6.1 Vegetative propagation

Where the propagation cycle includes a period in open ground, the site requirements for a bare-root nursery also apply to establishing a new nursery exclusively devoted to vegetatively propagated planting stock.

2.6.2 Container systems and fully housed propagation systems

Where plant production is entirely inside propagating or container houses, there is no longer any need to ensure soils with appropriate pH; however, most of the other factors, including good soil drainage also apply. In addition, maintenance of uniform water pressure between and within houses is more important, and is facilitated if the ground is sufficiently flat for all the houses to be laid out on the same level on the site. Particular care should also be taken to ensure that the water supply will be reliable both in quality and quantity.

2.7 First crops in new nurseries

2.7.1 Land freshly taken in from heathland or woodland

Where ground, before being taken in, showed *no* signs of weeds, there is much to be said for

23

sowing seedbeds on such land. There has been experience over many years of excellent first crops in these circumstances without resort to presowing treatment with dazomet; see Chapter 12, section 12.3.1. Seedling yields may be slightly lower if there is a lot of partially broken down organic matter in the soil and the ground cannot be compacted as much as would be wished; however, the risk of bringing in undesirable organisms, especially weed seeds is avoided.

Transplants are obtained from the first year's crops of seedlings.

No special steps are needed to introduce mycorrhizal fungi into new nurseries; sufficient inocula are available in the soil and plants pick these up if nutrition and soil pH are adequate (Levisohn, 1965).

2.7.2 Land formerly under agricultural crops

If, however, the site is on former agricultural land or there are reasons to believe there will be a significant residual weed seed population, then more immediate management considerations can determine whether to sow seed and line out home production, or whether to import seedlings for lining out in the first year, and similarly, whether dazomet should be used for controlling weeds in the first year, and if not, what other means of weed control should be used.

REFERENCES

BUCZACKI, S.T. and HARRIS, K.M. (1981). *Pests, diseases and disorders of garden plants*. (Collins Guides series). Collins, London.

BAXTER, Sheila M. (1985). *Windbreaks for horticulture*. ADAS Booklet 2280. MAFF, Alnwick.

DAVIES, D.B. (1982). *Subsoiling*. ADAS Leaflet L 617. HMSO, London.

GARNER, J.R. (1988). *Windbreaks for fruit crops*. ADAS Pamphlet 3150. MAFF, Alnwick.

HSC (1991). *First aid at work. Health & Safety (First-aid) Regulations, 1991. Approved Code of Practice*. Revised, 1991. HMSO, London.

HSE (1989). *A guide to the Offices, Shops and Railway Premises Act, 1963*. Health & Safety Executive Booklet HS(R)4. HMSO, London.

LEVISOHN, I. (1965). Mycorrhizal investigations. (Supplementary paper in *Experiments in nutrition problems in forest nurseries*.) Forestry Commission Bulletin 37, Vol. I, 228–235. HMSO, London.

NSCA (1985). *Trees & shrubs for farm planting*. NSCA Leaflet 50. North of Scotland College of Agriculture, Aberdeen.

PEPPER, H.W. (1992). *Forest fencing*. Forestry Commission Bulletin 102. HMSO, London.

PHILLIPS, D.H. and BURDEKIN, D.A. (1992). *Diseases of forest and ornamental trees*. Macmillan, London.

Chapter 3
Forest nursery soils

D. G. Pyatt

To ensure steady output from forest nurseries, first and foremost the soil must be sufficiently acid for the crop being raised and sufficiently light and well drained to be workable during the larger part of the winter. Freedom from weeds is an advantage, though less important than formerly because of the availability of herbicides.

Formerly, plants in forest nurseries largely depended for their nutrients on what was stored in the soil. Farmyard manure or lime might have been applied but this was as much to benefit a greencrop as forest trees. Only the soils with better reserves – the traditionally more fertile soils – could sustain any worthwhile crops.

Now it is generally accepted that each crop must be given a plentiful supply of mineral nutrients if vigorous stock is to be raised; large nutrient reserves and high organic matter contents are useful but any consequences of deficiences in these properties can largely be made good.

3.1 Physical characteristics

The soil is composed mainly of particles derived from the parent rocks together with humus and partly decayed residues of dead plants and soil animals. The texture (section 3.1.1) of the soil is determined by the proportions of different sizes of mineral particle; the structure (section 3.1.3) of a soil is determined by the extent to which the particles adhere together to form natural aggregates.

The growth of crops and their response to fertilisers can be very much affected by the physical condition of the soil. If drainage becomes impeded, for example if a plough pan or compacted layer is formed by cultivating when the soil is too wet, poor aeration and slow drainage in the soil may give rise to poor plant growth and yield, in spite of the most carefully conceived fertility regime.

3.1.1 Texture

Soil texture is defined by the proportion of particles of different size in the soil.

Sand (particles from 2 to 0.06 mm diameter) and silt (particles from 0.06 to 0.002 mm) consist mainly of minerals derived from parent rock unchanged by weathering; in contrast, the clay fraction (< 0.002 mm) consists predominantly of colloidal minerals formed as products of weathering and not found in unweathered rocks. The origin or composition of the particles does not affect the definition of texture. Thus the sand particles may be 90–95% quartz – e.g. in soils derived from sedimentary deposits; alternatively the sand particles may include substantial proportions of felspar or mica, for example if derived from granitic rocks, or they may be composed of calcium carbonate as in seashore dune sands where particles of broken seashells abound.

Clay particles in the soil have two important properties: the ability to hold or combine with nutrients required by plants, and the property of swelling and shrinking as the soil becomes wetter or drier. This latter property has a major influence on the structure of the soil and the ability of the soil to form aggregates, such as the 'crumbs' composing the surface of seedbeds at sowing time on loamy or heavy clay soils.

Natural drainage channels in clay soils occur only between aggregates of particles and are open only when some shrinkage has taken place in the clay. The spaces between individual clay particles are minute and when filled with water do not drain under the force of gravity.

Classification by texture

The proportions of sand, clay and silt present in each soil can be the basis of an objective soil classification. Several alternative classifications have been made; one of the best known, shown in Figure 3.1, is used by the Soil Survey of England and Wales (Hodgson, 1985; Avery, 1990).

Texture of forest nursery soils

An ideal nursery soil should be well drained, stone-free, and have a maximum of 10% clay and 10–15% of silt. Soils within these limits fall into the texture classes; sands, loamy sands and sandy loams. Good nursery crops can also be grown on soils with less than 10% silt and clay – by definition sands – though more attention has to be paid to the supply of nutrients on such soils, and to ensure plants do not suffer from drought.

Some soil characteristics such as pH and nutrient status can be modified fairly readily within certain limits by the nursery manager. Soil texture, however, can only be modified at a greater expense than is generally acceptable. Only if the soil is of the right texture is it possible to produce successful annual crops of tree seedlings and transplants regularly.

On the heavier soils, winter work may become impossible in wet periods and frost-lift may also be a serious problem, limiting autumn lining out. In addition, within the range of soils commonly encountered in forest nurseries, the heavier the texture, the easier it is to create a cultivation pan (section 3.1.5).

3.1.2 Organic matter and humus

Organic matter is not taken into account in the standard soil texture classifications. Nevertheless humus in the soil holds moisture and nutrients as clay does, but without its stickiness. Soils low in clay but relatively high in organic matter are probably the ideal from the point of view of texture for forest nurseries.

Organic matter in soil varies considerably. One important practical distinction however is between raw organic matter and humus. Raw organic matter consists mostly of remains of plants, usually partially decomposed, but still retaining part of the original plant structure. During decomposition, the proportion of cellulose and hemicellulose in plant tissues is usually reduced in relation to the lignin constituent. This lignin breaks down much more slowly and its colloidal, dark-coloured residues form the bulk of what is called humus. Any chemical determination of organic matter may include raw organic matter besides humus proper, as well as the live tissues of soil bacteria and fungi, though these last two sources form a relatively small part of the organic matter so determined. However, colloids derived from bacteria may form an important constituent of humus.

Humus swells or shrinks in response to wet or dry conditions respectively and thereby assists in establishing and maintaining good soil structure. Raw organic matter can also have an important effect on soil structure, partly by its own physical presence as a dis-

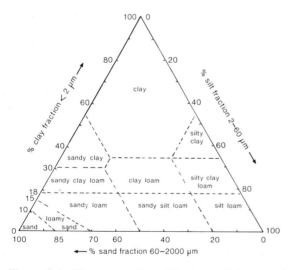

Figure 3.1 The composition of the textural classes of soils. (Based on the system used by the Soil Survey of England & Wales and ADAS; reproduced with permission.)

continuity in the soil mineral matter and partly as a site of bacterial and fungal activity where organic colloids are present in far greater concentrations than normal.

When a new nursery is established on land previously under semi-permanent heathland, woodland or perennial grass vegetation, the organic matter content of the soil diminishes until in equilibrium with the new soil condition associated with annual cropping. The breakdown of the initial 'surplus' of organic matter may be quite rapid, especially if the soil pH is raised by liming. The improved aeration resulting from cultivation is an important factor stimulating this biological decomposition of organic matter. As breakdown proceeds, plant nutrients are released, thus giving rise to the outstanding growth of plants in the first years of many heathland nurseries. See also Chapter 4, section 4.4.

3.1.3 Structure

In contrast to texture, structure describes the way the soil particles are aggregated. Soils have their individual particles clustered together into crumbs, clods, blocks, etc., though in sandy soils these are weakly developed and easily break up. The shape and size of these aggregates principally determine the structure. How densely aggregates are packed together also is part of the description of the structure of any soil.

One, if not the most important effect of a good soil structure is to ensure good drainage and aeration, the gaps between individual aggregates being the main channels for the movement of excess water. Loss of structure implies that soil becomes denser, the larger pores disappear and drainage is impeded. See also section 3.1.5.

3.1.4 Air and water, pore space and compaction

Soil may be described as a mass of particles, more or less aggregated together and permeated with a network of channels and pores. Some fundamental soil properties derive from the geometry of this pore space, for example,

the amount of air or water present, the rate at which air diffuses and the rate at which water percolates down through the soil.

In a soil with a good structure, between 40 and 60% of the volume should be occupied by pores and $1/3–1/2$ of the total pore space should be filled with air. If the air-filled pores are reduced to 10% of the soil volume or less, plant growth becomes impossible.

Pore size has a most important effect on the tenacity with which water is held in the soil. In pores with a diameter of less than about 0.03 mm, the water is held with a force greater than that of gravity, while in pores larger than this the water can drain away. Thus clay soils with a large proportion of very small pores hold much water while sandy soils have few small pores and retain little. Plants extract 'available water' from the soil until they can get no more, when they reach 'wilting point'.

Only about 21 mm of water is 'available' in the top 15 cm of sands; on heavy clays, up to 27 mm of stored water is available, while on loamy soils with a high proportion of fine sand, 30–35 mm of water is available. (Hodgson, 1985). Plants on very coarse-textured soils, with a small reserve of available water are therefore more likely to suffer from drought than plants on medium-textured soils. See also Chapter 11, section 11.2.

The pore-size distribution in soil is determined partly by the texture and partly by the structure, which in the upper layers of cultivated soils can be markedly affected by management. In a loamy soil, a crumb structure, whether produced by skilful cultivation or by substantial additions of organic matter, will not only increase the amount of pore space but also the proportion of large pores, so improving the natural drainage and surface aeration.

Sandy soils with a high proportion of *fine* sand are liable to drain more slowly following heavy rain or irrigation and to be more liable to compaction damage if machine-lifting or other operation involving repeated passage of machines has to take place while the soil is still very wet. On such soils, checks for compaction should be made regularly and also whenever there is a suspicion that drainage is slower than expected.

Heavy dressings of organic matter can have a marked effect on the moisture-holding capacity of light soils, and increases of up to 70% have been reported in agricultural practice. A similar effect was observed in the woodland nursery at Teindland in Moray, where regular dressings of hopwaste maintained the original exceptionally high organic matter content and the water-holding capacity of the soil, while without hopwaste both have fallen markedly; the stability of the very small soil crumbs has also been improved. (Table 4.9, page 58; Low and Sharpe, 1973.)

3.1.5 Plough pans and soil capping

A plough pan is a compacted layer where soil aggregates are more densely packed and some may have lost their structure by being rubbed and pressed together.

Once present, the pan may interfere with free drainage and thus cause temporary waterlogging leading to root death, or it may interfere with root penetration.

A pan will usually develop whenever soil is frequently cultivated to the same depth, whether by repeated passes of the plough share and tractor wheel, by rotovating or by repeated passes of a plant lifter. Pans are most readily formed when any of these operations is undertaken when the soil is wet.

There is a strong risk of plough pan formation when ground is repeatedly cultivated during fallow periods to control weeds. This risk can be minimised by ensuring that mid-season cultivations are to a depth of at least 5 cm less than the final autumn ploughing which should be to full cultivation depth. Any plough pan formed during the summer should be broken up before the winter by use of a winged subsoiling tine at 0.9–1.3 m intervals. Winged tines are more efficient and will allow the disruption of the pan in one pass (see Davies, 1982). If a winged tine is not available, an unwinged tine should be used, working first in one direction and then at right angles to it. The soil should be dry at the time of subsoiling.

Plough pans can easily form and any slowness in disappearance of water following heavy rain or any unexpectedly poor health of stock, especially transplants, should immediately lead to a test to determine whether a plough pan is present. Lodgepole pine transplants of inland origins seem particularly sensitive to temporary waterlogging of this sort.

A pan may be detected by digging carefully into the suspect area. The spade should be handled very gently and only a shallow layer of soil removed at a time. A pan will be apparent by the occurrence of compact soil at a depth of between 10 and 20 cm according to the depth of cultivation. Once the pan is passed through, the soil may become less compact again. An alternative method of detection is to dig a pit to a depth of 25 to 30 cm, carefully expose a clean face on one wall and with a pencil point probe the soil at intervals down the profile. Any compact layer can be detected by greater resistance to the probe. A cruder alternative is to probe vertically with a sharp strong rod.

Visually, compacted layers sometimes appear to be lighter or greyer in colour than the soil either side. In extreme cases, the pan gives off hydrogen sulphide (the smell of rotten eggs), and has an olive hue which rapidly darkens on exposure to air.

All these methods require a sensitive touch, but this can be acquired with a little practice. Any nursery forester should acquire the skill to test for plough pans at the earliest opportunity.

Capping

Capping of the soil, i.e. the formation of a thin, smooth, almost impermeable crust, is common after heavy rain, and may be particularly common on sandy loams and on silty soils low in organic matter. Water will run off a capped soil more rapidly in heavy storms than if the soil surface is loose, thereby rendering the rainfall less effective in replenishing soil-moisture reserves. Such rapid run-off also occasionally leads to soil erosion. Otherwise, there is no evidence that soil capping is harmful in forest nurseries. Surface cultivation can break up the cap, but when a vigorous crop of seedlings or transplants is growing, the cap is unlikely to be damaging. Capping is less prevalent where the organic matter content of soil is high and it is unlikely to be serious in seedbeds where a suitable grit cover is used, or on fallow ground which is cultivated regularly.

3.2 Soil pH

Soil acidity or soil reaction is commonly referred to in terms of the pH scale where a value in the range 6.5–7.5, measured in water, indicates a neutral soil, values from 5.5 to 6.5 indicate slightly acid soil, from 4.5 to 5.5 acid soil, and less than 4.5 very acid soil. Soil pH values of 3.5 or less are rare. Soil pH values above 7.5 indicate alkaline soils.

In the laboratories of the Forestry Commission, the Agricultural Development and Advisory Service and the Macaulay Land Use Research Institute, the pH of soil is measured electrically after the soil has been mixed with water. Some workers have used solutions of calcium chloride. Measurements made in calcium chloride solution are usually about 0.6 less than those made in water. This difference has to be remembered when examining the pH response curves given in Forestry Commission Bulletin 37 *Experiments on nutrition problems in forest nurseries* (diagrams 7–13, pages 36–44) (Benzian, 1965).

The pH, as determined in the field or laboratory, varies a little not only with method of measurement but also with time of year and crop. It will tend to be higher in cool, moist weather and in winter than in hot dry weather and in summer; it will also be higher in summer under a crop than under bare fallow. Thus differences in soil pH of less than 0.2 should be ignored. Where possible, comparisons should be based on samples taken at the same time of year and following a similar crop. For production nurseries, sampling in the autumn on fallow land is the ideal.

3.2.1 Plant growth and pH
Most seedling conifers grow best in soil with a pH between 4.5 and 5.0. Spruces, hemlock, lodgepole pine and larch grow more slowly in soils with a pH much outside this range and, under otherwise identical conditions, may be less than half as tall on neutral soils (pH 6.5–7) as on acid soils. Scots pine, Corsican pine, Norway spruce and Douglas fir are less intolerant of slightly acid or near-neutral soils, though these species still do best in acid conditions. Western red cedar on the other hand grows better on slightly acid soil (pH 5.5–6.5) than on acid soil, but this is the only commonly planted conifer for which this response has been established.

There has been little research into the pH responses of hardwoods while in the nursery. However, practical experience and limited research show that seedlings and transplants of the broadleaved species most commonly planted in woodlands, e.g. oak, alder, beech, birch and sycamore, grow well in the nursery on acid soils (pH 5.0–5.5) but that poplars and ash require slightly acid or nearly neutral soils (pH 5.5–6.5) and will not tolerate acid conditions.

For most crops, an acid soil is therefore either essential or at least satisfactory. If both conifers and poplars are to be grown, an acid soil should nevertheless be sought as it is easy to make an acid soil less acid by adding limestone or chalk but more difficult to acidify a neutral soil. Some nursery managers have limed a section of an otherwise acid nursery and keep this section solely for the production of hardwoods.

3.2.2 Changes in pH
The pH of soils is most readily changed by liming which raises the pH and makes the soil less acid (see the following section). Liming is usually a deliberate and controlled attempt to influence soil acidity, but the pH of soils can also be altered by certain fertilisers sometimes used in forest nurseries, some fertilisers acidifying soil more rapidly than others. (See section 4.2 *et seq.* for details.)

The rate at which soil pH may change depends on the soil texture. The resistance to change, the 'buffer capacity', is largely proportional to the organic matter and clay content of the soil (and in neutral and alkaline soils, the carbonate content, but this last is not relevant to forest nursery soils). A strongly buffered soil is likely to provide a more constant environment for plants than a soil that is weakly buffered; light sandy soils are however usually in the latter category, unless very well provided with humus.

3.2.3 Making soils less acid

Where the soil is too acid, it can readily be brought to the optimum for the crop by adding lime in one of its several forms. For forest nurseries, however, several warnings must be given. Firstly, many light sandy soils are weakly buffered, therefore, the pH of such soils may be very readily raised by liming; secondly there is only a moderate range of pH over which optimum growth is obtained. To these must be added the fact that most weeds are less vigorous on very acid soils. Thus it is of the greatest importance:

- to apply lime evenly,
- not to apply excessive doses,
- to keep if anything on the acid side of the optimum.

The amount of lime required depends on a combination of the buffer capacity of the soil – this is most readily related to texture – and the extent to which the pH has to be raised. A guide which can be used in the absence of any other information is given in Table 3.1. Soils are grouped in four texture classes.

Within each soil texture class, three columns are given. Use the values in the first column (to raise the pH to 5.0) whenever the sections to be treated are likely to be used for conifer production. Values in column two (to raise the pH to 5.5) may be used if the sections to be so treated are for hardwoods only, while the values in column three should only be used for sections devoted to the raising of poplar or ash.

Soils laboratories are also able to determine the 'lime requirement' of soil (i.e. the amount of lime required to raise the pH to a given value) from samples sent in for analysis. If the lime requirement is to be determined, the laboratory must be told the desired optimum pH for the soils being analysed; the recommendations resulting from the analysis must be checked against the values shown in Table 3.1 for the pH and soil textures of the samples. If the 'lime requirement' exceeds the value derived from the table by more than 600 kg ha^{-1}, the divergence should be discussed with the soil chemist doing the analysis. If in doubt, always adopt the lower value of the two.

Liming materials (See also sections 3.2.1 and 3.2.4)

The forms of chalk and limestone from the various geological deposits are, when finely ground, approximately equal in value as means of raising the pH of soils even though there may be small differences in the amount of other materials present.

Dolomitic limestone provides Mg in addition to lime and can be used where, in addition to raising the pH, the Mg reserves in the soil have also to be increased.

Dolomitic limestone may be taken as equivalent weight for weight to ordinary ground limestone or chalk, and at the same time, equivalent weight for weight, to Epsom salts as regards supplying magnesium.

Magnesian limestone contains less Mg than dolomitic limestone but may be considered as its equivalent for all practical purposes.

Basic slag has been recommended in the past. However, because of changes in the steel industry, it is no longer available.

Lime-free seedbed grit

In the past, the pH of many nursery soils was raised unwittingly, when grits containing lime were used as seedbed covers and when basic slag or composts made with liming materials were applied to greencrops and trees. In recent years, foresters have understood such dangers and have used lime-free grits, etc. Periodic checks must be carried out however to ensure that in particular, the grits currently in use for covering seed are lime-free.

If in doubt about the suitability of a grit,

take a sample (about a tablespoonful), put it on a clean saucer or shallow bowl and pour over it a little dilute hydrochloric acid. If the grit fizzes or individual particles of the grit fizz, limestone is present and the grit is unsuitable.

Hard water has also raised the pH of sections which have been heavily irrigated for several years.

A fuller discussion of the different liming materials available is contained in Whinham, 1976.

3.2.4 Acidification of soils

While it is easy to neutralise an acid soil, it is more costly to acidify a soil when the pH is too high. Where a substantial amount of free lime is present, acidification is practically impossible. Every forester should, therefore, avoid measures which make the soil less acid than is required and, of course, a soil with a naturally high pH should never be chosen for a nursery.

Soil without free lime may be acidified over a period of several years by regular use of ammonium sulphate applied as top-dressings to crops. The ammonium-nitrogen in this fertiliser is either taken up directly by the plant, or on soils with a pH over 5.5 is converted to nitrate in the soil, leaving the free sulphate which is the principal acidifying agent. The nitrate-nitrogen also acidifies as long as it is not taken up by plants.

More rapid acidification can be achieved by

Table 3.1 Tonnes per hectare of magnesian limestone, ground limestone or ground chalk to raise the pH of soil to approximately 5.0 (for normal forest nursery production); 5.5 (for sections devoted to hardwoods); or 6.0 (for sections devoted to poplars)

	Soil texture class														
	1 Sands, loamy sands			2 Sandy loams			3 Silt loams, sandy silt loams, sandy clay loams			4 Clay loams, silty clay loams, clay			5 (Soils in class 4 but high in organic matter)		
	Tonnes lime per hectare to raise soil pH														
Soil pH (suspension in water)	up to 5.0	5.5	6.0	up to 5.0	5.5	6.0	up to 5.0	5.5	6.0	up to 5.0	5.5	6.0	up to 5.0	5.5	6.0
3.0	5.0	6.3	7.5	6.0	7.6	9.0	8.1	10.1	12.1	10.0	12.5	15.0	11.9	14.9	17.9
3.2	4.5	5.8	7.0	5.5	7.0	8.5	7.3	9.4	11.4	9.0	11.5	14.0	10.8	13.6	16.6
3.4	4.0	5.3	6.5	4.9	6.4	7.9	6.5	8.5	10.5	8.0	10.5	13.0	9.5	12.5	15.5
3.6	3.5	4.8	6.0	4.3	5.8	7.3	5.6	7.8	9.8	7.0	9.5	12.0	8.4	11.3	14.3
3.8	3.0	4.3	5.5	3.6	5.1	6.6	4.9	6.9	8.9	6.0	8.5	11.0	7.1	10.1	13.1
4.0	2.5	3.8	5.0	3.0	4.5	6.0	4.1	6.1	8.1	5.0	7.5	10.0	6.0	8.9	11.9
4.2	2.0	3.3	4.5	2.5	4.0	5.5	3.3	5.3	7.3	4.0	6.5	9.0	4.8	7.8	10.8
4.4	1.5	2.8	4.0	1.9	3.4	4.9	2.5	4.5	6.5	3.0	5.5	8.0	3.6	6.5	9.5
4.6	1.0	2.3	3.5	1.3	2.8	4.3	1.6	3.6	5.6	2.0	4.5	7.0	2.4	5.4	8.4
4.8	0.5	1.8	3.0	0.6	2.1	3.6	0.9	2.9	4.9	1.0	3.5	6.0	1.3	4.1	7.1
5.0		1.3	2.5		1.5	3.0		2.0	4.1		2.5	5.0		3.0	6.0
5.2		0.8	2.0		1.0	2.5		1.3	3.3		1.5	4.0		1.8	4.8
5.4		0.3	1.5		0.4	1.9		0.4	2.5		0.5	3.0		0.6	3.6
5.6			1.0			1.3			1.6			2.0			2.4
5.8			0.5			0.6			0.9			1.0			1.3

Note: If the soil contains more than 10% organic matter, use the next higher soil texture class; e.g. if the soil is a loamy sand, the values in the first set of three columns would normally be appropriate. However, if the soil organic matter of such a soil exceeds 10%, use the set of columns headed 'Sandy loams'.

a single heavy winter dressing of sulphate of ammonia. A dressing of 3750 kg ha^{-1} has reduced the pH by between 0.75 and 1 unit. (Benzian, 1965). However, such heavy winter dressings may result in excessively high concentrations of soluble salts and risk of scorch to plants during the subsequent growing season.

Alternatively, soils can be acidified by additions of screened rock sulphur, or flowers of sulphur. Rock sulphur has been used successfully in several Scottish forest nurseries. However, the risk of damage in a dry spring is greater with sulphur than with ammonium sulphate. In either case, the sulphur is oxidised in the soil and forms sulphuric acid. Sulphuric acid has also been applied direct to soils experimentally. Ferrous sulphate is used in horticulture for acidification but not, so far as is known, in British forest nurseries.

The quantity of sulphur required for acidification depends on the pH of the soil and the pH required. In experiments in England, 1250 kg ha^{-1} of sulphur were required to procure a drop of between 0.75 and 1.0 pH unit, while in Scotland 500–600 kg ha^{-1} have had the same effect. In some nurseries, the soil once acidified has stayed acid while in others the pH has slowly drifted back towards its original value.

3.2.5 Maintaining the status quo; and the effect of nitrogen fertiliser on pH

Several proprietary nitrogen fertilisers are available which combine a nitrogen compound with calcium carbonate, so that the fertiliser can be used with little effect on soil pH. 'Nitrochalk' with 15.5% N was used as a top-dressing for seedbeds in research programmes for many years and had no effect on soil pH. Currently, however, the content of N in this and similar proprietary fertilisers is higher and the ratio of acidifying to neutralising constituents changed. Light nursery soils are likely to become more acid with repeated use of such compounds, but the rate of change will be slow.

The acidifying effect of ammonium sulphate is described in the previous section. Ammonium nitrate is also likely to acidify soils, but not as strongly as ammonium sulphate. The effects of slow release fertilisers depend on their constituents and no generalised comment can be made.

Because pH is so important for plant growth and because it can be altered by the nutrient regime, soil samples should be taken, at least for pH measurement, every 3 years as a matter of routine.

3.3 Soil analysis

Many attributes of the soil can be the subject of chemical or physical analyses. However, only those which can be influenced by management are discussed below. Permanent attributes such as texture (section 3.1.1) while of critical importance in selecting sites, are of small significance in relation to day-to-day control of fertility.

While chemists have been examining agricultural soils for many years, forest nursery soils have received much less attention. Cooke (1967) discusses fully the values and the limitations of soil analysis and emphasises the risks of extrapolating results from one crop to another, or from one soil series to others derived from unrelated parent material.

Soils are normally analysed for P, K, Mg, pH and lime requirement. Some laboratories also determine the percentage of organic matter. The analytical methods, especially in England and Wales, have been based on agricultural crops and agricultural soils; for forest nurseries it seems at present best to treat the results of soil analyses as indicators of any need to boost reserves in the soil *in addition* to supplying, through fertilisers, the current needs of the crop.

In paragraphs 3.3.1 *et seq.*, tables are given showing the range of values likely to be obtained when analysing soil for P, K and Mg. The two sets of values and indices given are those currently in use by the laboratories most likely to analyse forest nursery soils, i.e. the Agricultural Development and Advisory Service (ADAS) for England and Wales, and the Macaulay Land Use Research Institute in Scotland.

The recommendations in paragraphs 3.3.1–3.3.3 are adequate for sandy loams and loamy sands of moderate organic matter content (say, between 2.5 and 7%). For heavy soils, or soils with a much higher organic matter content, they will be less reliable.

It has usually been considered that balance, i.e. a similar analysis index for P, K and Mg, is as important as the actual values, and if P and K, or K and Mg are badly out of balance, then deficiency symptoms are more likely to appear in plants.

3.3.1 Phosphorus

Results of soil analysis for P indicate whether it is necessary to boost the reserve of P by means of an extra application at the first opportunity after analysis.

3.3.2 Potassium

Forest nursery soils which are light and acid usually contain little K and may have a limited capacity to store any reserves. Additional fertilisers containing potassium should therefore be added as a matter of routine as top-dressings for each crop on such soils. Soils containing more adequate levels of K will need less top-dressing with K or possibly none at all.

3.3.3 Magnesium

The presence or absence of deficiency symptoms and results of soil analysis should determine whether to apply magnesium for each crop until the next analysis, or alternatively whether to apply magnesian limestone both to raise pH and increase reserves of Mg.

3.3.4 Interpretation of results of soil analyses

While a soil analysis is a highly informative guide to managers, it is most important to realise that it is not an exclusive basis for recommendations for any fertiliser regime. The nursery forester has other sources of information which may support or modify recommendations based on soil analyses. The most important of the other sources is the knowledge of the plants' performance over the last 2–3 years in relation to the fertiliser used. This and the knowledge of what can be achieved in productive nurseries should give a good idea of the extent by which current practice needs to be modified to achieve such aims as high out-turns of usable 1-year seedlings, 1+1 transplants or undercut seedlings. The forester should also know whether the plants show deficiency symptoms at any time during the year. The forester should

Table 3.2 Phosphorus content of soils by analysis

ADAS analysis		Action recommended in addition to standard treatment*		Macaulay analysis	
Analysis results (parts per million P)	Index			Analysis results (mg kg^{-1} P)	Index†
0–9	0	Apply 1250 ⎫		<7	VL
		875 ⎬ kg of ground mineral		7–22	L
10–15	1	625 ⎭ phosphate per ha respectively		23–35	SL
16–25	2	Apply		35–48	S–SL
26–45	3	standard ⎫		48–109	S
46–70	4	treatment ⎬		>109	H
		only ⎭			

(ADAS scale goes up to 9 but the higher indices are relevant mainly to glasshouse soils)

* Standard treatment is to add for each crop 60–120 kg ha^{-1} of P (25–30 kg ha^{-1} for greencrop); see Table 4.4.
† VL, very low; L, low; SL, slightly low; S, satisfactory; H, high.

have some idea of how the soil handles, and its texture, structure and capacity to retain nutrients, as well as being aware of features of local climate which affect responses to fertilisers, e.g. high summer rainfall or regular spring drought.

Where in doubt, and where information is not otherwise available, properly designed and laid-out fertiliser trials can provide information leading to more confident prescriptions for fertility maintenance.

3.3.5 Recommendations to apply lime

One particular aspect of soil analysis that should always be looked at critically and checked against Table 3.1 and section 3.2.3 is any recommendation to apply lime. Many soil laboratories are accustomed to handling agricultural soils and to applying agricultural standards of lime requirement, and an error could easily occur here. If any lime recommendation seems excessive, ask for confirmation of the figure recommended, making it quite clear

Table 3.3 Potassium content of soils by analysis

ADAS analysis		Action recommended in addition to standard treatment*	Macaulay analysis	
Analysis results (parts per million K)	Index		Analysis results (mg kg^{-1} K)	Index†
0–60	0	Top dressing with K essential especially on light soils. See Table 4.2	<12	VL
			12–42	L
61–120	1	Perhaps top-dress with K	42–66	SL
			66–91	S–SL
121–240	2		91–208	S
241–400	3	No top-dressings necessary	>208	H
401–600	4			
(Index scale goes up to 9)				

* Standard treatment is to apply 125–185 kg ha^{-1} of K in spring to each crop; see Table 4.4.
† VL, very low; L, low; SL, slightly low; S, satisfactory; H, high.

Table 3.4 Magnesium content of soils by analysis

ADAS analysis		Action recommended in addition to standard treatment*	Macaulay analysis	
Analysis results (parts per million Mg)	Index		Analysis results (mg kg^{-1} Mg)	Index†
0–25	0	Apply 60 kg ha^{-1} magnesium to each crop.	<12	L
26–50	1	Use magnesian limestone whenever pH has to be raised. See Table 4.3.	12–24	SL
51–100	2	Annual magnesium applications probably not necessary. Use magnesian limestone whenever pH has to be raised. See Table 4.3.	24–36	S–SL
101–175	3		>36	S
176–250	4			

* Magnesium is not normally applied unless shown to be necessary by foliage discoloration or soil analysis.
† L, low; SL, slightly low; S, satisfactory.

what is the desired optimum pH for the nursery soil.

3.3.6 Sampling of soil for analysis

Before any samples of soil are taken, contact should be made with the laboratory doing the analysis. Agreement must be reached about when and how many samples are required and the sampling and labelling procedure to be followed. Laboratories which may analyse forest nursery soils are listed in Appendix Ib. The method of sampling likely to be recommended is given in section 3.3.7. Samples should be taken in the autumn unless otherwise agreed, so that variations according to the time of year are minimised. It is preferable that soils should be sampled regularly every 3–4 years.

Analysis may take some time; allow for at least 6 weeks between sending samples and getting the results. Each section is best sampled before greencropping or during bare fallow, whichever is normally part of the rotation. Samples should be taken in dry weather, but if this is impossible, the soil laboratory should be consulted before any drying of soil is attempted. In England and Wales, soils are preferred undried.

Any covering letter and accompanying label on the soil sample should, between them, give the following details:

- Name and address of sender (to whom results will be returned).
- Location of nursery if different from above.
- Number of samples sent and source nursery section of each sample.
- Analyses required.
- Optimum pH desired for each section.
- Date and reference of previous soil analyses.
- Crops and fertilisers since the last analysis.
- Any relevant information, e.g. deficiencies observed, high summer rainfall, soil map if available, soil type if known.

3.3.7 Method of soil sampling

First decide what areas should be sampled.

Normally, each nursery section should be sampled separately unless two or more sections are of the same soil type have similar drainage conditions and have been treated identically for several years.

Any subsection or part of a section which differs visibly from the rest of the section, or on which plants regularly grow markedly better or worse than elsewhere in the section, should be sampled separately.

It is important to determine the normal depth of cultivation, especially in heathland nurseries.

For each section to be sampled, the aim is to get as representative a soil sample as possible. This can be done by collecting about 24 small equal samples from points evenly distributed over each sample area. Small sections may be less intensively sampled, but a minimum of 10 samples should always be taken. Sections may be traversed following a W pattern, and taking six samples from each leg of the W; other sampling patterns may be used if preferred.

Samples may be taken with an auger or a spade. An auger is preferable and if samples are to be taken regularly, a suitable tool should be obtained for this purpose. Sampling by spade necessitates additional work mixing samples and sub-dividing to reduce the bulky sample to the amount required for analysis.

Sampling by auger

There are special soil augers of approximately 3 cm diameter for taking samples; wood augers of similar size can also be used if the shank is lengthened. Screw the auger into the soil to the full depth of normal cultivation, pull it out with the soil sticking to it, then take the soil off and put it in a clean bucket. Continue this procedure, as outlined in the preceding paragraph, until the whole section has been covered and sufficient soil collected (i.e. about 1 kg). The soil should then be well mixed and put in a polythene or cotton bag.

Sampling by spade

If using a spade, ensure it is clean before sampling, then at each sampling point, dig to expose a smooth face of soil the width of the spade and to the depth of cultivation. From this face, remove a slice of soil not more than 3 cm thick from the whole depth of the exposed face and put it in a clean bucket. All samples from a given section should then be mixed thoroughly in the bucket and the mixed sample reduced by repeated halving until about 1 kg soil is left. This should be put in a strong polythene or hessian bag – the best size is one which the sample will fill half to two-thirds full.

For further reading, see Russell, 1988.

REFERENCES

AVERY, B.W. (1990). *Soils of the British Isles.* CAB International, Wallingford.

BENZIAN, B. (1965). *Experiments on nutrition problems in forest nurseries.* Forestry Commission Bulletin 37. HMSO, London.

COOKE, G.W. (1967). *Control of soil fertility.* Crosby Lockwood & Son, London.

DAVIES, D.B. (1982). *Subsoiling.* ADAS Leaflet L 617. HMSO, London.

HODGSON, J.M. (1985). *Soil Survey field handbook.* Technical Monograph 5. Soil Survey of England & Wales, Harpenden.

LOW, A.J. and SHARPE, A.L. (1973). The long-term effects of organic and inorganic fertiliser regimes at Teindland nursery. *Scottish Forestry* **27**, 287–295.

RUSSELL, E.W. (1988). *Soil conditions and plant growth,* 11th edtn, ed. A. Wild. Longmans, London.

WHINHAM, N.W. (1976). *Lime in agriculture.* ADAS Leaflet L 542. HMSO, London.

Chapter 4

Plant nutrition

M. F. Proe

Introduction

During the last two decades, new systems of production have been introduced into British forest nurseries. Many of these make greater use of cold storage, precision sowing, undercutting, containerised stock and vegetative propagation. Such diverse production systems require a thorough understanding of the principles of plant nutrition.

Pressure for land has now made fallowing and greencropping more difficult to incorporate into nursery management plans. Many traditional sources of organic amendments have disappeared or are so remote from nurseries that transport costs prohibit their use. On the other hand, many new formulations of fertilisers are now available, including slow release and liquid products.

Environmental concerns over loss of inorganic fertilisers to drinking water supplies (especially in southern England) threaten further constraints to nursery management.

Nutrient regimes in forest nurseries must, therefore, ensure that intensive production can be sustained without long-term soil degradation. In addition, the supply of nutrients must be carefully matched to plant demand, thereby minimising losses through leaching. Nutrient supply must also be manipulated, in conjunction with production techniques, to produce stock of correct size specifications and in the correct physiological state to maximise their chance of survival and rapid early growth when planted out to forest sites.

This chapter focuses upon nutritional regimes for the production of bare-root planting stock.

4.1 Foundations

The regulation of a balanced nutrient supply is one of the nursery manager's most important duties. Inadequate nutrient supply can cause failure in the achievement of production targets. No one nutrient is more important than another for plant growth, though in any particular nursery one nutrient may be in relatively short supply compared with others because of the local soil type or climate.

4.1.1 Essential nutrients

Carbon dioxide and water provide the carbon (C), oxygen (O) and hydrogen (H) necessary for the production of carbohydrates during photosynthesis. In addition, plants require a further 13 mineral elements derived primarily from the soil. Six of these are required in relatively large amounts – nitrogen (N), phosphorus (P), potassium (K), magnesium (Mg), calcium (Ca) and sulphur (S). The first four nutrients have to be applied deliberately in the forest nursery or plants may not grow. Calcium and sulphur are constituents of fertilisers such as superphosphate and are almost always present in the soil in sufficient quantities to maintain good plant growth. Trace amounts of seven other elements are required for growth – iron (Fe), manganese (Mn), boron (B), zinc (Zn), copper (Cu), molybdenum (Mo) and chlorine (Cl). These are rarely deficient in British forest nurseries.

4.1.2 Nutritional targets

The nursery manager should aim to provide a balanced supply of nutrients capable of supporting healthy and vigorous plant growth while also ensuring adequate root development and plant hardiness.

Ideally, nutrient regimes should be used in conjunction with other cultural practices such as undercutting and irrigation to maintain growth so that plants reach the optimum size for sale at the end of their final growing season in the nursery. However, in practice, this is not always possible because of the unpredictability of summer temperature and rainfall. These affect both the rate of nutrient supply from the soil and the rate of demand for nutrients by growing plants. Erring on the cautious side may lead managers to apply heavier dressings than are necessary. This can lead to what has sometimes been referred to as 'luxury uptake'. In this case nutrients may be supplied in excess to plant demand with no return in increased growth. If the effects of over-application of fertiliser are limited to 'luxury uptake', the economic penalty incurred is small in terms of overall crop production costs. However, over-application of fertiliser can lead to toxicity ('fertiliser scorch'), excessive shoot growth both in relation to the nursery manager's objectives and in relation to the size of the root system (poor shoot:root ratio).

The concept of 'luxury uptake' has been questioned in recent years. There is now substantial evidence that nutrient uptake continues in late summer and autumn when plant growth may be minimal. Storage of N during winter has been shown to influence growth the following spring in both sycamore and Sitka spruce (Millard and Proe, 1991a and 1991b). Uptake of N and K late in the season can also increase overwinter frost resistance although late season N applications may induce earlier flushing in the following season, thereby increasing the risk of spring frost damage (Benzian *et al.*, 1974).

Below optimum levels, there is a critical range in which plant nutrient levels are marginal and growth may be slightly reduced without any visual signs of deficiency. As plant nutrient levels decline, visual symptoms do appear and growth is markedly reduced.

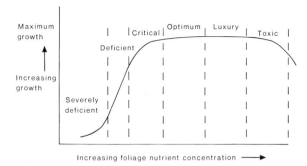

Figure 4.1 Plant response to increasing nutrient supply. (Modified from Morrison, 1974)

Eventually, deficiency becomes so severe that growth ceases and plants may die.

The general relationship between plant nutrient concentration and growth is illustrated in Figure 4.1. Marginal ranges of nutrient concentrations for different species are given in Table 4.8. These values are based upon broadleaved foliage sampled in July/August, or the tops of conifer seedlings taken at the end of the growing season. Little information exists regarding how these values change throughout the growing season. In practice, there is seldom enough time to collect and analyse foliage samples for the prescription of remedial fertiliser applications within the same growing season. Foliage analyses can be used, however, to check how soil analysis data relate to plant nutrient status in a specific nursery.

4.1.3 Soil fertility

Aspects of soil fertility have already been discussed in Chapter 3. In terms of plant nutrition, however, it is through the soil that plants obtain most of their nutrients and some factors affecting nutrient availability are described in the following sections.

Nursery managers should try to prevent the occurrence of nutrient deficiencies by matching the supply of nutrients with the expected removal from the nursery in planting stock. This must also take account of any applied fertiliser lost from the site by leaching, or immobilised within the soil by

Table 4.1 Nutrients removed in Sitka spruce (kg ha^{-1})

Crop and nursery	Dry matter	N	P	K	Ca	Mg
Sitka spruce seedlings						
Teindland, Moray	–	55.0	8.2	41.8	13.2	4.4
Wareham, Dorset	3201	48.4	7.7	22.0	19.8	4.4
Kennington, Oxford	3938	75.9	12.1	47.3	24.2	4.4
Sitka spruce transplants						
Wareham, Dorset	4435	69.3	11.0	40.7	24.2	5.5
Kennington, Oxford	7392	110.0	15.4	66.0	42.9	7.7
Devilla, Kincardine	–	115.5	14.3	62.7	18.7	7.7

competing micro-organisms or through soil chemical processes; such processes include, for example, **phosphorus fixation** in which soluble forms of P react with iron or aluminium in the soil and become unavailable for plant growth (Brady 1974, p.462).

Nutrient removal

The quantity of nutrients typically removed in crops of Sitka spruce are given in Table 4.1. What is actually removed within any particular crop will depend upon the soil, plant size, stocking levels, fertiliser regimes and climate. In general, however, quantities of nutrients removed in forest nursery crops are of the same order as those removed in the harvesting of cereals, hay or potatoes. The quantity of fertilisers required to supply these nutrients is comparatively large due to poor recovery of applied nutrients by plants. In an extreme case of a sand low in clay and organic matter, 70% of the potassium applied was lost from the top 42 cm of the soil profile due to leaching, while only 22% of applied phosphorus was either taken up by the plants or retained within the top 25 cm of the soil (Bolton and Coulter, 1966).

Cation exchange capacity

The extent to which nutrients are retained within a soil in forms available to plants depends, to a large extent, upon soil **cation exchange capacity** (CEC). Cation exchange capacity is conventionally expressed as milli-equivalents per 100 g of soil (meq 100 g^{-1} soil).

Clay particles and well-humified organic matter typically possess negative charges. Soil electrical neutrality is maintained by the adsorption of positively charged 'cations' (H$^+$, K$^+$, (NH$_4$)$^+$, Ca^{2+}, Mg^{2+}, etc.) that are important for plant nutrition. There are a number of techniques by which soil cation exchange capacity can be measured (Bache, 1976). The most usual method is to displace exchangeable cations with a saturating salt (e.g. ammonium acetate) buffered to a pH of 7. However, because CEC can vary with soil pH, measurements taken often over-estimate the CEC that is operating in forest nursery soils where pH values are usually within the range 4.5 to 6. Target values for some North American forest nursery soils have been set within the range 7–12 meq g^{-1} soil (Youngberg, 1984). Values in UK nurseries usually fall within this range.

Soils with a high cation exchange capacity can retain nutrients in an available form to plants, so resisting leaching losses following fertiliser application. Cation exchange capacity increases with increasing organic matter content, provided this is well decomposed (Figure 4.2), and also with increasing clay content.

Base saturation

Nutrient availability depends not only upon the cation exchange capacity but also on the proportion of this capacity occupied by nutrient elements as opposed to hydrogen ions – the **base saturation**. This, in turn, is largely reflected by soil pH (Figure 4.3).

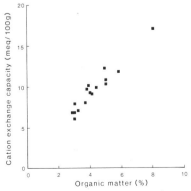

Figure 4.2 Relationship between cation exchange capacity and percentage soil organic matter.

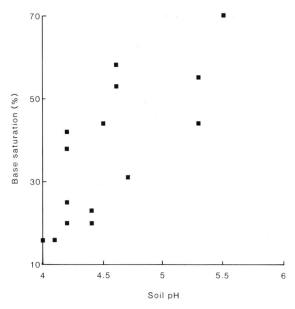

Figure 4.3 Relationship between soil pH and percentage base saturation.

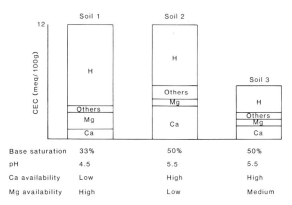

	Soil 1	Soil 2	Soil 3
Base saturation	33%	50%	50%
pH	4.5	5.5	5.5
Ca availability	Low	High	High
Mg availability	High	Low	Medium

Figure 4.4 Relationship between cation exchange capacity, soil type, base saturation and nutrient availability for three contrasting soils.

The effects of cation exchange capacity and base saturation upon nutrient availability are illustrated in Figure 4.4. The first two soils have CECs of 12 meq $100\,g^{-1}$ soil while the third has a CEC of 6 meq $100\,g^{-1}$. The nutrient holding capacity of the soil depends, to a large extent, on the total cation exchange capacity. Nutrient availability, however, depends more upon the proportion of exchange sites occupied by each nutrient. Soil 2 and soil 3 have base saturations of 50% and their pH values are 5.5. Soil 1 has a base saturation of 33% and, consequently, a lower pH of 4.5. In soil 1 the *amount* of exchangeable calcium is the same as in soil 3 but the *availability* will be greater in soil 3 because the *proportion* of exchangeable sites occupied by calcium is greater. Similarly, magnesium availability will be greater in soil 3 than soil 2 even though the amounts are similar.

In soil analysis, an attempt is made to estimate the potential availability of nutrients to plants rather than the total soil content. Nitrogen is rarely analysed since its availability through a season is very difficult to

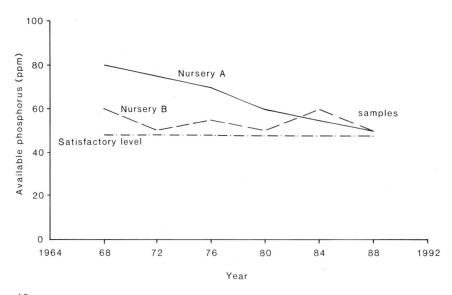

Figure 4.5 Soil analysis interpretation: available phosphorus in two soils over a 20-year period.

determine from a single analysis, as it takes part in many microbe-related reactions and not just in cation exchange.

To get the best out of them, soil analyses should be based upon regular sampling together with careful records of fertiliser use and plant performance. In this way each analysis can be seen in the context of historical trends within specific nurseries. For example, a given value in one nursery may indicate stable and adequate nutrient levels whereas the same value in another may show a rapid decline toward possible deficiency levels within the near future (Figure 4.5). Record keeping should include details of the timing and rates of past fertiliser treatments, any organic materials added to the soil, amounts and duration of rainfall and irrigation and the timing of undercutting and any other important cultural operations.

4.2 Use of fertilisers

The particular nutritional requirements of individual crops vary greatly depending upon plant and soil characteristics, together with the type of management adopted. The guidelines given here include a representative range of fertilisers used in common practice, but each nursery should tailor its fertiliser regime to fit its own requirements, normally with the help of a soil analytical service. A wide variety of products are currently available to nursery managers. Traditionally, a dressing of phosphorus and potassium has been applied as solid fertiliser before the growing season and top dressings of nitrogen, sometimes with potassium, applied several times during the season. Advances in technology and improved understanding of the relationships between nutrient supply and plant performance have led more recently to the development and use of both liquid and various types of slow-release fertilisers. Current trends are towards applying fertilisers through nursery irrigation systems (particularly container systems under polythene), thereby achieving a better match between nutrient supply and plant demand

(Burt, 1988). Nevertheless, solid fertilisers are likely to remain in use as long as bare-rooted stock continues to be produced.

4.2.1 Soluble fertilisers

Most materials used in forest nurseries are readily soluble compound fertilisers comprising various combinations of nitrogen (N), phosphorus (P) and potassium (K). The most widely used products are nitrogen fertilisers, nitrogen/potassium and phosphorus/potassium compounds.

Single nutrient ('straight') fertilisers

Nitrogen is usually supplied as ammonium nitrate, ammonium sulphate or urea (Table 4.2). N-fertilisers are often granular or prilled for ease of application and are readily soluble in water. The positively charged ammonium ions tend to be held within the cation exchange complex of soils and are less prone to leaching than are nitrates. Pure ammonium nitrate (34.5% N) is slightly acidifying and this is sometimes counteracted by adding calcium carbonate to provide a neutral fertiliser with a nitrogen content in the region of 27%. Applications of ammonium sulphate are three times as acidifying as ammonium nitrate. This is due to microbial activity which produces sulphuric and nitric acids. On soils with relatively high pH values, ammonium sulphate can be used to lower the pH gradually towards optimum levels.

Prilled urea, which is widely used in plantation forestry, is rarely used in the nursery due to the high concentrations of nitrogen present (44%) and the tendency for losses to occur through volatilisation. Where urea is used, an initial reduction in soil acidity is followed by subsequent acidification, with an overall net acidifying effect similar to that of ammonium nitrate (Brady,1974).

Phosphorus is much less mobile within the soil than highly soluble nutrients such as N and K. Nevertheless, it can be leached from very sandy soils, but, at the other extreme, it can become unavailable to plants by becoming closely adsorbed on clay minerals in the soil.

Phosphorus is currently applied as phosphate. Phosphates vary in water solubility from virtually insoluble, to moderately soluble. Water-insoluble forms are, however, slightly soluble in citric acid. This often provides the basis for expressing the availability of phosphate to plants in such materials.

Phosphorus is usually applied in combination with other nutrients but there are some 'straight' phosphate fertilisers (Table 4.2).

Superphosphate is the principal phosphate fertiliser currently used. It is manufactured by treating rock phosphate with sulphuric acid to produce a material containing approximately 30% phosphates, 50% gypsum (calcium sulphate) and 20% impurities. Triple superphosphate is produced by treating the raw rock phosphate with phosphoric acid to increase the phosphate content more than two-fold.

Rock phosphate is the least soluble of all phosphate fertilisers and must usually be ground to a powder (ground mineral phosphate, or GMP) if it is to become available for plant uptake. Finely ground rock phosphate is most effective when added to soils high in organic matter. Availability of GMP as a powder is now limited. Coarser material may have a role in maintaining P levels in difficult soils where leaching or fixation on to clay minerals is a problem. Where rock phosphate is used, North African sources are preferred and the properties of various sources are discussed more fully in Forestry Commission Leaflet 63 (Binns, 1975).

'Bonemeal' is an alternative source of P used in horticulture but its high cost usually precludes its use in forest nurseries.

Potassium is obtained from mining underground salt beds and is usually applied as potassium chloride (muriate of potash) or potassium sulphate (sulphate of potash). All potash salts used as fertilisers are water soluble and have little effect upon soil pH even when applied in large amounts. Occasional damage to plant tissues has been recorded with potassium chloride and potassium sulphate is now generally preferred for forest nurseries.

Magnesium, if required, is usually applied as magnesium sulphate. This can be as 'Epsom salts' or in the more concentrated form of kieserite (Table 4.2). If soils are particularly acidic then magnesian limestone or dolomitic limestone can be used.

Compound fertilisers

There are several chemical compounds used as fertilisers which contain more than one of the major nutrients applied in forest nurseries. Potassium nitrate contains both potassium and nitrogen. Monammonium phosphate (MAP) and diammonium phosphate (DAP) contain both nitrogen and phosphorus.

'Compound' fertilisers usually comprise a number of 'straight' products mixed to provide a number of different nutrients, although potassium nitrate, MAP and DAP may also be used.

Individual formulations vary between manufacturers and also change with time. Constituents used include potassium salts, ammonium nitrate, superphosphates and ammonium phosphates. Examples of different products currently available are given in Table 4.3.

4.2.2 Slow-release fertilisers

On sandy, well-drained soils in areas of moderate to heavy rainfall, soluble salts of nitrogen and potassium are particularly vulnerable to losses through leaching. The usual method of overcoming this problem is to apply top-dressings every 4–6 weeks throughout the season thus incurring increased costs of application. An alternative is to use slow-release fertilisers, many of which are now on the market. Allen (1984) described the potential benefits from slow release fertilisers:

- better utilisation by the crop due to the release rate being more closely related to plant demand;
- reduced losses from leaching, volatilisation or denitrification;
- reduced toxicity due to their lower salt indices;

Table 4.2 Single nutrient 'straight' fertilisers

Nitrogen

Material	Formula	% N	Properties	Uses
Amonium nitrate	$NH_4\,NO_3$	34.5	Water soluble crystals – slightly acidifying	Top dressings
Amonium nitrate + Calcium carbonate	$NH_4\,NO_3$ + $Ca\,CO_3$	27	Granular – water soluble: little effect on soil pH	Top dressings
Ammonium sulphate	$(NH_4)_2\,SO_4$	21	Water soluble crystals: acidifies soil	Top dressing
Urea	$CO\,(NH_2)_2$	44	Water soluble – prilled initially reduces but then increases soil activity	Basis of many slow release N fertilisers

Phosphorus

Material	Formula	% P_2O_5 (%P)	Properties	Uses
Rock phosphate	Complex	25–35 (11–15)	Insoluble – slow acting. Preferred as ground powder if available	Longlasting and used to increase soil P status
Super phosphate	$Ca(H_2PO_4)_2$ + $Ca\,SO_4.2H_2O$	18–20 (8–9)	Water soluble powder/granules	Seedbeds and transplants
Triple super phosphate	$Ca(H_2PO_4)_2$	46 (19–20)	Water soluble granules	Quick acting on seedbeds and transplants

Potassium

Compound	Formula	% K_2O (%K)	Properties	Uses
Muriate of potash – potassium chloride	KCl	60 (50)	Water soluble crystals	Top dressing but can cause foliage scorch
Sulphate of potash – potassium sulphate	$K_2\,SO_4$	50 (42)	Water soluble powdery crystals	Top dressing – causes less scorch than KCl

Magnesium

Compound	Formula	% MgO (%Mg)	Properties	Uses
Epsom salts	$Mg\,SO_4.7H_2O$	17 (10)	Soluble crystals	Restricted to remedial foliage sprays due to cost
Kieserite	$Mg\,SO_4.H_2O$	29 (17)	Slowly soluble crystals	Applied to soil several weeks before sowing/lining out
Magnesian limestone and dolomite*	$Mg\,CO_3$ + $Ca\,CO_3$	16–21 (10–13)	Slightly soluble powder – reduces soil acidity	Used to correct low soil Mg levels on acid soils

* Dolomite is composed of approximately $7CaCO_3$ + $6MgCO_3$. Magnesian limestone contains a higher proportion of $CaCO_3$.

Table 4.3 Some currently available fertiliser products

Manufacturer	Product	Formulation N : P_2O_5 : K_2O % % %			
Readily soluble fertilisers					
Hydro Agri	Double Season PK	0	24	24	Check when available in year*
	NK Silage	24	0	17	
	Extran	34.5	0	0	
ICI Fertilizers	Nitram	34.5	0	0	
	Kaynitro	25	0	16	
ICI Horticulture	'5 Star' Stabilised N	25	1	0	+ 1.5% Mg + trace elements
	Enmag	4	19	10	+ 7.5% Mg
Kemira	Nitraprill	34.5	0	0	(formerly UKF)
	Kayenne	26	0	15	
Controlled release fertilisers					
Fisons	Ficote 70	14	8	8	} Short term
		16	10	10	CRF
	Ficote 140	14	8	8	} Medium term
		16	10	10	CRF
Grace Sierra	Osmocote Mini	18	6	12	2 - 3 months CRF
		18	6	11	5 - 6 months CRF
	Osmocote	18	11	10	8 - 9 months CRF
		17	10	10	12 - 14 months CRF
		16	8	9 + 3% MgO	16 - 18 months CRF

* PK fertilisers similar in composition to 0:24:24 may also be obtainable from fertiliser blenders, e.g. Scotphos, Ayr.

- lower application costs.

Slow release nitrogen fertilisers are essentially of two types (Sharma, 1979):

- those comprising organic and inorganic compounds of low water solubility;
- conventional, soluble fertilisers coated with insoluble or slowly soluble materials (sometimes referred to as controlled release or CRF fertilisers).

Nitrogen fertilisers with low solubility include urea–formaldehyde (UF), isobutylidene diurea (IBDU) and magnesium ammonium phosphate. Rate of release of nitrogen from slowly soluble materials depends mainly upon particle size together with soil conditions and climate.

Various materials have been used to coat soluble fertiliser granules to control the rate of nutrient release including gums, oils, waxes, resins, sulphur and plastics. These provide slow or delayed release by a number of different mechanisms. Water may diffuse through a semipermeable coating causing the granules to swell and burst the coating. Other products may have small pores in an impermeable coating through which the soluble fertiliser diffuses slowly while in others the impermeable coating is designed to degrade slowly due to chemical or biological action.

Apart from slow-release nitrogen fertilisers, studies have also been made into the performance of potassium metaphosphate as a slow-release source of both phosphorus and potassium. Results of tests in Britain showed that on the lightest soils it sustained a supply of K better than potassic superphosphate. It was not, however, as effective at maintaining soil K levels as was a regime of potassic super-phosphate in the spring plus a top dressing of K (prilled potassium nitrate) in the summer (Benzian *et al.*, 1969).

Many slow-release fertilisers are now on the market including Enmag, Gold-N (sulphur-coated urea), 5-Star Fertilisers, Ficote and Osmocote. Modes of action vary as do individual formulations with some including trace elements in addition to several of the major nutrients. If these products are to be used, advice should be sought regarding rates of application, timing and use of supplementary dressings.

4.2.3 Liquid fertilisers

In recent years there has been a growing interest in the use of liquid fertilisers in forest nurseries. Early experience suggests liquid fertilisers are every bit as safe as granular fertilisers when used carefully. They are particularly important for nurseries using irrigation systems through which liquid feed can be applied at frequent intervals. They also give nursery managers greater choice of rate and time of application and enable a more even application of fertiliser to seedbeds and transplants, thus reducing the risk from scorch on young plants.

Liquid fertilisers usually contain various combinations of urea, ammonium nitrate, potassium chloride, ammonium phosphate and ammonium polyphosphates depending upon their specific formulation. There is a limit ('concentration barrier') to how much of these compounds can be dissolved into solution so that liquid fertilisers usually contain less nutrient per unit weight than do solid fertilisers.

A wide variety of true solution fertilisers is now available. When used, particular care must be taken to control the quantity of spray applied together with the droplet size and nutrient concentration.

On the whole, liquid fertilisers are more expensive than their solid counterparts.

Attempts have been made to overcome the concentration barrier imposed by liquids through the development of 'suspension' fertilisers in which slurries of solid particles are kept in suspension by means of suspending agents and by regular agitation. Such materials require specialised skills and equipment for their correct application and are not widely used in UK forest nurseries.

The use of slow release fertilisers together with liquid fertilisers provides a possible mechanism for matching nutrient supply to plant demand, thereby minimising the dangers of excessive salt levels in the soil and losses due to volatilisation or leaching.

All the developments in slow-release and liquid fertilisers have been led by demands in the ornamental nursery trade; there has been little research into optimum regimes for forest nursery stock. As a consequence, recommendations for their use have to be based on extrapolations from the use of conventional fertilisers in forest nurseries. As a working rule, slow-acting or soluble fertilisers should be applied at rates which, for the season as a whole, do not exceed the rates recommended for conventional fertilisers.

4.2.4 Rates of fertiliser application

Fertilisers must be applied to forest nurseries:

- to maintain soil nutrients at levels which ensure adequate availability to plants;
- to provide a supply of nutrients to meet current uptake requirements;
- to counteract processes which reduce nutrient availability such as leaching, volatilisation and immobilisation within the soil.

The nutrient content of fertilisers offered for sale in the UK has, by law, to be stated. The analysis may be expressed in terms of elements or their oxides. To convert from the oxide to the element the following factors should be used:

$$P = P_2O_5 \times 0.44$$
$$K = K_2O \times 0.83$$
$$Mg = MgO \times 0.60$$

For example, to calculate how much of each element 150 kg Scottish Agricultural Industries Enmag will supply (6%N, 20% P_2O_5, 10%

Table 4.4 Fertiliser application rates applied before sowing or transplanting (kg of element ha^{-1})

Crop type	Nitrogen* Standard	Phosphorus Standard	High[+]	Potassium Standard	High[+]
Seedbeds	(60)	55–65	65–75	100–120	120–145
Transplants	(50)	45–55	55–65	85–100	100–120

* If nitrogen is applied then a slow release formulation should be used.
[+] High rates used if soil reserves low or levels difficult to maintain.

K$_2$O, 8.5% Mg) the following procedures are necessary:

Nitrogen $\ = (6 / 100) \times 150 \quad\quad = 9.0 \,\text{kg N}$
Phosphorus $= (20 \times 0.44 / 100) \times 150 = 13.2 \,\text{kg P}$
Potassium $\ = (10 \times 0.83 / 100) \times 150 = 12.5 \,\text{kg K}$
Magnesium $= (8.5 / 100) \times 150 \quad\quad = 12.8 \,\text{kg Mg}$

Initial fertiliser dressings

Forest nursery production can place heavy demands upon soil for nutrients. Each crop will have its own requirements depending upon species, age, management system, soil and climate. In addition, fertiliser recovery rates are always well below 100% so that application rates must exceed rates of removal in planting stock.

Typical rates of nutrients applied as initial dressings are given in Table 4.4. Phosphorus and potassium are usually applied as readily soluble compound fertilisers. Phosphorus applications may well last the entire season whereas on sandy soils with moderate rainfall, potassium top dressings may be necessary to supplement the initial application. Where nutrient levels are difficult to maintain, the higher range of dressings given in Table 4.4 should be used. If soil reserves are low then, once again, higher rates of readily soluble fertilisers should be used. Nitrogen is rarely applied before sowing or transplanting, but slow release formulations can be useful in reducing leaching and volatilisation losses early in the season. When used, slow release fertilisers should be supplemented by top dressings later on. Where phosphorus levels are low and potassium satisfactory, Enmag can be useful as it provides twice the usual

ratio of phosphorus to potassium together with some magnesium and a slow-release form of nitrogen.

Additional fertilisers

Soil nutrients must be maintained so that adequate supplies are normally available. For a typical nursery soil (sandy loam with a bulk density at 1.5 g cm^{-3}) available* nutrients to 15 cm depth should be of the order 200 kg P, 300 kg K and 100 kg Mg per hectare. These would correspond to approximate analysis values of 90 p.p.m. P, 140 p.p.m. K and 45 p.p.m. Mg. Once values fall to two-thirds of those quoted above, nutrient availability could be reduced and the higher rates recommended for initial dressings in Table 4.4 should be used.

Where analysis shows available nutrients to have fallen below one-half of the levels quoted above then further measures must be taken:

- Ground mineral phosphate will increase soil phosphorus reserves and, because it is slow acting, it should have a prolonged effect. Rates of application should be between 500 and 800 kg ha^{-1} depending upon the level of phosphorus reported in the soil analysis.

- Magnesian limestone and kieserite are also slow acting and can be used to increase soil magnesium levels. Where soil pH is high, kieserite should be used in preference to magnesian limestone. Rates of application to correct soil magnesium levels are 600 kg ha^{-1} for magnesian limestone and 300 kg ha^{-1} of kieserite. Materials should be applied a few weeks before drilling or transplanting.

---

* Extractable with 0.43M acetic acid at 20°C.

46

Table 4.5 Top dressing application rates (kg of element ha^{-1} y^{-1})

Crop	Nitrogen	Potassium
Seedbeds	100–150	50–75
Transplants	75–100	35–50

Note: A single top dressing should not apply any more than 25 kg of nitrogen ha^{-1}.

- Potassium salts are very soluble and may be quickly leached on very sandy soils, low in organic matter. More frequent top dressings should be used if soil potassium levels are low.

If problems persist then expert advice should be sought. Reasons could include phosphorus fixing soils (Smilde, 1973), low cation exchange capacity, or heavy rainfall causing excessive leaching.

4.2.5 Top dressings

Nitrogen and, to a lesser extent, potassium can be quickly lost from the soil by leaching in periods of heavy rainfall or by denitrification. To minimise such losses, several dressings are usually applied throughout the growing season. Typical rates of application per year are given in Table 4.5. For nitrogen responsive species such as larch, Douglas fir, alder and birch, rates of application should be reduced to between half and two-thirds of usual levels. Where liquid fertiliser regimes are used, phosphorus can also be included in top dressings, making a corresponding reduction in the fertiliser applied at the time of sowing or lining out.

4.2.6 Timing of fertiliser applications

Granular fertilisers can feasibly be spread at any time of the year. Ground mineral phosphate and low doses of magnesian limestone can be applied at any convenient time before sowing or transplanting. Soluble compound fertilisers and slow release formulations used as initial dressings should be spread and cultivated into the top 7–10 cm of soil as near as possible to the time of sowing or transplanting. Where large additional dressings of soluble fertilisers are to be used or salt sensitive species are to be produced (Norway spruce and *Abies*), then the risk of fertiliser scorch can be minimised by earlier applications – approximately one month before the ground is to be used.

Top dressings of nitrogen are usually given as three or four equal applications during the season. On soils with low potassium retention (sandy with low organic matter and high rainfall), NK fertilisers are usually used for one or two top dressings. The traditional pattern of application has been to wait 5–7 weeks after germination of seedlings (by which time the primary needles/leaves should have appeared) before making the first application. Thereafter, applications are given at regular intervals of not less than 4 weeks with a final application in late August. Transplants should receive their first dressing in mid-May (provided a minimum of 4 weeks has passed since transplanting). Thereafter, dressings are again given at intervals of not less than 4 weeks with a final dressing in late August. Fertilisers should not be applied to any crop during hot weather or when the soil is dry. Between consecutive dressings at least 25 mm of rain or 12 mm of irrigation should have occurred but if very heavy rain occurs soon after top-dressing then a second application should be considered to replace any losses due to leaching. For nitrogen responsive species (larches, Douglas fir, alder and birch) mid-season dressings can be omitted. If slow-release compounds are used as pre-sowing/transplanting dressings then early top-dressings may be reduced or omitted. On crops which are to be stood-over then it is usual to apply half of the top-dressings one year and half the next.

In recent years, research under carefully controlled conditions has shown that much greater efficiency of fertiliser use by trees can be obtained by using frequent, low-rate applications of nutrients matched to the rate of plant growth (Ingestad, 1977; Ingestad and Lund, 1986). This must, however, be seen in the context of increased costs associated with multiple applications.

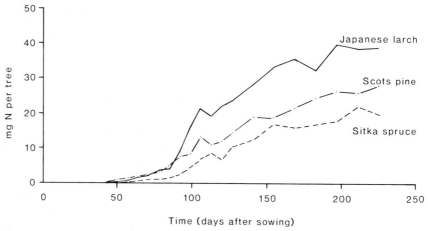

Figure 4.6 Seasonal variation of nitrogen in conifers.

While it is not yet possible to predict, with any degree of confidence, the nutrient requirements for a given crop at a given time, it is becoming clear that the use of a small number of equal top dressings during the season is not the most efficient schedule. Preliminary research on container stock grown in the polyhouse clearly demonstrated that, for a range of conifer species, rates of N uptake varied markedly during the growing season (Figure 4.6). Rates of N uptake were slow for the first 10–12 weeks, followed by a short period of rapid uptake and a more extended period of moderate N uptake. Care must be taken in extrapolating such results to the open nursery seedbed where sowing densities differ between species, temperatures are lower and the vagaries of climate must be considered. The general pattern of N uptake is, however, likely to hold with only the absolute values changing. Based upon such preliminary information it is reasonable to speculate that a nitrogen top dressing regime in which the first application was reduced to provide only 20% of the season total N fertiliser, followed by a second dressing supplying 40%, a third pro-

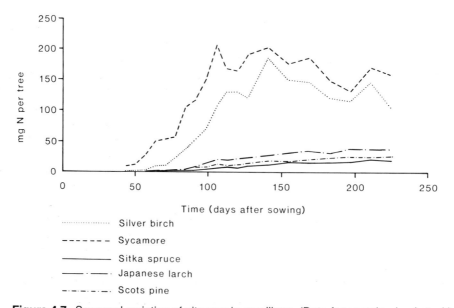

.... Silver birch

– – – – – Sycamore

————— Sitka spruce

———·——— Japanese larch

–·–··–··–. Scots pine

Figure 4.7 Seasonal variation of nitrogen in seedlings. (Data for containerised stock)

48

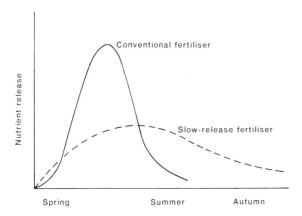

Figure 4.8 Fertiliser release characteristics.

viding 30% and a final dressing in August to make up the last 10% may prove beneficial. If more than four dressings can be applied then so much the better.

Information on broadleaves is very limited, but the same piece of research mentioned above suggested the pattern of N uptake may be quite different (Figure 4.7). Demand for N was much greater earlier in the season and top dressings should probably reflect this. Seedlings became 'pot-bound' approximately 3 months after sowing. Further research is necessary to confirm these results in open nursery seedbeds but there is already sufficient information to suggest equal top dressings throughout the growing season are likely to be inefficient.

There may well be scope for greater use of the more complex slow release fertiliser compounds developed to provide a closer match between rate of nutrient supply and plant demand (Figure 4.8). However, it will still be necessary to supplement slow release products, applied at sowing or transplanting, with top dressings later in the season. One suitable regime might be to apply 50% of the annual N fertiliser as a slow release at the start of the season with a further 30% in early summer and the final 20% as a final top dressing in August.

These new top dressing regimes are currently based largely upon theory and preliminary research on containerised stock. It is important to do small-scale trials within the nursery before implementing these new regimes on a larger scale.

4.2.7 Nutrition and outplanting performance

Careful attention to nutrition within the nursery can have significant effects upon yield from plantations through improved survival and accelerated establishment. Evidence suggests that initial seedling size, as influenced by nursery nutrition, can have a strong influence on early field performance and tree growth (Fisher and Mexal, 1984). Studies in North America have shown that needle %N in 2 + 0 Douglas fir and Sitka spruce was positively correlated with survival, total height and current height growth after 3 years in the forest (Van den Driessche, 1984). The same study also reported that Douglas fir maintained similar relative growth rates after planting out such that any differences in seedling dry weights at the time of planting continued to influence growth for several years. Late-season applications of nitrogen (after bud set) have also been reported to advance bud break of Sitka spruce when planted out in UK forests, without any deleterious effects upon survival, except in very exposed locations where frost damage was increased (Benzian *et al.*, 1974). This, in turn, increased height growth during the first season in the field but differences became small in relation to tree size in later years. The increased survival of Douglas fir following late season fertilisation was thought to be a result of elevated mineral nutrient reserves increasing the capacity for root growth, although direct evidence for such an effect is still required (Van den Driessche, 1985).

In the past it has often been assumed that late season applications of potassium may improve cold hardiness. Benzian *et al.* (1974) showed potassium fertiliser increased growth of trees soon after planting on forest sites but found no significant effect upon frost damage. In a thorough review of the literature, Pellett and Carter (1981) concluded that adequate nutrition to promote rapid growth, without compromising the shoot:root ratio, should enable plants to acclimatise to cold better than those suffering severe nutrient deficiency or supra-optimum fertilisation. There is also evidence that potassium is important in regulating plant water status through stomatal control and late-season applications may increase drought tolerance of transplanted seedlings (Fisher and Mexal, 1984). Other work on Douglas fir, again in North America, showed frost hardiness to be more closely related to the ratio of K to N present in tissues, rather than to the level of an individual element (Timmis, 1974).

4.3 Nutrient deficiencies and remedial fertilisers

4.3.1 Deficiency and damage

In the course of the growing season, plants exhibit a range of colours. For most plants, these remain within the range of shades of green until tints associated with natural leaf senescence develop. A few species adopt a more bronzed or purple hue over winter, namely western red cedar and seedling pines, but for most species the untimely appearance of red or yellow hues or browning of foliage is a sign of distress due to one, or a combination of the following:

Nutrient deficiency
Nutrient excess (fertiliser scorch)

Damage by: frost
           insects
           fungi
           wind
Waterlogging of soil
Drought
Sunscorch
Pesticides (residues or faulty application)

The first step in determining the cause of any discoloration is always to dig up and examine carefully a sample of the affected plants, paying particular attention to the roots. Possible causes of observed symptoms are shown in Table 4.6.

Pests and diseases, the effects of climate and damage due to weedkillers used in forest nurseries are described elsewhere.

Plants markedly deficient in one or more nutrients show this by poor growth and by developing characteristically discoloured foliage; foliage may be smaller than normal and in certain extreme cases, shoots may die back. In addition, plants may be more susceptible to damage by frost, drought, insect and fungal attack.

While it is easy to ascribe symptoms to deficiencies induced in experiments, it is not always easy to make correct diagnoses from foliage symptoms alone, as more than one nutrient may be lacking. Diagnosis usually involves weighing up probabilities, taking into account:

Table 4.6 Symptoms and possible causes of deficiencies and damage

Observed symptoms	Possible cause
Withering or drying (green) foliage.	Weedkiller; sun scorch; fungal attack; insect feeding on roots.
Straw or light-brown foliage (not autumn colours of deciduous species).	Fertiliser excess; weedkiller; heat scorch; wind burn; fungal attack; copper deficiency.
Yellow, red or purple discoloration; foliage remains fresh.	Nutrient deficiency; root damage; lime-induced chlorosis; weedkiller.
Spotting or blotching of foliage.	Fungal attack; insect attack; weedkiller.
Dead roots.	Waterlogging; fungal attack; dessication or mechanical damage during lining out; maltreatment before lining out; insect feeding.
Visible loss of bark on roots, or loss of foliage.	Insect attack; mechanical damage by implement; hail.
Dead root collar (or stem at soil surface) but roots and stem healthy.	Weedkiller, sun scorch, fungal attack.

- what fertilisers have been put on and when;
- rainfall and irrigation in relation to fertiliser applications;
- soil characteristics; and, if possible,
- knowledge of the situation with similar crops in other nurseries.

The following sections outline the major roles of each nutrient in plant growth. Visual symptoms of deficiency are described for three groups of seedlings (Benzian, 1965; Hacskaylo et al., 1969; Huttl, 1986; Ingestad 1957, 1959, 1960; Lavender and Walker, 1981; Leaf, 1968; Morrison, 1974; Stone, 1968; Swan, 1960 and Worley et al., 1941):

1. needle bearing conifers based mainly on descriptions for pines and spruce;
2. conifers which have scale-like leaves based upon descriptions for western red cedar, and
3. broadleaves such as birch and elm.

A brief description of the fertilisers available for supplying each element is then given.

While recommendations for remedial fertilisers are given, these will only restore nutrient levels in plants to the extent that the plants are physiologically capable of taking them up. For example, foliage showing severe deficiency symptoms may not be able to recover. Also, plants which failed to grow rapidly because of nutrient deficiency, may resume rapid growth following remedial treatment but will not be able to grow faster to compensate for the earlier lost growth.

4.3.2 Nitrogen

Role

Nitrogen is a constituent of amino acids (the basic building blocks of proteins), the nucleic acids (RNA and DNA), many metabolic intermediates and is an essential component of chlorophyll. When nitrogen is deficient, the chlorophyll content of many of the otherwise green parts of the plant is reduced (Bould et al., 1983).

Deficiency symptoms

Needle bearing conifers (pine, spruce, larch, fir, hemlock, etc.)
A general yellowing and reduced growth of needles occurs, the extent of which increases with the severity of the deficiency. Very severe deficiency produces short, stiff needles yellow-green to yellow in colour. Occasionally the tips of needles in seedlings may turn pink or purple and this is sometimes followed by needle necrosis at the end of the season. Needles exposed to full sunlight appear to develop more discoloration than those in shade. Typically, seedbeds become saucered with the seedlings at the outer edges being taller and greener than those toward the centre. Symptoms can be recognised as soon as seedlings are large enough for different shades of green to be recognised.

Conifers bearing scale-like leaves (e.g. western red cedar)
Foliage is yellowish, very sparse and stems may be reddish in young seedlings. Dying of the older foliage is conspicuous but there is little *shattering* (Hacskaylo et al., 1969 – see glossary).

Broadleaves (e.g. birch, elm)
Seedlings become stunted and leaf size may be markedly reduced. Foliage is pale green or yellow with anthocyanin spots developing on the underside. Older leaves die and stems or petioles that are normally green may take on pink or reddish colours.

Remedial fertiliser
Observed nitrogen deficiencies can develop very rapidly when the crop is growing fast and demand for N is large (Figure 4.6). Deficiency can be corrected by a standard top dressing of ammonium nitrate or ammonium sulphate at 125 kg ha^{-1} supplying around 25–40 kg ha^{-1} N). However, loss of growth may not be recovered.

Where nitrogen deficiency symptoms occur in early/mid season and N top dressings have been withheld to avoid excessive growth, colour can be restored by addition of a light top dressing in the same season (25 kg ha^{-1} N). Plants left undisturbed into the winter, usually green up by the time of lifting. However, if repeated undercutting is proposed, a top dressing should be put on deficient plants (and, where possible, watered in) a few weeks before the first undercut.

4.3.3 Phosphorus

Role

Phosphorus forms high-energy phosphate bonds which are the chief medium for energy transfer in plants. It also affects the functioning of many enzymes and plays a key role in many biosynthetic reactions.

Deficiency symptoms

Needle bearing conifers

Phosphorus deficiency is associated, primarily, with a reduction in growth. Sitka spruce does not exhibit any characteristic colour symptoms when deficient in phosphorus either as seedlings or transplants. Visual symptoms have, however, been reported for a number of other spruce species, pines and western hemlock. Young needles are green or yellow-green while older needles develop a purple tinge that deepens with severity so that in extreme cases all needles of seedlings may turn purple. Symptoms are typically patchy over the seedbed.

Conifers bearing scale-like leaves

Young foliage retains a good green colour whereas older foliage and stems develop reddish or purplish tinges during the first year, turning a reddish brown in older seedlings and followed by necrosis. The oldest foliage dies but does not shatter.

Broadleaves

Leaf size appears to be unaffected in birch. Foliage becomes dark green with some reddish/purple discoloration on the underside due to the presence of anthocyanin. In elm, leaves may be slightly reduced in size and a gradation in colour can occur from dark green in the older leaves to very light green in the youngest. Lower portions of the usually deep green stems turn a dark brown.

Remedial fertiliser

Top dressings of phosphatic fertilisers are relatively ineffective (Van den Driessche, 1980). If problems are apparent, an early season dressing of monammonium phosphate (MAP) can be used at 250 kg ha^{-1} to supply approximately 60 kg ha^{-1} P, although this may have little effect in the same growing season.

4.3.4 Potassium

Role

The processes of photosynthesis, protein synthesis and carbohydrate translocation all require potassium. It is also involved in the osmotic regulation of water conditions within the plant which, in turn, can affect resistance to drying winds and frost.

Deficiency symptoms

Needle bearing conifers

First signs in the seedbed usually appear in August but can occur as early as June. Typically, needle-tip chlorosis occurs and the tips may take on a purplish tinge. As the season progresses, the discoloration extends back from needle tips and a range of colours may develop including blue-greens, purple, red, reddish-yellow and yellow. Tips may eventually turn brown and necrotic. Symptoms are more pronounced in the youngest needles with the discoloration much reduced toward the base of seedlings. The autumnal colours reminiscent of hardwoods help to distinguish potassium deficiency from the 'hard yellows' of magnesium deficiency. Earlier in the season, potassium can be distinguished from nitrogen deficiency because the chlorosis (yellowing) is most marked at the young shoot tips, in contrast to nitrogen where the discoloration is more uniform. Symptoms in transplants are similar and may occur from June onwards, the previous year's shoots usually being the most discoloured.

Conifers bearing scale-like leaves

Foliage appears sparse and stems become limper, causing a droopy appearance. Foliage at the branch tips maintains a good, green colour but older foliage may be necrotic or dying. Many of the lower leaves and branches turn brown and die.

Broadleaves

Chlorosis and necrosis of foliage occurs from the leaf margins inward. There is typically a sharp boundary between the white/yellow chlorotic area and the normal green. After chlorosis, leaves become brown and dry.

Remedial fertiliser

Dressings of potassium sulphate at a rate of 200 kg ha^{-1} to supply 84 kg ha^{-1} K, can be used to correct potassium deficiency. Sulphate rather than muriate of potash is preferable because risk from fertiliser scorch is less (Armson and Sadreika, 1979).

4.3.5 Magnesium

Role

Magnesium is an important constituent of chlorophyll and its absence reduces the chlorophyll content of the foliage and slows the processes of photosynthesis. Magnesium is also involved in carbohydrate metabolism, cell division and energy transfer within the plant.

Deficiency symptoms

Needle bearing conifers

Magnesium deficiency usually occurs late in the season, typically from late August through to October. Needle tips turn bright yellow and the discoloration develops along the entire length of young needles although this is rare in older foliage. There is, characteristically, very little gradation between bright yellow and healthy green portions of seedbeds, individual seedlings or individual needles. Severe

deficiency may cause needle tip necrosis with occasional bud death, particularly at the time of autumn frosts.

Conifers bearing scale-like leaves

With magnesium deficiency the youngest foliage usually remains green but older branches become yellow or white before turning brown and have a tendency to shatter. As a result seedlings develop a tuft of green at the top with bare branches below.

Broadleaves

In magnesium deficient birch, foliage first turns yellow. Leaf margins may become grey or brown, eventually spreading over the whole leaf blade and resulting in leaf mortality. Interveinal chlorosis and curling under of leaf margins can occur in lime while elm seedlings can be very stunted with their leaf size much reduced. Oldest leaves are usually most affected with a typical progression of mottled chlorosis accompanied by whitening edges that spread over the blade until it becomes entirely white, the green veins being the last regions to succumb.

Remedial fertiliser

Epsom salts (magnesium sulphate) applied at a rate of 150 kg ha^{-1} (15 kg ha^{-1} Mg) should reduce or eliminate deficiency symptoms. Alternatively, plants can be sprayed in July or August with 1400 l ha^{-1} of a solution containing 25 g Epsom salts and 0.5 ml of liquid detergent per litre of solution.

4.3.6 Calcium

Role

Calcium is an important constituent of plant cell walls and a number of different enzymes.

Deficiency symptoms

Calcium is an unavoidable constituent of many regularly used fertilisers. Deficiencies of calcium rarely, if ever, occur in UK forest nurseries and the symptoms reported below are based upon laboratory studies.

Table 4.7 Trace element deficiency symptoms

Nutrient	Deficiency symptoms		Remedy
Role	Conifers	Broadleaves	
Copper (Cu) Enzyme component and catalyst	'Tip burn' – needle ends near growing points dry and become straw coloured. In Sitka spruce, onset sudden during dry weather in late summer. Very short transition from healthy to affected tissue. Upper needles of apparently healthy plants near affected ones may show spiral twist. If sunny weather prolonged, growing points may die.	Blackening of leaf tips, then general marginal scorch of youngest leaves. Inverveinal yellowing follows. Leaf edges become taut and brittle causing cupping of leaves. On acutely affected plants, the youngest leaves fall, leaving main shoots and side branches bare.	Copper sulphate broadcast dry at 20 kg ha^{-1} or 10 kg in 2000 litres water ha^{-1} in June and again in July.
Iron (Fe) Constituent of chlorophyll	Lime-induced chlorosis (iron deficiency) is a well known disorder of acid loving plants when planted on alkaline soils. On a forest nursery, its occurrence indicates that the site is unsuitable and that another site should be sought. NB: Zinc toxicity symptoms strongly resemble those of iron deficiency – see under zinc below.		
Energy carrier in photosynthesis and respiration	More or less uniform chlorosis of new foliage eventually, needles and plants become dwarfed.	Chlorosis in interveinal tissue; veins remaining green, often sharply etched. Wholly chlorotic tissues die slowly, producing apical or marginal scorch.	
Boron (B)	Deficiency in Britain (nursery and forest) limited to two possible cases. Reported from overseas, especially New Zealand. Immobile in plant; meristem areas may be deficient even though levels in foliage appear adequate.		
In sugar translocation water absorption and transpiration	Death of apical shoots or 'rosetting' – progressive reduction in leaf spacing and size. In pines, shoot, shoot tip or bud die-back abrupt, sometimes preceded by wilting or abnormal growth.	Foliage dwarfed and discoloured. Uneven mesophyll growth producing blistered appearance; some spp. may show interveinal chlorosis or browning.	10–20 kg ha^{-1} borate fertiliser or borax. Bulk up with sand for even distribution, or 0.1 – 0.2% w/v soluton of 'Solubor' at 1000–1500 l ha^{-1}.

Needle bearing conifers

Deficiencies of calcium can cause serious injury to meristematic regions. A general chlorosis is usually followed by needle necrosis, especially at branch tips. Severe deficiency can lead to the death of terminal buds, top dieback and excessive resin exudation.

Conifers bearing scale-like leaves

Good green colour may be maintained in the lower foliage but tips of leaders and branch shoots turn brown and become necrotic.

Broadleaves

Terminal leaves become chlorotic, stunted and delicate. Discoloration occurs first at leaf tips and then spreads inwards to produce whitened leaf margins progressing toward midrib. Eventually, terminal buds become necrotic.

4.3.7 Sulphur

Role

Sulphur is an essential constituent of amino acids used in protein synthesis. It also occurs

Table 4.7 *continued*

Nutrient	Deficiency symptoms		Remedy
Role	Conifers	Broadleaves	
Manganese (Mn)	Neither deficiency nor toxicity reported from British forest nurseries.		
Plant respiration	Difficult to distinguish from Fe or Mg deficiency. Needles chlorotic at emergence, may 'green-up' in later months.	Chlorosis begins near leaf margin, developing as V-shaped areas extending inward between major veins. Symptoms usually develop late in the season.	$8\,kg\,ha^{-1}$ of manganese sulphate or chloride in 500 litres water ha^{-1}.
	Symptoms of toxicity include smaller leaves, severe chlorosis, necrotic spots and discoloration.		
Zinc (Zn)	Deficiency symptoms not reported from British nurseries, but found in culture.		
Enzyme systems	Extreme shortening of needles and needle spacing and general yellowing and occasional bronzing of needle tips.	Chlorotic mottling of interveinal areas. Frequently proceeds up stem, associated with leaf-fall. Terminal rosettes may form; severe deficiency causing die-back.	$5\,kg\,ha^{-1}$ zinc sulphate + $2.5\,kg\,ha^{-1}$ calcium hydroxide in 500 litres ha^{-1} water.
	Zinc toxicity has been observed occasionally in forest nurseries, usually associated with the presence of galvanised or zinc coated wire mesh, especially where rolls of netting have remained for several weeks rolled up at the ends of seedbeds. In such localised situations, seedlings may fail to germinate; those that do may be stunted and show a chlorosis similar to that resulting from iron deficiency.		
Molybdenum (Mo)	Deficiency symptoms not reported in British forest nurseries; amounts required are minute compared with other elements. Availability falls with increasing acidity in soils.		
Enzyme system also metabolism of N-fixing bacteria	Chlorosis followed by necrosis of tissue, beginning at the tip and eventually covering the entire needle.	For N-fixing alders, symptoms resemble N deficiency – pale N leaves with marginal scorch.	$200\,g\,ha^{-1}$ sodium molybdate as a 0.01% solution.

in a number of co-enzymes and is contained in chlorophyll.

Deficiency symptoms

Needle bearing conifers

Needles may be thin and spindly. General chlorosis develops although this is most pronounced in the terminal regions where necrosis may occur.

Conifers bearing scale-like leaves

Foliage becomes yellowish, especially in younger portions. Older foliage is paler than usual, in contrast to iron deficiency in which older foliage retains good, green colour. (NB all young foliage tends to become yellowish for a time, particularly during periods of rapid growth.)

Broadleaves

Plants may be stunted and younger leaves become yellowish green – similar in appearance to nitrogen deficiency but no anthocyanin discoloration on undersides of foliage. Older leaves retain their dark green colour.

Remedial fertiliser

Sulphur deficiencies are not known on the range of soil normally encountered in forest nurseries. It is frequently applied as an unspecified constituent of many fertilisers including superphosphates, Enmag and ammonium sulphate. If deficiencies are encountered then flowers of sulphur can be used at 20–30 kg ha^{-1} or ammonium sulphate at approximately 100 kg ha^{-1}. More usually, sulphur is used as a means to lower soil pH (Chapter 3, section 3.2.5).

4.3.8 Trace elements (micronutrients)

Trace element deficiencies in UK forest nurseries have rarely been reported. Most of the information reported in this section relates to induced deficiencies within experiments or to experience overseas. Under field conditions it is difficult to diagnose trace element disorders due to problems with sample contamination and the high degree of variability within plant tissues. Table 4.7 summarises the available information.

4.3.9 Tissue analysis

While soil analysis provides a 'snap-shot' of the nutrient reserves in the soil, at the time of sampling, *tissue analysis* (or foliage analysis) provides a means of assessing the success with which plants are able to extract nutrients from the soil, and translocate them within the plants.

A general guide to the critical or marginal range of nutrient concentrations (see Figure 4.1) that could be expected in nursery planting stock is given in Table 4.8. Plants with levels above those given in the Table 4.8 should have adequate supplies of nutrients whereas values below those quoted are usually indicative of nutrient deficiency. The values given in Table 4.8 are for current shoots in late autumn for conifers and for the foliage of broadleaved species in midsummer when concentrations are most likely to be stable (Figure 4.9).

In addition to the absolute value of foliage nutrient levels, it is also important to ensure the balance between nutrients is correct. Imbalances can occur, for example, between levels of calcium and magnesium, nitrogen and phosphorus, nitrogen and potassium or nitrogen and sulphur all of which may lead to physiological disorders and unsatisfactory growth.

Table 4.8 Marginal range of nutrient concentrations in forest nursery stock

| | Major nutrients | | | | | |
	N	P	K (% oven dry weight)	Ca	Mg	S
Pines	1.5–1.8	0.16–0.18	0.6–0.7	0.06–0.10	0.07–0.10	0.15–0.20
Spruces	1.2–1.6	0.16–0.18	0.5–0.7	0.10–0.15	0.06–0.08	0.13–0.18
Larches	2.0–2.5	0.20–0.25	1.0–1.2	0.20–0.25	0.10–0.12	0.16–0.20
Other conifers	1.6–1.8	0.18–0.20	0.7–0.8	0.15–0.20	0.10–0.12	0.16–0.18
Alder, birch, sycamore, cherry, lime, willow, Norway maple	2.3–2.8	0.18–0.25	1.0–1.2	0.15–0.20	0.10–0.15	0.14–0.20
Other broadleaves	1.7–2.3	0.14–0.20	0.7–1.0	0.20–0.30	0.15–0.20	0.16–0.20

| | Trace elements | | | |
	Cu	Fe (μg/g)	Mn	B
Pines and spruces	3–5	20–40	20–40	15–30
Other conifers	3–5	40–60	40–60	20–40
Broadleaves	3–5	30–80	30–80	20–40

1. Below marginal levels indicative of deficient status.
2. Above marginal levels indicative of satisfactory status.
3. Conifers = current shoots in late autumn.
4. Broadleaves = foliage in midsummer.

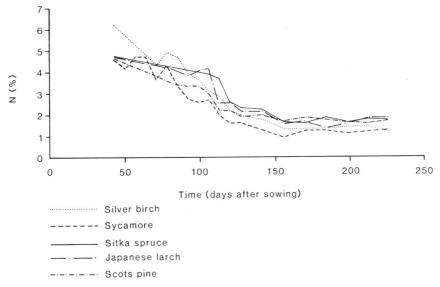

Figure 4.9 Seasonal nitrogen concentrations in seedlings.

At present, tissue analysis as a guide to plant health and nutrition in forest nurseries is still in its infancy. There is only an imperfect understanding of the relationship between the results of soil and tissue analysis, and their interaction with season (e.g. rainfall, temperature, moisture deficit), site (e.g. soil texture and pH), nursery practice (e.g. timing of operations, quantities of fertiliser, irrigation) and incidence of pests and diseases.

Samples are often taken when visual deficiency symptoms appear with the aim of either taking remedial action with respect to the crop sampled or, at least, to prevent any recurrence in future crops. Such samples are often taken with little standardisation with respect to tissues sampled or time of sampling. This makes interpretation of results particularly difficult since the evidence that is available shows considerable variation in nutrient concentration throughout the season. For example, the potassium content of Sitka spruce seedlings can fall from 3% dry matter in midsummer to 1% or less by late autumn; it can also vary markedly from one season to another (Benzian *et al.*, 1969).

Foliage sampling *should* be conducted on a regular basis similar to that carried out for soils. This is the best method for detecting any areas in the nursery in which nutrient concen-

trations are 'critical', affecting growth or performance without any visible deficiency symptoms. Information would then be available relating soil and foliage analyses for each nursery block or soil type thus enabling better interpretations of analytical results to be made and nursery-specific fertiliser recommendations to be given.

Taking plant samples

Before samples are taken for analysis it is essential that the laboratory that will conduct the analyses be consulted regarding the type and quantity of sample required, the time at which samples should be taken and the way in which samples should be handled to avoid any contamination. The amount of material required will depend upon the analyses to be carried out but where deficiency symptoms are observed, at least two samples should be taken from apparently healthy areas and two from those areas where symptoms are apparent. If possible, intermediate levels of deficiency should also be included. For analyses of major nutients the tops of sufficient plants to provide approximately 20–30 g of material per sample should be taken while for trace elements considerably more material may be required. Care should be taken to avoid inclusion of soil in the samples.

Owing to the range of factors that can affect plant nutrition, some within and some outwith the nursery manager's control, information from historical records can be crucial in diagnosing problems. A summary of such information should always accompany samples sent for analysis.

4.4 Soil organic matter

Soil organic matter comprises three principal components: (1) live microbes, flora and fauna within the soil; (2) plant, animal and microbial residues in various stages of decomposition; and (3) humic substances representing the final stages of a series of predominantly biochemical reactions (Davey and Krause, 1980).

In the soil, free-living micro-organisms use organic matter as a source of both energy and nutrients necessary for the synthesis of their own tissues. Energy is obtained through the process of respiration during which the carbon contained in organic matter is oxidised to carbon dioxide and then liberated into the air. Thus, there is a natural tendency for organic matter contents of soils to decline unless they are continually replenished.

Nursery management practices tend to increase the rate at which soil organic matter is decomposed. Tillage of the soil increases aeration by reducing soil bulk density; it also kills and buries most residual vegetation, hastening its break-down. Adequate moisture supply also enhances microbial activity, thus accelerating the processes of decomposition of residues compared with drier soils, or those in which moisture contents are sufficiently high to cause reduced aeration. Within certain limits, microbial activity increases with increasing soil temperature and the elevated temperatures found in forest nurseries compared with those in forests usually result in increased biological activity. Microbes also require various nutrients for growth and these are frequently available in forest nurseries where comparatively heavy fertiliser regimes are used.

4.4.1 Properties

Fresh organic material, particularly green

Table 4.9 Effect of six annual applications of 63 000 kg ha^{-1} raw hopwaste on some physical properties of a sandy loam soil at Teindland Nursery, Moray

	Percentage organic matter	Moisture equivalent	Percentage microaggregate stability
Control	11.0	20.8	11.4
Hop waste	18.0	29.3	15.0
Least significant difference at 0.1%	3.7	3.4	2.4

crops incorporated into the soil, break down very rapidly during the initial stages of decomposition. During this phase, bacteria involved produce a number of polysaccharide gums that enhance soil structure. This is illustrated in the microaggregate stability figures given in Table 4.9. The high metabolic activity within the soil can also result in the suppression of various pathogens due to elevated carbon dioxide levels and the production of certain antibiotics within the soil. This period of high activity may last for several weeks and during the first week or two soil oxygen may become limiting and lead to the production of a range of volatile organic compounds and acids which can be toxic to germinating seeds and young plants (Aaron, 1976). These substances break down rapidly once oxygen levels return to normal but care should be taken to ensure that seed is not sown into soil that has received additions of readily decomposable material in the preceding 10 days. Composts or peat produce no such problems because they have already undergone this initial phase of rapid decomposition.

As decomposition proceeds, fungi predominate as celluloses and eventually lignin are slowly degraded. Over periods of many years, humus is formed which differs physically and chemically from the original material from which it was derived.

Humus and partly decomposed organic matter affect soil properties in a number of important ways:

• It is dark coloured at the soil surface, absorbs more of the sun's heat and so

Table 4.10 Nutrient contents of various bulky organics (from FC Bulletin 37, Tables 80 and 81)

	Percentage moisture content of fresh material	Percentage in dry matter				
		Organic matter	N	P	K	Mg
Hopwaste	84–87	85–89	4.8–5.1	0.9–1.3	0.2	0.4
Peat	47	93	2.1	0.0	0.1	–
Sawdust	44	99	0.2	0.0	0.1	0.0
Bracken/hopwaste compost	72–81	70–83	3.2–3.9	0.5–0.9	1.3–2.1	0.3
Straw/hopwaste compost	73–82	66–78	3.6–4.3	0.9–1.0	0.4–0.8	0.4
Farmyard manure	76	75	2.2	0.3	2.8	–
Sewage sludge	20–55	39–42	1.6–2.8	1.4–2.3	0.3–0.4	–

increases ambient soil temperatures with consequent effects upon the rate of biological activity.

- Water retention within soils has been shown to be directly related to total organic matter content. This is especially important in nurseries with sandy soils and low clay contents.
- Humus can also combine with clays to stabilise soil structure.
- It has a high cation exchange capacity and in most forest nursery soils it is the organic fractions that contribute the largest share of cation exchange sites.
- The influence of soil organic matter on cation exchange capacity makes it a major factor affecting the buffering capacity of a soil in relation to changes in soil acidity resulting from the use of inorganic fertilisers or hard irrigation water.
- Soil organic matter can also have direct effects upon the availability of nutrients for plant uptake.

Table 4.10 shows the analysis of a range of bulky organic soil amendments.

The addition of nitrogen-rich, coarse organic matter can enhance nitrogen availability in forest nurseries. However, materials low in nitrogen, or with a high C:N ratio like sawdust, reduce availability due to immobilisation by microbes during early phases of decomposition. Supplemental inputs of inorganic nitrogen may, therefore, be required following the application of materials with high C:N ratios.

In contrast, soil organic amendments can increase phosphorus availability by directly supplying phosphate and by the eventual chelation of insoluble iron and aluminium phosphates into more available forms. This latter process can be significant in newly established nurseries on podzolic soils in which the B horizon's considerable potential for phosphate fixation can be counteracted by organic soil amendments. Trace element availability may be affected by additions of organic matter either through changes in soil reaction (pH) or by the chelating properties of soil organic matter. Boron availability, for example, has been shown to be highly correlated with soil organic matter content (Martens, 1968). Similar results have been obtained for extractable copper in Scottish agricultural soils (Berrow and Reaves, 1985).

Results from a number of long-term experiments comparing inorganic to organic nutrient regimes have usually failed to show significant differences between treatments. The only result reported consistently was a reduction in seedling numbers on beds receiving bulky organics in the year of sowing. Such reductions could be due to increased fungal action perhaps in response to the large amounts of added nitrogen. Alternatively, bulky organics may interfer with the capillary rise of water in sandy soils where good consolidation is vital to satisfactory germination. In this context, Benzian (1967) reported difficulty in consolidating seedbeds at Wareham when the quantity of added organic matter was increased to 75 t ha^{-1} y^{-1}.

Transplants growing on light sandy soils were found to benefit from incorporation of bulky organics (Benzian, 1967). It therefore seems logical on sands and very light loams (which form a large proportion of forest nursery soils) to recommend the application of bulky organics to transplants and to grow seedlings using inorganic fertilisers plus any residues from the manuring of transplants. Such a regime should benefit from organic residues without incurring associated losses on seedbeds.

4.4.2 Optimum levels

Levels of organic matter in soils vary from nursery to nursery and it is difficult to provide guidelines for optimum values. Although the individual attributes of soil organic matter are well known, experiments studying the performance of seedlings grown with and without additions of bulky organics have tended to be inconclusive with no definite evidence of improved performance compared with those using inorganic fertilisers alone (Aldhous, 1972; Benzian, 1965; Benzian *et al.*, 1972; Low and Sharpe, 1973). Soil organic matter content is determined, to a large extent, by the soil factors of moisture, temperature, fertility and texture. Organic matter tends to accumulate under conditions where the soil is fertile and the growing season long, moist and cool whereas a long, moist, warm growing season favours decomposition. Clay tends to associate closely with humus, retarding breakdown by soil microbes so that fine-textured soils usually have higher organic matter contents than coarse-textured soils in similar climatic locations. In areas with moist, mild winters saprophytic fungi are active almost all year and organic matter levels can be very difficult to maintain. Organic matter contents above 10% sometimes occur in British forest nurseries but usual levels lie between 2 and 8% (Figure 4.2).

There are two basic methods of increasing organic matter contents of forest nursery soils.

Crops can be grown on the land and incorporated into the soil (greencropping) or materials can be brought into the nursery from outside.

4.4.3 Greencrops

The incorporation of greencrops has been claimed to improve the humus content of soils and to provide a readily available supply of nutrients for the succeeding crop. However, the nutrient supply can only be increased significantly if the organic matter in the incorporated greencrop is broken down quickly, whereas to build up humus in the soil such organic matter must be fairly resistant to decomposition. If the greencrop is ploughed under while still soft and green, plant material will be broken down rapidly with the risk of losing any nitrate so released by leaching before the planting of a tree crop in the following spring. There is also some evidence that the decomposition of nutrient rich organic matter can act as a 'primer' and increase the rate of breakdown of native soil organic matter (Broadbent, 1947; Hallam and Bartholemew, 1953). If, on the other hand, greencrops are allowed to mature then fibrous matter, low in nitrogen, will be formed in the later stages of growth. These will persist in the soil and immobilise nitrogen during their breakdown, perhaps at a time when plants could advantageously use more nitrogen.

The risk of production of coarse woody materials and immobilisation of nitrogen during their consequent decomposition may be avoided if nitrogen fixing species are used for the greencrop. Symbiotic associations with N fixing bacteria allow these plants to utilise atmospheric sources of nitrogen unavailable to most plants. As a result, the soil N capital increases and such increases can offset consequent immobilisation during decomposition. Coarse N fixing species include peas, lupins and oil-seed rape.

Recommendations for greencrops

Greencrops must be suited to the pH of the nursery. Mustard is likely to fail if the soil pH is less than 5.5; oats do best at a pH above 5.5

and are likely to fail at any pH less than 5.0. Blue or yellow lupins and also ryegrass grow well at the range of pH optimum for most conifers. Lupins are more expensive than oats. See also Chapter 7, section 7.3 for details of Rhizobial inoculation.

Lupins should be sown in May or June at 450 kg ha^{-1}. This and all other greencrops should be raised on ground given 45–55 kg ha^{-1} N, 50–65 kg ha^{-1} P and 70–95 kg ha^{-1} K before sowing. The crop should be ploughed in no sooner than the time flowers first open but before seeds have set. On very light soils, seedlings of yellow lupins grown as a greencrop have suffered because of excessive uptake of P when grown on ground given superphosphate (Warren and Benzian, 1959).

Oats should be sown in May at 400–500 kg ha^{-1} of Yielder or Castleton potato oats. These should be ploughed in when the ears are visible but still green.

Ryegrass can be used as either a summer or autumn grass crop. The early crop should be sown in April at 33 kg ha^{-1} of perennial ryegrass, or 22 kg and 11 kg, respectively, of perennial ryegrass and Italian ryegrass. It should be cut regularly and ploughed in, in late August. The late crop should be sown in late August or early September depending on site. If the autumn is mild and grass is sown too early, top growth of ryegrass can become so luxuriant as to be an embarrassment by the time it should be dug in as a preliminary to lining out. At this time, the greencrop should be no more than 10–15 cm high.

4.4.4 Imported organic materials

Hopwaste

Hopwaste is a well proven material providing substantial amounts of nitrogen and phosphorus. It is a waste-product from breweries where the hops are boiled to extract flavouring and can be applied directly to the soil as a weed-free organic amendment. There is no benefit from composting hopwaste which, if kept at the nursery, should be stored under cover to minimise loss of nutrients by leaching. Traditional rates of application have been approximately 25 t ha^{-1} to seedbeds and 12.5 t ha^{-1} to transplant lines. More recent recommendations have been toward applying 25–40 t ha^{-1} to lines and none to the seedbeds owing to possible reductions in seed germination following applications of bulky organics (see section 4.4.1 above). If this recommendation is followed and seedbed applications are reduced then 50 kg more phosphorus per hectare should be included in the pre-sowing fertiliser dressing on the seedbeds and one or perhaps two additional top-dressings of nitrogen used. When available, hopwaste is a very suitable organic material for use in forest nursery soils. However, it has become increasingy difficult to obtain.

Bracken–hopwaste compost

At the beginning of the post-war period of intensive research into plant nutrition in forest nurseries, which culminated with the publication of Bulletin 37 (Benzian, 1965), it was necessary to establish a satisfactory, widely available 'standard' compost against which to assess experimental fertiliser regimes. Bracken–hopwaste compost became this standard material. However, in practice, it is no longer made, being replaced where a bulky organic supplement is required, by uncomposted hopwaste.

Bark chippings and sawdust

The direct use of organic residues such as bark chippings and sawdust, which contain much woody tissue, can deplete the supplies of available nitrogen in the soil during their decomposition. If these materials are composted and supplementary inorganic fertilisers added then the resulting material is suitable for use in forest nursery soils although, as for any compost, the cost may be high. Suitable methods for composting bark have been described in detail by Solbraa (1979). Additions of nitrogen, superphosphate (with sulphur) and, probably, micronutrients are necessary to attain maximum rates of decomposition. Solbraa recommends adding to the compost 2.0 kg m^{-3} of urea and 1.5–2.0 kg m^{-3} of superphosphate together with 0.2 kg m^{-3} fritted trace elements (e.g. SAI FTE-253A). Moisture content and aeration should be maintained by regular turning of the compost and irrigation. For piles of 4–5 m³ this entailed turning the compost up to four times. The compost was considered suitable for use once the temperature within the pile fell below 20°C, usually after 4–6 weeks. Modern methods of composting using microfloral inoculations and careful control of the environment may reduce this time quite considerably (Campbell *et al.*, 1990a and 1990b).

Sewage sludge

The use of sewage sludge as a fertiliser and soil amendment has received increasing attention in recent years due to rising costs of fertilisers and environmental problems of sewage sludge disposal on agricultural land. Sewage sludge has rarely been used in forest nurseries for several reasons.

- Its high water content makes it expensive to transport.
- It may be very unpleasant to handle.
- It may be a major source of weed contamination.
- It may contain varying amounts of trace elements and heavy metals.

New methods of processing sewage can now provide, at a cost, a solid, easily handled and nearly odourless end product that is weed and disease free. Certain elements are, however, found in concentrations approximately 40 times greater than in soils, particularly copper, tin and zinc (Berrow and Weber, 1972). Zinc, especially, is present in sewage sludges in a highly soluble form often exceeding 500 times that found in the soil. Additional problems may arise due to high levels of nickel and manganese. *Sewage sludge should only be considered for use in the nursery if the supplier can guarantee a sustained supply, entirely free from toxic heavy metals and noxious materials such as broken glass.*

Other materials

Farmyard manure

Farmyard manure was used extensively in forest nurseries up to 1945 but fell out of favour because it was a major source of weeds and because lime was mixed with the manure in the farmyard. When this was applied in forest nurseries, growth of conifers could sometimes be depressed on all but the most acid nursery soils. Its use has increased recently due to difficulties in obtaining other suitable materials and changes in farm husbandry practices which have reduced these causes for concern.

Peat

Acid peat has been used only occasionally as a supplement to forest nursery soils. In one nursery on a heavy textured soil, it was considered to have improved the working properties of the soil and to have acidified it.

Litter

Broiler house litter has been used successfully in at least one forest nursery but care must be taken to avoid scorch from the ammonia generated from fresh piles of such material, and to ensure that the litter is totally free from carcasses.

Mushroom compost

Spent mushroom compost appears to provide an alternative material for use as a soil organic matter amendment. The lime content of such material should be analysed to ensure that no detrimental effect upon soil pH is likely to occur. In one nursery the soil pH was increased by over one unit for at least 4 years following application.

Other materials may become available in the future. A comprehensive chemical analysis should be obtained, and advice sought, before any decision is taken to use a new material.

REFERENCES

AARON, J.R. (1976). *Conifer bark: its properties and uses.* Forestry Commission Forest Record 110. HMSO, London.

ALDHOUS, J.R. (1972). Comparison of organics and bulky inorganics on seedbeds cropped annually for thirteen years. In *Nursery practice* (1st edtn). Forestry Commission Bulletin 43. HMSO, London, 147–152.

ALLEN, S.E. (1984). Slow-release nitrogen fertilisers. In *Nitrogen in crop production.* ASA-CSSA-SSSA, 677 South Segoe Road, Madison, WI 53711 USA, 195–206.

ARMSON, K.A. and SADREIKA, V. (1979). *Forest tree nursery soil management and related practices.* Ontario Ministry of Natural Resources, Toronto.

BACHE, B.W. (1976). The measurement of cation exchange capacity of soils. *Journal of the Science of Food and Agriculture* **27,** 273–280.

BENZIAN, B. (1965). *Experiments on nutrition problems in forest nurseries* (2 Volumes). Forestry Commission Bulletin 37. HMSO, London.

BENZIAN, B. (1967). Manuring young conifers: experiments in some English nurseries. *Proceedings, Fertiliser Society* **94,** 5–37.

BENZIAN, B., BOLTON, J. and MATTINGLY, G.E.G. (1969). Soluble and slow-release PK fertilisers for seedlings and transplants of *Picea sitchensis. Plant and Soil* **31,** 238–256.

BENZIAN, B., BROWN, R.M. and FREEMAN, S.C.R. (1974). Effect of late-season top-dressings of N (and K) applied to conifer transplants in the nursery on their survival and growth on British forest sites. *Forestry* **47,** 153–184.

BENZIAN, B., FREEMAN, S.R.C. and PATTERSON, H.D. (1972). Comparison of crop rotations, and of fertiliser with compost, in long-term experiments with Sitka spruce (*Picea sitchensis*) and other conifers grown in English forest nurseries. *Forestry* **46,** 55–69.

BERROW, M.L. and REAVES, G.A. (1985). Extractable copper concentrations in Scottish soils. *Journal of Soil Science* **36,** 31–43.

BERROW, M.L. and WEBER, J. (1972). Trace elements in sewage sludges. *Journal of the Science of Food and Agriculture* **23,** 93–100.

BINNS, W.O. (1975). *Fertilisers in the forest: a guide to materials.* Forestry Commission Leaflet 63. HMSO, London.

BOLTON, J. and COULTER, J.K. (1966). Distribution of fertiliser residues in a forest nursery manuring experiment on a sandy podsol at Wareham, Dorset. In *Report on forest research for the year ended March 1965.* Forestry Commission. HMSO, London, 90–92.

BOULD, C., HEWITT, E.J. and NEEDHAM, P. (1983). *Diagnosis of mineral disorders in plants.* Volume 1. HMSO, London. (170 pp.)

BRADY, N.C. (1974). *The nature and properties of soil.* Collier Macmillan Publishers, London.

BROADBENT, F.E. (1947). Nitrogen release and carbon loss from soil organic matter during decomposition of added plant residues. *Soil Science Society of America Journal* **12,** 246–249.

BURT, A.C. (1988). *Media and mixes for container-grown plants.* Unwin, London. (309 pp.)

CAMPBELL, C.D., DARBYSHIRE, J.F. and ANDERSON, J.G. (1990a). The composting of tree bark in small reactors – self-heating experiments. *Biological Wastes* **31,** 145–161.

CAMPBELL, C.D., DARBYSHIRE, J.F. and ANDERSON, J.G. (1990b). The composting of tree bark in small reactors – adiabatic and fixed temperature experiments. *Biological Wastes* **31,** 175–185.

DAVEY, C.B. and KRAUSE, H.H. (1980). Functions and maintenance of organic matter in forest nursery soils. In *Proceedings of North American Forest Tree Nursery Soils Workshop,* July 28 to August 1, 1980, Syracuse, New York, 130–165.

FISHER, J.T. and MEXAL, J.G. (1984). Nutrition management: a physiological basis for yield improvement. In *Seedling physiology and reforestation success,* eds M.L. Duryea and G.N. Brown. Martinus Nijhoff/Junk, The Netherlands.

HACSKAYLO, J., FINN, R.F. and VIMMERSTEDT, J.P. (1969). Deficiency symptoms of some forest trees. Ohio Agricultural Research Development Centre. Research Bulletin 1015. (68 pp.)

HALLAM, M.J. and BARTHOLEMEW, W.V. (1953). Influence of rate of plant residue addition in accelerating the decomposition of soil organic matter. *Soil Science Society of America Journal* **17**, 365–368.

HUTTL, R.F. (1986). *Forest fertilisation: results from Germany, France and the Nordic countries.* Fertiliser Society, London. (40 pp.)

INGESTAD, T. (1957). Studies on the nutrition of forest tree seedlings. I. Mineral nutrition of birch. *Physiologia Plantarum* **10**, 418–439.

INGESTAD, T. (1959). Studies on the nutrition of forest tree seedlings. II. Mineral nutrition of spruce. *Physiologia Plantarum* **12**, 568–593.

INGESTAD, T. (1960). Studies on the nutrition of forest tree seedlings. III. Mineral nutrition of pine. *Physiologia Plantarum* **13**, 513–533.

INGESTAD, T. (1977). Nitrogen and plant growth; maximum efficiency of nitrogen fertilisers. *Ambio* **6**, 146–151.

INGESTAD, T. and LUND, A.-B. (1986). Theory and techniques for steady state mineral nutrition and growth of plants. *Scandinavian Journal of Forest Research* **1**, 439–453.

LAVENDER, D.P. and WALKER, R.B. (1981). Nitrogen and related elements in nutrition of forest trees. In *Proceedings Forest Fertilisation Conference,* eds S. P. Gessel, R. M. Kenady and W. A. Atkinson, Washington, USA University of Washington, 15–22.

LEAF, A.L. (1968). K, Mg and S deficiencies in forest trees. In *Forest fertilisation ... theory and practice.* Tennessee Valley Authority, Muscle Shoals, Alabama, 88–121.

LOW, A.J. and SHARPE, A.L. (1973). The long term effects of organic and inorganic fertiliser regimes at Teindland nursery. *Scottish Forestry* **27**, 287–295.

MARTENS, D. C. (1986). Plant availability of extractable boron, copper and zinc as related to selected soil properties. *Soil Science* **106**, 23–28.

MILLARD, P. and PROE, M.F. (1991a). Leaf demography and the seasonal internal cycling of nitrogen in sycamore (*Acer pseudoplatanus* L.) seedlings in relation to nitrogen supply. *New Phytologist* **117**, 587–596.

MILLARD, P. and PROE, M.F. (1991b). Storage and internal cycling of nitrogen in relation to seasonal growth of Sitka spruce. *Tree Physiology* **10**, 33–43.

MORRISON, I.K. (1974). *Mineral nutrition of conifers with special reference to nutrient status interpretation: a review of literature.* Department of the Environment, Canadian Forestry Service, Publication No. 1343, Ottawa, Canada. (74 pp.)

PELLET, H.M. and CARTER, J.V. (1981). Effects of nutritional factors on cold hardiness of plants. *Horticultural Review* **3**, 144–171.

SHARMA, G.C. (1979). Controlled-release fertilisers and horticultural applications. *Scientia Horticulturae* **11**, 107–129.

SMILDE, K.W. (1973). Phosphorus and micronutrient metal uptake by some tree species as affected by phosphate and lime applied to an acid sandy soil. *Plant and Soil* **39**, 131–148.

SOLBRAA, K. (1979). Composting of bark. III. Experiments on a semi-practical scale. *Reports of the Norwegian Forest Research Institute* **34** (15), 387–439.

STONE, E.L. (1968). Microelement nutrition of trees. A review. In *Forest fertilisation .... theory and practice.* Tennessee Valley Authority, Muscle Shoals, Alabama, 132–175.

SWAN, H.S.D. (1960). *The mineral nutrition of Canadian pulpwood species. 1. The influence of nitrogen, phosphorus, potassium and magnesium deficiencies on the growth and development of white spruce, black spruce, jack pine and western hemlock seedlings grown in a controlled environment.* Pulp and Paper Research Institute of Canada, Woodland Research Index 116. (66 pp.)

TIMMIS, R. (1974). Effect of nutrient stress on growth, bud set, and hardiness in Douglas-fir seedlings. In *Proceedings of North American Containerised Forest Tree*

Seedling Symposium, eds R.W. Tinus, W.I. Stein and W.E. Balmer, Great Plains Agricultural Council Publication No. 68, 187–193.

VAN DEN DRIESSCHE, R. (1980). Health, vigour and quality of conifer seedlings in relation to nursery soil fertility. In *Proceedings of North American Forest Tree Nursery Soils Workshop,* July 28 to August 1, 1980, Syracuse, New York, 100–120.

VAN DEN DRIESSCHE, R. (1984). Relationship between spacing and nitrogen fertilisation of seedlings in the nursery, seedling mineral nutrition, and outplanting performance. *Canadian Journal of Forest Research* **14,** 431–436.

VAN DEN DRIESSCHE, R. (1985). Late-season fertilisation, mineral nutrient reserves, and retranslocation in planted Douglas-fir (*Pseudotsuga menziesii* (Mirb.) Franco) seedlings. *Forest Science* **31,** 485–496.

VAN DEN DRIESSCHE, R. (ed.) (1991). *Mineral nutrition of conifer seedlings.* CRC Press, Boston, USA.

WARREN, R.G. and BENZIAN, B. (1959). High levels of phosphorus and die-back in yellow lupins. *Nature (London)* **184,** 1588.

WORLEY, C.L., LESSELBAUM, H.R. and MATTHEWS, T.M. (1941). Deficiency symptoms for the major elements in seedlings of three broad-leaved trees. *Journal of the Tennessee Academy of Science* **16,** 239–247.

YOUNGBERG, C.T. (1984). Soil and tissue analysis: tools for maintaining soil fertility. In *Forest nursery manual: production of bareroot seedlings,* eds M.L. Duryea and T.D. Landis. Martinus Nijoff/Dr W. Junk Publishers, The Hague, 75–80.

Chapter 5

Seed

P. G. Gosling and J. R. Aldhous

Introduction

The use of seed from stands of high inherent quality is widely recognised as the best means of ensuring fast-grown and healthy plantations capable of yielding good quality wood. Seed guaranteed to have been collected in nationally registered seed orchards or seed stands* may be two or three times more expensive than seed collected from unregistered stands of unknown quality. The higher cost is due to the additional labour and supervision needed to ensure that the seed is true to its description, and for seed orchards, the cost of their management. Nevertheless, even the highest of these seed costs adds little to the cost of newly established plantations, and this is amply covered if the plantation raised from the registered seed grow only a few percent faster than plantations from unregistered seed (Faulkner, 1992; Gill, 1983; Lee, 1990; Rook, 1992.)

Forestry Commission seed manuals

Two current Forestry Commission publications describe in detail, many aspects of seed collection, storage, handling, etc., relevant to the forest nursery manager.

Forestry Commission Bulletin 59. *Seed manual for ornamental trees and shrubs* (Gordon and Rowe, 1982).

Forestry Commission Bulletin 83. *Seed manual for forest trees* (Gordon, 1992).

Nursery managers are recommended to include both volumes in their collection of readily available reference books.

---

* For explanation of terms, see glossary (Appendix II) and also Chapter 15, section 15.1.

Contents of the seed manuals are summarised below.

Subject	Bulletin 59 (broadleaves & ornamentals)	Bulletin 83 (forest trees)
Flower, fruit & seed development	Chapter 3	Chapter 6
Collection methods & times	Chapter 4 & Appendix 3	Chapters 7 & 8
Extraction & processing	Chapter 4	Chapter 9
Seed yields	Appendix 4A	Table 9.1
Storage	Chapter 5 & Appendix 5	Chapter 10
Testing	Chapter 6	Chapter 11
Seed & plant identity number systems	–	Chapter 4

5.1 Choice of seed origin

5.1.1 Improved seed

Much effort has gone into 'tree improvement' through selection and testing programmes. As a result, supplies of seed are available from open-pollinated seed orchards and from controlled pollination of genetically superior parent trees in the tree improvement programme. Unfortunately, lack of resources has restricted work in the UK to a very small number of species.

Seed of Scots pine is available from 'approved' and untested seed orchards in reasonable quantity. For Sitka spruce, increasing amounts of 'approved' seed are available; initially, most of this is reserved for vegetative propagation programmes. The yield of hybrid larch from open pollinated seed orchards has been much less than anticipated; however, supplies of seed from controlled pollination in polyhouses should become commercially available in small quantities in the mid 1990s. This is also being reserved for vegetative propagation programmes.

Wherever seed from such improved sources is available and appropriate, it should be the grower's first choice and nursery managers should ensure that stocks are on offer. Nevertheless, for many species, such improved seed is not yet in production, so that the grower will have to seek stock from home-grown or imported seed.

5.1.2 Home-grown seed

If home-grown seed is being sought, as a first principle, seed should be chosen from the very best stands in the locality where it is intended to plant, ensuring that these are 'registered' when relevant (see Chapter 15, section 15.3). If such seed is not available, the second choice should be from the nearest registered seed source on a similar site. Failing a local registered source, information on other registered sources may be obtained by consulting the register of seed sources held at the Forestry Authority national offices, addresses of which are given in Appendix I.

5.1.3 Origins of imported seed

If only imported seed is available, the origins given in Table 5.1 are to be preferred.

Table 5.1 Suggested sources of seed when home-collected registered or improved sources are not available

Species	Suggested source
Scots pine	Should not normally need to be imported because seed-orchard seed available. Where grant-aid is linked to use of particular local native sources of SP, the requirements of the relevant grant schemes must be observed.
Corsican pine	For southern sites, registered stands in Corsica: second choice France, region 01(2A) or 01(2B). For planting north of the Midlands, seed from second generation Calabrian CP stands in Belgium (e.g. Koekelare) or France (e.g. Les Barres) are also suitable.
Lodgepole pine	No simple recommendation; see footnote to table.
Sitka spruce	Queen Charlotte Islands is a well-proven general purpose seed source. For favourable sites in Wales and southwest England, origins in Washington and northern Oregon may be used; for very exposed and frosty sites in north Scotland, consider Alaskan origins. Improved seed from seed orchards is also available.
Norway spruce	For timber production, eastern Europe Romania, Poland, the Czech and Slovak republics; for Christmas tree production, south Germany (German seed zone 84013).
European larch	Carpathian and Sudeten Mts of the Czech and Slovak republics (native stands); if not available, low elevation stands in Austria and Germany.
Japanese larch	Suwa region of Nagano (elevation 1500–1800 m); if not available, Nikko region of Tochigi (1500 m) and plantations on Hokkaido.
Douglas fir	Washington coast and foothills of W. slope of Cascades (US seed zones 012, 030, 041, 202, 241, 403, 411, 412).
Grand fir	Olympic Peninsula and Puget Sound (US seed zones 030, 202, 212, 221, 231, 241); if not available, Vancouver Island (British Columbia zone 1020).
Noble fir	Larch Mountain, Oregon, 975 m, (US seed zones 042, 440, 452).
Western hemlock	Vancouver Island (BC zone 1010); if not available, coastal Washington (US zones 030, 012, 011), or Queen Charlotte Isles. For sheltered sites in northern Britain, Alaskan origins are hardiest but grow more slowly.
Western red cedar	Washington Olympic Mts below 150 m (US Zone 030, 012, 011, 221); if not available, Vancouver Island, e.g. BC zone 1020.
Oak, pedunculate sessile	Registered seed sources in woodland in northern France and northwest Germany.
Beech	Belgium (Forêt de Soignes); if not available, any registered seed source in Belgium, Holland, northern France or northwest Germany.
Birch, downy silver	Western european sources from low elevation at latitudes similar to Britain.

More detailed information can be found in: Forestry Commission Bulletin 66 *Choice of seed origins for the main forest species in Britain* by R. Lines (HMSO, 1987).

5.2 Seed identity numbers

Forestry managers have for many years, used numbering systems as brief alternatives to names describing the origin of seed, both in the United Kingdom and elsewhere. The advent of seed stand registration under EEC legislation, has given a further impetus to establish systems that indicate the quality as well as the location of origin or provenance of seed lots. Systems in current use in Europe, USA and Canada, and those used in the past in the United Kingdom, are described comprehensively in Chapter 4 of Bulletin 83. The following is a summary of current practice in the United Kingdom.

5.2.1 The Forestry Commission seed identity number system

Seed Identity Numbers currently being allocated have three parts:

> species name;
> crop year;
> source.

While called identity 'numbers', letters or names may also be incorporated.

Species name

The species name is an essential part of a seed identity, without which it is unlikely to be unique.

Seed crop year

The first two digits of all Forestry Commission identity numbers denote the 'seed crop year', 1st August – 31st July. This is identified by the last two digits of the calendar year in which the crop year begins, e.g. the first two digits for seed collected in January 1991 is '90'.

Source

The letters and digits that follow the seed crop year indicate whether the seed was grown in Great Britain or was imported and whether the seed is from a tree improvement programme or other special category.

The letters and digits indicating source are enclosed in a bracket with supplementary information following.

5.2.2 Identity numbers for seed collected in Great Britain

General collections

Great Britain is divided for general seed collection purposes into four regions of provenance, numbered 10, 20, 30, 40. These are shown in Figure 5.1. Within any region of provenance, seed may have been obtained from 'registered' or 'unregistered' stands. Registered stands of a species in a region of provenance are serially numbered; the source identity consists of the region of provenance number followed by the registered stand serial number.

Seed from unregistered sources is given only the region of provenance number; it could have been derived from a single stand or from a number of unregistered stands within the region of provenance.

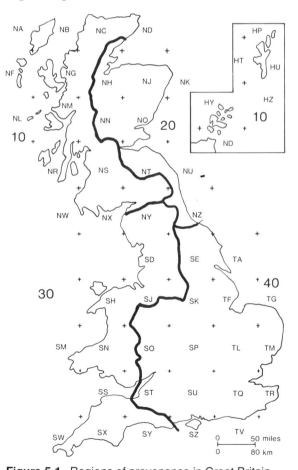

Figure 5.1 Regions of provenance in Great Britain.

For example: SS 88(1006) denotes Sitka spruce collected in crop year 88 in stand 6 of region 10;

POK 89(40) denotes pedunculate oak collected in crop year 89 from unspecified stands (or stand) in region 40.

Native Scots pine

Within the range of native Scots pine, approximately 40 woodlands in seven collection zones are included in a national register (Forestry Commission, 1993). The collection zones are shown in Figure 5.2. Seed collected from such stands is indicated by the initial letter 'N' (i.e. native), followed by a digit showing the zone number followed by two digits for the stand; e.g. SP 89(N502) is native Scots pine seed collected in crop year 89 from stand 2 of zone 5.

Improved seed from seed orchards

Seed orchards in Britain are numbered consecutively from 1 within each species. Seed from such orchards is identified by that number. This is preceded by 'A' if the component clones in the orchard have been approved as a result of a completed test programme, or

by 'NT' if the testing programme for the orchard is not yet completed, e.g. SP 90(A70) denotes seed from seed orchard 70 the components of which have been approved. SP 87(NT45) denotes seed from Scots pine seed orchard 45 for which tests have not yet been completed.

A small number of Scots pine seed orchards are composed of clones from native sources. The letter 'N' is then added followed by the native pine zone number.

SP (NT37)N2 denotes Scots pine seed from seed orchard 37, this being made up of clones collected from within native tree region 2 (see Figure 5.2).

Hybrid larch

Collections of seed from orchards of mixed clones of Japanese and European larch are sometimes made from clones of one species only. The letters 'E' or 'J' are used to indicate this.

HL 84(NT8)E denotes seed from hybrid larch seed orchard 8 from European larch cones only.

Family mixtures for vegetative propagation

Mixtures of seed from controlled pollination of proven genetically superior families are now used for the commercial production of rooted cuttings. These mixtures are numbered sequentially starting with 0001, and prefixed by the letter 'M'.

SS 85(M0014) is mixture 14 from controlled pollination of tested families of Sitka spruce.

5.2.3 Identity numbers for imported seed

For imported seed lots, name and crop year conventions are the same as for home collected seed.

The source information for imported seed is based on the Universal Decimal Classification (UDC) code for countries or parts of countries and is placed within brackets. A list of the more important UDC codes for countries from which seed is imported can be found in the current Forestry Commission Seed Catalogue or Forestry Commission Bulletin 83 *Seed manual for forest trees*.

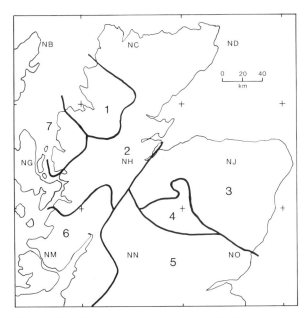

Figure 5.2 Native Scots pine seed collection zones.

In addition, details of region of provenance provided for the exporting country may be provided, following the bracketed digits. For example:

(492)3	region 3 of the Netherlands,
(436)VII/4	region VII/4 of Austria,
(711)C4	coastal zone 4 of British Columbia,
(795)051	zone 051, Oregon
(8331)	Malleco province, Chile

5.2.4 Lot numbers

Lot numbers may be allocated where, for operational reasons during collection, handling, storage or processing, seed which would otherwise have had a single identity number has become divided.

5.3 Procurement of seed

By far the largest quantities of seed sown by nursery managers are purchased. The principle exceptions are the larger seeded broadleaved and ornamental species within easy reach of a nursery.

For recommendations for methods of handling, extraction and storage of locally collected seed, see Forestry Commission Bulletins 59 and 83.

For details of administrative procedures to be followed under the Forest Reproductive Material Regulations for species covered by those regulations, see Chapter 15, section 15.3.

5.3.1 Sources of seed

Seed may be purchased either from seed merchants or from the Forestry Commission. A list of members selling tree and shrub seed may be obtained from the Horticultural Trades Association, 19, High Street, Theale, Reading, Berks, RG7 5AH.

Prospective purchasers from the Forestry Commission should write for a current seed catalogue to: Plant and Seed Supply Branch, Seed Trading, Alice Holt Lodge, Wrecclesham, Farnham, Surrey, GU10 4LH.

5.3.2 Legislation governing purchase and sale of seed

Trade in tree seed is covered by legislation, of which the most immediate is the Forest Reproductive Material Regulations; see Chapter 15, section 15.1 and also section 15.8.2.

The Forest Reproductive Material Regulations affect fewer species than had been included in the earlier, now repealed, 1920 Seeds Act. Species currently covered are listed in Table 15.1 (page 224).

5.3.3 Classes of seed

Seed is classified in current seed catalogues as:

'unregistered'
'registered' – either from 'selected seed stands' or from 'seed orchards' (either 'untested' or 'approved').

Registered seed conforms to that category of seed under the Forest Reproductive Material Regulations, but is extended for convenience and consistency to species not covered by the regulations, but which may for example be marketed under OECD rules. See Chapter 15, sections 15.1 and 15.4.

The bulk of conifer seed used in forestry plantations falls into the 'registered/selected' category. Some seed is also available from 'approved' and from 'untested' seed orchards. Legally, both types of seed have to be placed with 'selected' seed lots because there are currently no EEC categories 'approved' or 'untested seed orchard seed'. In practice, however, 'approved' seed should be considered equivalent to the EEC 'tested' seed while 'untested' should be considered intermediate between 'selected' and 'approved' (Chapter 15, section 15.1.2).

Seed of oak and beech is from time to time available from registered seed sources; however, trees do not bear seed crops every year, nor can seed be stored easily from one year to the next. Consequently, in many years, unregistered seed sources have to be used (Chapter 15, section 15.1.5).

Seed of other broadleaved species comes almost entirely from unregistered stands.

Table 5.2 Prescriptions for seed sampling

(a) Seed lot in sacks or other containers

Number of containers in the lot	Minimum number of containers to be sampled (Samples to be taken from at least 5 positions)
1–5 (inclusive)	Each container
6–14	Not less than 5 containers
15–30	At least one container in 3
31–49	Not less than 10 containers
50 or more	At least 1 container in 5

(b) Undivided bulk seed lot

Weight of bulk seed

Exceeding	Not exceeding	Number of positions to be sampled
–	50 kg	Not less than 4
60 kg	1500 kg	Not less than 5
1500 kg	3000 kg	At least 1 for each 300 kg
3000 kg	5000 kg	Not less than 10
5000 kg	20000 kg	At least 1 for every 500 kg

Table 5.3 Seed testing: fees (as at 1.10.93); minimum sample weight; maximum seed lot weight; purity standards

EEC species	Fee for statutory seed test (£)	Minimum sample weight (grams)	Maximum seed lot weight (kg)	Maximum impurities % by weight** %
Silver fir	£75*	240	–	0.1%
Beech	£110†	1000	5000	0.1%
European larch	£75‡	25	–	0.5%§
Japanese larch	£100*	25	–	0.5%§
Norway spruce	£75‡	40	–	0.5%
Sitka spruce	£100*	25	1000	0.5%
Austrian and Corsican pine	£75‡	100	–	0.5%
Scots pine	£75‡	40	–	0.5%
Weymouth pine	£75*	90	–	0.5%
Douglas fir	£100*	60	–	0.5%
Red oak	£95	500#	–	0.1%¶
Pedunculate oak	£95	500#	5000	0.1%¶
Sessile oak	£95	500#	–	0.1%¶

* Seed test: purity; weight of 1000 pure seeds; germination without prechilling.
† Seed test: purity; weight of 1000 pure seeds; viability by tetrazolium method; germination with prechilling.
‡ Seed test: as for * plus germination with prechilling.
§ Purity test standard allows 1% of other *Larix* seed.
¶ Purity test standard allows 1% of other *Quercus* seed.
\# Minimum *number* of acorns to be submitted in sample.
** Maximum permitted percentage by weight of fruits and seeds of other forest tree species.

remixed or it must be treated as two or more uniform seed lots.

Where a uniform seed lot has been divided between a number of sacks or containers for storage or transport, these must be sampled as specified in Table 5.2. Where it is not divided, samples should be taken as in Table 5.2.

Where there are more than five containers in a lot, the containers to be sampled should be selected at random, if possible, using a walking stick sampler. Where the seed is stored in bulk, samples should be taken with a stick sampler at random throughout the bulk, from at least the number of positions indicated in Table 5.2 (see Bulletin 83 for fuller details).

Sample size

Samples should be of a weight that will contain a minimum of 5000 seeds (500 for *Quercus* spp., minimum weight for *Fagus* spp. 1 kg). Minimum weights for species covered by regulations are included in Table 5.3.

Sample despatch

Samples should be sent in rigid containers by the fastest available means. Samples for moisture content tests must be sent in moisture-proof containers.

For the United Kingdom, seed may be sent for testing to: The Official Seed Testing Station, The Forestry Authority, Research Division, Alice Holt Lodge, Wrecclesham, Farnham, Surrey, GU10 4LH.

With each sample, there should be enclosed:

- full name and address of sender;
- species name;
- date of sampling;
- stock number or reference;
- quantity of seed represented by sample;

- a statement of whether the seed is or has been kept in cold storage;
- number of Master or other Certificate of Provenance, or if not available, details of seed provenance;
- tests required;
- remittance for cost of tests.

Seed test fees

Fees for seed tests (at October, 1993) are included in Table 5.3.

5.6.2 Tests of physical quality

Purity

The object of the purity analysis is to determine the percentage by weight of four fractions:

- seed of the species under test;
- seed of other forest species;
- other seed;
- inert matter.

The maximum impurities (content of fruits and seeds of other forest species + inert matter) permissible in any seed lot covered by the FRM Regulations is given in Table 5.3.

Weight of 1000 pure seed

The weight of 1000 pure seed is an expression of seed size and is determined by weighing a counted number of seeds

The weight of 1000 pure seed is required, together with figures for purity percent and the results of the germinability or viability tests, to calculate the number of germinable or viable seeds per kilogram for any seed lot.

Moisture content

Control of moisture content is essential if seed is to be stored successfully. The moisture content of seed is expressed as a percentage of the fresh weight of the seed.

A method of determining moisture content in the nursery, using a balance and an infrared lamp to dry seed quickly, is given in Bulletin 59, pages 18 and 19. From such a pro-

cedure, the moisture content percent of the seed is:

$$\frac{(\text{fresh weight} - \text{dry weight}) \times 100}{\text{fresh weight}}$$

This will be a sufficient guide to the moisture content of locally collected seed, to indicate whether the seed requires any further drying before storage.

5.6.3 Tests of physiological quality

There are broadly two types of tests of physiological quality, 'germination' tests and 'viability' tests.

The germination test, as its name implies, measures the proportion of seeds in a given sample that is capable of germination under standard test conditions.

Alternatively, one of a range of viability tests may be made which permit seeds to be classified as either alive (i.e. viable) or dead, the inference being that live seeds are capable of germination. Seeds with some live tissue, but also significant amounts of dead tissue are usually counted as dead/incapable of germination.

The choice of test depends on circumstances and in particular, whether there is any statutory requirement for certain tests to be made, and how soon the nursery manager wants to sow the seed.

The germination test directly measures the characteristic which the nursery manager wishes to reproduce in the nursery, but it takes time. Viability tests may be sought if seed has to be sown as soon as possible, or because the seed is dormant and the full germination test results will not be available for many weeks.

For example, ash, cherry, beech, hawthorn, rowan and lime can require between 6 and 18 months low temperature pretreatment to overcome dormancy; the germination test at a higher temperature may take a further 6 weeks.

5.6.4 Germination tests

In its simplest form, i.e. without any seed pretreatment, a laboratory germination test consists of incubating seeds under standard conditions, as near optimal as possible, until no more seeds germinate.

Non-dormant seeds normally take between 2 and 5 weeks. At the end of the test, germinated seedlings are classified as normal or abnormal and ungerminated seeds are classified as fresh, empty or dead; see Gordon, 1992 for details of germination testing procedures.

However, a simple test of untreated seed is inadequate for most conifer seeds, and also for broadleaves such as alders and birches because such seeds exhibit shallow dormancy (see section 5.7.1).

Pretreatment by 3–4 weeks of cool moist chilling at 3–5°C is necessary for such species. The treatment breaks any shallow dormancy and conditions the seed to be able to achieve the maximum rate of, and total percentage germination when transferred to germination test temperatures. For seeds that may be shallowly dormant, therefore, the whole test procedure to assess germination capacity usually takes about 8 weeks.

Double tests of germination

Wherever there is doubt about the potential effect of 3–4 weeks prechilling, 'double' tests are performed – with and without pretreatment. Hence, two germination capacity assessments are obtained. Comparison of mid-test and end-of-test germination figures show whether pretreatment stimulated, or reduced germination, or whether it left it unaffected. Advice is given on seed test certificates on the basis of this test.

Pretreatment is recommended where, in the test, pretreatment clearly increased total germination by the end of the test period. It is also recommended where, although there was no clear benefit at the end of the germination test period, during the test, pretreated seed germinated more quickly than untreated seed.

5.6.5 Viability tests

The tetrazolium (TZ) and excised embryo (EE) tests are normally applied to those species where the combined time to pretreat and germinate seeds is longer than 8 weeks.

The 'cut' test, is applied to 'recalcitrant' seeds (see section 5.5.1 above), which cannot

be dried and therefore have a very limited storage life.

Occasionally, viability tests may be applied to the faster germinating species without storage problems, such as pines and spruces, but only if very quick results (less than 2 weeks) are required.

Cut test

The cut test is the simplest, oldest and crudest method of assessing the potential performance of seeds or fruits. It relies on the fact that only full and physically undamaged seeds have the potential to germinate.

When seeds or fruits are cut open, some may be entirely empty; in others the embryo may be present but is immature, shrivelled, mouldy or insect damaged. Clearly, none of these is viable. The only fruits and seeds which are viable are those which appear clean, full, firm and apparently healthy.

Although the cut test can be applied to any seed, it is most commonly applied to oaks, horse and sweet chestnut.

- It gives a rapid viability estimate on fruits that are notoriously short lived.

- The resultant partially dissected fruits can be transferred to a suitable germination medium where the pericarp removal (a part of the cut test) acts as a 'pretreatment' which speeds up germination.

Interim report based on cut test

In Great Britain, the Official Seed Testing Station routinely provides customers requesting tests on these species with an interim report based on the cut test results, the germination test results following a few weeks later. The cut test report normally states:

- total percent viable, including sprouted;

- percent sprouted (and therefore viable);

- total percent dead, including insect damaged;

- percent insect damaged (and therefore not viable).

Tetrazolium (TZ) test

In this test, seeds are soaked in a colourless solution of 2, 3, 5 triphenyl tetrazolium chloride (TZ). Live tissues turn red, their cells having the enzymes capable of converting the colourless TZ salt to an insoluble red product. The pattern of red staining on the seeds is then used to distinguish live (viable) seeds from dead.

Excised embryo tests

Embryos are surgically removed from seeds and maintained under conditions similar to those for germination. Viable embryos either remain firm and fresh or actually show visible evidence of growth or greening over the course of incubation. Non-viable embryos show signs of decay.

5.6.6 Seed Test Certificates

Nursery managers purchasing seed must be familiar with the results of seed testing as presented on Seed Test Certificates. All Official and most Advisory Seed Test Certificates issued in the United Kingdom include the following information:

- number of Seed Test Certificate;
- purity (percent);
- germination percent;
- number of live seeds per kilogram (of seed as supplied);
- number of seeds capable of germinating, per kilogram;
- weight of 1000 pure seeds in grams;
- year in which the seed ripened;
- whether the seed has been kept in cold storage.

Species covered by the 1977 FRM Regulations, when marketed, must be accompanied by a current 'Supplier's Certificate'. This includes the information from Official Seed Test Certificates, listed above. In addition, the 'Suppliers Certificate' must include the description 'EEC Standard', or a statement that sub-standard seed has been authorised for marketing (Chapter 15, section 15.2.1.).

How to use seed test certificate data to obtain best performance from tree seed

An example of a Forestry Commission Seed Test Certificate is shown in Figure 5.3. Most of the contents are self-explanatory. However, a few minor comments can be made.

Quality for sowing into containers and for precision sowing

Germination and viability data on the test certificate are expressed as percentages. In this form they can be used to assess whether a seed lot is suitable for precision sowing, or any cell or container method of intensive plant production. See Chapter 8, section 8.2.1 for undercut production and Chapter 9, section 9.5.1. for discussion of alternatives when it appears that an appreciable number of cells or containers will be unstocked if one seed is sown per cell and no other seed is available.

Appraisal of seed quality

Germination and viability percentages combined with purity and seed weight results indicate the overall quality of the seed and provide the starting point for calculating sowing densities, and a basis for comparing different seed lots.

Pretreatment

Pretreatment recommendations are given under 'General remarks' on the test certificate. The majority of broadleaf species (but not alders, birches, oaks and chestnut) exhibit seed dormancy and for such species, pretreatment is strongly recommended.

Where the certificate relates to shallowly dormant species, the results of an ISTA 'double' test will be given; see section 5.6.4 on page 75.

5.6.7 Seed tests for species not covered by the Forest Reproductive Material Regulations

The tests described above can be undertaken for any other forest species. Such tests are carried out to the same standards and at the same cost, and are supported by 'Official' certificates.

TEST CERTIFICATE

The Official Seed Testing Lab.
The Forestry Authority, Research Division
Alice Holt Lodge, Wrecclesham, Farnham
Surrey, GU10 4LH

SENDER OF SAMPLE

Seed description

Genus and species :
Common name :
Ident No. :
Master Certificate of Provenance no. :
OR Licence to Market no. :
Region of Provenance :
Place of Provenance :
Place of origin :
Altitude (metres) :
Date of sampling :
Date of sample receipt :
Quantity represented :

Test results

Test Certificate no. :

It is hereby certified that the results of the official test are as follows:

Purity analysis (full)

Purity :
Other forest seed :
Weight of 1000 pure seed :
Number of pure seeds/kg :

Germination test

No pretreatment (Results at day 21) :
Normal germ. + Abnormal germ. + Fresh = Viability

Pretreatment (Results at day 21 after 21 days pretreatment) :
Normal germ. + Abnormal germ. + Fresh = Viability

Number of germinable seeds/kg :
Number of viable seeds/kg :

Viability test

% Viable by i)   Tetrazolium: ii) Excised embryo:
iii) Cut test: (Sprouted:)   (Insect damaged:)

Number of viable seeds/kg :
Remarks on foreign seed :
Remarks on pure seed : Ave. % empty :   Moisture content :
Remarks on inert matter : Wing Pieces, Broken Seed, Resin,
Organic Matter, Cone Parts.

General remarks
This seed will not benefit from pretreatment.

Officer in charge ....

Date

Figure 5.3 Sample seed test certificate.

Advisory tests for seed

For seed of species where the quantity of seed is small, 'advisory' tests may be more appropriate as they require less seed and the fees are lower. For current fees, contact the Official Seed Testing Station.

The efficiency of an advisory test will depend to a very large extent upon the efficiency of the sampling. The sample should be truly representative of the bulk, containing seed and inert matter in their true proportions. The size of the sample is at the discretion of the grower but for all except the bulky broadleaved species one containing between 200–2000 seeds (with accompanying inert matter) is adequate. Samples of the larger seeded species should not contain fewer than 100 seeds.

All results will be given in terms of germinable or viable seeds per kilogram depending on the test applied. When results are supplied as the number of viable seeds per kilogram, providing pretreatment is optimal and nursery conditions reasonable at the time of sowing, a similar number of seeds should germinate.

Quick information test (for results in about 14 days)

This advisory test employs ISTA prescribed analyses but is applied to fewer seeds than are used in an Official test, and always relies on a 'viability' test. Quick information tests cannot be applied to species with very small seeds, e.g. alders, birches.

It must be specified in writing when rapid results are desirable and a quick information test is required. The Seed Testing Station will then endeavour to meet reasonable deadlines.

Moisture content test

The moisture content of tree seeds is a useful property for potential purchasers to know. Seeds of most species possess greater longevity at low moisture levels, and obviously the higher the moisture content the less seed and the more water is being purchased per unit weight.

Moisture content results are determined by drying the seed and assuming that any loss in weight reflects a loss of water.

5.6.8 Correlation of laboratory test results with field emergence

A germination test measures the maximum germination percentage attainable by a seed lot under standard laboratory conditions which are near ideal. Tree seeds are however notorious for germinating less well when conditions are not ideal; seedling yields in the nursery similar to germination percentages in the laboratory are extremely rarely achieved because conditions, temperatures in particular, are seldom optimal and because seedlings once emerged have to survive the hazards of the growing season.

Viability test results are an even more indirect measure of potential seed performance.

Local 'field survival factors'

A 'field survival factor' for an individual sowing can be obtained by dividing the number of usable seedlings available for transplanting at the end of the season, by the number of germinable or viable seed sown.

The implementation of nursery production plans, and specifically, sowing programmes, are more secure if long-term records of nursery performance are available.

Table 5.4 Field survival factors – common conifers (numbers in 000)

	Average number of germinable seeds per kg	Average number of usable seedlings		Field survival factors	
		1+0	2+0	1+0	2+0
Scots pine	140	80	75	0.6	0.55
Corsican pine	55	30	–	0.6	–
Lodgepole pine	270	160	135	0.6	0.5
European larch	60	33	–	0.55	
Japanese larch	100	60	–	0.6	–
Hybrid larch	50	28	–	0.55	–
Douglas fir	70	38	32	0.55	0.45
Norway spruce	110	85	80	0.6	0.55
Sitka spruce	320	170	150	0.55	0.45
Grand fir	20	8	7	0.4	0.35
Noble fir	12	5	4	0.4	0.35
Western hemlock	420	180	170	0.45	0.4
Western red cedar	500	225	210	0.45	0.4
Lawson cypress	230	100	90	0.45	0.4

Table 5.4 contains field survival factors, based on long-term averages from Forestry Commission nurseries.

5.7 Seed dormancy

Mature seed of most woody plant species from temperate zones frequently exhibits dormancy. A dormant seed is one that can be shown to be alive, but will either not germinate at all, not germinate promptly, or only germinate over a narrow range of environmental conditions. In dormant seed lots, significant numbers of individual seed remain dormant under conditions normally suitable for germination. This can be a serious handicap both to reliable plant production and to seed testing.

5.7.1 Breaking dormancy

In order to bring about the germination of a dormant seed lot, a suitable 'dormancy breakage' procedure or 'pretreatment' has to be identified and applied, before seed testing or sowing in the nursery.

Table 5.5 lists several alternative pretreatment procedures which overcome dormancy of temperate tree species. However, no one pretreatment is universally effective and for some species, even when the most suitable pretreatment has been selected, differences in for example, seed moisture content, duration of pretreatment, etc., can materially affect its success.

The most effective and widely used dormancy-breaking pretreatment is to 'prechill' seed, i.e. to expose imbibed (moist) dormant seed to low temperatures – i.e. between 2° and 5°C.

The optimum duration of prechilling depends largely on species; however, the geographical location, the environmental conditions under which seed has developed and matured, time of collection, and how seed has been processed and stored may also affect the depth of dormancy and hence the period of prechilling required.

Dry storage and prechilling

Dormant, orthodox tree seeds, kept in long

Table 5.5 Techniques to overcome seed dormancy

1. Outdoor overwintering of moist seed (stratification).
2. Cold treatment of moist seed at *c.* 2.5°C (prechilling).
3. Alternate warm (*c.* 20°C) then cold (*c.* 2.5°C) treatment of moist seed, under controlled conditions.
4. Mechanical scarification of hard coated seed.
5. A short immersion in hot (*c.* 70°C) or even boiling water.
6. Treatment with a corrosive chemical, e.g. sulphuric acid.
7. Treatment with non-corrosive chemicals, e.g. KNO_3, KCN, NaOCl, H_2O_2.
8. Treatment with plant growth substances, e.g. gibberellic acid.

term storage at the normal moisture content for dry storage (6–8%) *do not* lose dormancy. This is in complete contrast to cereal grains which *do* lose dormancy in dry storage. Tree seeds which respond to prechilling *must* be chilled under *moist* conditions for dormancy to be broken.

Deep dormancy

Species which do not germinate at all until pretreated and require in excess of 8 weeks moist prechilling to bring about any response, are commonly referred to as 'deeply' dormant. As an example of deep dormancy, Figure 5.4 illustrates the results of germination tests at a range of temperatures with a lot of beech seed. The unchilled seed was incapable of germinating at any temperature; 15 weeks moist prechilling stimulated germination and 19 weeks was even more effective (Gosling, 1991).

Shallow dormancy

Shallowly dormant seed lots respond to prechilling but do not require the duration of treatment necessary for deeply dormant species. Figure 5.5 illustrates the response of a 'shallowly' dormant seed lot. Untreated, the seed reaches is best performance over a narrow temperature range; with 3–6 weeks' moist chilling, this range is considerably widened. In practice, this implies that pretreatment enables seed to germinate well over a range of weather conditions, and not only in the best.

5.7.2 Seed prechilling

In laboratory seed tests, small quantities of dry seed placed on moist filter paper and incubated at 3–5°C take up water slowly and commence pretreatment once their moisture content has increased sufficiently. For commercial production, full scale versions of this procedure have long been practised.

Stratification

Traditional methods of large scale pretreatment (stratification) are to mix seeds in suitable sized containers with a well-drained but moisture retaining medium such as peat or

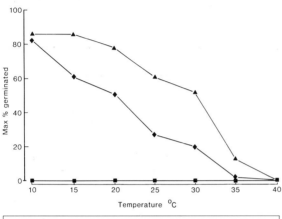

Figure 5.4 The effect of pretreatment on germination of beechnuts at different temperatures.

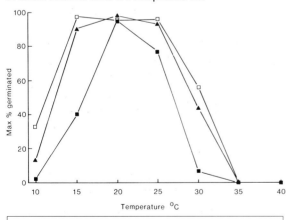

Figure 5.5 The effect of pretreatment on germination of Sitka spruce seed at different temperatures.

coarse sand or peat and sand, and to store the stratified seed in a vermin-proof well-drained pit out of doors (Anon., 1960). The naturally occurring low soil temperatures in the winter months are normally sufficient to meet the seeds' chill requirements; however, soil temperatures closely reflect the winter and early spring weather, and in mild early springs seed can be found to be germinating sooner than is desirable. Wherever out of door stratification is practised, it is essential to examine seed regularly and to be prepared to sow if germination appears imminent.

Prechilling instead of short-duration stratification

In the last 20 years, prechilling has largely replaced stratification especially for shallowly dormant species requiring shorter pretreatment periods. This has been due to the wider availability of refrigerated storage to regulate temperature, and the availability of polythene bags which make good containers for handling and storing moist seed; moisture loss during pretreatment is restricted to acceptable levels if bags are loosely tied at the neck.

Pretreatment of species requiring long-duration pretreatment

For the longer periods of pretreatment necessary for deeply dormant species, pretreatment may be carried out in a refrigerated store so that close control of temperature is maintained. However, a stratification medium is also necessary:

- the medium retards drying more effectively over the longer pretreatment periods required;
- it helps check the spread of any fungal infection, should it break out;
- it provides a greater mass to absorb heat from any seed respiration and reduces the risk of the temperature of the seed rising.

The drawbacks to using a moisture retaining medium are:

- peat and sand add considerably to the weight and volume of seed during pretreatment.

- any excess moisture present in the medium enables seeds which lose their dormancy first to absorb water and begin to germinate. These prematurely germinated seeds can be killed by mechanical damage during sowing. If they do survive, their early emergence will accentuate any unevenness of growth in the seedbed.

Prescriptions for the prechilling of shallowly and deeply dormant seeds are given in Table 5.6.

5.7.3 Varying the period of pretreatment for deeply dormant species

Different deeply dormant seed lots of the same species often exhibit different depths of dormancy. Thus, the recommended duration of prechilling based on average requirements may be too short or long for any particular lot. Similarly, within a lot of seed, individual seeds can require different periods of pretreatment in order to bring about subsequent germination.

Where a seed test has been carried out and a pretreatment prescription given with the test

Table 5.6 Prescriptions for prechilling shallowly and deeply dormant seed

Shallowly dormant	Deeply dormant

Preparation

1. Divide seed bulk into conveniently sized lots for pretreatment, taking into account: total quantity of seed; sowing density; total area of seedbeds and where natural breaks will occur in relation to sowing areas and programme; the risk that larger volumes of seed may heat up during pretreatment by respiration.

2. Place conveniently sized seed lots into suitable pretreatment containers. Polythene bags able comfortably to hold about four times the seed volume are ideal, but need rigid support from a bucket, drum or box during operations 3–5 below.

Soaking

3. Carefully add about three volumes of cold water (at about 5°C) to one volume of seed. Ensure that none of the seeds adhere to the sides of the container or remain unwetted.

4. Place the now soaking seeds in refrigeration at about 5°C for 48 h to imbibe.

5. Drain off excess water – either decant, or poke holes in the bottom of the bag (as long as the seed is big enough not to escape!).	5. Drain off excess water *without making holes in the bag.*

DO NOT LEAVE STANDING WATER IN THE BAG – local waterlogging will drown seeds, act as a site for bacterial or fungal growth, and may also encourage premature germination of some seeds.

6. Lightly tie the neck of the bag, leaving a large air space above the seeds. This will allow aeration without excessive drying. A length of plastic pipe can be used as a breather tube, and the open end of the bag gathered around it.	6. Mix the now imbibed seeds with moist peat and sand. First mix approx. one volume of peat to one volume of sand, moistening it so that when squeezed, it does not quite release free water. Mix about one volume of seed to one volume of the peat/sand mixture. Lightly tie the neck of the bag, leaving a large air space above the seeds.

Prechilling

7. Return the now moist seeds to about 5°C to begin their period of prechilling.	7. Return the mixture of peat, sand and seed to about 5°C to begin their period of prechilling.
8. Aim to prechill for at least 3 weeks, but not more than 10 weeks, removing seed when sowing conditions are considered suitable.	8. Aim to pretreat each deeply dormant species for the duration of each warm/cold period recommended in Bulletin 59, Appendix 7. The warm storage of these treatments should be at 15–20°C.

9. Open bags once a week, gently mix the seeds and check for signs of either mould growth or premature germination.

Table 5.6 *continued*

Shallowly dormant	Deeply dormant
Surface drying before sowing	
10. At the end of the dormant period, the seed, still in lots for sowing, should be *surface* dried. Seed will surface dry if spread thinly on towels, newspapers or trays, in a room which is either naturally well ventilated, or ventilated with the help of an electric fan. NEVER USE AN ELECTRIC FAN-HEATER. Occasionally, *gently* stir seeds to ensure even surface drying. Surface drying is complete when the seeds *just* begin to flow freely enough to pass sowing machinery. NEVER CONTINUE DRYING BEYOND THIS STAGE: NEVER APPLY ARTIFICIAL HEAT. Overdrying &/or heating reimpose dormancy and may ultimately kill the seed if internal drying is severe.	10. Surface drying is not necessary for deeply dormant seed.
Temporary storage before sowing of surface dried seed	
11. If soil conditions in the nursery deteriorate when sowing should be in progress, pretreated seed should be put back into store in its surface dry state, in loosely tied polythene bags ± plastic breather tube, and stored at about 5°C until required. Most surface dried seed can be stored refrigerated in this way for a few weeks, but should be checked at least weekly for mould growth and premature germination.	11. Sowing programme delays are an insignificant part of the time necessary for deeply dormant seed pretreatments, therefore special procedures for temporary storage are unnecessary. Seed should be left in pretreatment until conditions in the nursery are suitable for sowing.
Sowing	
12. Surface dry seed can be either broadcast, drill or precision sown.	12. Seed can either be sown with the pretreatment medium, or sieved from the medium and broadcast, drill or precision sown.

results, it is simplest to follow the recommendation. Because of variation with a seed lot, a proportion of the seed may germinate prematurely and may be lost but this is usually very small, especially if a check examination has been carried out in the 2–3 weeks before sowing.

Where test results for a seed lot are not available (e.g. because there has not been time for a test to be completed), there are three options:

1. Adopt the standard pretreatment recommendations.

2. Commence pretreatment as though the seed were an average lot, but from 4–6 weeks before the nominal end of the treatment period, inspect the seed regularly, waiting until about 10% of the seed has chitted before sowing, expecting that the remaining seeds are now close to germinating.

3. Inspect the seed regularly during the latter stages of pretreatment and at suitable intervals, remove chitted seed (by flotation and/or

sieving) and sow them. Return the seed to store and repeat the process at frequent intervals until no more seeds germinate.

Exposed radicles of chitted seed are very susceptible to mechanical damage; such seed must be handled very gently if this is to be avoided. Option 3 is also very time consuming and is only worth considering for very valuable seed or when seed of the variety is in short supply.

5.7.4 Monitoring pretreatment

To assess whether pretreatment is progressing successfully, take a representative sample of 100–200 seeds at least 4 weeks before the anticipated sowing date and incubate the sample under moist conditions at room temperature (15–20°C). The germination which occurs within about 4 weeks is a good indicator of how effectively the pretreament is progressing.

FURTHER READING

YOUNG, J.A. and YOUNG, C.G. (1992). *Seed of woody plants in N. America.* Dioscorides Press, Portland, Oregon, USA. (Revision of US Forest Service Handbook 450.)

REFERENCES

ANON. (1960). *Collection and storage of ash, maple and sycamore seed.* Forestry Commission Leaflet 33. HMSO, London.

ANON. (1962). *Collection and storage of acorns and beech mast.* Forestry Commission Leaflet 28. HMSO, London.

FAULKNER, R. (1992). In *Seed manual for forest trees.* Forestry Commission Bulletin 83. HMSO, London.

FORESTRY COMMISSION (1993). *List of native Scots pine seed collection areas. 1st June 1993.* The Forestry Authority, Edinburgh.

GILL, J.G.S. (1983). Comparison of production costs and genetic benefits of transplants and rooted cuttings of Sitka spruce. *Forestry* **56** (1), 61–73.

GORDON, A.G. and ROWE, D.C.F. (eds) (1982). *Seed manual for ornamental trees and shrubs.* Forestry Commission Bulletin 59. HMSO, London.

GORDON, A.G. (ed.) (1992). *Seed manual for forest trees.* Forestry Commission Bulletin 83. HMSO, London.

GOSLING, P.G. (1991). Beechnut storage: a review and practical interpretation of the scientific literature. *Forestry* **64** (1), 51–59.

LEE, S.J. (1990). *Potential gains from genetically improved Sitka spruce.* Forestry Commission Research Information Note 190. Forestry Commission, Edinburgh.

LINES, R. (1987). *Choice of seed origins for the main forest species in Britain.* Forestry Commission Bulletin 66. HMSO, London.

ROBERTS, E.H. (1973). Predicting the storage life of seeds. *Seed Science and Technology* **1**, 499–514.

ROOK, D.A. (ed.) (1992). *Super Sitka for the 90s.* Forestry Commission Bulletin 103. HMSO, London.

Chapter 6

Production of bare-root seedlings and transplants

W. L. Mason

This chapter covers all operations involved in the production of seedlings and transplants, producing 1+1, 2+1, 1½ + 1½ and similar transplanted stock. It starts with seedbed preparation and sowing density, and finishes with transplant spacing and maintenance. The nutrient requirements of seedlings are given in Chapter 4, while weed control methods are described in Chapter 12. Undercutting systems are considered separately in Chapter 8.

Seedling production

6.1 Preparation of the ground for sowing

6.1.1 Cultivation of the seedbed area and incorporation of bulky organic manures

Where the seedbed area has carried a previous crop, the ground should be sprayed with a contact or translocated herbicide soon after lifting to remove any weeds. See Chapter 12, section 12.3. Fallow land should be treated in the same way. The ground should be ploughed in late autumn to level the area and give the soil time to weather overwinter. If ground is ploughed too early in the autumn, weed seed will germinate and weeds will grow and spread during mild spells in the winter unless controlled by herbicides.

Magnesian or ordinary limestone, ground mineral phosphate or any other material prescribed to adjust pH or to correct a nutrient deficiency should be spread on fallow land in late autumn or early winter. See Chapter 3, section 3.2.2, and Chapter 4, section 4.2.4.

It is normally preferable to apply bulky organics to land to be used for transplanting rather than for seedbeds. However, if organics are to be used, any bulky organic matter such as hopwaste or peat should be spread evenly in late autumn or winter by agricultural dung-spreader, or by hand. Uneven distribution leads to uneven growth in the subsequent season. After spreading, the organic material should be ploughed or rotovated into the top 15 cm of the soil. Any bulky organic matter used must be weed and lime-free. See Chapter 4, section 4.

The normal sequence of cultivation is to plough to 20–30 cm depth using a chisel plough, followed by rough harrowing to break up any clods and rotovation to prepare a fine tilth. Ploughing normally takes place in the autumn with any clods left to weather over-winter. Harrowing and rotovating occur in the spring.

Ploughing at depths of more than 30 cm is undesirable since it may bring subsoil to the surface.

If there is any compacted soil horizon or cultivation pan, this should be broken up with a winged tine *before* the ground is ploughed.

6.1.2 Size of seedbeds

Beds are normally 1.1 m wide with alleys or paths between beds 0.5 m wide. This bed width is traditional, being just narrow enough to permit easy handweeding from either side. However, it is also well suited to the distance between tractor wheelings and the width of the wheels. Beds are raised above the alleys which define them and provide drainage channels so minimising erosion of the sown area by storm water. Where the annual rainfall is no more than 1000 mm, raising the beds 5–8 cm is sufficient. With an annual rainfall over 1000 mm beds need to be raised to 10–15 cm.

6.1.3 Throwing up seedbeds

The method will depend on the size of the nursery. Mechanical equipment is normally used for most of the work. However in smaller nurseries, some or all the work of preparation may have to be done by hand.

In larger nurseries, and especially where soils are light, beds should be thrown up using two potato-ridger ploughs set at a distance of 1.6 m apart centre to centre. A wooden board or pair of metal bars should be fixed between the ridgers to level off the bed to an appropriate height. In this way beds are both thrown up and levelled in a single operation. Suitable ridgers can be made by removing the centre unit of any three-unit potato ridger which fits the three-point linkage of the nursery tractor. The additional bar, or bars, to level off the bed can usually be made locally and various forms are in use in different parts of the country. When using this implement, it is important that sufficient soil is moved from the edges of the bed to the middle, otherwise the subsequent rolling only consolidates the edges of the bed and leaves the middle loose. It is also possible to use specialist bed forming machinery to prepare the beds.

Where beds have to be prepared by hand, the beds should be marked out 1.1 m wide with 0.5 m alleys between beds. Garden lines are run out to mark the edges of the beds, and soil is thrown from the alleys on to the beds by spade, each bed on either side of the alley receiving a spadeful alternately.

Beds may be thrown up at any time during winter or early spring while the soil is workable; the sooner they are prepared, the better. Where the soil is very sandy and does not require frost in order to obtain a tilth, beds may be rolled or raked level and should be left to pack down as hard as possible over the winter and early spring. However, where the soil is loamy, it is essential to fork up the surface of the newly made beds as roughly as possible to allow the soil to dry out and ensure maximum exposure to frost, so that a good tilth is obtained.

6.1.4 Partial soil sterilisation

Partial soil sterilisation is a useful tool in seedbed management. Pretreatment of the formed seedbed area with dazomet in the autumn before sowing can reduce weed germination during the following season and can increase seedling growth (Williamson *et al.*, 1993). Part of the benefit from soil sterilisation is due to an increase in available ammonium nitrogen. While partial soil sterilisation may control pathogens such as nematodes (and is recorded as having done so), such control of itself is not sufficient to explain the effects observed. See discussions in Benzian, 1965, pp. 137–163; also, Aldhous, 1972, pp. 159–161. It is sensible practice for seedbed areas to be sterilised at regular intervals (e.g. 3–4 years) to prevent build-up of pest populations.

Recommended procedure for seedbed sterilisation with dazomet

In forest nurseries with responsive soils, seedbed sterilisation with dazomet should be carried out in autumn (preferably early to late October) before the soil temperature has fallen appreciably below 7°C at a depth of 15 cm. Spring application is generally not feasible because the need to wait until the soil temperature is high enough together with the length of the treatment period would delay sowing unacceptably.

Before sterilisation, the area should be ploughed and cultivated to provide a reasonable tilth, but seedbeds should not be thrown up at this stage. At the time of treatment, the soil must be moist but not wet; moisture is necessary for the chemical breakdown of dazomet, but the presence of excess soil moisture leads to uneven distribution of the sterilant gas as well as making soil working difficult.

The prilled dazomet should be broadcast over the soil surface at 380 kg ha^{-1}. Uniform distribution is essential and is best achieved using a machine such as the Sisis 'Truspred' (hand-drawn) or 'Lospred' (tractor-mounted) spreader. The material is incorporated into the upper 15–20 cm of the soil by thorough rotovation; the area is then sealed by rolling with a heavy smooth-surfaced roller to leave the soil surface firm and without cracks. (On small areas, polythene sheeting weighted down with soil (Plate 2), or water could be applied after rolling to provide a more complete seal, but this is not usually practicable for large-scale use.)

Not less than 4 weeks after application of the chemical, the soil can be opened up by further rotovation to release any residual gas. Great care should be taken to avoid cultivating deeper than the treated zone and so bringing up unsterilised soil. Where release cultivation is carried out before the onset of winter, seedbeds can then be thrown up roughly to weather over winter. However, there is no reason why the treated area should not be left undisturbed until early spring if this accords with local practice, provided that release cultivation is carried out at least 2 weeks before seed sowing.

Before final seedbed preparation, a 'cress test' should be used to check the soil for freedom from residual gas. The test procedure is detailed in a leaflet provided by the suppliers of dazomet, and compares cress germination in sealed jars containing soil samples from the treated area and from adjacent untreated land.

6.1.5 Incorporation of inorganic fertilisers

For a full discussion of the quantities of fertilisers to apply see Chapter 4, section 4.2. Inorganic fertiliser is generally applied in granular form, the rate depending on the nutrient content of the particular brand selected and the requirements of the crop and the levels of nutrient reserves in the soil.

Granular fertiliser can be spread either by hand or by fertiliser distributor. It should be incorporated in to the topmost 5–10 cm of the bed by light raking or rotovation before the bed is finally consolidated. Fertiliser has sometimes been pressed into the surface by roller at the time of final bed preparation, but this is a practice which in dry conditions can reduce germination because of the close proximity of seed and fertiliser resulting in salt damage to the emerging radicle. There is no consistent benefit to be obtained by leaving the application of fertiliser to the last moment; it can be applied any time in the 9 weeks before sowing.

In studies of placed fertiliser in drills in relation to band-sown seed, drills of fertilisers containing potassic superphosphate substantially reduced the seedling yield per kilogram of seed, although the seedlings that were obtained were appreciably larger than those from broadcast-sown beds in which the fertiliser was mixed evenly with the soil. Fewer losses occurred with placed phosphate than with potassium sulphate.

6.1.6 Consolidation and tilth

Correct control and timing of cultivation operations to achieve well consolidated seedbeds is an essential prerequisite for seedbed management. Inadequate consolidation or creation of a cultivation pan can each seriously reduce seedling growth and development.

Beds must be well consolidated before sowing so that soil moisture can reach the surface layers by capillary action and prevent germinating seed from drying out in warm dry weather. This is especially important for coniferous and small seeded hardwood species. One effective and simple test is to press the surface of the bed firmly with the flattest part of a clenched fist. Consolidation is adequate when no more than a moderate indentation (i.e. 1 cm deep) can be made. It is important that consolidation is uniform throughout the upper 15 cm of a bed and that there is no compaction or 'plough pan' which will impede water movement. The creation of a pan is a particular risk if the soil is worked when too wet since all the benefit of the previous winter's weathering can be lost by compression and aggregation of soil crumbs.

Beds which will be consolidated soon after they have been thrown up should have a roller weighing 100–250 kg drawn one or more times over the bed according to the soil type, after which no further raking should be necessary. Suitable rollers may be adapted from agricultural rollers; these should be wide enough to cover a single seedbed and be arranged to fit the three-point linkage of the tractor. A specially manufactured hollow roller, the weight of which can be varied between 120 and 350 kg by adjusting the amount of water inside, is also available.

On very sandy soils, beds thrown up early and consolidated naturally should be disturbed as little as possible before sowing. The natural consolidation following exposure to winter and early spring rain can scarcely be equalled by rolling beds which have been loosened or which were newly thrown up shortly before sowing. Particular care must be taken when incorporating inorganic fertilisers not to cultivate too deeply and lose the benefit of natural consolidation.

On loamy soils, a fine tilth has to be created in the top 5–8 cm of soil immediately before consolidating. This can be achieved by working the soil with a small rotary cultivator, or with a rotovator or spading machine attached behind a tractor. Rotary cultivators, or rotovators if used when the soil is too wet can create a plough pan through the 'smearing' action and downward pressures of the blades of these machines. This is less of a risk with spading machines. On loamy soils, the interval between preparation of a fine tilth, consolidation of the soil and sowing must be kept to a minimum. If heavy rain intervenes after cultivation but before consolidation, the soil often loses its structure, becomes saturated with water and handles like porridge, and if dry weather follows, may set hard. In these circumstances, the soil should be roughly forked up while moist and left to dry out again.

6.2 Preparation of seed for sowing

Seed should be ordered for delivery well in advance of sowing so that the necessary pretreatments can be given. This is particularly important with deeply dormant species where up to 26–30 weeks of stratification may be required. Seed certificates should be checked carefully to ensure that a given seed lot is not damaged by pretreatment (e.g. pine seed lots where germination is reduced by moist prechilling).

6.2.1 Storage awaiting sowing

Short-term storage methods are described in Chapter 5, section 5.5.3. Long-term seed storage regimes are fully described in Forestry Commission Bulletins 59 and 83 (Gordon and Rowe, 1982; Gordon, 1992).

6.2.2 Seed pretreatment

Recommendations for pretreatment are given in Table 5.6, p.81, and Chapter 5, section 5.7.

Careful handling of seed is essential if optimum germination is to be obtained and thought must be given to the management of the cold store or refrigerator to ensure space is available for seed to be pretreated. Seed should be inspected regularly to check for the presence of fungal pathogens, that moisture content is correct and that premature chitting is not occurring. It is also important to monitor the temperature of the pretreatment environment regularly to check that refrigerators are maintaining the required temperature.

6.2.3 Seed dressings

In agriculture and horticulture, it is common practice to dress seeds with a fungicide, insecticide or repellent. In forest nurseries, the most serious and widespread losses of seed in the past were often due to depredations by birds, and to a lesser extent, mice. Formerly, seeds were regularly dressed with red lead, believing that this gave some protection against small birds, etc. However, in very many nurseries, this was found not to be the case and physical protection by netting became the principal protection against birds.

One advantage of red leaded seed was that it showed up clearly against the soil and gave the sower an indication of how evenly he was sowing. However, lead compounds are not considered environmentally desirable as seed dressings and the use of red lead is no longer recommended.

Currently, the large majority of nurseries sow mechanically and find that a seed colourant is not essential. Also, much of the seed is pretreated and often just chitting; in this condition it is much more susceptible than dry seed to mechanical damage during the additional handling and is best sown without a seed dressing.

6.3 Sowing

6.3.1 Date of sowing

The correct timing of sowing is a most important part of seedling production. For instance if seed is sown too early in a cold spring, germination can be slow and, although the seedlings may grow to a good size by the end of the season, the yield will be low and the crop variable. If sown too late in a dry spring, germination may be lower than expected. The normal date of sowing in Britain is between early March in southern England and mid May in northern Scotland. Actual dates will depend upon the season, seed pretreatment, the target crop (i.e. 1 or 2 year seedlings) and local nursery factors such as the availability of irrigation and the risk of spring frosts.

The temptation to leave sowing until lifting has been completed must be resisted, unless it is the policy to produce 2-year-old seedlings, and a regular high germination of late-sown seed can be guaranteed. Lining out and planting programmes will scarcely be affected by the delay while seedbeds are sown, but if sowing is late, it will often make the difference between seedlings that can be lifted after 1 year and those that have to be grown on for 2 years.

6.3.2 Factors affecting sowing density

Recommendations for the density of sowing of the commonly used conifer and broadleaf species are given in Tables 6.1 and 6.2. The density at which seed should be sown depends on many controllable factors such as the variation in species and seed quality, the known productivity of the nursery, local techniques (e.g. drill or broadcast sowing), and preference for either 1-year or 2-year seedling stock.

In contrast, seasonal factors such as distribution of summer rainfall and critical spells of drought cannot be predicted, yet they also may have a profound effect on nursery yields. Because of these uncontrollable factors, it is not possible to make precise forecasts of seedling yields from given densities of sowing.

An estimate of the average *total* yield of seedlings is given in columns 8 and 9 of Table 6.1 and column 8 of Table 6.2. It must be realised however, that figures are averages and that variations of ±25% are commonplace.

Germination / survival factor and field survival factor

It will be apparent from Tables 6.1 and 6.2 that more germinable seeds are recommended to be sown per square metre (columns 6 and 7) than are expected as seedlings at the end of the season. The 'Germination Survival Factor' (column 12) is the number of live seedlings at the end of the season, expressed as a percentage of the number of germinable seeds sown. The difference is accounted for by the seeds which do not germinate, are eaten by birds, killed by fungi, etc. If nursery managers find that consistently they obtain better or poorer yields of seedlings at the end of the season than are given in the tables, they should make an appropriate adjustment to the sowing density in subsequent years. The 'Field Survival Factor' mentioned in section 5.6.8 is the 'Germination Survival Factor' reduced by whatever allowance is appropriate in the nursery for culls. In Table 5.4 15% of live seedlings have been allowed as culls. Nursery managers should always critically examine the reasons for a particular 'Field Survival Factor' to see whether it can be improved, either by reducing the proportion of unusable seedlings produced, or by increasing the overall consistency of germination.

Changes in recommended sowing densities

The densities listed in Tables 6.1 and 6.2 are designed to give fully stocked seedbeds in average seasons in productive nurseries and should be used if individual calculations for each seed lot are not to be made. The conifer densities represent a substantial reduction on the densities prescribed in the previous edition of this Bulletin (Aldhous, 1972; Table 23). This reduction reflects the major impact that bird netting and the use of pre-emergence herbicides to eliminate weed competition have had in raising seedling yields. They also reflect increasing recognition that allowing wider spacing between seedlings produces sturdier and better quality planting stock. In seasons when germination and growth are good, even these spacings may be too close due to seedlings being taller than average or too densely stocked, or both. However, periodic slight overcrowding is inevitable if seedbeds are not to be understocked in all except the most favourable seasons. There is no evidence that the yield of usable plants is reduced in good seasons because of high seedling density following sowing at the densities recommended; the percentages of culls may be somewhat higher, but the total number of usable plants from a given number of germinable seeds is usually above average in a good season in spite of apparently crowded beds.

The figures for numbers of pure seeds, germination and/or viability percentage are derived from laboratory tests. They represent an adjustment to the tables in the previous edition of this Bulletin to allow for more recent information (e.g. Gordon and Rowe, 1982).

The broadleaved species given in Table 6.2 include only those commonly grown in forest nurseries. Recommendations for minor broadleaved species can be obtained by referring to Gordon and Rowe (1982, Appendix 6a) or extrapolating from the most appropriate species listed in Table 6.2.

Table 6.1 Seed quality, sowing density and expected yields: major conifers

Common name	Seed qualities			Sowing density for standard seed; number of germinable seeds per m² (1000s)		Expected yield in productive nurseries				
	Average number of pure seeds per kg (1000s)	Germination percentage		Number of germinable seeds per kg			Total number seedlings per m² at end of season (1000s)		Average height of usable seedlings at end of season (cm)		Germination survival factor (%)
		Standard	Low		1+0	2+0	1+0	2+0	1+0	2+0	
(1)	(2)	(3)	(4)	(5)	(6)	(7)	(8)	(9)	(10)	(11)	(12)
Scots pine	165	85	50	140	0.9	0.8	0.6	0.5	5–10	8–15	60–70
Corsican pine	70	80	50	55	0.6	0.5	0.4	0.3	4–8	8–15	60–70
Lodgepole pine	300	90	50	270	0.9	0.8	0.6	0.5	5–10	8–15	60–70
European larch	170	35	15	60	0.8	(0.7)	0.5	(0.4)	10–20	(12–25)	50–60
Japanese larch	250	60	30	100	0.7	(0.6)	0.5	(0.4)	10–20	(12–25)	60–70
Hybrid larch	210	25	10	50	0.8	(0.7)	0.5	(0.4)	10–20	(12–25)	50–60
Douglas fir	88	80	50	70	0.8	0.7	0.5	0.4	7–15	10–20	50–60
Norway spruce	145	80	50	110	1.0	0.8	0.7	0.5	4–8	10–15	60–70
Sitka spruce	400	80	50	320	1.0	0.8	0.6	0.4	4–8	10–15	50–60
Grand fir	45	40	15	20	1.0	0.8	0.5	0.4	4–8	7–15	40–60
Noble fir	40	30	15	12	1.0	0.8	0.5	0.4	4–8	7–15	40–60
Western hemlock	650	65	30	420	1.2	1.0	0.7	0.6	4–8	7–15	50–60
Western red cedar	850	60	30	500	1.2	1.0	0.7	0.6	4–8	7–15	50–60
Lawson cypress	460	50	30	230	1.2	1.0	0.7	0.6	4–8	7–15	50–60

Notes: 1. Figures in brackets refer to species which are rarely sown for 2+0 production.
2. Germination survival factor gives an estimate of *average* survival factors.
3. Note that columns 8 and 9 are *total* numbers including unusable seedlings.

Table 6.2 Seed quality and seedling production: broadleaves

Common name (1)	Average number of seeds per kg (2)	Average purity (%) (3)	Average germination (%) (4)	Average viability (%) (5)	Average Number of germinable or viable (v) seeds per kg (6)	Number of germinable/ viable seeds sown per m² (7)	Average yield of seedlings per kg (8)†	Average seedling height at 1+0 (cm) (9)
Common alder	770 000	85	40	–	250 000	2000	66 000	5–20
Italian alder	410 000	85	30	–	108 000	2000	60 000	5–20
Grey alder	1 500 000	80	25	–	300 000	2000	60 000	5–20
Red alder	1 400 000	75	55	–	575 000	2000	60 000	5–20
Ash	13 000	90	60	65	7 800 (v)	600	2 500	10–25
Beech	4 500	97	60	70	3 000 (v)	500	1 300	10–20
Silver birch	1 900 000	30	25	–	150 000	2000	100 000	5–20
Downy birch	3 500 000	30	30	–	320 000	2000	105 000	5–20
Bird cherry	20 000	99	–	75	14 700 (v)	800	1 000	10–25
Wild cherry	5 000	99	75	80	4 000 (v)	800	1 000	10–25
Horse chestnut	100	100	80	85	90 (v)	120	45	15–25
Sweet chestnut	240	100	80	65	175	100	110	10–30
Wych elm	90 000	95	45	–	37 000	600	20 000	10–20
Hawthorn*	11 000	95	–	70	7 900 (v)	2000	1 300	10–20
Hazel	800	100	70	60	480	500	200	10–15
Holly	35 000	99	80	75	22 000	1200	9 000	5–15
Hornbeam	25 000	96	45	65	14 500	600	3 000	5–10
Large-leaved lime	8 500	97	70	75	6 500	1000	550	10–20
Smalled-leaved lime	30 000	95	70	80	22 000	1000	2 000	10–20
Field maple	13 500	92	55	70	8 900 (v)	500	3 300	5–20
Norway maple	6 500	85	40	70	3 900 (v)	350	2 000	15–30
Sycamore	9 000	90	40	60	5 000 (v)	250	2 200	15–40
Pedunculate oak	250	99	80	80	220 (v)	250	180	10–20
Red oak	300	99	80	85	240 (v)	250	160	10–25
Sessile oak	300	100	80	85	270 (v)	250	180	10–20
Rowan	290 000	96	70	85	245 000 (v)	2000	8 000	10–25
Whitebeam	55 000	89	–	65	31 000 (v)	2000	2 200	10–25
Nothofagus obliqua	115 000	90	25	–	25 500	700	5 200	10–25
Nothofagus procera §	90 000	89	25	–	20 500	700	6 000	10–25
Common walnut	100	100	80	85	85	40	55	10–25

Notes: * Hawthorn figures are for *Crataegus monogyna* and should be adapted for other species.
  † Column 8 includes usable and non-usable seedlings.
  § Now re-named *Nothofagus nervosa*.

6.3.3 Calculation of seedbed sowing area

For seed for which there are germination test data, the normal broadcast sowing area per kg of seed may be calculated by dividing the number of germinable or viable seeds per kilogram from the test results by the number of germinable or viable seeds per square metre in Tables 6.1 or 6.2. This gives the figures for sowing area in m². If estimates of both germinable and viable seeds are available, the former should always be used since this provides a better indication of seedling yield.

Adjustments to the normal broadcast sowing area are given below; drill sowing for undercutting is covered in Chapter 8, section 8.2.2.

1. *Low quality seed:* should the germination percentage fall below the value given in column 4 of the table, the calculated area *per kg* should be reduced by 20%;

2. *Local experience:* experience in a particular nursery may indicate that growth, or germination and survival of a particular species, is consistently higher or lower

than normal. This may be allowed for as follows:

(a) if seedlings of any particular species at 1 year or 2 years are regularly 20–35% taller than average (for conifers, see columns 10 and 11, Table 6.1), increase the sowing area per kg by 33%. If regularly 35–50% taller, increase the sowing area per kg by 66%;

(b) where the germination/survival factor of conifer sowings regularly departs by 20% or more from the value given in column 12, the sowing area should be increased or decreased in proportion.

Example 1

To determine the sowing area for 1 kg of Sitka spruce seed with 70% germination and 300 000 germinable seeds per kilogram, to be sown broadcast to produce 1-year seedlings:

First step, calculate sowing area at normal broadcast sowing density:

$$\text{Sowing area} = \frac{\text{Number of germinable seeds per kg}}{\text{Recommended number of germinable seeds per m}^2}$$

$$= \frac{300\,000*}{1\,000\dagger}$$

$$= 300 \text{ m}^2 \text{ per kg}$$

* Figure available with seed.

† Column 6: Table 6.1

Example 2

To determine the sowing area for 0.5 kg of rowan seed with 85% viability and 240 000 viable seeds per kilogram, to be sown broadcast to produce 1-year seedlings:

$$\text{Sowing area} = \frac{\text{Number of viable seeds per kg}}{\text{Recommended number of germinable seeds per m}^2}$$

$$= \frac{240\,000}{2\,000}$$

$$= 120 \text{ m}^2 \text{ per kg}$$

i.e. 60m^2 for 0.5 kg

In both examples, note that germination or viability percent is used in the calculation of ger-

minable or viable seeds per kilogram and is *not* used directly in the sowing density calculations.

6.3.4 Broadcast sowing

The aim of broadcast sowing is to distribute seed as evenly as possible over the sown area so that each seedling has as similar a space as possible in which to grow. All broadcast conifer and hardwood seed are sown on to raised seedbeds. During the season, the edges of beds usually crumble away and any seedlings growing there may be lost; hence it is advisable to leave 8 cm unsown on each edge of the bed.

The sowing techniques described below can be used for most conifer and many smaller hardwood seeds. There are exceptions; stratified seed is damp and bulky and so is not easily sown by machine, and may have to be sown by hand. The large seeded hardwoods which are covered with soil cannot be sown by the machines designed for conifer seed and the techniques for such seed are described at the end of this section.

Broadcast sowing by hand

Where seed is sown by hand, it may be sprinkled or cast over the bed, so that it does not fall beyond the edges of the bed, or it may be cast or thrown diagonally across the bed so that some of the seeds rebound from a wooden 'bouncing' board between 20 and 60 cm high by about 1 m long. The board is held vertically with one edge on the margin of the sowing area and is moved along as sowing proceeds. Best results come from casting seed but small-winged seed like that of Lawson cypress or birch can only be sprinkled.

Whether or not a board is used, best results are obtained if the seed for a bed is divided into two equal parts and one part sown working from one side and the other from the other side of the seedbed. Uniform sowing by hand can only be achieved by practice and novices must expect some unevenly distributed seed.

Broadcast sowing by machine

The machines most commonly used for seed

sowing were originally designed to spread fertiliser and sow lawn seed. They are tractor drawn and essentially consist of a hopper on wheels (Plate 4). At the base of the hopper is a moving belt which carries seed out at a rate regulated by a metal slide or grate. Seed is brushed off the belt to ensure uniform distribution. Do not use the same machine for both seed sowing and applying fertilisers since fertiliser corrosion to the metal slide can cause the rate of seed sowing density to be wrong.

Prechilled seed should be air dried just enough to flow without sticking; if the seed is too moist, then the seed will be clumped on the bed.

6.3.5 Larger broadleaved seed

Whereas almost all other forest tree species are best sown on the soil surface and covered with sand or grit, the seed of the larger seeded broadleaves such as oak, beech and sweet chestnut are best sown and covered with a 2.5–4 cm thick layer of soil.

When broadcast sowing by hand, seed can be spread over the surface of the bed before the alleys are dug and the soil from the alleys can then be spread evenly over the seed. The alleys so formed may be 10 cm below the seedbed surface. If there is more soil than is required to cover the seed, the surplus may be taken evenly away from the sowing area using rakes or 'cuffing boards', i.e. flat boards roughly 10×50 cm on the end of long handles.

Large broadleaved seeds may also be sown in bands between 2 and 5 cm wide and 15–20 cm apart. Bands can be prepared using a pair of plough shares set very shallow to open a trench on the first pass and spread a shallow covering of soil in the next. There are specialist machines available for this task.

6.3.6 Rolling after sowing

If the seed bounces up while being covered with grit after sowing, it should be pressed into the surface of the soil either by a light roller, approximately 20 cm in diameter (Plate 5) or by a light board 10 cm wide fitted to a broom handle. This is probably more necessary where grit cover is spread by hand than where a machine is used, the reason being that when covering by hand the grit has further to fall and hits the ground with greater momentum.

6.3.7 Grit covering

Seed covered with coarse sand or fine grit germinates more quickly and gives higher yields than if nursery soil is used. If the nursery is sheltered, coarse sand is quite suitable but in many nurseries, sand may be blown off by wind and a fine grit passing a 3–5 mm sieve is preferable. Table 6.3 gives examples of the particle size distribution of several grits that have been successfully used in Britain.

In some localities, 6 mm grit is readily available but this grade of grit should only be used if nothing finer can be obtained. Where there is a choice between crushed flint and a

Table 6.3 Particle sizes of grits that have proved successful in forest nurseries (percentage of particles in each size category)

Name	Particle size (mm)					
	<0.425	0.425–1.00	1.00–2.00	2.00–2.80	2.80–4.75	>4.75
1. Leighton Buzzard	1.5	5.9	30.0	51.9	9.2	1.5
2. Quartzag	3.4	0.7	0.6	9.5	64.7	21.1
3. Edzell	3.0	10.0	19.0	28.0	22.0	18.0
4. Aukley	19.9	15.0	12.3	26.2	17.5	9.1

Notes: 1.   All grits are light coloured and have no free lime.
2.   The first grit (a washed river gravel) is probably the best in terms of uniformity. The others tend either to have too much fine material (e.g. sample 4) or too much large material (samples 2, 3).

rounded material of approximately the same size, the latter is preferable, especially in weedy nurseries, as workers' fingers may be cut by sharp edges on the crushed flints.

It is essential that the grit is free from silt and from lime. It is also preferable to use a light-coloured grit rather than a dark one. If the grit is silty, it will cake and may reduce the germination of seedlings; if it contains lime, it will ultimately ruin the nursery by making the soil pH neutral or even alkaline when it should be acid (section 3.2.3). If in doubt, add vinegar or dilute hydrochloric acid to a sample of the grit; if it fizzes, it contains too much lime to be used with safety.

The colour of the grit affects the temperature at the seedbed surface; black or dark-grey grit can be several degrees warmer at the soil surface on a hot day than a very light coloured grit. This could make the difference between little injury and severe heat injury to conifers at the root collar. Table 6.4 illustrates the effects of particle size and colour on the yields of seedlings in a hot summer. In the experiment from which these results are taken, maximum temperatures, recorded just under the grit, were 49°C and 55°C for the white and dark grey grits respectively.

The quantity of grit required depends on the size of the grit and the size of the seed. As a rough guide, the depth of covering required should slightly exceed the length of the seed on its longest axis. This should be sufficient to cover the seed so that it disappears completely from view. On average, one tonne of grit should be expected to cover about $80\,m^2$ of conifer seedbed.

Grit is normally applied using a grit box which fits on the three-point linkage of a tractor (Plate 6). The grit runs out through an adjustable slit at the bottom of the box. The depth of grit is controlled by the combination of speed of the machine travelling over the ground and the width of the adjustable slit. This normally spreads a layer of grit over the whole width of a bed. However, where seed is sown in drills, baffles or stops can easily be made and fitted by the nursery manager so that only sown drills are covered and the remaining inter-row space left uncovered; the cost of grit is quite substantial and the saving by this simple modification is well worth having.

When covering by hand, the grit should be shovelled on to 6 mm mesh riddles or sieves held chest high and shaken so as to distribute the grit evenly over the nearer half of the bed, the other half being covered from the other alley.

6.3.8 Protection against birds and mice

Seed-eating birds (e.g. finches, pigeons) can cause serious damage to germinating seedlings (Tee and Petty, 1973). Failure to guard against this type of damage is a major reason for low stocking in seedbeds and it is a false economy not to protect seedbeds. The most effective measure is to cover beds with a

Table 6.4 Effect of the colour and size of grit used as a seedbed covering on the yield of Sitka spruce seedlings per m²: Kennington Nursery, Oxford 1955

| Colour of grit | Grade of grit | | | | | |
| | Fine | | Medium | | Coarse | |
	Number (m⁻²)	Height (cm)	Number (m⁻²)	Height (cm)	Number (m⁻²)	Height (cm)
White	763	4.6	821	4.6	293	3.1
Light grey	307	1.5	425	3.1	377	3.1
Dark grey	305	1.5	274	1.5	274	2.5

The white grit was a quartz from St Austell, Cornwall, the light grey material was a granitic sand from Penmaenmawr, Gwynedd, and the dark grey material a basalt from Clee Hill, Shropshire. The particles in the fine material ranged from 0.2 to 2 mm diameter, the medium from 2 to 6 mm while the coarse particles were more than 6 mm in diameter.

2cm (¾ inch) plastic mesh ('bird netting') which is supported on wire hoops made of No 8 or 10 gauge galvanised wire (see Plate 8). Bird netting should be laid over the beds within 1–2 days of sowing. Care should be taken to peg down the netting at the side of the seedbed. The netting can be removed once the first true leaves of the seedlings are well developed and the seed caps have been dislodged. Bird-netting is not necessary if seedbeds are covered with cloches or floating mulches (see below), except for large seeded broadleaves where crows can pierce the mulch sheet to get at the seeds.

Mice can also be a serious pest of seedbeds, particularly with large seeded species such as oaks, chestnut and Macedonian pine. The problem can be particularly bad on seedbeds adjoining hedges, woodland or disused ground. Bird netting will not serve as adequate protection and baited spring-traps must be laid at intervals along the beds. The traps should be inspected daily and rebaited as required. Mice are rarely a problem once seedlings have passed the first true leaf stage.

6.3.9 Cloches and floating mulches

The main objective of seedbed management is to obtain rapid and uniform germination. Delayed or inadequate germination can result in patchy stocking and variable seedling size, neither of which can easily be corrected. Frequently the germination rate is restricted by cold temperatures, particularly on heavier soils and/or in more northerly nurseries. One way of compensating for this is to use polythene or woven fabrics to improve the seedbed microclimate. When such materials are laid flat on the surface of the bed, they are called 'floating mulches' (Plate 9). If they are raised off the bed and supported on wire hoops in the same way as for bird-netting they are termed 'cloches'. These are somewhat akin to 'low tunnels' used in horticulture (Plate 7).

Transparent polythene cloches and translucent mulches provide a favourable microclimate for germination and growth as a result of higher soil and air temperatures, higher relative humidity (i.e. lower vapour pressure

deficit), lower nutrient leaching and more favourable soil moisture conditions when compared with uncloched control beds. For instance, a 12°C increase in daily maximum air temperature was recorded under clear polythene cloches during May–August compared with controls (Biggin, 1983). Minimum temperatures were also increased, but only by about 1°C. The effect of these higher temperatures is to speed germination and growth. Thus, 50–100% increases in germination percentage and height over controls were reported by Biggin (1983) when lodgepole pine, Corsican pine, Douglas fir, Japanese larch and Sitka spruce were grown under clear polythene cloches for 16 weeks after sowing.

A wide range of types of polythene and of fabric materials have been tested to examine their effect upon seedling growth. However, those in general use are clear polythene, 'white' polythene and woven polyester fabrics (e.g. Agryl P17 or Vlies). The fabrics differ from polythene sheet in being porous to air and water; consequently the magnitude of the temperature increase is less. The same is true of various types of 'breathable' polythene sheeting which have holes or slits at intervals in the sheet. The porous fabrics and perforated polythene sheets are best used as floating mulches whereas the standard (unperforated) polythene sheets are to be preferred as cloche covers. White polythene should be used if the crop species is thought to be sensitive to high temperatures (see below) since the temperature increase is generally rather less under this type of cover (Biggin, 1983).

Cloches

Cloches are normally supported by wire hoops or similar supports in the same way as bird netting. In profile, the cloche describes a flattened semi-circle above the bed, standing some 30 cm above the centre of the seedbed. A heavy duty polythene is best used, since lighter gauge material may be damaged by the wind. The cloches should be put on as soon as possible after the completion of sowing, gritting and herbicide application. Normal pre-sowing fertilisers are used. Cloches should be used with sterilised seedbeds so that weed competition is minimised. If the weather has been dry, then the bed should be well irrigated before the cloche is put on. The sides of the cloche should be dug into the alley and well secured so that an airtight seal is achieved and to prevent the cloches lifting in the wind. An extra 25 cm of alley between seedbeds must be allowed to ensure that the polythene can be dug in. Once the polythene has been dug in, the cloche should be left undisturbed for around 8–16 weeks depending upon the crop and management objectives. The shorter period will only promote germination, whereas the longer will also increase growth. The only problems that are likely to occur are from weed regrowth and the cloche drying out. If large weeds develop, then the polythene should be lifted, the weeds removed by hand and the polythene replaced. The soil moisture status can be easily checked by looking at the polythene on warm days. Under such conditions there should be a film of condensation all over the inner surface of the polythene as a result of water vapour condensing on the cooler polythene. If this film is not present, then humidity within the cloche is too low and young seedlings could be damaged. The solution is temporarily to remove the cloche (but *not* in very warm conditions), irrigate and then replace the polythene.

Seedlings grown under cloches have to be carefully hardened-off to prevent physiological stress from windy or warm conditions after cloche removal. Removal should ideally take place in cool weather or in the evening. Irrigation may be necessary to prevent wilting. Cloches should never be kept on after the beginning of August because of the risk of seedlings being damaged by an early autumn frost.

If seedlings appear to be suffering from fungal attack, the cloches should be removed for the season and appropriate fungicides applied.

Floating mulches

As noted earlier, floating mulches are laid flat over the seedbed after the completion of sowing, gritting and herbicide application. Sheets of material can be laid over one or more beds as convenient and are dug into the alleys. It is not so critical to ensure the bed is moist before covering with a mulch because the materials used are porous to water and irrigation can be applied if dry conditions occur. Mulches are normally removed once the germinating seedlings have started to lift the cover off the surface of the bed. It is important not to delay removal since the growing tips can be damaged if they penetrate the fabric of the covering sheet. Materials with circular or slitted perforations are not recommended as floating mulches on conifer seedbeds since leading shoots of the crop will frequently emerge through the perforations and make it impossible to remove the cover without damage to the seedlings.

The provision of a favourable germination environment under cloches or floating mulches can result in extremely high seedling yields. Experience over more than 5 years in Forestry Commission northern research nurseries suggests that, using cloches on pine seedbeds, yields of 90–100% of the germinable seed are attainable. The good germination and rapid early growth mean that sowing densities should be reduced over normal recommendations to prevent seedlings becoming too spindly. Recommendations are given in Table 6.5, based upon experience with conifers. There is limited experience with broadleaves; both oak and birch have shown good response, but beech has proved sensitive to high temperatures. A floating film may give useful protection against frost where autumn sown seed has germinated and there is no other shelter.

Cloches or floating mulches should be seriously considered by any nursery manager who seeks to improve seedling yields and produce more uniform crops. The use of cloches is particularly appropriate in northern nurseries where the increase in seedling growth can ensure that crops are of transplantable size in one year. Floating mulches could be used on many nursery sites in Britain where the more modest temperature increase that is produced

Table 6.5 Sowing density for conifer species under cloche cover

Species	Sowing (germinable seed per m²)	Remarks
Scots pine	400	Clear polythene cover
Lodgepole pine	400	Clear polythene cover
Corsican pine	450	Clear polythene cover
Macedonian pine	500	
Sitka spruce	600	
Norway spruce	600	White polythene cover (germinating seedlings can be damaged by warm conditions)
Douglas fir	600	
Larch spp.	600	

(Other species: a general rule of thumb is to use between 25 and 50% of normal densities)
NB: Densities for floating mulches should be slightly higher than those used for cloches.

can provide rapid, uniform germination. This may be of particular importance with techniques such as drill sowing. However, the interested manager will need to spend adequate time determining the technique that is most appropriate for a particular crop and nursery.

6.4 Subsequent care

After beds have been sown and covered, weeds, insect, animal or fungal pests must all be controlled, and shelter or watering provided as necessary, together with appropriate fertiliser top-dressings.

6.4.1 Weed and pest control

The control of weeds and of pests is of paramount importance both for the best growth of the crop sown and for subsequent crops. Growing crops should be inspected frequently to check for any signs of damage. Details of techniques for control of pests are given in Chapter 13 and of weeds are given in Chapter 12 (see also Williamson *et al.*, 1993).

6.4.2 Protection against sun and frost

In normal years, damage from sun is a rare occurrence in British nurseries. Untimely frosts can be a more serious source of damage. Building up a good knowledge of the local microclimate is the key to avoiding damage from frost. The use of shelters against sun and frost and of irrigation against frost are described in Chapter 13, section 13.1 and Chapter 11 section 11.4.3 respectively.

6.4.3 Top dressings

Nitrogen top dressings will normally be required to promote seedling growth. In many nurseries, top dressings of potassium fertilisers are also likely to be beneficial. The quantities to apply are set out in Chapter 4, Table 4.5 and section 4.2.5, while the timing of top dressings is prescribed in Chapter 4, section 4.2.6. The danger of scorching seedlings by applying inappropriate fertilisers such as potassium chloride and urea must be remembered.

Irrigation

Adequate irrigation is an essential part of modern nursery management; planned schedules of fertiliser application and undercutting regimes can only be relied on to produce the designed size and type of crop if irrigation is available to make up for deficiencies in the pattern or amount of summer rainfall. Detailed consideration of irrigation is given in Chapter 11.

6.4.4 Special methods of seedling production

Production of containerised seedlings is covered in Chapter 9. For other techniques (e.g. Dunemann beds), the reader should consult the previous edition of this Bulletin (Aldhous, 1972).

Transplant production

6.5 Transplanting

The objectives of transplanting or 'lining out' are to provide greater space for young plants to develop, and to encourage the formation of a more fibrous and compact root system, together with a higher ratio of root to shoot than would develop if seedlings were allowed to grow undisturbed in seedbeds. It also gives an opportunity for grading and culling seedlings to produce more uniform transplants.

6.5.1 Preparation of ground

Ground for lining out must be free-working and not hard or compacted. In many nurseries, it is preferable to cultivate only as much ground each day as is required for that day's lining-out. On very sandy soils, there is little harm in cultivating more than a day's ground at a time but on heavier soils, heavy rain can destroy the tilth of unplanted ground.

The sequence of operations preceding lining out depends on the type of previous crop, when it was lifted, the soil condition and predicted weather.

6.5.2 Late autumn ploughing

If the ground has been fallow, or has carried a greencrop or for any reason has been cleared in the autumn, it should be ploughed in October or November and left rough. Any annual weeds will be buried and the ground will be in a state to benefit from weathering by frost and rain during the winter. Any dressing of ground mineral phosphate or magnesian limestone, etc., prescribed to correct nutrient deficiencies should be applied before this ploughing.

6.5.3 Ploughing in bulky organic matter

If hopwaste or other bulky organic manure is to be applied, this should be spread and ploughed or rotovated in a few weeks before lining out. Organic matter can be spread and ploughed in the autumn, but the longer the interval between spreading and transplanting, the more nutrients in the organic matter will be lost by breakdown and leaching before transplanting.

6.5.4 Ploughing in crop residues

If the ground has been under seedbeds or lines, it will normally need to be ploughed to level out paths between seedbeds or strips of transplants and to bury any remaining plants. This operation can be combined with either of the two preceding operations if convenient.

6.5.5 Lining out following late greencrop

Where a greencrop of rye grass has been sown late in the summer and is no more than 10–12 cm tall, this may be ploughed in as lining out progresses; it should otherwise be ploughed in or cultivated 2–3 weeks beforehand; this may be necessary where the crop has grown more than expected (e.g. because of mild winter weather) and is too bulky to be ploughed in as part of the lining out process.

6.5.6 Incorporation of inorganic fertilisers

In most circumstances, inorganic fertilisers should be spread not more than 3 weeks before lining out. They do not need to be ploughed in and can be worked in as lining out progresses, or they can be rotovated in shortly beforehand. Inorganic fertilisers supplying the crop's nutrients for the season should not be applied as early as the autumn if plants are to be lined out in the spring following. However, any lime or remedial additional fertilisers may be applied at that time.

On very sandy soils, Norway spruce and grand, noble and European silver fir transplants lined out in late spring may be damaged by normal rates of inorganic fertilisers, if prolonged dry conditions follow shortly after lining out. This risk is minimised by spreading the inorganic fertiliser no later than mid-March, even though the plants in question may not be lined out for several weeks; alternatively the regime outlined in section 4.2.6 may be adopted.

6.6 Plants for transplanting

6.6.1 Spacing

Plants which are overcrowded in the lines or in the seedbeds become drawn and spindly and do not survive forest planting as well as sturdy plants; adequate nursery spacing is essential. See Tables 6.6. and 6.7.

There are two factors in plant spacing, the area and the shape of the growing space. What little critical work has been done on transplants in forest nurseries shows, as one would expect, that a greater growing area increases the size of the plants produced, particularly the root collar diameter. In a series of experiments, doubling the growing space from 75 to 150 cm² per plant increased the stem diameter of plants by an average of 20–30% but height by only 5–10%. The shape of the growing space had little effect on plant size; nevertheless plants tended to be sturdier when planted with a square rather than a rectangular spacing (i.e. more space between plants with rows closer together compared with the same area per plant, but plants closer in the row and the rows further apart).

In practice, mechanisation of transplanting and subsequent operations are so greatly facilitated by a standard spacing between rows that the only easy variation is of the distance between plants. Current practice is to space rows at 17.5, 20 or 22.5 cm with plants at 3.7, 5 or 7.5 cm in the row.

Plants to be lifted after one growing season may be grown at a closer spacing than if they are expected to remain *in situ* for two growing seasons. (This assumes that the 1-year (+1) plants will not be as big at the end of the season as plants 2 years in the lines (+2). If the 1-year plants are expected to be the same size at the end of the year as other +2s, they should be given similar growing areas.)

Table 6.6 Recommended growing area for transplants

Average height expected at lifting (cm)	Recommended growing area (cm²)
<20	75–100
20–40	100–125
40–60	100–150
>60	125–200

The growing area available to plants should be determined by the size they are expected to reach at the time of lifting.

Table 6.7 Number of transplants per unit area (excluding area of alleys) at different spacings

Spacing of plants in row (cm)	No. of plants per 100 m² Spacing between rows (cm)			
	15	17.5	20	22.5
3.75	17 800	15 240	13 330	11 850
5.0	13 330	11 430	10 000	8 890
7.5	8 890	7 620	6 670	5 930
10.0	6 670	5 710	5 000	4 440

6.6.2 Lifting for transplanting

Seedlings

Seedlings are usually lifted by hand from the seedbeds and transplanted either at the end of their first, or during or at the end of the second growing season. Seedlings less than 4 cm tall are too small to be handled easily and quickly, and are usually discarded. If more than 40% of all seedlings in a bed are less than 4 cm tall, the whole bed should be grown on for a second year. Nevertheless, special circumstances may justify planting such small plants, and experience has shown that if handled with care, many will survive and grow well. Small plants should not be transplanted until the risk of frost-lifting has past.

Often only a proportion of seedlings in a bed are large enough to be handled easily while the remainder are too small for handling. A decision has to be taken whether to lift the seedbed and waste a proportion of the seedlings or to let the bed stand over, and possibly be undercut, with the risk that bigger plants may grow too large while the smallest are suppressed. The decision will depend on factors such as the need for plants, whether leaving the beds will make cultivation of adjoining land difficult, and a prediction of the risk of disease – in particular grey mould – spreading if the seedlings become too dense.

A third possibility is that the whole bed can be loosened using a lifter passed at 15–20 cm deep so that the larger plants can be picked out without excessive stripping of roots and the small ones left. This technique is most suited to beds where up to 30% of the seedlings are clearly larger than the rest, as may occur when seed germinates over a long period instead of germinating all at once. Often a proportion of the smaller seedlings get buried during the loosening or subsequent lifting.

Lifting transplants

In the same way as seedbeds can be picked over, so transplants which have been in lines for 1 or 2 years can be sorted at lifting into those large enough for the forest and those too short or too spindly for planting out. (See also Chapter 14.) While there is no evidence that segregation of seedlings by size has any penalty in terms of genetic potential, seedling size being determined primarily by seed size and date of germination, repeated segregation of transplants can result in only the least vigorous stock as the residue held in the nursery. Normally, plants should be re-transplanted only once. At the end of the second period in the lines, stock should either be sent to the forest or should be burned. Exceptions to this rule should only be made for stock solely for amenity planting where larger than normal plants are required, and in the rare cases where late spring frost has caused extensive damage to shoots and there is a reasonable chance of recovery, given another year in the nursery.

6.6.3 Handling seedlings after lifting

Roots of all plants to be transplanted must always be protected from drying by placing the plants in buckets or boxes lined with damp moss, or in polythene bags or by heeling the plants in. Plants in clear polythene bags must always be kept out of direct sunlight; see Chapter 14, sections 14.2.6 and 14.5. Plants can also be placed in cold store to reduce the risk of desiccation.

6.6.4 Grading of seedlings for transplanting

Grading of usable seedlings is the separation before lining out into two or more size categories. This is worthwhile if there is such a wide range in the heights of seedlings that the smaller plants need an extra year to grow to a usable size compared with larger plants. Seedling grading should also be carried out if the variation in size is such that two grades may be produced from the transplant lines. Studies have shown that grading at the seedling stage will produce more uniform transplant beds with limited requirement for a final grading. If grading is required, seedlings should normally be separated into only two grades.

6.6.5 Time of transplanting

It is possible to lift plants of cold temperate species at almost any time of the year and transplant them with success. However, so much care has to be given to plants moved during the growing season to ensure good survival that in practice most plants are lifted in the dormant season, i.e. after the time in late autumn when shoot growth has ceased, shoots hardened off and winter buds formed, and before the time when the buds have begun to swell in the spring. During this dormant period, plants, ideally, should be lifted and transplanted immediately without temporary storage. However, where there are a large number of plants to be lifted at one time, these must be stored safely until they can be transplanted. (See Chapter 14.) If it is likely that planting will continue after the normal time of bud break, the plants involved should be lifted while still fully dormant and should be kept in a cold store until needed. (See Chapter 14, section 14.7.4.)

The best time for lifting and transplanting is in late February and March in England and Wales, and in March and early April in Scotland (see later for summer lining out). By this time, the worst of the winter weather has usually passed, the soil is moist and the roots have not yet started to grow. Ideally, average soil temperatures for planting should be nearing 5–6°C so that root growth will begin soon after transplanting. If transplanting is done in autumn or winter on soils that retain moisture, there is a risk of seedlings being lifted out of the ground by frost.

Deciduous species such as larch, oak, beech and other hardwoods should be lined out first, followed by the pines and then by the spruces, silver firs (*Abies* species), Lawson cypress, hemlock and western red cedar. Douglas fir should always be left to last – indeed it is sometimes said that this species should be transplanted just as the buds break. Corsican pine should be transplanted before the end of March although good results have also been obtained with autumn lining out.

Monterery pine (*Pinus radiata*) is a warm temperate species and must not be lined out or planted at the soil temperatures found in the forest in the UK in winter. In the few experiments in the south of England on date of planting, almost all plants of this species lined out in February or March have died while 90–100% survival has followed planting in September and 60–80% survival was found after planting in May. The reason for this difference is thought to be due to cold soil temperatures in spring. *Pinus radiata* can be transplanted without difficulty in many countries with Mediterranean or sub-tropical climates and would appear to require warm soil if newly transplanted stock is to grow well.

6.6.6 Summer transplanting

In northern nurseries, many species can be transplanted with great success in late June, July or August after the spring growth has hardened off, provided the soil is moist at the time of transplanting. This technique can only be used for seedlings in their second growing season, and for this reason it is not commonly practised in England unless the plants have been cold stored. Unless irrigation is available, the timing of summer transplanting is very dependent upon rainfall. The plants resulting from mid-summer transplanting are frequently better than those left for 2 years and then lined out. This technique reduces the risk of late-season attack by *Botrytis* (grey mould) damaging densely-stocked second year seedbeds.

There are three prerequisites if summer lining out is to be a regular feature of nursery production:

1. sufficient fallow land for the work to proceed without interfering with plants for early autumn transplanting or early throwing up of seedbeds;
2. a labour force that is not already fully occupied by a weeding programme or other essential work;
3. adequate irrigation.

6.6.7 Nutrient regime for transplants

This is fully discussed in Chapter 4, sections 4.2.4 *et seq*. See also Tables 4.4 and 4.5.

6.7 Technique and methods of lining out

There are several methods for transplanting seedlings and each has its particular merits and requirements. However, all of them require certain standards.

6.7.1 Position of plant

Plants must be set upright with roots radiating symmetrically downwards from the root collar. The stems of plants set askew will straighten up but the base of the stem will remain curved and the young trees will be more difficult to plant in the forest. Similarly, plants set with all roots bent towards the horizontal in one direction will shoot satisfactorily but their roots will remain and grow in the position in which they were placed and will thicken and harden in this shape. Such root systems are often described as 'hockey stick

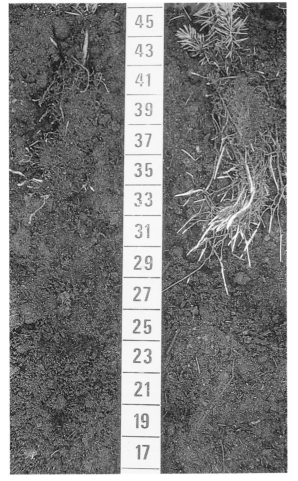

Plate 1. *Four types of Sitka spruce planting stock. Left to right: cutting ($C^1/_2 + 1^1/_2$), containerised seedling (P1 + 0), transplant ($1^1/_2 + 1^1/_2$), undercut (1 u 1). (50182)*

Plate 2. *Soil sterilisation using Dazomet. Polythene sheet seal being spread; edges are covered by soil, turned over by small shares one in each alley. (A3184)*

Plate 3. *Plants from root growth potential test, in position in gutter; white roots are clearly visible in one and weakly developed in the other. (38107)*

Plate 4. *Seed being sown broadcast by Sisis Lospred.* (E8835)

Plate 5. *Light seedbed roller for pressing seed into soil surface, showing:*
i) roller,
ii) scraper to remove adhering soil,
iii) brush to break any surface crust formed by rolling. (39771)

Plate 6. *Covering seedbeds with grit.* (39769)

roots' and may persist after planting in the forest with detrimental effects on stability, especially in the pines, larches and Douglas fir. These root deformations are not acceptable under the British Standard for Forest Nursery Stock (BSI, 1984), nor EEC standards (EEC, 1971; EEC 1974). Straight plants with good roots can be grown provided the trench, notch or slit made is vertical and not sloping and is wide and deep enough to accommodate the roots of the plants being handled. The collar should be at or just below the soil surface. Good supervision is essential if this standard is to be achieved. The risk of root distortion during transplanting can be reduced by trimming any roots longer than 10–15 cm. Such trimming does not affect subsequent performance.

6.7.2 Prevention of drying of the roots

Roots of seedling forest trees will die if allowed to dry out and this can occur in a very short time on a warm breezy spring day. Once lifted, plants must therefore be kept in boxes, buckets, polythene bags or crates, etc., out of the sun and wind until required. Plants must not be left out of the ground in lining out boards or in open bags at any time.

Plant roots are sometimes dipped in water or in a slurry of soil and water but, though this practice can be traced back to ancient Greek times, there is no clear evidence that in Britain the proportion of plants surviving is increased. Materials such as alginates and waterholding polymers which make water more viscous are currently on the market. Roots dipped in viscous or 'thickened' water retain more of it on roots than if plain water had been used. However, this and other forms of dipping are costly and are only likely to be effective if conditions are otherwise unsuitable for lining out, i.e. dry soil or severely drying winds.

6.7.3 Firmness in the ground

Following transplanting, plants must be firm enough in the ground that they cannot be uprooted by a gentle, steady pull. Plants which are loose take longer to become established and are also more likely to suffer drought injury in dry weather through inadequate contact between roots and soil. If simazine or other herbicides are used to control weeds and the soil is loose, these can be washed down by rain into the rooting zone of the crop plants rather than into the top 1.5–2.5 cm in which weeds germinate, thereby increasing the risk both of crop damage and of inadequate weed control.

6.7.4 Hand laying

The simplest system requires no more than a garden line and a dibble with which to make a hole and put in seedlings one by one. Alternatively, a V-shaped trench 13–15 cm deep may be dug with a spade, one face of the trench being vertical. Plants are then placed in position by hand against the vertical face. Each plant is secured in place individually by pressing a handful of soil against the roots to hold them to the trench until a 1–1.5 m length of trench has been set with plants when the trench is filled in, and the ground to the side consolidated by treading and levelled.

6.7.5 Lining out, using boards

In the board system, plants are laid side by side on a board until it is full, when a second board (or lid) is secured so that the plants are gripped between the two boards and can then be moved to the trench. The two parts may be hinged together or free. The two types of boards most widely used are the 10 ft ('Ben Reid') hinged board and the 6 ft 4 inch ('Paterson') unhinged board (approximately 3 m and 2 m long respectively). These are discussed in full in the previous edition of this Bulletin.

6.7.6 Transplanting machines

Almost all transplanted planting stock is lined out by machine, of which there are several types in use in forest nurseries.

The most successful types are based on the 'Accord' and 'Super-prefer' (Plate 11) transplanter units. All units have a planting wheel into which plants are placed like spokes with the roots projecting beyond the margin of the wheel (Plate 12). Plants are gripped in place on the wheel either by soft rubber or by a spring-loaded catch, and are held firmly until in position in the ground when they are released. A narrow parallel-sided trench is opened by a share and closed by compacting wheels immediately the plants are released. The machines using spring-loaded catches are preferable since they provide a more precise spacing and planting depth and therefore a more uniform quality of plant. The 'Super-prefer' units give five rows to the standard seed-bed whereas the 'Accord' provides six rows.

The advantages of transplanting machines are that they eliminate both the hard manual work of digging trenches and the need to fill boards. They are also capable of very high rates of work, but:

- Transplanting machines travel very slowly and have to be drawn by a tractor fitted with a low reduction gear box. Self-propelled versions of both machines are available.
- While the workers avoid the bulk of the physical labour of carrying and digging, they have little scope to move and can get very cold, even though screens may be fitted to give some protection from the wind.

Plants raised following mechanical transplanting have been satisfactory except where roots have dragged back on the share on entering the ground, when plants with a 'hockey-stick' root system have developed. This trouble may be reduced by enlarging the share by deepening by 3–5 cm, and by ensuring that any unduly long roots are cut off.

6.7.7 Irrigation and transplants

See Chapter 11, sections 11.4.1–11.4.3.

6.8 Tending

6.8.1 Weed control in transplant lines

Elimination of weeds ensures that there the

growth of the crop is not hampered by competition for nutrients or moisture. If weeds are prevalent, herbicides should be used for control (see Chapter 12, section 12.4, or Williamson *et al.*, 1993). If for any reason these cannot be used, the same freedom from weed competition can be achieved by regular and very frequent light cultivations of the soil surface, using tractor-mounted tines, brush hoes or rotary hoes, supplemented by hand weeding of weeds growing between plants in the lines.

It is bad management, and disastrous in the long term, to allow the number of weeds to build up towards the end of the year. While such weeds will undoubtedly by buried when the ground is ploughed following clearance, and while it is also true that the transplants themselves will suffer little, nevertheless many weeds will release viable seeds, especially the annual meadow grass *Poa annua*, groundsel *Senecio jacobea* and willowherb *Epilobium* sp. Such seeds will germinate in subsequent years and cumulatively increase the weeding problem and costs of control.

FURTHER READING AND REFERENCES

ALDHOUS, J.R. (1972). *Nursery practice.* Forestry Commission Bulletin 43 (first edition). HMSO, London.

ALDHOUS, J.R. and GLEDHILL, H. (1960). Temperatures at the soil surface. *Journal of the Forestry Commission* **29**, 48–50.

ALDHOUS, J.R. (1962). A survey of Dunemann seedbeds in Great Britain. *Quarterly Journal of Forestry* **56** (3), 185–196.

BENZIAN, B. (1965). Stunted growth and the effects of partial sterilization and related treatments. *Experiments on nutrition in forest nurseries.* Forestry Commission Bulletin 37, Vol. 1, 134–163. HMSO. London.

BENZIAN, B. (1979). Nutrition of young conifers and soil fumigation. In *Root diseases and soil-borne pathogens.* Part Proceedings First International Congress of Plant Pathology, London 1968, eds T. A. Tousson *et al.* University of California Press, 222–225.

BIGGIN, P. (1983). Tunnel cloches – development of a nursery technique for growing conifers. *Forestry* **56**(1), 45–59.

BRIND, J.E. (1965). Studies on the effect of partial sterilization on the soil micropopulation. (Supplementary paper in) *Experiments on nutrition problems in forest nurseries*. Forestry Commission Bulletin 37, Vol. 1, 206–209. HMSO, London.

BSI (1984). *Nursery stock. Part 4 – Specification for forest trees*. BS 3936: part 4. British Standards Institution, London.

EDWARDS, M.V. (1953). *Effects of partial soil sterilization with formalin on Sitka spruce and other conifer seedlings*. Forestry Commission Forest Record 16. HMSO, London.

EDWARDS, M.V. and HOLMES, G.D. (1951). Effect of height and diameter on growth and survival of planted-out seedlings. *Report on Forest Research 1950*, 22–23.

EEC (1971). Council Directive No. 71/161/EEC on external quality standards for forest reproductive material marketed within the community. *Official Journal of the European Communities*, L87, 17.4.71, p.14.

EEC (1974). Council Directive No. 74/13/EEC, amending Directive No. 71/161/EEC, on the external quality standards for forest reproductive material marketed within the community. *Official Journal of the European Communities*, L15, 18.1.74, p.12.

FAULKNER, R. (1957). Experiments on seedbed compaction. *Report on Forest Research 1956*, 113–123.

FAULKNER, R. and HOLMES, G.D. (1954). Placement of fertilisers. *Report on Forest Research 1953*, 20.

FAULKNER, R. (1953). Notes on choosing a suitable conifer seedbed cover with some recent experimental results used for illustration. *Scottish Forestry* **7** (4), 121–124.

FAULKNER, R. (1953). Summer, autumn or spring lining out. *Scottish Forestry* **12**, 127–134.

GORDON, A.G. (ed.) (1992). *Seed manual for forest trees*. Forestry Commission Bulletin 83. HMSO, London.

GORDON, A.G. and ROWE, D.C.F. (eds) (1982). *Seed manual for ornamental trees and shrubs*. Forestry Commission Bulletin 59. HMSO, London.

TEE, L.A. and PETTY, S.J. (1973). *Survey of losses of first year conifer seed and seedlings in Forestry Commission nurseries 1972*. Forestry Commission Research and Development Paper 103. Forestry Commission, London.

THOMPSON, S. (1980). The growth of lodgepole pine seedlings raised under clear polythene cloches at five seedbed densities. *Canadian Journal of Forest Research* **10**, 426–428.

WILLIAMSON, D.R., MASON, W.L., MORGAN, J.L. and CLAY, D.V. (1993). *Forest nursery herbicides*. Forestry Commission Technical Paper 3. Forestry Commission, Edinburgh.

Chapter 7

Mycorrhizas, actinorhizas and rhizobia

C. Walker and C. T. Wheeler

Some soil organisms interact with plants to improve nutrient availability or uptake, or to provide protection against pests or pathogens. These may act indirectly (e.g. free-living nitrogen fixing bacteria, phosphate mineralising bacteria, and antibiotic producers), or directly (some symbiotic species of bacteria, actinomycetes, or fungi). Except for leguminous nitrogen fixers, commercial preparations of such organisms are not available in Great Britain, though there are recommendations for introducing nodulating bacteria to nursery beds of alders.

Although there are currently only limited prospects for using these micro-organisms in nurseries, the background information included in this chapter may help the nursery manager to assess future developments.

7.1 Mycorrhizas

Mycorrhizas are specialised structures which develop where certain fungi colonise the tissues of fine roots of plants (Figure 7.1). The fungi assist in the mineral nutrition of the plant in exchange for carbohydrates and other necessary substances, such as vitamins. This mutually beneficial relationship is termed 'symbiotic' or a 'symbiosis'. The fungal hyphae permeate soil more intimately than plant roots, and take up nutrients which they transfer to plants, thus effectively increasing the soil volume exploited by the rooting system. Because of their rapid turnover, hyphae more readily respond to changes in soil conditions than do the roots. Their main action is to enhance mineral nutrient uptake (especially phosphorus), but they may reduce

drought stress and provide protection from some pathogens (Harley and Smith, 1983).

The three main types of mycorrhizas found on tree roots are ectomycorrhizas, endomycorrhizas and ectendomycorrhizas (Walker, 1986, 1989 b). Ectomycorrhizas and ectendomycorrhizas occur principally with members of the Pinaceae (e.g. pines, firs, Douglas fir, western hemlock, larches and spruces), the Fagaceae (beeches and oaks), and the Betulaceae (birches and alders). Endomycorrhizas form with most other hardwoods (notably maples, including sycamore, cherry, ash and planes) and on members of the Cupressaceae and Taxodiaceae. A few species, such as alders and willows, can have all three kinds on the same root system.

7.1.1 Ectomycorrhizas

Ectomycorrhizas are formed mainly by basidiomycetes such as the many species of *Boletus* and *Amanita* (many of the common toadstools found in the forest belong to ectomycorrhizal fungi) and a few ascomycetes (truffles are ectomycorrhizal ascomycetes). These fungi can be grouped loosely by the age of the plants with which they form mycorrhizas (Mason *et al.*, 1986). Some are found mainly with young plants and are termed 'early stage' fungi. Others, known as 'late stage' fungi, occur only with relatively mature trees, and are not found in nature with seedlings. The early stage fungi are those which may be of interest to the nursery manager. Some ectomycorrhizal fungi are host-specific. For example, *Suillus grevillii* is found only with larch. Most early stage fungi, however, are not specific to host.

One of the most common early stage ectomy-

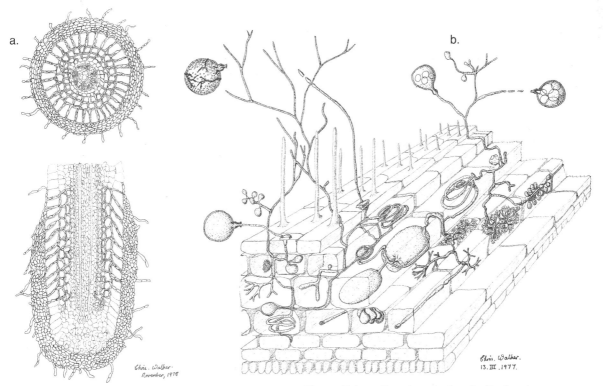

a.

b.

Chris. Walker.
November, 1978

Chris. Walker.
13. III. 1977.

c.

C

d.

L

Figure 7.1 a. Drawing of a longitudinal and cross-section of an ectomycorrhiza.
b. Perspective drawing representing a portion of an arbuscular mycorrhiza. (Only the outer cells of part of the root are drawn.)
c. Sitka spruce seedling, control treatment (C) with non-mycorrhizal roots.
d. Sitka spruce seedling with mycorrhizal roots following inoculation with *Laccaria proxima* (L).

corrhizal fungi is *Thelephora terrestris*. The fruiting body of this fungus is velvety, of various shades of brown, and often fan-shaped (Phillips, 1981), hence its common name of 'earth fan'. This fungus may form fruiting structures around the stem and lower needles of young conifers in the nursery, a habit which has lead to the erroneous conclusion that it is pathogenic. Because of this, it was once known as the 'smothering fungus', and attempts were made to eliminate this helpful symbiont. *Thelephora* is often found in nurseries together with the two other early stage fungi, *Laccaria proxima* and *L. laccata*. These, and other early stage fungi, can improve growth of young trees in both nursery and forest soils (Holden *et al.*, 1983; Thomas and Jackson, 1983).

7.1.2 Ectendomycorrhizas

Ectendomycorrhizas are particularly common in nurseries, especially with pines. They seem to be adapted to high-nutrient or stressful situations. They are formed mainly with species of Discomycetes which may be found fruiting in nursery beds or on the surface of soil in containers (Molina and Trappe, 1984). They may be beneficial in nurseries, but little is known about their role in the forest (Castellano and Molina, 1989).

Ectomycorrhizas and ectendomycorrhizas can be seen with a magnifying glass because the fungus forms a sheath around the root tip, suppresses root hair formation, and usually modifies the morphology of the short roots. They can, however, be distinguished with certainty only by microscopical observation of cut sections, since the chief distinction between them is in whether the fungus penetrates the cortical cells (ectendo-) or merely grows between them (ecto-).

7.1.3 Endomycorrhizas

There are several types of endomycorrhiza, but the one likely to be found with trees is usually known as an arbuscular mycorrhiza (AM). This type of symbiosis can only be detected by chemically clearing and staining roots for observation under a microscope, since no sheath is formed, and root hairs are not suppressed. The fungal partners in AMs are Zygomycetes. They do not have obvious fruiting bodies, but produce large spores in the soil. There are no airborne spores, their spread being by either root-mycorrhizal contact (e.g. by transplantation of colonised plants), by movement of spores by small animals, or by transport in soil (e.g. by water, wind or humans). There seems to be little host-fungus specificity with AM fungi, though there is some evidence that different strains of a fungus can produce different growth responses with the same plant species.

The presence of a well-developed root system on nursery stock is an essential aim of the nursery manager. Ectomycorrhizas and ectendomycorrhizas contribute to this by enhancing the production of short roots. Nursery managers can help to ensure a well-balanced, mycorrhizal root system, even though no active inoculation is carried out, by keeping soil aeration high, reducing use of fungicides to a minimum, and by applying only as much inorganic fertiliser as is absolutely necessary. Endomycorrhizas too help in producing high quality planting stock. Normal nursery practice results in the loss of AM inoculum, and if endomycorrhizal plants are desired, then active inoculation with soil containing propagules of AM fungi will be necessary.

7.1.4 Recent advances

Recently, there has been an upsurge of research into the more practical aspects of the production and use of mycorrhizal inocula (Marx et al., 1984). Mostly, this has been with pines and Douglas fir (ectomycorrhizal species), but there has also been progress with citrus and other endomycorrhizal plants. Nevertheless, commercial use is limited. In the southeastern United States, some nurseries now routinely introduce the fungus *Pisolithus tinctorius* into seedbeds before sowing loblolly pine (*Pinus taeda*). Spore-based inocula of both ectomycorrhizal fungi and AM fungi are available in the USA, as is vegetative mycelium of ectomycorrhizal fungi for incorporation into seedbeds or containers (Castellano and Molina, 1989). Such products are not yet available for ectomycorrhizas in Great Britain, recent attempts at production and marketing having failed. In France, experiments with Douglas fir and Norway spruce have shown that inoculation in the nursery with a suitable strain of ectomycorrhizal fungus can lead to both reduction of root disease and enhanced forest performance. Trials are being carried out in independent nurseries, and have shown great promise. Favourable results, however, are restricted to relatively warm soils, where pathogen problems necessitate fumigation of nursery soils. This is an important factor in the success achieved. Commercially available inoculum of AM fungi is now available through AGC (see address in section 7.3), but has not yet been tested in forest nurseries.

Recent experiments in Great Britain

During the past decade, research has been carried out into the introduction of ectomycorrhizas to Douglas fir and Sitka spruce seedlings, both in seedbeds and in containers (Walker, 1987; 1988; 1989 b).

Mycorrhizas have been successfully established in undercut beds of Douglas fir by use of spores of the DF-specific fungus *Rhizopogon vinicolor* (Walker, 1989 a). However, although there have been some minor successes, generally results have been discouraging with Sitka spruce. In one experiment, for example, carried out in the south of England in a disused sandy nursery, seedling growth was considerably stimulated by the addition of mycorrhizal fungi (Thomas and Jackson, 1983). On the other hand, when the same fungi were tried in more typical nurseries in the north of Britain, no growth effects were obtained (C. Walker, unpublished; Wilson *et al.*, 1990).

Plant handling can damage mycorrhizas. Evidence from root growth potential tests shows that one of the results of poor plant handling is a reduction in the number of active mycorrhizas (see also Chapter 14). There are no immediate prospects of using mycorrhizal inoculation as a routine in the nursery. Nevertheless, as progress is made in other countries, products may become available in Britain, and, in theory, they could be beneficial. The nursery manager should keep a 'weather eye' open for announcements in the horticultural press, but initially should beware of commitment to anything other than a trial, of any commercial products that become available. Advice on the latest situation can be obtained from the Forestry Authority Research Division at the Northern Research Station near Edinburgh.

When land which has not been under recent tree cover is converted to nursery use, it is likely that there will be few, if any, ectomycorrhizal fungi in the soil. Natural invasion through 'spore rain' will be slow and patchy. Such sites should be used for lining out before establishment of seedbeds. Mycorrhizal fungi will then be transferred with the transplanted seedlings. Unless the soil is later fumigated, they will then remain in the soil and become available to future seedlings.

7.2 Non-leguminous nitrogen fixers

These organisms may be symbiotic or free-living (Fitter and Hay, 1987). The importance of the latter is not well understood, and they are not likely to be used in the management of forest nurseries.

Actinomycetes in the genus *Frankia* form nitrogen fixing nodules with a wide range of perennial woody species, distributed between some 24 different genera in eight plant families. Such plants are now usually designated 'actinorhizal plants', to distinguish them from leguminous species nodulated by *Rhizobium*. Casuarinas are widely planted and economically important examples of actinorhizal plants in the tropics and sub-tropics. In temperate regions, species of the genus *Alnus* constitute the most widely used actinorhizal trees but species such as the Russian olive (*Elaeagnus*) and sea buckthorn (*Hippophoae*) are utilised for land reclamation/stabilisation and others for fruit production (Wheeler and Miller, 1990).

7.2.1 Nitrogen-fixing nodules formed on alders by species of *Frankia*

The nodules formed following infection with *Frankia* are perennial structures and can achieve cricket ball or larger size as a result of seasonal growth. Nodule masses so formed on a plant may contain one or several *Frankia* strains that can vary widely in effectiveness in nitrogen fixation (Hooker and Wheeler, 1987). The continued growth of the nodules ensures the persistence over several years of the symbiosis with the *Frankia* strain(s) responsible for the initial infection. This is of particular advantage for the nitrogen nutrition of the host plant if the infecting strain is of high effectiveness.

Frankia is a slow growing micro-organism compared with *Rhizobium* or some ectomycorrhizal fungi and techniques for its isolation from nodules and its culture in the laboratory have been developed only during the last 12 years (Lechevalier and Lechevalier, 1990). Strains of *Frankia* isolated from nodules of an actinorhizal plant can vary widely in their competitiveness and effectiveness for nodulation, even when re-inoculated on to plants of the same species (Wheeler, McLaughlin and Steele, 1981; Hooker and Wheeler, 1987). Many *Frankia* strains are promiscuous in their infectivity and can nodulate plants of species in families different from that from which they were isolated. Sometimes this can result in a satisfactory symbiosis, but in other cases, it may be less efficient, or even completely ineffective. Often, poorly effective nodules are produced on plants introduced into areas containing well nodulated plants of different species of the same genus (Hall *et al.*, 1979).

Frankia is often found in natural plant communities where actinorhizal species have been absent for many decades (Arveby and Huss-Danell, 1988). Its introduction to such areas may be as spores, as these can be widely water- or wind-dispersed. *Frankia* may also survive in a vegetative condition by saprophytic growth in association with the roots of non-nodulated species such as birch (Smolander *et al.*, 1990). Survival seems to be poorest in highly organic soils such as peats (Arveby and Huss-Danell, 1988). It is not unusual, therefore, for nursery soils where alders are to be grown to contain *Frankia* which will give rise to nodules, of varying effectiveness in nitrogen fixation, on the roots of seedlings grown in unsterilised seedbeds. If alders are grown in the nursery for some time, then the levels of *Frankia* in the soil will gradually increase. However, not all nursery soils contain *Frankia*, or the strains present may be poorly infective or ineffective in fixation. In addition, even if a nursery soil contains *Frankia*, sterilisation of the seedbed before sowing will prevent nodulation of the seedlings until the organism is re-introduced. Poor nodulation of seedlings in the nursery will reduce seedling growth and vigour and may seriously affect the successful establish-

ment and growth of transplants on nitrogen deficient sites from which *Frankia* is absent, e.g. spoil reclamation areas.

Recent research in Great Britain

Strains of cultured *Frankia*, effective on alders, have been identified for use in Britain (Hooker and Wheeler, 1987) and their applicability has been proven at Forestry Commission research nurseries, near Edinburgh, Lothian, and Farnham, Surrey (Wheeler *et al.*, 1991). Inoculated plants can be sent from the nursery as 1+0 seedlings instead of, as is more usual, 1+1 transplants. Enhanced growth compared with uninoculated controls can be observed for at least 3 years following outplanting on mine reclamation sites (McNeill *et al.*, 1989 and 1990). It is important that alders destined for planting out on reclamation land are well nodulated.

7.2.2 Availability and recommendations for application of inoculum

Techniques for the large scale inoculation with *Frankia* are available in countries such as Canada for the inoculation of alders (Perinet *et al.*, 1985). The market in Britain is not sufficiently large to justify the investment required for such a venture but interested readers are referred to Benoit and Berry (1990) for further details. Nodulation with crushed nodules is an easy and successful technique, however, and it is recommended that seedbeds be treated in this way until commercial inoculum is available.

Healthy nodules, free of blackening or obvious fungal attack, should be collected from an existing stand of the appropriate species. The nodules should be freed of roots, washed well with running water and, with a blender, homogenised in water (preferably not tap-water, which usually contains chlorine). The resulting mixture should be strained through muslin or a fine sieve to remove large particles and the liquid retained. Approximately 10 g fresh weight of nodules should be ample to treat $10 \, m^2$, when diluted in 9 litres of water. It should be applied to the seedbed with a watering can, fitted with a coarse rose. The inoculum can be applied successfully to the seedbed at sowing or, in drought conditions, shortly after seed germination. Some inoculated plants should be retained in the nursery in 30 cm pots containing nursery soil mixed with 'Perlite' to act as a future source of nodules. While a plant may have only 1–2 g nodules after one year's growth, nodule weight should have increased to 10 g or more per plant by the third year. New potted plants should be established each year to provide a continuous supply of nodules as the older trees outgrow their pots. Alternatively, a permanent hedge of inoculated alders can be established in the nursery from which nodules can be gathered as required.

Although a small amount of mineral nitrogen aids nodulation by reducing stress on the seedling before infection and thus encouraging the development of functional nodules, it should be emphasised that nodulation is sensitive to excess fertiliser nitrogen and that even very small amounts of ammonium nitrate can inhibit nodulation of some actinorhizal plants (Righetti and Munns, 1982). It is unlikely that the nitrogen content of most nursery soils will be so low as to require the application of fertiliser before seeding. Application of phosphorus will aid nodulation and soil pH also is important in the nodulation process, although many alder species can tolerate a wide pH range from pH 4.0–7.5 (Dixon and Wheeler, 1983).

7.3 Legumes and their nitrogen-fixers

Nitrogen fixing root nodules on legumes are formed by symbiosis with bacteria (termed 'rhizobia') belonging to the family Rhizobiaceae. Two genera, *Rhizobium* and *Bradyrhizobium*, are of particular interest for temperate forestry. Of these, the former is better known. The best known of the latter, *B. japonicum*, nodulates soybean, but bradyrhizobia also nodulate many of the legume tree species (Allen and Allen, 1981).

Rhizobia exhibit some specificity for nodulation of particular plants, e.g. *R. loti* nodulates lotus, *R. leguminosarum* biovar *trifolii* nodulates clover; *Bradyrhizobium* spp. nodulate lupins, though cross inoculation often occurs between groups of *Rhizobia*.

Many legumes are nodulated effectively by the natural populations of rhizobia present in the soil. Thus, *R. leguminosarum* nodulates peas, and occurs widely in British soils, as do strains that will nodulate shrubs such as broom or gorse. As with *Frankia*, a crushed preparation of effective nodules (recognised by their pink colour on slicing) can be used for inoculation. However, effective rhizobia may be absent from the area to be planted and be unavailable locally. Consideration of the type of rhizobia required for inoculation of nursery stock is then important, particularly if outplanting is to be to a nitrogen poor location.

Unlike *Frankia*, commercial inoculum has been available for legumes for many years, There is an American supplier (The Nitragin Company, Liphatec, Milwaukee), and at least one company in Britain, AGC MicroBio Division, NPPL Building, Rothamsted Experiment Station, Harpenden, Hertfordshire, produces such a product. These firms produce catalogues of strains available for purchase. Inoculum is usually supplied in a peat-based carrier. It can be applied by incorporation into the soil or by coating the seed before sowing. Instructions are supplied with the inoculum ordered but application of a minimal bacterial number must be achieved for successful nodulation. Small-seeded species require at least 10 000 bacteria per seed while large seeds, such as soybean, will require as many as a million bacteria per seed to ensure inoculation.

The main uses of legume inoculation in the UK are likely to be with leguminous green cover crops, e.g. clovers and annual lupins. Although several legume trees such as *Laburnum* or *Robinia* are grown as ornamentals, their use in forestry is limited. *Cytisus* can have an important role in reclamation work (Skeffington and Bradshaw, 1980) and in biomass production (Wheeler *et al.*, 1987).

Tree lupins have been used successfully for sand dune rehabilitation in Australia and New Zealand, and as nurse crops, e.g. for conifers on china clay wastes in Cornwall (Thomas, 1988). It should be noted that many strains of *Rhizobium* are ineffective at soil acidity lower than pH 4.5–5.0.

REFERENCES

ALLEN, O.M. and ALLEN, E.E. (1981). *The Leguminosae. A source book of characteristics, uses and nodulation.* Macmillan, London. (812 pp.)

ARVEBY, A.S. and HUSS-DANELL, K. (1968). Presence and dispersal of infective *Frankia* in peat and meadow soils in Sweden. *Biology and Fertility of Soils* **6**, 39–44.

BENOIT, L.F. and BERRY, A.M. (1990). Methods for production and use of actinorhizal plants in forestry, low maintenance landscapes and revegetation. In *The biology of Frankia and actinorhizal plants,* eds C.R. Schwinzer and J.D. Tjepkema. Academic Press, New York, 281–294.

CASTELLANO, M.A. and MOLINA, R.J. (1989). Mycorrhizae. In *The container tree nursery manual,* Volume 5, eds T.D. Landis, R.W. Tinus, S.E. McDonald and J.P. Barnett. *Agricultural Handbook* 674. Washington DC: U.S. Department of Agriculture Forest Service.

DIXON, R.O.D. and WHEELER, C.T. (1983). Biochemical, physiological and environmental aspects of symbiotic nitrogen fixation. In *Biological nitrogen fixation in forest ecosystems: foundations and applications,* eds J.C. Gordon and C.T. Wheeler. Martinus Nijhoff/W. Junk, The Hague, 107–171.

FITTER, A.H. and HAY, R.K.M. (1987). *Environmental physiology of plants,* 2nd edtn. Academic Press, London.

HALL, R.B., McNABB, H.S., MAYNARD, C.A. and GREEN, T.L. (1979). Toward development of optimal *Alnus glutinosa* symbioses. *Botanical Gazette* **140** (Suppl.), S120–S126.

HARLEY, J.L. and SMITH, S.E. (1983). *Mycorrhizal symbiosis.* Academic Press, London.

HOLDEN, J.M., THOMAS, G.W. and JACKSON, R.M. (1983). Effect of mycorrhizal inocula on the growth of Sitka spruce seedlings in different soils. *Plant and Soil* **71**, 313–317.

HOOKER, J.E. and WHEELER, C.T. (1987). The effectivity of *Frankia* for nodulation and nitrogen fixation in *Alnus rubra* and *Alnus glutinosa. Physiologia Plantarum* **70**, 333–341.

LECHEVALIER, M.P. and LECHEVALIER, H.A. (1990). Systematics, isolation and culture of *Frankia.* In *The biology of Frankia and actinorhizal plants,* eds C.R. Schwinzer and J.D. Tjepkema. Academic Press, New York, 35–36.

MARX, D.H., CORDELL, C.E., KENNEY, D.S., MEXAL, J.G., ARTMAN, J.D., RIFFLE, J.W. and MOLINA, R.J. (1984). Commercial vegetative inoculum of *Pisolithus tinctorius* and inoculation techniques for development of bare-root tree seedlings. *Forest Science Monograph* 25.

MASON, P.A., WILSON, J., LAST, F.T. and WALKER, C. (1986). The concept of succession in relation to the spread of sheathing mycorrhizal fungi on inoculated tree seedlings growing in unsterile soils. *Plant and Soil* **71**, 247–256.

McNEILL, J.D., HOLLINGSWORTH, M.K., MASON, W.L., MOFFAT, A.J., SHEPPARD, L.J. and WHEELER, C.T. (1990). *Inoculation of alder seedlings to improve seedling growth and field performance.* Arboriculture Research Note 88/90/SILN. DoE Arboricultural Advisory and Information Service, Farnham, Surrey.

McNEILL, J.D., HOLLINGSWORTH, M.K., MASON, W.L., SHEPPARD, L.J. and WHEELER, C.T. (1989). *Inoculation of Alnus rubra seedlings to improve seedling growth and forest performance.* Forestry Commission Research Information Note 144. Forestry Commission, Edinburgh.

MOLINA, R.J. and TRAPPE, J.M. (1984).

Mycorrhiza management in bareroot nurseries. In *Forest nursery manual: production of bareroot seedlngs,* eds M. L. Duryea and D. Landis. Martinus Nijhoff/Dr W. Junk, The Hague.

PERINET, P., BROUILLETTE, J.G., FORTIN, J.A. and LALONDE, M. (1985). Large scale inoculation of actinorhizal plants with *Frankia. Plant and Soil* **87,** 175–183.

PHILLIPS, R. (1981). *Mushrooms and other fungi of Great Britain and Europe.* Pan Books, London. (288 pp.)

RIGHETTI, T.L. and MUNNS, D.N. (1982). Nodulation and nitrogen fixation in *Purshia:* inoculation response and species comparisons. *Plant and Soil* **65,** 383–396.

SKEFFINGTON, R.A. and BRADSHAW, A.D. (1980). Nitrogen fixation by plants grown on reclaimed china clay. *Journal of Applied Ecology* **17,** 469–477.

SMOLANDER, A., RONNKO, R., NURMIAH-LASSILA, E.L. and HAAHTELA, K. (1990). Growth of *Frankia* in the rhizosphere of *Betula pendula,* a non-host tree species. *Canadian Journal of Microbiology* **36,** 649–656.

THOMAS, G.W. and JACKSON, R.M. (1983). Growth responses of Sitka spruce seedlings to mycorrhizal inoculation. *New Phytologist* **95,** 223–229.

THOMAS, R.J. (1988). A review of the use of nitrogen-fixing shrubs and trees in agroforestry and farm forestry systems in N. Europe. *Research and Development in Agriculture* **5,** 143–152.

WALKER, C. (1986). Mycorrhizas in forestry – has inoculation a future? *Forestry and British Timber* **15** (5), 20–21.

WALKER, C. (1987). Sitka spruce mycorrhizas. *Proceedings of the Royal Society of Edinburgh* **93B,** 117–129.

WALKER, C. (1988). Mycorrhizas. *Report on forest research 1988,* 37. HMSO, London.

WALKER, C. (1989a). Friendly fungi poised to boost nursery growth. *Horticulture Week* **205** (1), 18–19.

WALKER, C. (1989b). Mycorrhizas. *Report on forest research 1989,* 40. HMSO, London.

WHEELER, C.T. and MILLER, I.M. (1990). Current and potential uses of actinorhizal plants in Europe. In *The biology of Frankia and actinorhizal plants,* eds C.R. Schwinzer and J.D. Tjepkema. Academic Press, New York, 365–385.

WHEELER, C.T., HELGERSON, O.T., PERRY, D.A. and GORDON, J.C. (1987). Nitrogen fixation and biomass accumulation in plant communities dominated by *Cytisus scoparius* L. in Oregon and Scotland. *Journal of Applied Ecology* **24,** 231–237.

WHEELER, C.T., HOLLINGSWORTH, M.K., HOOKER, J.E., McNEILL, J.D., MASON, W.L. and SHEPPARD, L.J. (1991). The effect of inoculation with either cultured *Frankia* or crushed nodules on nodulation and growth of *Alnus rubra* and *Alnus glutinosa* in forest nurseries. *Forest Ecology and Management* **43,** 153–166.

WHEELER, C.T., McLAUGHLIN, M.E. and STEEL, P. (1981). A comparison of symbiotic nitrogen fixation in Scotland in *Alnus glutinosa* and *Alnus rubra. Plant and Soil* **61,** 169–188.

WILSON, J., INGLEBY, K. and MASON, P.A. (1990). Ectomycorrhizal inoculation of Sitka spruce; survival of vegetative mycelium in nursery soil. *Aspects of Applied Biology* **24,** 109–115.

Chapter 8
Production of undercut stock

W. L. Mason

Chapter 6 describes a traditional bare-root production system where seed is sown at high density (800–1500 seeds per m²). The resulting seedlings are lifted after one or two growing seasons and lined out ('transplanted') at low densities at 100–150 plants per m². These transplants are then grown on for a further period before being lifted and dispatched to the forest. The purpose of this two-stage production system is to provide strong, sturdy plants with adequate root fibre that can withstand planting in the forest better than untransplanted seedlings.

This traditional system has a number of drawbacks. Firstly, seedlings in broadcast seedbeds invariably are unevenly distributed, creating localised interplant competition and resulting in appreciable variation in seedling size. Secondly, all methods of transplanting, if done badly, have a tendency to produce trees with a swept, J-rooted root system. This distortion can make trees difficult to plant and could cause serious stability problems in species with limited potential for adventitious root regeneration. Finally, transplanting is a labour-intensive operation and is an additional hazard in the production system, exposing seedlings to the risk of damage during the lifting and lining out process.

8.1 Potential of undercutting

An alternative approach to bare-root transplant production is to sow seedlings for undercutting, at about a quarter of the density of conventional seedbeds (e.g. 200 seeds per m²). The resultant seedlings are usually grown on for two seasons. A 1-year production cycle is only possible with fast-growing species (e.g. larches, radiata pine) in southern Britain. In the final season before lifting, a sharp blade is passed horizontally through the seedbed to sever the tap-root and any other roots below a given depth. The initial undercutting is often followed at intervals by further manipulations of the root system by 'wrenching'. This involves passing a blade at an angle (c. 35° front to rear) through the bed at or just below the depth of the undercut. Wrenching breaks off any secondary roots growing down below the initial undercut and stimulates proliferation of root fibre (Sharpe *et al.*, 1988). Drill sown beds may also be sidecut.

It is important to differentiate between 'multicut' stock purposely produced by regimes like the above, and 'casual undercutting' carried out as a last minute decision to check excessively vigorous plants or to attempt to salvage unsold stood-over stock. Plants produced by these 'casual' undercutting regimes will not be of the same quality as produced following the recommendations in section 8.3 below.

The purposes of planned and managed undercutting are:

- To promote and manipulate root development so that the maximum amount of root fibre is produced in the upper layers of the soil. This ensures that as much of the root system as possible is recovered at lifting.
- To control height growth so plants achieve a desired specification.
- To decrease the shoot:root ratio so that postplanting check is reduced.
- To avoid the risk of producing transplants with distorted roots.

8.1.1 Root response to undercutting

The speed of root regeneration after undercutting is largely dependent upon soil temperature, being faster at higher soil temperatures. This implies that, under British conditions, undercutting should normally take place in June or July, which tend to be the warmest months of the growing season. The later undercutting is delayed into the autumn, the slower and more limited will be the amount of root response obtained that year.

When undercutting, the lower part of the root system is severed, reducing the supply of water to the shoots. An imbalance rapidly develops between the demand and supply for water particularly during summer, moisture stress develops in the shoots and growth is reduced. Figure 8.1 shows patterns of shoot water potential (a measure of moisture stress) during the weeks following undercutting of Sitka spruce. Each point shows the maximum level of moisture stress recorded during a 24-hour period and is the mean of ten samples. The values show that undercut plants are significantly more stressed than non-undercut plants for at least 2 months after undercutting.

The root system has to be regenerated to maintain adequate supplies of water to the shoots. Studies have shown that, after undercutting, there is a substantial increase in the flow of photosynthate and nutrients towards the undercut root system (e.g. Rook, 1971). This change in the pattern of distribution of plant foodstuffs will continue until the root system is regenerated.

8.1.2 Plant quality and forest performance

Because of a more favourable shoot:root ratio, increased sturdiness and the greater amount of fibrous roots, undercut conifer planting stock has generally been found to be superior to transplant material in most recent British experiments. Since 1985, some 30 forest experiments have been established with Sitka spruce, Douglas fir, lodgepole pine, Scots pine, Corsican pine, Japanese and hybrid larch (Mason, 1988). In nearly all instances, the undercut stock has out-performed the transplants in terms of either survival and/or early height growth. The differences have tended to be most notable with species that are considered difficult to establish such as Douglas fir or Corsican pine.

Undercut stock has also shown greater resistance to the stresses imposed by storage and other aspects of the handling system. This improvement in performance appears to reflect the greater fibrosity of the root system, making the plant more resistant to different levels of damage. Various aspects of forest performance of undercut stock are discussed by Deans *et al.* (1989); Mason *et al.,* 1989; McKay and Mason (1991); Nelson and Howes (1991) and Sharpe *et al.* (1990).

The undercut plants used in these experiments were produced using the intensive undercutting regimes described later in this chapter.

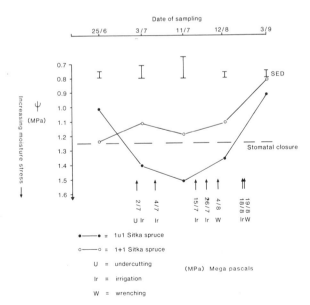

Figure 8.1 Shoot water potential (ψ) of undercut (1u 1) and non-undercut (1+1) Sitka spruce during the last third of the growing season.

8.1.3 Physiological effects of undercutting

During the growing season, the amount of height growth made by a seedling will be influenced by the moisture and nutrients being supplied via roots. Thus, a seedling grown under dry conditions with limited nutrients will be shorter and have poorer foliage nutrient status than one grown under moist fertile conditions. The former will also tend to have a larger root system in relation to the shoot size since more of the products of photosynthesis ('photosynthate') are diverted to developing a root system to supply the plant's requirement for water and nutrients. Undercutting is intended to divert photosynthate from shoot growth to the creation of a superficial and much branched root system.

The nursery manager has four key ways to influence the root system through the effect of undercutting:

1. The depth at which the initial undercut is made – the shallower the undercut the more intense the moisture stress the plant undergoes. Earlier work that showed inadequate response to undercutting was generally the result of undercutting at depths (e.g. 15 cm) where only a small amount of root was removed with only a very short-term effect upon the plant.

2. The timing of the first undercut and any subsequent operation – it should occur in high summer so that the soil is warm enough to allow root regeneration.

3. By wrenching and sidecutting to continue the manipulation of the root system so that roots develop in the upper layers of the soil and in a configuration which is convenient for lifting and planting. Continued root disturbance until the end of the growing season ensures that photosynthate continues to be channelled towards the root system.

4. Finally, regulation of irrigation is essential for effective application of undercutting regimes. Without remedial irrigation, plants can die if the undercut is followed by dry, warm weather. However, it is also a mistake to overwater undercut stock since there is some evidence that physiological quality at the end of the season is improved if the plants have been subjected to moderate

water stress. While the critical levels of plant moisture status before or after undercutting have not been well defined, the art of successful undercutting regimes is to bring plants close to the point of wilting without letting them die.

8.2 Sowing for undercut production

The main difference between sowing for undercut production compared with transplant regimes is the much lower sowing densities used in the undercut system. Table 8.1 gives recommended densities for precision sowing of a representative range of the major conifer and broadleaved species. The figures assume that the seed lots are of high quality with over 90% germinability or viability. The density chosen will depend upon the quality of seed lot, the equipment available for sowing, the ability to maintain favourable germination conditions in the seedbed, and the number and sturdiness of usable seedlings desired per m^2.

In general terms, at lower densities (i.e. wider spacings), plants will have greater root collar diameter in relation to their height and will have larger root systems with more fibre (see Deans *et al.*, 1989). In precision sown beds, densities are calculated on *actual*

Table 8.1 Sowing densities for precision sowing for undercut production with some conifer and broadleaved species

Species	Density (seeds per m^2)
Corsican pine	150
Scots pine	150
Larches	200
Sitka spruce	200
Douglas fir	200
Birches	200
Sycamore	150
Beech	150
Oaks	125

Note: Assumes seed lots with over 90% germinability/viability.

number of seeds sown rather than number of germinable seeds.

Clearly, the low sowing densities used in undercut systems mean that any failure in germination because of poor seed, poorly cleaned seed, temperature, drought, bird predation, mouse damage, etc., can be very costly. Table 8.2 shows how the recommended density for Douglas fir can be adjusted to take account of seed lots with lower germinability. Similar calculations can be undertaken for the other species. In general, it is not worthwhile sowing seed lots with less than 60% germination for undercut production without first attempting to upgrade the seed quality by removing any empty or damaged seeds. If seed is sown at relatively high density (e.g. 400 seeds per m²) and high germination results, then it is advisable to respace the seedlings to a lower density at the end of the first season. If this is not done, then plant quality will suffer, with the trees being tall and spindly with poor root development.

8.2.1 Freedom from stones

Successful conditions for growing undercut plants require that the upper soil horizons are free of large stones than might deflect an undercutter blade. This is to ensure that the undercutter can be kept at a constant depth in the soil. If stones or other large objects such as root debris are present, the undercutter will ride up over them and cut off roots very close to the surface. Plants treated in this way will often die or at best will have very inadequate root systems. The nursery manager should

seek to destone any sections where stone may be a problem, before sowing takes place. Standard agricultural destoners are perfectly acceptable, provided these lift the stones on a belt so that they can be deposited in a trailer and removed. Destoners that bury stones in the alleys or under the wheelings should not be used.

8.2.2 Seed sowing

A range of mechanical sowers is available for use in the production of undercut plants. The simplest option is to use the broadcast sowers used in conventional seedling production but to sow at a lower average density. The main problem with this approach is the inability to control lateral spread of seedling roots, and also a risk of uneven seed distribution so that individual plants do not have uniform growing space. A better approach is to sow the seed in bands ('drills') along the length of the bed. Depending upon the sower used, between six and eight drills can be obtained on a 1 m wide seedbed so that a side cutter can be used to sever roots crossing between drills. A further advantage of sowing in drills is that weed growth between the rows is more readily controlled.

Conifers

Most drill sowers available on the British market were designed for use in agriculture and they are not very easy to use with tree seeds. The main exception is the Matco-Fahse Mini-Air which can sow up to six drills on a preformed seedbed, and gives reasonable spacing between seeds of conifers.

The most accurate conifer seed sower on the British market is the Summit Precision Sower (see Front Cover and Plate 13) which was designed in New Zealand for sowing *Pinus radiata* and has been successfully adapted for use with a range of British conifer species. This machine can make and sow a seedbed in one pass. A vacuum inside the sowing drum ensures that seed for each drill is held on the drum for controlled delivery to the soil at regular intervals (Plate 14).

Table 8.2 Sowing density for seed lots of differing germinability for precision sowing of Douglas fir

Germination (%)	Target density (seed per m²)	Germinable seeds per m²
>90	220–200	180–200
81–90	250–220	198–225
71–80	285–250	177–228
61–70	320–285	174–224
<61 do not sow for undercutting without upgrading seed lot		

Whatever seed sower is used, it is important that the seed purity be high since seed wings and other debris can easily clog orifices or metering mechanisms and result in blank drills on the seedbed. It is worth checking that a sower can cope with a particular species by carrying out a small preliminary test.

Broadleaves

Large seeded broadleaves are treated rather differently, shallow drills being opened in the bed surface and seeds being fed down funnels to the drill which is then covered over.

Drill spacing

Drill-sowing for undercut production must be carried out with particular care since the placing of the rows affects all aspects of subsequent management. Wind can be a serious problem since seeds can have 5–20 cm to fall before making contact with the soil. Strong winds can blow the light seeds during their fall so that they lie outwith the drill. If seed has to be sown under windy conditions, heavy polythene skirts should be fixed round the drill to shield seed from the wind. Care is also necessary when sowing on side slopes since the sower can 'crab' or move downhill and become misaligned so that outside rows on one side are too close to the edge of the bed and are destroyed in subsequent operations.

8.2.3 Tending

Most other aspects of seedbed preparation and management follow the procedures outlined in Chapter 6. Seed is sown on the top of the seedbed and covered with grit in the normal manner, except for large seeded broadleaves which are drilled into the top layers of the soil. Presowing fertilisation and first year top dressing regimes should follow the standard prescriptions for the nursery.

Careful weed control is essential for successful management of a precision sowing and undercutting regime. Since the seedlings are sown at wide spacing, they are particularly vulnerable to weed competition in the first growing season. Soil sterilisation should be considered before sowing if the particular nursery section was weedy under the previous crop.

A standard pre-emergence herbicide should be applied immediately after sowing and further application of herbicide may well be necessary during the first season to ensure that no weed growth becomes established. Weed control during the second season can be less intensive, using a standard transplant product at the beginning of the season and following this at a later date by mechanical inter-row hoeing to remove any surviving weeds (see also Chapter 12, section 12.4).

8.3 Recommended undercutting regimes

The following recommendations are largely based upon experience with conifers at the Forestry Commission nursery at Wykeham in North Yorkshire. The nursery soil is a stone-free, coarse loamy sand derived from Jurassic passage beds and irrigation is available from an adjacent reservoir. While the basic principles should apply to all species and nurseries, they may need to be adapted to particular situations.

8.3.1 Time of first undercut

The initial undercut should take place in June or July of the second season with exact timing depending upon the growth of the plants. Earlier undercutting is possible if the aim is to reduce the rate of height growth. However, in such circumstances it is better to have an initial undercut, leave the root systems to regenerate for 6–8 weeks and then restart in late July to early August. Depth of undercut should be around 8 cm; shallower depths risk severely damaging the plants, while greater depth will not give adequate conditioning.

Subsequent operations

Undercutting should be followed after 2–3 weeks by wrenching at 10–15 cm depth (i.e. below the initial undercut) and this should be repeated at similar intervals until early

Plate 7.
Seedbeds under polythene continuous cloches.
(J.R. Aldhous)

Plate 8. *Seedbed being covered with polythene netting against birds showing:*
i) hoops to hold netting above bed, man feeding them out,
ii) netting roll on rotating spindle,
iii) netting edges being secured (with pegs). (39386)

Plate 9. *Seedlings grown under floating mulch, showing mulch being removed.* (W.L. Mason)

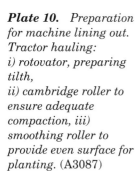

Plate 10. *Preparation for machine lining out. Tractor hauling:*
i) rotovator, preparing tilth,
ii) cambridge roller to ensure adequate compaction, iii) smoothing roller to provide even surface for planting. (A3087)

Plate 11. *Transplanting using Super-prefer. A general view showing shelter for workers against wind and cold. (E8833)*

Plate 12. *Inserting seedlings into holders on rim of planting wheels. (38222)*

Table 8.3 End of season height as a percentage of height at time of first undercutting in four conifer species for two growing seasons

Species	Percentage height	
	1986*	1987†
Scots pine	103	109
Corsican pine	110	
Sitka spruce	185	
Douglas fir	180	165

Data are from Wykeham nursery.

* 1986: trees were first undercut on 2/7 followed by wrenching on 4/8; 19/8; 5/9; 19/9; 6/10; 29/10.

† 1987: trees were first undercut on 16/7 (SP) or 31/7 (DF). Wrenching on 21/8; 3/9 and 14/9.

October. In some tap-rooted species (e.g. Corsican pine, oaks), it may be necessary to undercut the crop for a second time if wrenching does not remove roots regenerating downwards from the tap-root. Where beds have been drill sown, one or two sidecuttings will also be necessary during the period from July to October to prune roots growing across the drills.

Sidecutting can be undertaken using discs set to a depth of 15 cm passing between drills (Plate 17).

The crop's response to undercutting and wrenching should be monitored closely. It can take up to 3–4 weeks before roots show any sign of response to undercutting in July. The best way of monitoring the crop is to lift plants with a spade at weekly intervals to check upon root development. Beds should be irrigated if the leading shoots of the crop show signs of wilting.

The effect of undercutting upon height growth varies with species. Conifers which make a single flush of growth such as Scots and Corsican pine make little growth after the initial undercut, whereas those capable of growth throughout the season (e.g. larches, Douglas fir) may grow another 5–10 cm in height after the initial undercut (Table 8.3). The difference is species response means that undercutting on its own cannot always be used to control height growth, and that fertilisation regimes must also be considered.

8.3.2 Fertilisation of undercut stock

A common observation is that undercut and/or wrenched plants develop pale, chlorotic foliage in the later part of the final growing season (Coker, 1984). This response occurs because nutrients, particularly nitrogen, are redistributed from the foliage to the regenerating root system. This symptom may take at least a month to develop after undercutting and fertiliser regimes should anticipate the problem rather than wait for it to develop. This response is also found in other species such as Scots pine and Douglas fir.

Figure 8.2 (see also Table 8.4) shows how nitrogen deficiency develops in undercut Sitka spruce over the course of a growing season. A standard regime of nitrogen applied at regular intervals was unable to maintain N status in the undercut seedlings even though it was adequate for plants that were not undercut (2+0). By contrast, a more generous regime with five applications of nitrogen in liquid form, four applied at close intervals following undercutting, was able to maintain and improve the nitrogen status of the foliage. This high nitrogen regime involved the application of over one-and-a-half times as much elemental N as the standard regime.

Other results suggest that increasing the amount of nitrogen top-dressing by a factor of 1.5–2.0 compared with transplant stock is a reasonable rule-of-thumb to adopt. However, there is no evidence to suggest that levels should exceed $150 \, kg \, N \, ha^{-1}$ in one growing season. Fertiliser should be applied in small doses in a 'little and often' approach. Application of nitrogen in a liquid form will enhance the speed of uptake provided it is adequately diluted. Care should be taken to avoid formulations involving urea, since these can scorch plants particularly when they are under stress following undercutting.

Deficiences of P, K and Mg have not been observed in British nurseries on undercut stock given standard nutrient regimes. However, P and K deficiencies are noted in the literature (Racey and Racey, 1988). Where levels of these elements tend to be marginal, a

Figure 8.2 Response to undercutting of Sitka spruce plants in their second season of growth: nitrogen status of foliage.

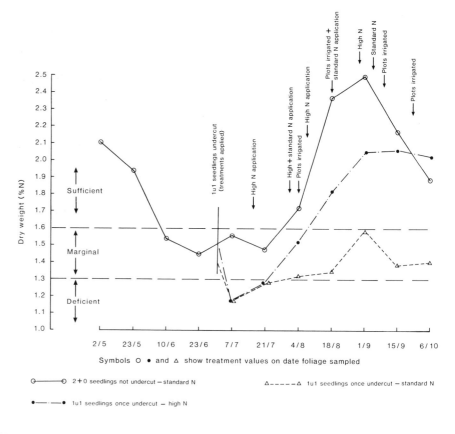

Symbols O ● and △ show treatment values on date foliage sampled

O———O 2+0 seedlings not undercut – standard N   △-----△ 1u1 seedlings once undercut – standard N

●—·—● 1u1 seedlings once undercut – high N

Table 8.4 Response of Sitka spruce 1u1 plants to undercutting: nitrogen status of foliage (see Figure 8.2). Details of regimes

18 June	Kay-nitro (25-0-16) at 75 kg ha⁻¹ to standard treatments.	8 August	Nitrogen liquid feed to high N treatment (70 litres ha⁻¹).
	Nitrogen liquid feed (35-0-0) at 70 litres ha⁻¹ to high N treatment.	18 August	Kay-nitro to standard treatment (75 kg ha⁻¹).
2 July	Undercut standard and high N treatment.	19 August	Wrench standard and high N treatments.
16 July	Nitrogen liquid feed to high N treatment (70 litres ha⁻¹).	29 August	Nitrogen liquid feed to high N treatment (70 litres ha⁻¹).
1 August	Nitrogen liquid feed to high N treatment (70 litres ha⁻¹).	4 September	Kay-nitro to standard treatment (75 kg ha⁻¹).
	Kay-nitro to standard treatment (75 kg ha⁻¹).	5 September	Wrench standard and high N treatments.
4 August	Wrench standard and high N treatments.	19 September	Wrench standard and high N treatments.
7 August	Side-cut standard and high N treatments (70 litres ha⁻¹).	6 October	Wrench standard and high N treatments.

Notes: 1. 2+0 plants received the standard regime.

2. Standard treatment received 75 kg elemental N ha⁻¹ over season; high N received 120 kg elemental N ha⁻¹ over the same period.

3. Mean height of plants at the end of season was; 2+0 non-undercut – 21.3 cm; 1u1 standard – 16.2 cm; 1u1 high N – 17.4 cm.

Table 8.5 A provisional fertiliser regime for precision sown undercut conifer stock being produced on a 2-year cycle

Basal fertiliser	Top dressing
Year 1	
PK plus other nutrients at recommended rate for the section following soil analysis.	N applied at 50–100 kg element ha⁻¹ over the season. Two to four applications. K applied at 75 kg ha⁻¹ K₂O at the end of season.
Year 2	
PK applied in spring at $^1/_2$–$^3/_4$ of rate applied the previous year. Applied between rows and incorporated.	N applied at 100–150 kg element ha⁻¹ at 5–6 intervals over the season. K applied at 75 kg ha⁻¹ K₂O at the end of season.

sensible precaution is to apply a supplementary dressing at the beginning of the second growing season. This can be incorporated into the soil by applying it in bands between the rows and using the sidecutters or a rotary brush hoe to mix the fertiliser into the top layer of the soil.

Table 8.5 sets out a fertiliser regime for precision sown and undercut conifer stock based upon experience at Wykeham. There are a number of areas that still require confirmation, particularly the role of late season top-dressing in alleviating nitrogen deficiency. However, the nursery manager should realise that undercutting regimes require additional nutrient inputs compared with transplant production, and that production of chlorotic plants is not inevitable.

8.3.3 Mechanical aspects of undercutting

Successful undercutting can only be achieved if adequate equipment is used (van Dorsser and Rook, 1972). The prerequisites are a sharp, reciprocating (i.e. side to side action) blade which can be carefully maintained at the proper depth (Plates 15 & 16). Sharp blades ensure that root systems are cut cleanly and not dragged. Blunt blades often do not cut roots, but drag them so that a swept root system results. Soil texture has an important effect on the need to resharpen blades since sharp sands will rapidly blunt a blade while smoother soils have little effect. Soil conditions at the time of undercutting are also important. In dry spells, the soil in the upper horizons can be quite hard so that the undercutting blade has difficulty in moving through the bed. In such situations, the blade will bow towards the centre so that seedlings in the middle are undercut at perhaps only 2 cm depth. This problem can be avoided either by loosening the soil before the start of undercutting by passing a lifting blade through the soil below the target undercut depth or by side cutting or by irrigating the beds before undercutting. Up to 12 mm of water should be applied if the latter approach is adopted. Plate 17 illustrates a disc side-cutter.

At the end of the final growing season when plants have been intensively undercut and wrenched, the upper 8–10 cm of the seedbed may be quite loose, so that it is possible to lift plants easily by taking the leading shoot between the thumb and forefinger and pulling the plant from the soil with only limited root damage. The looseness of the soil can cause difficulties when plants are lifted using a single-row lifter. This is because successful operation of such machines requires firm soil in front of the plough share if there is to be a regular flow of plants taken up by the lifting belts. One solution to this problem is to use some form of whole-bed lifting system to harvest the plants. Such a system has the added advantage of reducing the risks of soil compaction that are the result of single row lifters travelling every part of the seedbed. Alternatively, a heavy application of irrigation 2–3 weeks before lifting may settle the soil back around plants sufficiently to enable lifters to work.

If long lateral roots remain, which will impede subsequent planting, these should be carefully trimmed back to 15–20 cm (Nelson and Howes, 1991).

8.4 Use of undercutting with other systems

In southern Britain, it is possible to produce faster growing conifers and many broadleaves on a ½u½ production cycle. Most aspects of this system follow the general principles discussed for 2-year undercut production. However, the key factor is to sow early (March to April at the latest) and to force the early height growth using floating mulches, so that the seedlings are tall enough to start undercutting in July or early August at the latest. If this is not done, then the nursery manager runs the risk of either producing very small plants (if not brought on) or of producing taller plant with poor root systems (if not undercut effectively). Neither will make satisfactory planting stock.

There is no major reason why undercutting cannot be used in transplant lines to improve the quality of the root systems. However, for this to be done effectively, it is desirable that the transplants are lined out on to a raised bed. This makes it easier to operate the undercutter at the correct depth. It is very much more difficult to operate a reciprocating undercutter on flat transplant lines since the arms of the blade tend to plough up the alleys and the undercutter may be damaged. Otherwise, a fixed blade may be used.

8.5 Implications for nursery management

The results of forest and plant handling experiments generally indicate that a precision sown and repeatedly undercut and wrenched (or 'multicut') plant is a superior product to the conventional bare-root transplant. The fact that the labour-intensive transplanting operation can be eliminated means that it is possible to produce a plant of better quality at a reduced cost. However, this requires full stocking, which in turn depends upon use of good quality seed, high germination and survival being achieved, leading to evenly spaced, well-stocked seedbeds. The system also requires good quality nursery soil (i.e. stone-free loamy sands on level or uniform sloping ground) with adequate irrigation to allow undercutting at the most appropriate time. The system cannot be successfully employed in all nurseries, particularly small units with dif-

ficult soil. It is also important to recognise that the system involves more intensive disturbance of the plants than is usual in traditional bare-root production. Correct application of the system requires a good grasp of the principles of plant growth, physiology and nutrition, plus sensitivity to seasonal variation.

REFERENCES

COKER, A (1984). Nitrogen status of *Pinus radiata* seedlings after undercutting: changes in total, soluble and insoluble nitrogen. *New Zealand Journal of Forestry Science* **14** (3), 277–288.

DEANS, J.D., MASON, W.L., CANNELL, M.G.R., SHARPE, A.L. and SHEPPARD, L.J. (1989). Growing regimes for bare-root stock of Sitka spruce, Douglas fir and Scots pine. I. Morphology at the end of the nursery phase. *Forestry* **62** (suppl.), 53–60.

MASON, W.L. (1988). *Precision sown and undercut conifer planting stock. I. Quality and performance.* Forestry Commission Research Information Note 129. Forestry Commission, Edinburgh.

MASON, W.L., SHARPE, A.L. and DEANS, J.D. (1989). Growing regimes for bare-root stock of Sitka spruce, Douglas fir and Scots pine. II. Forest performance. *Forestry* **62,** (suppl.), 275–284.

McKAY, H.M. and MASON, W.L. (1991). Physiological indicators of tolerance to cold storage in Sitka spruce and Douglas fir seedlings. *Canadian Journal of Forest Research* **21,** 890–901.

NELSON, D.G. and HOWES, R.E.J. (1991). Root pruning of planting stock after lifting. *Forestry Commission Report on forest research 1991*, 9. HMSO, London.

RACEY, J.E. and RACEY, G.D. (1988). *Undercutting and root wrenching of tree seedlings: an annotated bibliography.* Ontario Ministry of Natural Resources. Forestry Research Report 121. (78 pp.)

ROOK, D.A. (1971). Effect of undercutting and wrenching on growth of *Pinus radiata* D. Don. seedlings. *Journal of Applied Ecology* **8,** 477–490.

SHARPE, A.L., HOWES, R.E.J. and MASON, W.L. (1988). *Precision sown and undercut conifer planting stock. II. Nursery regimes.* Forestry Commission Research Information Note 132. Forestry Commission, Edinburgh.

SHARPE, A.L., MASON, W.L. and HOWES, R.E.J. (1990). Early forest performance of roughly handled Sitka spruce and Douglas fir of different plant types. *Scottish Forestry* **44** (4), 257–265.

VAN DORSSER, J.C. and ROOK, D.A. (1972). Conditioning of *Radiata pine* seedlings by undercutting and wrenching: description of methods, equipment and seedling response. *New Zealand Journal of Forestry Science* **17,** 61–73.

Chapter 9
Container production of tree seedlings

R. L. Jinks

The majority of forest tree seedlings are raised on open-ground nurseries and are dispatched in a bare-root condition; however a small but increasing number of plants are produced in containers, the technique having a place for producing plants for smaller planting schemes and for stock of special genetic quality (Mason and Biggin, 1988; Mason and Hollingsworth, 1989; Mason and Jinks, 1990). A container-grown plant is one which has been raised in a cell, bag or pot filled with an artificial growing medium and has growing medium surrounding the roots when the seedling is planted out. The term 'cell-grown' is often used to distinguish tree seedlings raised in modular trays from the larger container plants which are produced for ornamental planting and which are grown for more than one year on the nursery.

Although container seedlings can be more expensive to grow than bare-root stock, the root systems are less likely to be damaged during lifting and transport, and planted seedlings may have a better chance of survival in certain situations. Container production also offers several advantages for the nurseryman. The production period is short, allowing a quick response to changes in demand; if necessary two or more crops could be sown each year in appropriately equipped nurseries. Nurseries exclusively producing containers, whatever their size, are not confined to sites with a suitable soil type and there is less risk of a build up of soil problems. However, a higher capital investment is required in growing facilities and ancillary equipment (e.g. polytunnels, irrigation systems, benching, etc.).

Container production offers opportunities for the more precise control of growth through the regulation of mineral nutrition, spacing, temperature, irrigation, light intensity and day length. Such scheduled production should lead to more uniform and reproducible growth as long as stock is not overcrowded. This chapter describes the equipment and techniques required for the production of tree seedlings in modular trays.

9.1 Container systems

There are several types of proprietary container systems which are specifically designed for growing tree seedlings, most of these have originated in North America and Scandinavia. A detailed discussion on the types of container available in the United States and Canada can be found in Landis *et al.* (1990); (see also Hollingsworth and Mason, 1989).

The Japanese paper pot is a degradable container system which is used in the UK for the production of Corsican pine seedlings. The paper is bonded together with a soluble adhesive forming a honeycomb pattern of cells; the pots are readily separated and are planted with the paper still surrounding the media and roots. Three different grades of paper are available which have different breakdown times, the medium resistance, F grade, is suitable for forestry use. The Ecopot system is similar to Japanese paper pots except that the paper is coated with a layer of plastic and is stripped off the root plugs at planting.

Most of the non-degradable systems are made from moulded plastic or polystyrene. All have slits or ribs on the inner walls of the cells to prevent root coiling and they have large holes at the base for drainage and to encourage air pruning of roots when the trays are placed on mesh covered benches or pallets. The cells are arranged in pre-formed plastic trays (e.g. Rigipots and Styroblocks) or as hinged books (Rootrainers) and are offered in a range of cell volumes and numbers of cells per tray (Plates 18–20).

Several factors influence the choice of container system. The design of the cells must be biologically suitable for growing tree seedlings and must include features for preventing root coiling and for encouraging root pruning at the base of the cells. The cell volume must match the final size of the seedling and this will be a function of both the species being grown and the duration of the growing period. Volumes of 50–100 cm^3 appear adequate for most conifers, while larger volumes of up to 300 cm^3 are appropriate for many broadleaved species. In 'Honeycomb' systems with water-permeable walls such as Japanese paper pots, water is able to move laterally between pots, compensating to some extent for any unevenness of watering in the polyhouse.

The spacing between the cells also influences the morphology of the seedlings, particularly the root collar diameter (RCD). Although close spacing maximises the number of seedlings able to be grown in a tunnel, some unwanted consequences may result from such spacing.

- It increases the competition for light between neighbouring seedlings, reduces seedling dry weight and RCD and may 'draw up', i.e. increase seedling height (e.g. Timmis and Tanaka, 1976);

- it can encourage the development of shade leaves, and cause the production of distorted stems, particularly along the edges of the trays;

- close spacing may also encourage fungal diseases and create problems with watering broadleaved species and faster growing conifers.

Most broadleaved species require a wider spacing than conifers because of the width and density of the leaf canopy. However, the larger volumes of the cells which are selected for these species usually result in a wider spacing between the cells in the trays. Exact relationships between cell volume, spacing and growth have yet to be determined for most species grown under UK conditions.

Besides the important biological considerations, other factors have also to be considered when selecting a suitable container system. Systems such as paper pot containers are used only once, a fresh supply being required for each crop of tree seedlings. Most plastic tray systems are designed to be used for raising more than one crop, the tree seedlings can be dispatched either in their trays or removed from them at the nursery and packaged for transport to the customer. If plants are sent out in the trays, a reliable procedure is needed to ensure their prompt return to the nursery after planting. The trays should also be robust enough to withstand any mistreatment after they have left the nursery. Reusable trays have to be cleaned, sterilised and then stored until required for the next crop. Trays can be cleaned by scrubbing or with high pressure hoses, and they should be sterilised by dipping in a suitable solution recommended by the tray manufacturer.

9.2 Nursery facilities

Many of the facilities and items of equipment required for the efficient production of container-grown seedlings are typical of any intensive horticultural nursery. Further details on nursery layout and facilities can be found in Stanley and Toogood (1981) and Macdonald (1986), only the particular requirements for growing trees being emphasised in this section.

9.2.1 Plastic tunnels and glasshouses

Container seedlings are most commonly grown in plastic tunnels. Glasshouses are equally suitable though more expensive. The tunnels can be either arranged as a series of separate structures or linked together as multi-span tunnels to enclose a much larger area. They should have wide doors to permit easy access for tractors and other equipment and the sides should be near vertical to allow full use of the covered area.

The floors of the tunnels should be isolated from the soil by covering with porous materials such as woven plastic sheets, gravel, or chipped bark, or even concrete block. Bare soil will turn to mud under the frequent irrigation regime and traffic inside the tunnels. Uncovered soil will also encourage the development of weeds and diseases.

Ventilation

Tunnels and glasshouses for raising tree seedlings must have an efficient ventilation system to prevent heat injury during sensitive stages of production such as germination and early seedling growth. Adequate ventilation is also needed for promoting hardening-off of the crop after the seedlings have reached their required size. The sides of tunnels should be clad with a netting material which extends well above the height of the crop and supporting benching, to provide side ventilation. Wind-up polythene skirts should also be installed so that the tunnel can be closed up in colder weather to maintain warmer temperatures for seedling growth. Tunnels which have variable roof vents are also available. A more expensive but flexible option is to install forced ventilation using thermostatically-controlled electric fans. The ability to shade areas within a tunnel will also reduce the heat load on containers during hot weather, particularly during germination.

9.2.2 Irrigation and liquid fertilisation systems

The volume of the cells used for raising tree seedlings is small and this limits the amount of water which can be stored between irrigations. Hence, frequent irrigation is required during hot weather, particularly when the crop has a large leaf area. Tunnels must be equipped with an efficient irrigation system which has the capacity to deliver sufficient water uniformly to the growing crop in a reasonable time. Hand watering is only practical when production is on a very small scale. It is very important that the irrigation water is evenly applied to ensure that all seedlings receive adequate water since the cells of many container systems are isolated from one another so that there is no transfer of water from wetter to drier cells. An inefficient irrigation system will result in some cells being overwatered while others remain dry. Overwatering causes leaching loss of nutrients; sufficient to bring about short-term waterlogging may encourage development of disease. The effects of irregular water distribution can often be seen as rings or zones of uneven seedling growth within a tunnel.

Irrigation systems in polyhouses fall into two categories: mobile and fixed systems. Further information on the design principles of irrigation systems can be found in Landis *et al.* (1989).

Mobile irrigation systems

Mobile systems consist of a horizontal boom with a series of regularly spaced nozzles. The boom is moved back and forth above a group of benches by an electric motor. These systems produce an even distribution of water and the nozzle types can be interchanged for different purposes such as applying pesticides. The quantity of water which is delivered is determined by the nozzle output per unit of time and the speed and number of passes which the boom makes over the crop.

Fixed systems

Fixed overhead systems consist of a series of irrigation lines with sprinklers or nozzles inserted at regular intervals to form a grid pattern (Plate 21). The distribution of water tends to be less even than for mobile booms but fixed systems should prove satisfactory if they are properly designed, installed and maintained. Fixed systems can waste more water than boom systems and drips falling from the nozzles on to the cells beneath after the irrigation has been switched off can also be a problem. It is recommended that advice is sought from an experienced irrigation supplier or consultant about the design of an appropriate irrigation system to ensure that the system fully meets the requirements for raising tree seedlings.

The performance of any irrigation system should be tested regularly to check both the quantity of water being applied and the distribution pattern. This can be simply done by catching water applied in a given period of time in a series of containers with similar size aperture, arranged in a grid pattern throughout a tunnel or bay. The results of such tests provide essential information for timing the duration of irrigation and also should identify any dry spots which may need supplementary hand watering or modifications to the sprinkler pattern.

Container seedlings are most commonly fertilised by applying liquid feed through the irrigation system either at every watering or at less frequent intervals. A range of dilutors and injectors of varying degrees of sophistication and cost are available for use in horticulture and the principles of operation of the different types are discussed by Bunt (1988) and Landis *et al.* (1989). The injection system must be compatible with the irrigation system and is usually installed on a by-pass line so that either irrigation water or liquid feed can be applied through the irrigation system.

9.2.3 Benching and pallets

One of the features of growing tree seedlings in containers is that the roots are air pruned at the base of the cells. This prevents roots from growing out of the containers and can also promote the development of a more fibrous root system. Seedling containers are designed with large drainage holes and must have an unrestricted air space beneath the trays to permit air pruning. The trays should be raised at least 15 cm above the ground by supporting them on mesh benches, trestles, or by some other means which exposes the base of the cells to air. Benches which are at about waist height are convenient for manual operations such as thinning seedlings, while low mesh-covered pallets placed on the ground

allow groups of trays to be readily transported by fork lift. The supporting system must be constructed of durable material and capable of withstanding the weight of full trays of recently watered containers (Plate 22).

9.2.4 Hardening-off and holding areas

Once stock has reached its desired size, it can be hardened off and held outside the tunnels before despatch. If moved outside during the growing season, some species may make more growth before the end of the season.

A suitable standing area should be constructed with a clean base, equipped with irrigation and wind protection. Alternatively, houses can be fitted with sides that can be wound up or removed; this avoids the need to find an additional hardening-off area.

9.2.5 Mixers and other machinery

Operations such as mixing the growing medium, filling trays and sowing seed can be carried out manually, but for a larger scale of production some or all of these procedures can be mechanised. These operations should be carefully integrated together into an efficient production line which makes the best use of labour and materials and prevents bottlenecks forming.

Suitable buildings are of course required for housing these operations and also for the storage of trays, ingredients for growing media, etc.

9.3 Growing media

A good quality growing medium is essential for successfully raising tree seedlings in containers. The medium should:

- drain well after irrigation and so be well aerated;
- hold adequate reserves of water for plant growth after irrigation;
- have a pH appropriate for the species being grown;
- hold reserves of mineral nutrients;
- be free from harmful insects, diseases and weeds;

- be free flowing to allow cells, particularly small ones, to be filled easily whether manually or mechanically;
- retain its physical structure during the lifetime of the crop and not decompose.

Thus a medium suitable for growing tree seedlings in containers has to have an adequate physical structure which is determined by the bulk ingredients used in the mix, and it also has to have an appropriate nutrient content which is determined by the amounts of added fertilisers. Detailed information on the physical and chemical properties of growing media are presented in Bunt (1988) and Landis *et al.* (1990).

Growing media can either be bought in ready mixed or made up on the nursery from the basic ingredients. Proprietary media have several advantages including the saving of time, labour and facilities needed for making up the media at the nursery. However, on-site mixing allows more flexibility in adjusting the composition of the medium to include new materials and recommendations; the grower can also experiment and adapt his mix to suit particular situations and crops. Mixing on a small scale can be carried out by hand but mixing by machine is far more efficient. It is important not to over-mix a medium since this can destroy its physical structure and also damage the coating of any controlled-release fertilisers in the mix. Two typical mixes which have been found suitable for use in containers are shown in Table 9.1.

9.3.1 Bulk ingredients

Peat

The main bulk ingredient used in container media is peat, and this is often amended with a coarse material such as perlite. It is likely that other materials will be developed as an alternative to peat in the future. Relatively undecomposed, medium grade sphagnum peats are generally suitable as they have a high 'total pore space' (TPS). Such peats have a high 'available water holding capacity' (AWHC), yet there are sufficient larger pores

Table 9.1 Growing media suitable for use with a liquid feed programme

Bulk ingredients (%)	
For general use:	
Medium grade sphagnum peat	100
For overwintering:	
Medium grade sphagnum peat	75
Perlite or vermiculite	25
Fertilisers (kg m^{-3})	
Ground magnesium limestone	2.5
Ammonium nitrate	0.2
Superphosphate	0.75
Potassium nitrate	0.4
Frit WM 253A	0.3

which will drain after irrigation and provide aeration (AFP – the 'air filled porosity'). The more decomposed sedge peats are best avoided since they are too fine and can become waterlogged; these peats also tend to break down quickly and so lose their physical structure. Fibrous peats should also be avoided for use in small cells since they can make filling cells difficult. Suitable medium grade peats are clean to handle; peats which leave the hands dirty are too decomposed to make good media.

Up to 25% of a relatively coarse amendment is often included in container mixes to change the physical properties of the medium, particularly if a crop will be exposed to rainfall during winter. Materials which contain fine particles (<0.5 mm) should not be used since they will reduce the AFP of the peat and so increase the risk of waterlogging. The main materials used as amendments include perlite, vermiculite, pine bark, and sands and grits.

Perlite

Perlite is available in several grades and the seed grade is suitable for container media. Perlite does not contain any plant nutrients nor does it absorb them from added fertilisers. Mixes containing perlite have a lower AWHC and are well aerated.

Vermiculite

Vermiculite is also available in several grades and it contains some available nutrients such as potassium and magnesium and can absorb these and other nutrient ions such as ammonium nitrogen from added fertilisers. The industrial grades used for insulation are not suitable for horticultural use. Vermiculite has a high total porosity and can hold water and air; while the particles are less stable than perlite, they should last long enough for tree seedling production.

Other amendments

Particles of pine bark can also be used as an amendment; such bark must be stacked and aged before use, to eliminate any toxicity. Coarse lime-free sands and grits can also be used in container mixes; in horticulture, these are usually added to increase the weight of a mix but this is generally not desirable in forest seedling production.

9.3.2 Base fertilisers

Lime and pH

Peat is a naturally acidic material and the pH of growing medium is commonly raised by the addition of ground limestone. Ground dolomitic limestone is often used because it supplies magnesium as well as calcium for plant growth. It is common practice to maintain the media pH between 5.5 and 6.5; the lower value is often recommended for growing conifers while the nearer neutral pH is advised for raising broadleaves. However, there is evidence that for many species there is no advantage to liming organic media above pH 5.5 (Wright and Niemiera, 1987), and it has been suggested that the addition of limestone should be discontinued since pH adjustment and the supply of calcium and magnesium can be efficiently carried out by liquid feeding (Landis *et al.*, 1989).

In some situations the addition of dolomitic lime can have an adverse effect on growth. Douglas fir seedlings can develop distorted and chlorotic shoots in media containing dolomitic lime (Dangerfield 1978; Dumroese *et al.*, 1990).

More research is needed to investigate fully the response of container seedlings to the addition of lime to container media before detailed recommendations can be made. However, the pH of container media should not be allowed to increase above 5.5 to reduce the risk of chlorosis developing. The amount of lime required to raise the pH of a medium depends on the types and quantities of material used in the mix. Mixes containing a large proportion of an amendment such as perlite will require less lime than one composed predominantly of peat. The lime requirement also varies between different types of peat (Bunt, 1988). The quantities listed in Table 9.1 are applicable to Irish sphagnum peat.

Low lime rates should also be specified when ordering proprietary mixes; media formulated for growing ericaceous plants such as *Rhododendron* spp. should be suitable. If dolomitic limestone is completely omitted from a medium, then it is important to include magnesium and calcium in the liquid feed.

Micronutrients

The micronutrient elements such as copper and iron which are required by plants in very small amounts are usually added to the medium either in a slow-release form as powdered glass frits or as soluble chemical salts. Some controlled-release fertilisers also contain micronutrients.

Nitrogen, phosphorus and potassium (N, P, K)

In most soil-less media, all seedlings' requirements for nitrogen, phosphorus and potassium have to be supplied as fertilisers. However, if all of the fertiliser requirement was applied as soluble fertilisers at mixing, the resulting high levels of dissolved salts in the medium would impair germination and damage seedlings. In addition, these nutrients are not readily retained by soil-less media and so will be leached out if excess irrigation water is applied. In practice, these elements can be applied either as slow-release fertilisers supplying their nutrients over a period of time or by frequent feeding with a dilute solution of soluble fertilisers.

A small amount of soluble fertiliser is often included in the mix to provide a starter supply of nutrients for early seedling growth before liquid feeding commences. Suitable fertilisers include ammonium nitrate, superphosphate and potassium nitrate; these are added in quantities which are unlikely to cause salt injury provided that the medium is not allowed to dry out.

Controlled-release fertilisers

Coated controlled-release fertilisers (CRF) can also be used as either a base dressing in combination with a liquid feed programme, or as the main source of the major elements. Several formulations are available, designed to last from 3 to 19 months. The rate of release from these fertilisers is governed by the nature of the coating and by temperature; the release rate increases at warmer temperatures. Because of the small size of tree seedling containers, it is difficult to obtain an even distribution of the relatively few large fertiliser granules required in each cell. However, two formulations of 'Osmocote' have a smaller granule size than other CRFs and so permit a more even distribution of granules between cells. Two longevities are available: 2–3 month (18-6-12) and 5–6 month (18-6-11).

Once a CRF has been incorporated in the mix, the grower has little control over the supply of nutrients since the fertiliser will continue releasing nutrients until the fertiliser salts have become depleted.

New formulations of controlled-release fertiliser come out on the market from time to time and it is always advisable to test any new material or procedure on a small scale to determine if there are any potential problems or whether the new product offers any significant advantages.

9.4 Liquid feeds

Applying nutrients as a solution through the irrigation system is the commonest method for fertilising container tree seedlings. The amounts of nutrient which are applied to the crop can be precisely controlled and varied to suit different stages of growth with little risk of damaging plants through over-fertilising. However, the nutrient solution has to be evenly applied to the seedlings; a well-designed irrigation system and injector or dilutor is therefore essential. Liquid feeding also requires some skill to mix the stock solutions and to monitor the performance of the feeding programme.

There are several proprietary liquid feeds available and these are convenient to use because the concentrated feed is already prepared as a powder or liquid. The concentrate is dissolved or diluted to make a stock solution which is then injected into the irrigation water at the required dilution. The alternative to proprietary feeds is to make up the concentrated stock solutions on the nursery from soluble chemicals. This is cheaper and allows more flexibility in the amounts of nutrients which are applied to the crop. In addition, the pH of the nutrient solution can also be adjusted by using acids such as nitric acid as one of the ingredients.

There are three criteria which have to be considered in selecting or formulating a liquid feed programme:

- the composition of the feed;
- the balance between the elements in the feed;
- the concentration at which the solution is applied to the seedlings.

9.4.1 Composition

Most solutions will contain N, P and K, and many will include Mg, Ca, S and micronutrients. Micronutrients should not be required in the nutrient solution if these have been included (e.g. as frit) in the growing medium unless a deficiency is subsequently diagnosed. Similarly Mg may not be required if dolomitic limestone has been used as the source of lime. The irrigation water may contain significant concentrations of certain nutrient ions such as NO_3^-, Ca^{++}, and Mg^{++} and these should be taken into account when formulating the feed; a detailed description of the appropriate calculations can be found in Landis *et al.* (1989). The form of nitrogen in the solution can also be important; both the ammonium and nitrate forms should be present, the proportion of ammonium-N not exceeding 50% of the total nitrogen concentration (Landis *et al.*, 1989).

9.4.2 Nutrient balance

Imbalances in the proportion of the nutrient elements can affect the pH of the medium and also cause interference in the uptake and utilisation of certain ions, or even lead to the development of nutrient toxicity if certain nutrients are in great excess. The ratios of nutrients are usually set relative to nitrogen and the ratios of 100N:15P:80K determined by Ingestad (1979) are often used in nutrient solutions for applying to container tree seedlings. In proprietary feeds the phosphorus and potassium contents are expressed as the proportion or percentage of the oxides P_2O_5 and K_2O in the concentrate, while the nitrogen content refers to the proportion of elemental N. (Factors for converting from the oxide to the elemental form are 0.436 for P_2O_5 to P and 0.83 for K_2O to K).

9.4.3 Nutrient concentration

The concentration of the final diluted solution is usually expressed as the concentration of nitrogen in the feed in p.p.m. (parts per million). Typical concentrations range from 50 to 200 p.p.m. N, the choice of concentration depending on the stage of growth and the frequency of feeding. When applying nutrients with every irrigation, 50 p.p.m. may be applied during the establishment phase and the concentration increased to 100–150 p.p.m. during the period of rapid growth. The higher concentrations of 150–200 p.p.m. are applied when feeding at less frequent intervals.

9.5 *Seedling production*

9.5.1 Preparation of seed for sowing

It is important that the highest quality seed is obtained for container production both in terms of purity and percentage germination;

seed purity is particularly important if the seed is to be sown by machine and is not to clog it. Seed should be correctly pretreated to break dormancy and to promote rapid, even germination. Regimes for seed pretreatment are covered in Chapter 5, section 5.7.

9.5.2 Seed sowing

It is essential that a high proportion of the cells produce a usable seedling and each cell must be sown with at least one germinable seed. Unfortunately the percentage germination of tree seed seldom approaches 100% and, particularly with some broadleaved species, the final percentage germination can be quite low and unpredictable. There are four options for achieving high stocking rates in containers.

- Seed with a high germination capacity, can be sown mechanically at the rate of one seed per cell (Plate 23).

- Cells can be sown with more than one seed and the seedlings thinned to a single plant per cell. This method is suitable for many conifer species where the percentage germination of a seed lot is reasonably predictable from laboratory tests. Table 9.2 gives simple guidelines. For a more detailed discussion of multiple seed sowing, see Tinus and McDonald (1979), Schwartz (1993), and Wenny (1993).

- Multiple sowing is not practical for trees which have large seeds because of the narrow diameter of the cells. Seed of these species can be allowed to begin germination during pretreatment (chitting), the germinating seed can then be separated out at intervals and sown into the cells.

Table 9.2 Number of seeds to sow per cell as a function of percentage germination

Percentage germination	Seeds per cell
85–100	1
75–85	2
60–75	3

(*Source:* Tinus and McDonald, 1979)

- Seed of species whose percentage germination is very low or unknown, for example exotic species, can be germinated, after pretreatment, in seed trays and the seedlings can then be pricked out into individual cells.

The procedure for sowing seed into containers depends on the size of the seed, whether it has been pretreated and, if appropriate, on its stage of germination.

Small ungerminated seed

Small seed which is sown directly into the cells should first be surface dried in air after pretreatment; this makes it more freeflowing and easier to handle. The seed is sown on to the surface of the growing medium and then covered with a layer of lime-free grit to a depth equivalent to the thickness of the seed to prevent drying out. The sown trays can be covered with white polythene sheet or a woven polypropylene sheet to maintain high humidities. The covers are usually removed once about 10% of the seeds have germinated.

Chitted seed

Chitted seed should be sown as soon as signs of germination are visible, usually when the seed coat splits and the radicle begins to emerge. The cells should be partially filled with growing medium to leave sufficient room for the seed and its covering of compost. The chitted seed should be placed on to the surface of the medium with the radicle pointing down, the cells are then filled with media sufficient just to cover the top surface of the seed. If germination is allowed to progress too far when the seed is chitting then great care must be taken not to damage the emerged radicles and the seedlings will have to be carefully pricked out into the medium. Cells sown with chitted seed are not normally covered with polythene or other materials since the seedlings should emerge at a rapid rate.

Protection

Sown seed must be protected from predation by birds, squirrels and rodents. All side vents and doors, if they are left open for ventilation, must be covered with bird-proof netting until the seedlings have fully emerged. Baited traps should also be set out among the trays to catch rodents.

Control of temperature

The seed of many species will begin to germinate at relatively cool temperatures normally experienced at sowing times between March and May. Earlier sowing dates usually require provision for frost protection to prevent freezing injury in cold weather. High temperatures after mid-May can limit later sowing unless the trays can be kept cool by shading and venting.

The environment has to be carefully controlled during germination and early seedling growth, in particular the temperature and the moisture relations of the germinating seed. The temperature of seed sown in containers can fluctuate widely since the upper layer of the medium, which is where the seed is situated, experiences the largest variation in temperature. Similarly, most of the water lost by evaporation from cells occurs at the surface of the medium and so these layers can also undergo wide fluctuations in moisture content.

To prevent damage occurring to the germinating seed, the growing medium temperature should not be allowed to fall below 0°C or exceed 30°C. It is important to measure the temperature of the medium, rather than just the air temperature, to determine if measures have to be taken to reduce the heat load on containers. In tunnels, the temperature of the medium may be several degrees higher than the air temperature during hot weather because of the absorption of solar radiation by the medium surface and the trays, especially if they are made from dark coloured plastic. Medium temperature can be easily checked by measuring the temperature at 1 cm below the surface using a hand-held electronic thermometer.

Several steps can be taken to cool the growing medium and reduce the rate at which the surface layer of the medium dries out.

Covering the surface of the medium with light coloured grit will reflect part of the incoming radiation; covering the trays with white polythene or a spun polypropylene material will also reduce the heat load at the medium surface as well as help retain moisture. Light coloured trays will reflect some of the incident heat radiation and so be cooler than dark coloured trays. Trays made from insulating materials like polystyrene will conduct less heat into the medium than thinner denser plastic trays. Tunnels should be adequately ventilated and can be shaded externally with shade-cloth in very hot weather. Frequent light irrigations during hot weather are required to replace water lost by evaporation. A high water content in the medium not only keeps the germinating seed moist but also provides a source of water for lowering the temperature of the growing medium by evaporative cooling.

9.5.3 Seedling establishment

During the earliest stages of seedling growth, it is important to avoid overwatering since reduced aeration in the medium can adversely affect root growth. Similarly 'damping off' may also become a problem. Liquid feeding is often started when the first true leaves have emerged, the original dressing of soluble fertiliser providing enough nutrients for the early stages of seedling growth. The exact time to start feeding will depend on the species, the amount of base fertiliser included in the medium and the amount of leaching that has occurred from excess irrigation. Species with large seeds can make appreciable growth using stored reserves and so are less dependent on the amounts of nutrients available early on.

9.5.4 Seedling growth

Once seedlings have become established they enter a period of rapid growth; correct irrigation, fertilisation and environmental control are essential to ensure the production of quality seedlings. High temperatures and humidities must be avoided, seedlings must not be exposed to water stress or allowed to become nutrient deficient or over-fertilised.

Control of irrigation

Container-grown seedlings require frequent irrigation during hot weather because of the limited water-storage capacity of the cells. There are several methods for determining when to irrigate. The simplest method is by careful observation of the growing medium and the condition of the seedlings. The moisture status of the medium is assessed by observing the ease with which water can be squeezed from a sample of medium and relating this to the status of the seedlings. This method is widely practised but does require experience and is subjective.

A more objective method for measuring the moisture status of the medium is to weigh a sample of trays, since the weight will decrease as water is lost by transpiration and evaporation. This technique requires a reasonably accurate weighing machine such as a pan balance on to which a tray can be placed or a spring balance from which trays can be hung. The trays are first weighed after excess irrigation and when drainage has ceased. This determines the 'saturation' weight. The trays are then weighed at regular intervals until it is determined that the seedlings require watering, this weight is the weight at which irrigation should be initiated. The water status of the seedlings can be determined either by examining the seedlings or, more accurately, by measuring the water potential (degree of water stress) of the seedlings using a pressure bomb (Landis *et al.*, 1989). To avoid problems of waterlogging or leaching of nutrients, trays are not normally irrigated to or beyond full saturation weight unless excess salts are being flushed out of the medium. The 'irrigation' weight can also be calculated from the water-release curve of the particular growing medium; this is a physical measurement made in a laboratory, of the availability to plants of water in the medium.

Control of liquid feeding

The frequency with which liquid feed is applied during growth depends on the rate of nutrient uptake by seedlings (i.e. the growth rate) and the rate at which nutrients are lost from the growing medium by leaching. Ideally the concentration of soluble nutrients in the medium should not be allowed to fluctuate widely; consequently, infrequent applications of a high concentration feed should be avoided.

If more nutrients are applied than the seedlings can absorb, the concentration of soluble salts can increase to high levels and cause salt damage to seedlings. To avoid this problem, containers should be periodically over-irrigated to ensure that a proportion of the nutrient salts are flushed out to prevent salt build up. The application of nutrients at a moderate concentration (50–100 p.p.m. N) with every irrigation is the simplest way of maintaining a relatively constant supply of nutrients in the growing medium.

In the UK, nutrients are more commonly applied at a higher concentration (150–200 p.p.m. N) in the liquid feed at set intervals between irrigations, typically once or twice weekly during periods of active growth. However, time-tabled feeding may not always supply adequate amounts of nutrients. It is advisable, therefore, to check the nutrient status of the growing medium periodically before applying liquid feed, to determine if the frequency of application is adequate.

Nutrient status of the growing medium

The concentrations of specific elements in samples of growing medium can be analysed by a soil science laboratory or by using a proprietary nutrient analysis kit. Laboratories usually provide guidelines for the interpretation of the analytical results. Very low concentrations of nutrients would indicate that feeding is too infrequent, assuming that the concentration of nutrients in the solution is correct and that the feed is being applied evenly for long enough. High concentrations of nutrients would suggest that too much feed is being applied by the fertiliser programme.

9.5.5 Conditioning seedlings

Once seedlings have reached their desired size during mid to late summer, steps must be taken to promote the cessation of growth, to encourage the onset of dormancy and to increase the hardiness of shoots and roots. Many species will cease growth and set bud naturally during late summer and such seedlings should be encouraged to remain dormant by stopping liquid feeding or switching to a low nitrogen feed, reducing watering and by maintaining cooler temperatures either by ventilation or by moving the plants out to a suitable outdoor standing area.

Other species can continue growing well into autumn if they remain in a productive environment under protection. This can delay shipment and may also reduce the degree of frost resistance of the plants. Hardening-off can be encouraged in several ways, such as by reducing or stopping the nutrient supply, and by exposing seedlings to mild drought, short days, and cool temperatures. A common and relatively simple method for promoting dormancy is to reduce or stop liquid feeding during late summer and to move the seedlings outside the tunnels to a prepared standing area. The combination of declining day length, cooler temperatures and reduced nutrient supply encourages the development of dormancy.

Exposure of seedlings to drought can also hasten bud set in certain species such as Douglas fir. However, the drying of the medium has to be carefully controlled to avoid damaging the seedlings. Ideally, the water status of the seedlings during drying should be carefully monitored by measuring shoot water potentials with a pressure bomb, but in practice the water status of the medium and seedlings is usually assessed subjectively.

Long periods of cloudy weather can reduce the rate of transpiration and so greatly increase the time taken before seedlings become exposed to mild water stress. Uneven drying of trays across a tunnel can also be a problem since some trays may dry more quickly than others and so require hand watering.

Artificial reduction in day length using blackout systems offers a precise method for inducing dormancy in species such as spruces and Douglas fir. The advantages of using pho-

Plate 13. *Precision drill sowing by Summit sower, showing:*
i) vacuum pump on tool frame immediately behind tractor,
ii) smoothing roller,
iii) (end visible, to right of white plate) vacuum roller which picks up seed at predetermined spacing from
iv) eight seed trays,
v) rollers pressing seed into soil surface. (39375)

Plate 14. *Seed sown using the precision sower. (A1002)*

Plate 15. *Undercutting. View from rear showing undercutter out of the ground with vertical reciprocating arms and trough shaped shares to restore the edges of seedbeds after the disruption by the reciprocating arms.* (E8272)

Plate 16. *Undercutting. View showing at far end of bed from left to right:*
i) depth control wheel,
ii) vertical coulter cutting track for
iii) small disc loosening soil ahead of vertical reciprocating arm carrying undercutting blade. (39556)

Plate 17. *Vertical discs cutting laterals between drilled seedlings. Position of discs controlled by steersman seated on tool-frame.* (39550)

toperiod to induce dormancy over drought and nutrient stressing are that seedlings are not stressed, crop response is uniform, and it is relatively easy to impose blackout treatments (Eastham, 1990).

9.5.6 Winter protection

If container seedlings have to be held at the nursery over winter it is important to protect them from freezing injury. The roots are particularly susceptible to damage because the roots of many young trees and shrubs are less frost resistant than the shoots; typically roots are injured when media temperatures fall below −5 to −15°C (Studer *et al.*, 1978).

Several features of container design increase the risks of frost damage during cold weather. Factors such as shallow depth and the isolation of the individual cells can increase the danger of media temperatures falling to damaging levels. The most certain way of preventing winter injury is to over-winter seedlings in tunnels provided with supplementary heat to prevent temperatures falling below 0°C.

If seedlings have to remain in unheated tunnels or outside during freezing weather, there are several measures which can be taken to reduce the risk of freezing injury occurring. It is important to ensure that the growing medium is well watered before the onset of freezing weather. While ice is forming, heat is released (the latent heat of fusion), which prevents the temperature of the medium from falling below 0°C. The root temperature will only fall below 0°C when all the water has become frozen, hence the higher the water content, the longer this delay will last.

Trays should be packed tight together and placed directly on the ground to reduce heat loss and allow heat to be conducted into the trays from below. Surrounding the trays with straw bales and covering them with materials such as polythene sheets, fleece, or a reflective thermal screen, will also reduce the rates of radiative and convective heat loss. Any snow which may cover trays overwintered outside should not be cleared away since snow is an excellent insulator.

The insulation provided by polystyrene trays will also reduce the rate of heat loss during cold weather and should be considered for nurseries where seedlings are likely to be exposed to sub-zero temperatures for long periods.

9.5.7 Handling and despatch

Cell-grown plants have the advantage over bare-rooted stock that the growing medium greatly reduces the risk of root damage between nursery and permanent planting site. Nevertheless, in other respects, the plants require the same care and protection as for bare-rooted plants. These requirements are fully described in Chapter 14.

REFERENCES

BUNT, A.C. (1988). *Media and mixes for container-grown plants: a manual on the preparation and use of growing media for pot plants.* Unwin Hyman, London.

DANGERFIELD, J.A. (1978). Influence of lime incorporated in soil mix on growth of Douglas-fir. *Fisheries and Environment Canada Bi-monthly Research Notes* **34** (1), 1–2.

DUMROESE, R.K., THOMPSON, G. and WENNY, D.L. (1990). Lime-amended growing medium causes seedling growth distortions. *Tree Planters' Notes* **41** (3), 12–17.

EASTHAM, A.M. (1990). Regulation of seedling height in container-grown spruce using photoperiod control. In *Target Seedling Symposium: Proceedings, Combined Meeting of the Western Forest Nursery Associations;* 1990 August 13–17; Roseburg, Oregon. Eds R. Rose, S. J. Cambell, and T. D. Landis. Gen. Tech. Rep. RM–200. US Department of Agriculture, Forest Service, Rocky Mountain Forest and Range Experiment Station, Ft Collins, CO. (286 pp.)

HOLLINGSWORTH, M.K. and MASON, W.L. (1989). *Provisional regimes for growing containerised Douglas fir and Sitka spruce.* Forestry Commission Research Information Note 141. Forestry Commission, Edinburgh.

INGESTAD, T. (1979). Mineral nutrient requirement of *Pinus sylvestris* and *Picea abies* seedlings. *Physiologia Plantarum* **45**, 373–380.

LANDIS, T.D., TINUS, R.W., McDONALD, S.E. and BARNETT, J.P. (1989). *Seedling nutrition and irrigation,* Vol. 4 of *The container tree nursery manual.* Agriculture Handbook 674. US Department of Agriculture, Forest Service, Washington, DC. (119 pp.)

LANDIS, T.D., TINUS, R.W., McDONALD, S.E. and BARNETT, J.P. (1990). *Containers and growing media,* Vol. 2 of *The container tree nursery manual.* Agriculture Handbook 674. US Department of Agriculture, Forest Service, Washington, DC. (88pp.)

LUCAS, R.E. and DAVIS, J.K. (1961). Relationships between pH values of organic soils and availabilities of 12 plant nutrients. *Soil Science* **92**, 177–182.

MacDONALD, B. (1986). *Practical woody plant propagation for nursery growers.* Batsford, London. (669 pp.)

MASON, W.L. and BIGGIN, P. (1988). Comparative performance of containerised and bare-root Sitka spruce and lodgepole pine seedlings in upland Britain. *Forestry* **61** (2), 149–163.

MASON, W.L. and HOLLINGSWORTH, M.K. (1989). *Use of containerised conifer seedlings in upland forestry.* Research Information Note 142. Forestry Commission, Edinburgh.

MASON, W.L. and JINKS, R.L. (1990). *Use of containers as a method for raising tree seedlings.* Forestry Commission Research Information Note 179. Forestry Commission, Edinburgh.

SCHWARTZ, M. (1993). Germination math: calculating the number of seeds necessary per cavity for a given number of live seedlings. *Tree Planters' Notes* **44** (2), 19–20.

STANLEY, J and TOOGOOD, A. (1981). *The modern nurseryman.* Faber and Faber, London.

STUDER, E.J., STEPONKUS, P.L., GOOD, G. L. and WIEST, S.C. (1978). Root hardiness of container-grown ornamentals. *HortScience* **13**, 172–74.

TIMMIS, R. and TANAKA, Y. (1976). Effects of container density and plant water stress on growth and cold hardiness of Douglas fir seedlings. *Forest Science* **22**, 167–172.

TINUS, R.W. and McDONALD, S.E. (1979). *How to grow tree seedlings in containers in greenhouses.* Gen. Tech. Rep. RM–60. US Department of Agriculture, Forest Service, Rocky Mountain Forest and Range Experiment Station, Ft Collins, CO.

WENNY, D.L. (1993). Calculating filled and empty cells based on numbers of seeds sown per cell: a microcomputer application. *Tree Planters' Notes* **44** (1), 49–52.

WRIGHT, R.D. and NIEMIERA, A.X. (1987). Nutrition of container-grown woody nursery crops. *Horticultural Reviews* **9**, 75–101.

Chapter 10

Vegetative propagation

W. L. Mason and R. L. Jinks

Introduction

Vegetative propagation is the term used to describe the production of plants by asexual means. Propagules are placed in an environment favourable for development so that each becomes an independent plant. Techniques include the rooting of cuttings and layers, grafting and budding, separation and division. Cuttings are usually made from shoots but roots may also be used. The original seedling plant from which vegetative propagules are taken is known as the 'ortet'; the cuttings taken from a particular ortet are known as 'ramets'. The attraction of vegetative propagation is that all the ramets are genetically identical to the ortet and potentially have similar form, timber quality, foliage colour and so forth. The resulting population of plants with the same genotype is known as a 'clone'.

Plants of tree species that are used in British forestry have generally been raised from seed. The basic reason for this is that there are only a few species which can be vegetatively propagated without the use of comparatively sophisticated propagation facilities. Species which can be easily rooted using stem cuttings include poplars, willows, London plane, some elms, Lawson cypress, western red cedar, clones of Leyland cypress, *Cryptomeria japonica*, coast redwood and giant sequoia. Until recently, the only genera where vegetative propagation was of importance in producing forest planting stock in Britain were the poplars and willows. Species in these genera possess latent root primordia in their stems which makes it relatively easy to root cuttings in the ground.

Over the last two decades there has been increasing interest in propagating vegetatively other tree species (e.g. Mason and Keenleyside, 1988) for three main reasons.

1. Tree breeders are increasingly able to identify genotypes which are more vigorous or have better form or timber quality or which are more disease resistant than the wild populations. These improved genotypes are generally available only in very small quantities (perhaps a few thousand seeds) and therefore they cannot be grown from seed in commercial quantities.

2. Propagation systems have improved considerably so it is now possible to maintain unrooted cuttings safely in humid conditions for several months while new roots develop.

3. We have a better understanding of the influence of the age of the donor plant upon the rootability of the cuttings (Davies *et al.*, 1988). Thus, cuttings taken from plants less than 3–4 years old from seed can be rooted fairly easily even though those taken from older plants can be difficult to root.

A wide range of forest tree species besides poplars and willows, in Britain have been successfully propagated using juvenile cuttings in intensively managed facilities (see Table 10.1). Thus cuttings could theoretically be used on a much wider scale for producing forest planting stock. However, cuttings cost around 1.5–3 times more per plant to produce than conventional seedlings. Therefore their use is normally justified only where the material propagated offers sufficient genetic superiority over unimproved seedlings to compensate for

Table 10.1 Tree species of commercial forest interest in Britain which have been successfully propagated using juvenile stem cuttings

Conifers	Broadleaves
Sitka spruce	Sessile oak
Norway spruce	Pedunculate oak
Hybrid larch	Red oak
European larch	Sycamore
Japanese larch	Beech
Lodgepole pine	Lime spp.
Scots pine	Birch spp.
Corsican pine	Gean
Macedonian pine	Ash
Western hemlock	Nothofagus spp.
Douglas fir	Common alder
Grand fir	Red alder
Noble fir	Sweet chestnut

Notes: 1. A revised version of Table 3 in Mason and Gill (1986).
2. Successful is defined as more than 60% rooting.

the increased price. This cost differential also means that some of the more intensive (and more expensive) propagation techniques used in other areas of horticulture may not be justifiable.

10.1 Propagation of broadleaves

10.1.1 Poplars

Most poplars raised commercially are propagated from hardwood cuttings taken during the winter. Poplars can also be propagated from seed, from softwood and root cuttings, and by grafting or budding. Raising from seed and grafting are generally only used in tree breeding programmes. Softwood and root cuttings are used for propagating those species which do not root readily from hardwood cuttings. Softwood cuttings are particularly useful for bulking up the numbers of a scarce clone in a short time.

A detailed discussion on the taxonomy and production of poplars can be found in Jobling (1990); see also Potter *et al.* (1990). Generally all the poplars in the *Aigeiros* section (the black poplars), apart from some forms of *Populus deltoides*, and in the *Tacamahaca*

section (the balsam poplars) are readily propagated from hardwood cuttings. In the *Leuce* section, the white poplars can also be propagated from hardwood cuttings, but the aspens and their hybrids are more difficult and are usually propagated from root cuttings.

10.1.2 Hardwood cuttings

Poplars can be marketed in different forms depending on their intended purpose. Stocks can be raised and sold as 1 or 2-year old rooted cuttings, and these are often used for wide spaced planting. Poplars required for high density planting such as for biomass, particularly the more recently introduced clones, or for new stool beds, are sold as unrooted cuttings or sets for direct insertion into the ground at the planting site.

Poplar cuttings and plants used for forestry purposes in the UK must be produced from stool beds which have been officially approved and recorded in the National Register of Basic Material under the Forest Reproductive

Table 10.2 List of poplar clones currently acceptable for registration under the Forest Reproductive Material Regulations, 1977

Preferred clone name	Poplar parentage
Fritzi Pauley	P. × trichocarpa
Scott Pauley	P. × trichocarpa
Columbia River	P. × trichocarpa
Trichobel	P. × trichocarpa
Balsam Spire (formerly 'TxT 32')	P. trichocarpa × P. tacamahaca
Canescens	P. alba × P. tremula
Casale 78 (formerly I-78)	P. deltoides × P. nigra
Eugenei	P. deltoides × P. nigra
Gelrica	P. deltoides × P. nigra
Heidemij (indistinguishable from Laevigiata)	P. deltoides × P. nigra
Robusta	P. deltoides × P. nigra
Serotina	P. deltoides × P. nigra
Primo	P. deltoides × P. nigra
Ghoy	P. deltoides × P. nigra
Gaver	P. deltoides × P. nigra
Gibecq	P. deltoides × P. nigra
Beaupré	P. deltoides × P. trichocarpa
Boelare	P. deltoides × P. trichocarpa

Material Regulations 1977. At present there are 18 clones of poplar which are acceptable for registration under these regulations. These are given in Table 10.2 (see also Chapter 15, section 15.3.4).

Poplar cuttings may be prepared at any time during the dormant season from 1-year-old fast grown shoots. Suitable shoots are best produced on specifically managed stock plants (stools), although shoots from 1-year-old rooted cuttings or other sources such as coppice may also be acceptable.

Stock plants / stool beds

Stock plants are established either by direct insertion of hardwood cuttings or by planting rooted plants at a spacing of at least 1×1 m in the nursery; the shoots are cut back to the ground annually during the winter to encourage the development of vigorous new shoots. Areas where such poplar stock plants are growing are normally called 'stool beds'. Many of the hybrid poplar clones are difficult to distinguish apart in the nursery. All stool beds must be clearly labelled and the layout of the beds must also be recorded on maps. Individual clones should be planted in separate rows to reduce the risk of mixing up cuttings or sets from different clones when cutting the shoots in winter. If more than one clone has to be planted in a row, it is important to leave a clear marker between clones, such as a large post, to emphasise the boundary. During the summer, stool beds should be checked for the growth of rogue plants which may arise from rooted pieces of discarded shoots left after winter pruning and cutting or from a previous stool bed. Any rogue plants should be removed or treated with herbicide to avoid the risk of producing batches of cuttings of mixed clones.

Cutting preparation

In British nurseries hardwood poplar cuttings are usually 20–25 cm long, with a diameter of 10–20 mm at their midpoint. Cuttings with a top diameter of less than 8 mm usually do not root well and so about the top third of the

anual shoot is often too thin for making cuttings. Cuttings are prepared from the well-budded remaining parts of shoots. Cuttings taken from the bases of shoots may be too thick for easy insertion into soil, and may be slower to shoot since many of the lateral buds may already have produced shoots during the first year. The top cut of the cutting should be made about 1 cm above a bud, while the basal cut should be made close to or just below a bud. Cuttings can be stored before use or dispatch in a cold store at +3 to 4°C. They must be enclosed in a labelled air-tight polythene bag to prevent water loss. Cuttings can also be stored outside by placing them upright and completely covering them in coarse sand.

Cuttings which are to be rooted in the nursery are usually inserted into the ground in late winter to allow roots to form before the buds break in the spring. Cuttings can be directly inserted if the soil has been suitably prepared. The cuttings should be pushed in vertically until the top cut surface is at soil level; subsequent soil settlement and some erosion will usually expose enough of the cutting to allow the rows to be readily identified. Spacings for inserting cuttings vary from as close as 30 cm within rows and 80–100 cm between rows, to 50×100 cm for the more vigorous clones. However, a spacing of 50×50 cm is commonly used.

The new shoots on rooted cuttings grow very vigorously and can reach heights in excess of 150 cm in the first year. Where more than one shoot emerges, the shoots should be singled to the straightest and most vigorous stem when the shoots are about 25 cm long. One-year rooted cuttings which have not reached a suitable size can be grown on for a further year in the nursery. The shoot system can be stumped back and the root stock transplanted in the winter to yield a source of cuttings and eventually to produce plants with 1-year-old shoots on 2-year-old root systems.

10.1.3 Poplar – softwood cuttings

All of the poplar species and cultivars which are raised commercially in nurseries in Britain can be propagated successfully from leafy summer cuttings. However, this is a more expensive method for propagating poplars than rooting winter-dormant woody cuttings because rooting softwood cuttings requires more attention and equipment. Nevertheless the leafy summer softwood cutting technique is a particularly useful means of rapidly increasing stocks of selected clones because of the rapid rate at which new roots are produced, typically after only 2 weeks, the high rooting percentages which can be obtained, and the large numbers of small cuttings which can, if necessary, be prepared from suitable shoots. Leafy cuttings can be rooted throughout the summer with little decline in percentage rooting and 90–100% rooting can be achieved with poplars from the sections *Aigeiros* and *Tacamahaca*. Rooting of softwood cuttings is a particularly successful method for propagating *P. × canescens* (grey poplar) and other poplars in the section *Leuce*.

Propagation facilities

An intermittent mist system is required if high percentages of rooted softwood cuttings are to be achieved. Mist installed in cold frames, glasshouses and polytunnels have all produced acceptable results. Bottom heat is not required for summer propagation; however, shading is essential for maintaining the turgor of cuttings. Maintaining light levels (total shortwave) at about $3\,MJ\,m^{-2}\,day^{-1}$ using Loach's (1988) shading scheme has produced successful rooting of even very soft tip cuttings. Further details on propagation systems and their management can be found in Hartmann, Kester and Davies (1990) and MacDonald (1986).

Cutting preparation

Softwood cuttings should be collected from vigorous shoots on stock plants which are cut back each winter. The cuttings are taken from current shoots and are usually 10–15 cm long and are cut just below a node; however cuttings as small as single-node cuttings can be successfully rooted. It is very important to prevent the cuttings from losing water before they are inserted in the rooting medium; cut-

tings should be collected in the early morning and stored away from direct sun in opaque polythene bags. Cuttings may be very soft at the beginning of the summer and require an efficient misting system to prevent wilting. The lower leaves are usually removed from the cuttings before they are inserted into a well drained rooting medium such as 1:1 peat: coarse sand or peat:vermiculite. The base of the cuttings can be dipped in a proprietary hormone rooting powder to increase the rate of rooting. Cuttings are also treated with a fungicide to prevent rotting.

Cuttings can either be inserted 3–5 cm apart in trays or in individual containers. The high rooting percentage which can be achieved with softwood cuttings makes the direct insertion of single cuttings into one litre containers a particularly efficient method of production because it eliminates the need to pot-up plants after the cuttings have rooted in trays. Peat:grit (3:1) amended with a low rate of controlled release fertiliser has been found to be a suitable rooting and growing medium. Cuttings inserted towards the end of summer are best rooted in trays and potted-up the following spring; potting-up in autumn may not allow sufficient time for the recently rooted plants to become established before winter.

After insertion, the misting frequency should be set quite high to prevent wilting, and the cuttings should be well shaded to avoid excessive water loss. After rooting the cuttings should be weaned-off by reducing the misting frequency and gradually increasing the ventilation around the cuttings.

Cuttings rooted in trays should be potted up as soon as possible after rooting to avoid the roots becoming too entangled. Cuttings which have been rooted in containers should be given occasional liquid feeds to maintain plant quality; however, too much fertiliser can promote excessive growth for the size of container.

The methods described here, while featuring poplars, can also be used for many other broadleaved species raised from cuttings taken during the growing season, while tissues are soft.

10.1.4 Aspen propagation from roots

Aspen (*P. tremula* L.) is a difficult species to root using stem cuttings. However, it suckers quite readily from the root system and this feature can be adapted by the nursery manager to provide planting stock of desired origins (Hollingsworth and Mason, 1991).

The simplest method is to dig up suckers in the forest with a sharp spade, making sure that sufficient root is recovered to support the shoot. These suckers can then be potted up at the nursery to grow on for a year before being planted out in the forest. The main problem is that this will only provide a small number of plants.

An alternative system involves the collection of roots from trees in the forest in late winter and bringing them to the nursery. The roots are then cut into lengths of 15–30 cm and are placed in seed trays in a greenhouse in a sphagnum moss peat:vermiculite 1:1 mixture to promote suckers. The suckers are harvested in early spring when 4–10 cm long, with a scalpel or sharp knife, by cutting just above the point where the suckers leave the root. They are immediately inserted into a freely draining substrate in an intermittent mist propagation unit. Up to 30 suckers may be produced per metre of root. Cuttings root within 2–3 weeks, after which they should be potted up and grown on for the remainder of the season. It is quite possible to produce 1-year-old plantable stock using this technique.

10.1.5 Willows

Many aspects of the propagation of willows are similar to those used for poplars. Willows can be planted as sets, hardwood cuttings or rooted plants.

Care must be taken not to mistake flower buds for vegetative buds. A substantial proportion of some current shoots of shrubby willows may be occupied by flower buds, such material being unsuitable for cuttings. Hardwood cuttings are usually 20 cm long and 12–25 mm thick with a single healthy vegetative bud about 1 cm from the top (White, 1990). Hardwood cuttings can be inserted 30 cm apart within rows and 60 cm between

rows and lifted after one year to produce a usable plant. Cuttings with shoots shorter than 50 cm are best transplanted and grown on for a further year. Sets are cut from shoots on stools and are usually 2.5–3 m long. They are planted at spacings of 30–60 cm x 60–90 cm and grown for 1 or 2 years according to size and growth rate or may be planted out direct into woodland. Many willows can also be successfully propagated from softwood cuttings and raised in containers.

10.2 Propagation of conifers

10.2.1 Propagation facilities

It is possible to root conifer cuttings in a traditional propagation frame with whitewashed glass and hand watering to maintain required levels of humidity. However, this is a labour intensive method which is generally not appropriate for propagation of more than a few hundred cuttings. Most commercial propagation of conifer cuttings takes place in polythene greenhouses using some form of intermittent mist irrigation (Plate 24). In this propagation system, the leaves are sprayed intermittently and are effectively cooled through the evaporation of the applied films of water (Loach, 1988). The lowered leaf temperature reduces the vapour pressure difference between the interior of the leaf and the surrounding air, and so restricts the rate of water loss from the cuttings and maintains them in a turgid condition. Under mist, much of the water that is lost by evaporation is not internal tissue water but external applied water.

The essential features required in a mist propagation unit are the polyhouse, the mist irrigation and controls, ventilation and some form of basal heating to promote rooting and prevent frost damage. General details of mist propagation facilities can be found in a number of standard horticultural texts (e.g. MacDonald, 1986). The following comments are specific to our experience with propagation of Sitka spruce and hybrid larch (Mason, 1989; Mason, 1992; Mason and Keenleyside, 1988).

Any normal type of commercial polyhouse is suitable for propagating conifer cuttings. Both single and multispan houses can be used, but the latter are to be preferred since they provide more constant air temperatures within the house. Either a clear or a white polythene cover can be used; the latter will provide shade and will therefore reduce the risk of scorch damage on unrooted cuttings. Additional shading may prove necessary during May–August to prevent high air and leaf temperatures increasing the rate of water loss and, if exceeding 30°C, also damaging the cuttings.

10.2.2 Temperatures in the propagating house

The target specification should be that air temperatures within the house remain between 5°C and 30°C; relative humidity should average 95% during rooting, but can be reduced to 50–60% when the cuttings are weaned. For this to be achievable, the facility must have some form of background heating to prevent frost damaging the cuttings or the irrigation system. High temperatures are normally controlled by forced air ventilation using fans, and by shading. Fans should be set to come on at temperatures between 25 and 30°C. Damp pads or similar devices should be placed over the louvres where the fan draws air into the house. This prevents dry air being drawn into the house and reducing the humidity to low, potentially damaging levels. If a propagation facility is operating under very warm conditions, there is always a trade-off to be made between ventilating the house to keep the crop cool, and maintaining high humidity and leaf wetness to prevent the crop drying out. In this situation, shading can help by reducing incident light intensity and the temperature build-up in the house. Attempts to cool a house by very frequent misting are often unsatisfactory since the rooting substrate may become saturated for long periods, creating anaerobic conditions at the base of the cuttings.

10.2.3 Mist

A wide variety of irrigation control systems are commercially available for producing intermittent mist. Before making a final decision in favour of a mist system, the water supply should be checked for pH, free lime and mains pressure. A hard water supply (> 130 p.p.m. free $CaCO_3$) should be acidified using nitric acid injected into the irrigation water (Landis *et al.,* 1989). A pressure of around 50–60 p.s.i. is desirable to ensure a fine mist spray with uniform distribution. The ideal mist system should be sensitive to ambient conditions and provide a variable frequency of misting according to evaporative demand within the house. There should be no mist applied overnight when humidity within the house will remain at near 100%.

10.2.4 Fogging

Alternative systems for propagating conifer cuttings include those based upon 'fog'. Fogging systems involve the creation of clouds of fine droplets less than 20 µm in diameter, which hang within the polyhouse. This maintains a stable, high humidity environment and because less water is deposited on plants and growing medium, reduces the amount of nutrient loss in the cuttings when compared with mist irrigation. Very good rooting can be obtained in a fogging unit. It is an expensive system requiring high pressures (> 100 p.s.i.). At present fogging is probably best seen as a research tool or as a technique for rooting very soft cuttings which would be prone to water stress, e.g. micropropagation material.

10.2.5 Types of cuttings and time of collection/insertion

Two types of cutting are normally distinguished in conifers. Hardwood (winter) cuttings are collected in early spring before the buds have broken; the cutting consists of tissue laid down in the previous growing season. Softwood or summer cuttings are taken in July when shoots are in active extension growth; the cutting consists of tissue laid down in the current growing season. Sometimes cuttings are taken in late August–September after resting buds have formed; these are known as semi-hardwood cuttings.

Hardwood cuttings are generally favoured by commercial nurseries propagating conifers for forestry. The use of dormant material reduces the risks of handling damage so that the cuttings can be safely cold-stored for short periods before insertion.

The normal size of cutting used is 8–10 cm. Both tip (i.e. with a terminal bud) and base (no terminal bud) cuttings can be rooted. The latter are particularly useful in achieving high multiplication rates. It is important not to collect thin, wispy cuttings since these are easy to damage during insertion and produce poor root systems.

10.2.6 Management of mother plants

Successful rooting of cuttings is influenced by nutrition of mother plants in the season before collection and insertion. Regimes should avoid the production of cutting material with either a very low or high nutrient status. The former are too deficient to root satisfactorily and the latter too soft to handle easily. It is particularly important to maintain adequate nitrogen status in the stock plants since this is an important nutrient for both root initiation and subsequent root development. The target should be to maintain adequate nitrogen levels (see Fig. 4.1 and Table 4.8) throughout the season before collection of cuttings.

Nursery managers should maintain mother plants of desirable genotypes in a juvenile state and collect cuttings over a number of years. There are two ways of achieving this. The first is to create a 'hedge' of mother plants of the desired genotype. These are cut back annually to a height of about 25 cm above ground and allowed to grow back. Cuttings are collected from this regrowth. The second method is to use 'serial propagation' where cuttings are collected from the previous crop of cuttings (known as a 'cycle'), this procedure being repeated over a number of cycles. Preliminary results have suggested that serial propagation is more effective than hedging in maintaining juvenility in Sitka spruce. However, it is not yet clear whether either technique will maintain cuttings in a juvenile state indefinitely.

10.2.7 Preparation and management of cuttings

Cuttings are normally collected with secateurs (Plate 25). These should have a scissor-type rather than the anvil type action to prevent crushing of the shoots. Provided the material is juvenile, there is no need to strip the needles, wound the base of the cutting or apply rooting hormone in order to achieve good rooting performance. Such techniques are expensive and increase the cost of producing the cuttings. They are of use only where the nursery manager is attempting to build up stocks of a desirable genotype that is hard to root.

Conifer cuttings can be successfully rooted in a wide range of substrates provided they give adequate support to the cutting and good drainage. The substrate needs to be adjusted to the type and intensity of misting regime being used. Thus, successful propagation under a system where there are long bursts of water applied at regular intervals will require a coarser, better drained substrate than one where misting is linked to evaporative demand. A substrate that has given good results over a number of years is 1 part sphagnum moss peat : 1 part composted pine bark : 1 part perlite (special seed grade, average size 1–3 mm) on a volume basis, all mixed together.

Normal practice is to root conifer cuttings in trays of the rooting substrate or in rooting beds. The former are generally easier to manage. Assuming a crop of hardwood cuttings is inserted in March, callus development is seen at the base of the cutting in May with root initiation shortly thereafter. At this stage, the misting intensity should be reduced at regular intervals as the cuttings develop self-sufficient root systems. The first roots that develop are typically white and fleshy and are termed 'water-roots'. These are brittle and easily damaged. An indication that propagation has been successful is when the roots turn brown and fibrous, similar to those of a seedling.

Fertilisers can be incorporated into the substrate but this is probably of little benefit unless the aim is to produce 1-year-old forest usable material. Cuttings are generally incapable of taking up external nutrients until new roots have been initiated. A heavy misting regime will also leach nutrients out of the substrate before they can be taken up. Cuttings propagated under mist become nutrient-deficient because of leaching of the foliage and of remobilisation of nutrients towards the rooting zone. For example, concentration of N, P and K in Sitka spruce cuttings declined by 51%, 61% and 37% respectively, after 3 months under mist compared with initial values.

Once mist frequency has been reduced at the start of weaning, regular liquid feeding should begin to restore the nutrient status of the cuttings. Fertiliser should be applied either once or twice a week with a balanced NPK feed at concentrations of around 200 p.p.m. N.

The high humidity present in mist houses can result in serious fungal attacks, particularly by *Botrytis* spp. Cutting material should be treated with an approved systemic fungicide 7–14 days before insertion. Once the crop has been inserted, the cuttings should be sprayed at weekly intervals as a prophylactic measure. It is essential that different products be used in sequence to guard against a build-up of resistance in the pathogen to a particular fungicide. The crop should also be inspected regularly and any diseased material removed. Particular points to watch out for are disease developing on damaged tissue, or under the bud scales of opening buds if they do not fall off. Fungicide, fertilisers and any other products should always be applied in the evening with the mist switched off for up to 12 hours after application. This will ensure that the chemicals are absorbed, while the time of application guards against any risk of scorch.

10.2.8 Production system

The current method of producing rooted conifer cuttings is to collect and insert the hardwood cuttings in March and to maintain them in the polyhouse until July–August. At this stage, the bulk of the crop should be well rooted (Plate 26); the cuttings are then lifted and lined out into a bare-root nursery, and grown on for a further 18 months when the cuttings should be 30–40 cm tall. At this stage, plants may either be used a source of further cuttings or they can be dispatched for forest planting. Blackwood (1989) has describes a commercial two-cycle propagation system of this type with a multiplication factor per ortet of 400 usable rooted cuttings (see section 10.2.9 following).

An alternative approach is to root the cuttings in seedling containers of the type described in Chapter 9. The advantage of this technique is that handling costs resulting from transplanting to the open nursery are eliminated. In addition, plantable cuttings can be produced in one year, reducing the time taken to produce bulk stock for planting. Propagation in containers uses similar techniques to propagation in trays or rooting beds, with one or two exceptions. These include incorporating a limited amount of small prilled controlled release fertiliser in each cell to boost growth after rooting. It is also necessary to lift up the containers after rooting to air-prune the cuttings and promote fibrous root development.

10.2.9 Sitka spruce vegetative propagation

Facilities have been established in the period 1989–91 at the Forestry Commission nursery at Delamere, Cheshire, for large scale production of vegetatively bulked up planting stock of genetically improved Sitka spruce from limited supplies of seed (Plate 27).

Table 10.3 gives details of the operations involved. These are spread over a 6-year period and involve three phases of production, each of 2 years.

Phase 1 starts with germination of the improved seed in small containers and intensive growth of the resulting seedlings, potting into larger containers during the first season (Plate 28). Plants are grown on under an intensive regime and should be at least 1 metre tall by the end of the second growing season. At this stage each seedling should be well enough furnished with side branches for the whole plant to be cut up and yield on average 80 cuttings per plant. All of this phase is carried out in polyhouses, the larger containers being on capillary sand beds.

Phase 2 (first cycle rooted stock production) commences in February/March at the beginning of the third year, when cuttings are taken. These are inserted into a mist propagation unit where they remain until July/August of that year, when the cuttings that are well rooted are lined out in open nursery ground. No attempt is made to maintain the identity of the individual original seedling trees from which the cuttings were taken.

Lined out cuttings remain in the open ground for the remainder of the year of planting and all the following year. By this time, they should have grown to the size of conventional forestry planting stock. Each plant should be big enough to yield about 9–10 cuttings per plant.

Phase 3 (second cycle rooted cutting production) commences in February/March at the beginning of the fifth year and is similar to the first cycle rooted stock production. Plants are cut to yield the maximum number of cuttings and these are inserted into a mist propagation unit, rooted cuttings being lined out in July/August of the fifth year for growing on until the end of the sixth season, when they should be suitable for forest planting.

At this stage, the plants will not look the same as conventional transplants. The rooted cuttings do not have such well developed lower lateral branches as conventional stock, because they lack the ring of buds associated with the terminal bud of a 1-year-old seedling. Some needles which developed while cuttings were rooting may also be smaller than usual, reflecting the effect of diversion of nutrients from shoot to root growth at that time. These differences should be pointed out to potential customers with the assurance that the genetically improved stock will grow better than plants from unimproved seed.

Table 10.3 Standard two cycle propagation system for Sitka spruce (source, Mason 1992)

Stage	Year	Month	Operation	Comments
1	0	February/March	Seed stratification	3–4 weeks moist prechilling at 2°C.
2	0	March/April	Sow seed	1 seed sown per cell in containers (100–200 ml cell capacity). Container substrate is sphagnum moss peat:vermiculite 3:1 by volume with Ficote 70 16:10:10 at 1.5 kg m^{-3}, ground limestone at 1 kg m^{-3}, magnesium limestone at 2 kg m^{-3} and fritted trace elements at 0.3 kg m^{-3}.
3	0	April–July/Aug	Germinate and grow on seedlings	Maintain seedlings in a polythene greenhouse under natural daylength at target temperatures of 20/15°C day/night with permitted maxima/minima of 30/5°C. Supplementary weekly liquid feeding using balanced NPK at 200 p.p.m. N will be necessary in July and August.
4	0	July/August	Pot on seedlings for stock plants	This should be done when seedlings are about 15 cm tall. Pot seedlngs into 4-litre containers with substrate of sphagnum moss peat:ground pine bark:grit in 6:3:1 ratio by volume. Incorporated basal fertiliser of Osmocote 18:11:10 (8–9 months) at 3 kg m^{-3}, ground lime at 1.2 kg m^{-3}, magnesium limestone at 2.4 kg m^{-3} and fritted trace elements at 0.3 kg m^{-3}. The role of the bark is to keep the substrate open and to provide a buffer against sudden release of nutrients in high temperatures. No liquid feeding should be required until May/June of year 1.
5	0–1	August–May	Grow on stock plants	Maintain polythene greenhouses frost-free overwinter. Keep plants spaced out so that laterals do not touch. Keep stock plants in polyhouse.

Table 10.3 *continued*

Stage	Year	Month	Operation	Comments
6	1	May	Pinch out leaders and side-shoots of stock plants to promote branching	This is best done with the fingers to prevent damage. Any plants of poor form should be culled out.
7	1	May/June–Sept	Stock plant management (target is plants up to 100 cm tall)	Feed up to twice weekly throughout the period of active growth (late May–August) using a high N product (e.g. NPK 2:1:1) at 200–250 p.p.m. N. Change to NPK 1:1:1 weekly feeding at 200 p.p.m. N in September and October. Feed to run-off to ensure that substrate is at correct nutrient balance. Target nitrogen levels in foliage should be > 1.5% dry weight. Use a conductivity meter for monitoring leachate. Water plants regularly (i.e. daily) especially during warm conditions. Respace plants at intervals to ensure laterals do not touch and cutting quality is maintained.
8	1–2	October–Feb	Overwintering stock	Can be done either in a frost free polyhouse or plants can be overwintered outside. If the second option is taken, the plants must be transferred outside before October to guard against early frosts. Roots may have to be protected against freezing temperatures.
9	2	February/March	Prepare to collect first cycle cuttings	Spray all plants with a systemic fungicide (e.g. 0.1% thiophanate methyl) 14 days before collection to guard against *Botrytis* infection.
10	2	February/March	Collect first cycle cuttings	A standard length of 8 (±2) cm is used. Both tip (with terminal bud) and base (no terminal bud) cuttings are collected. Only collect from wood laid down in the previous year (i.e. year 1). Minimum diameter of cuttings should be *c.* 2 mm (i.e. cuttings should withstand gentle bending between thumb and forefinger). Keep cuttings cool and shaded after collection. They can be cold-stored (+1°C) in polythene bags for 2–3 weeks without damage.
11	2	March	Insertion of cuttings	Insert to 3 cm depth in seed trays or similar that are 7 cm deep. Ideal spacing between cuttings is 4 cm, but 3 cm is acceptable. Seed trays should be placed on rooting benches or on fine sand. This prevents waterlogging at the base of the medium. Substrate should have an air filled porosity of >15%. Sphagnum moss peat:pine bark:grit (2–3 mm) or perlite in a 1:1:1 ratio by volume is our preference, but other alternatives are acceptable if they provide support and maintain good drainage. No rooting hormone is applied before insertion; stripping of basal needles is also unnecessary. No fertiliser is incorporated in the substrate.
12	2	March–June	Propagation of first cycle cuttings	Rooting trays are placed in a mist propagation unit under natural daylength. A white polythene cover or other shading is desirable to diffuse direct sunlight and reduce the risk of scorch. Target relative humidity levels are 90–95% during daylight hours. Peak misting frequency is a 5 s burst every 1–2 min. Mist frequency should be controlled by a device linked to ambient evaporative demand. Use fan ventilation to keep temperatures < 30°C. Fans should have moist pads on the outside to prevent dry air being sucked into the house. Fungicides are applied weekly in rotation to prevent *Botrytis* attack. Apply fungicides (and fertilisers) under dull conditions or in late evening to avoid scorch. Switch off the mist for 6–12 h after application. Start of callus initiation at base of cuttings 6–10 weeks after insertion.

Table 10.3 *continued*

Stage	Year	Month	Operation	Comments
13	2	June/July	Weaning of cuttings	After 50–70% of the crop has root initials, mist frequency should be reduced at weekly intervals until only one or two waterings per day are required. Burst length is increased so that there is a 'watering' rather than 'misting' regime. Raise trays of rooting plants to promote air pruning and encourage root proliferation within the tray. Start liquid feeding once weaning has begun, to counteract nutrient leaching during propagation. Use a 1:1:1 NPK feed at 200 p.p.m. N applied at 4 litres solution m^{-2} twice a week. Weaning is near completion when white fleshy roots ('water roots') have been transformed into brown fibrous roots.
14	2	July/August	Lift and line out cuttings	Cuttings should be lined-out in a bare-root nursery using standard lining out machinery. Space at 10 cm (50 plants m^{-2}) within rows to encourage branching. Apply normal basal fertilisers before lining out. Discard any poorly rooted or misshapen cuttings before lining out.
15	2/3	August–May	Care for lined out cuttings	Lining out should occur early enough so that cuttings make new root growth to guard against risk of frost lift. Normal herbicide regimes after lining out.
16	3	May–October	Maintenance of lined out cuttings (target is plants 40–50 cm tall)	Apply a balanced 1:1:1 feeding regime to provide around 100 kg of elemental N ha^{-1} over the growing season. If possible apply little and often to maximise height growth and yield of second cycle cuttings.
17	3/4	October–Feb	Overwintering	
18	4	February/March	Collect second cycle cuttings	Attempt to collect as many tip cuttings as possible to guard against risks of double leaders from basal cuttings.
19	4	March–July/Aug	Propagation and weaning of second cycle cuttings	Regimes are identical to first cycle.
20	4	July/August	Line out second cycle cuttings	As for first cycle except that spacing is now 5 cm ($\approx$100 plants m^{-2}).
21	4/5	August–May	Maintenance of lined out cuttings	As for first cycle.
22	5	May–October	Culturing of cuttings for forest planting (target is plants 25–35 cm tall)	One-two light top dressings of N (25 kg elemental N ha^{-1} in total) before undercutting at 8 cm in July. Follow by fortnightly or 3-weekly wrenching until end of growing season. Apply additional N and K to maintain nutrient status. Total of 50–75 kg of elemental N ha^{-1} over season.
23	5/6	Nov–March	Lifting of cuttings, grading and dispatch	Remove any double leadered plants. Plants with slight (up to 15–20°C deviation from vertical) stem bend are acceptable. Otherwise treat as normal forest planting stock.
24	6	Spring	Forest planting	

Notes: An alternative stock plant regime is to replace stages 4–8 inclusive with one where the stock plants are potted on in outdoor raised beds. These beds are 30 cm high and 1 m wide with a substrate of sphagnum moss peat:composted pine bark:grit in 1:1:1 ratio by volume. 16–18 month Osmocote 16:9:9:3 (Mg) is added at 4–6 kg m^{-3}, ground limestone at 3.0 kg m^{-3}, and trace element frit at 0.3 kg m^{-3}. Plants are spaced at 25 cm within and between rows. Target stock plant height is 50–75 cm. This system will give a lower yield of cuttings (30–40 per plant) compared with the standard polyhouse regime (60–70+ per plant) but it is less demanding on maintenance, especially watering.

Production areas

The following figures provide an approximate working guide to the numbers of plants and size of propagating facilities required to produce and sustain an annual production of 1 million rooted cuttings of genetically improved origins, suitable for planting in the forest, based on a 6-year production cycle.

The numbers are very dependent on the success of rooting of cuttings and achieving good survival in transplant lines. The factors shown are averages based on limited experience; a few minutes spent on the same sequence of calculations using other factors immediately illustrates the importance of striving for reliable high rooting percentage of cuttings and high percentage survival and growth following transplanting.

Production planning for 1 million rooted plants suitable for forest planting – the 6-year production cycle

1st year
- Seed to yield 2300–2500 seedlings; 4000 seeds should be sufficient, sown 1 seed per 100–200 ml capacity cell.
- Space in capillary bed house to accommodate 2500 seedlings potted on into 4 litre containers, maintained so that the plant laterals do not touch.

2nd year
Space to provide same specification as previously (but plants larger).

3rd year
- Mist propagation area to accept 190 000 (180 000–200 000) cuttings.
- Lining out area to accept 170 000 rooted cuttings.

4th year
Space to grow transplants on.

5th year
- Mist propagation area to accept 1 400 000 cuttings.
- Lining out area to accept 1 250 000 rooted cuttings.

Once committed to this type of planting stock, production is an ongoing rolling process, so that at any one time, there will be crops at each stage of growth. To maintain this scale of sustained production, approximately 500 m^2 of capillary house for seedling production, and 4200 m^2 of mist propagation house are required. However, because there is an inevitable build-up over the first 5 years, the capital investment in facilities can be spread over 4 years, the larger part of the mist unit requirement only coming into use at the beginning of the fifth year.

Production implications of any changes in technique involving cutting spacing or additional time spent in polyhouses when space is already fully allocated have to be carefully examined if the system is not to be disrupted. Nevertheless, there are obvious advantages in shortening the production time period so that developments to that end should be expected at some time.

10.3 Overview and future developments

It seems likely that vegetative propagation of tree species will continue to increase in importance as more superior genotypes are identified by tree breeding selection and testing programmes. More species are likely to be propagated by cuttings, including selected clones of the major broadleaves. As propagation techniques continue to improve, one can expect that the differences in price between cuttings and seedlings will become less. The use of vegetative propagation may become as important in forest nursery practice as it has in other areas of horticulture.

10.3.1 Micropropagation

An allied technique that is becoming increasingly important is micropropagation. This technique uses small pieces of tissue such as excised shoot, embryos or cells. The tissue is grown on a medium, usually containing growth promoting substances, in sterile conditions in a test-tube or similar container. The micropropagule proliferates shoots which are then subdivided to yield further material in a multiplication cycle. It may prove possible to multiply the selected genotypes by up to 1000 times in a year using these techniques. Micropropagation can be used to mass produce stock plants of selected genotypes which are then repropagated by stem cuttings. This combination of techniques makes it possible to see the advent of combined macro and micropropagation systems which mass produce selected clones for intensive production forestry (John and Mason, 1987). A similar type of system is already being used in horticulture to mass produce desirable cultivars of *Rhododendron* and other woody plant species.

REFERENCES

BLACKWOOD, C.H. (1989). Large scale production of genetically improved Sitka spruce by stem cuttings. *Forestry* **62,** (suppl.), 207–212.

DAVIES, T.D., HAISSIG, B.E. and SANKHLA, N. (eds) (1988). *Adventitious root formation in cuttings.* Dioscorides Press, Oregon.

HARTMANN, H.T., KESTER, D.E., and DAVIES, F.T. (1990). *Plant propagation: principles and practices.* 5th edn. Prentice-Hall, New Jersey, USA.

HOLLINGSWORTH, M.K. and MASON, W.L. (1991). *Vegetative propagation of aspen.* Forestry Commission Research Information Note 200. Forestry Commission, Edinburgh.

JOBLING, J. (1990). *Poplars for wood production and amenity.* Forestry Commission Bulletin 92. HMSO, London.

JOHN, A. and MASON, W.L. (1987). Vegetative propagagtion of Sitka spruce. *Proceedings of the Royal Society of Edinburgh* **93B,** 197–203.

LANDIS, T.D., TINUS, R.W., McDONALD, S.E. and BARNETT, J.P. (1989). *Seedling nutrition and irrigation.* Vol. 4 of *The container tree nursery manual.* Agriculture Handbook 674. US Department of Agriculture, Forest Service, Washington, DC. (119 pp.)

LOACH, K. (1988). Controlling environmental conditions to improve adventititous rooting. In *Adventititous root formation in cuttings,* eds Davies, T.D., Haissig, B.E. and Sankhla, N. Dioscorides Press, Oregon, 248–273.

MacDONALD, B. (1986). *Practical woody plant propagation for nursery growers.* Batsford, London. (669 pp.)

MASON, W.L. and GILL, J.G.S. (1986). Vegetative propagation of conifers as a means of intensifying wood production in Britain. *Forestry* **59** (2), 155–172.

MASON, W.L. and KEENLEYSIDE, J.C. (1988). Propagating Sitka spruce under intermittent mist and other systems. *Combined Proceedings International Plant Propagation Society* **38,** 294–303.

MASON, W.L. (1989). Vegetative propagation of hybrid larch (*Larix × eurolepis* Henry) using winter cuttings. *Forestry* **62,** (suppl.), 189–198.

MASON, W.L. (1992). Reducing the cost of Sitka spruce cuttings. In *Super Sitka for the 90s.* Forestry Commission Bulletin 103. HMSO, London, 25–41.

POTTER, C.J., NIXON, C.J. and GIBBS, J.N. (1990). *The introduction of improved poplar clones from Belgium.* Forestry Commission Research Information Note 181. Forestry Commission, Edinburgh.

WHITE, J.E.J. (1990). *Propagation of lowland willows by winter cuttings.* Arboriculture Research Note 85/90/SILS. DoE Arboricultural Advisory and Information Service, Farnham, Surrey.

Chapter 11
Irrigation

J. R. Aldhous

Introduction

Application of water by irrigation to promote survival and growth in dry periods is simple in concept. However, in order to use water effectively, it is desirable to have some understanding of the physical processes that underlie current practice in the UK. These are, unfortunately, complex, both in themselves, in their interaction and in their measurement. There is no easy, universally applicable means of estimating the day-to-day water requirements of crops. The literature on the subject is voluminous, much of it devoted to attempts to identify 'indicators' that are readily measured and can be used to predict when and how much irrigation to apply.

The transfer in 1990 of responsibility for water supply, to public companies owned by shareholders, and at the same time the increasingly stringent standards set for water quality within the European Community, have not yet had an obvious effect of availability or cost of water for crop irrigation. However, such effects cannot be ruled out for the future.

The sections following outline the more important theoretical and practical points affecting current irrigation practice. The first three sections focus on 'potentials', i.e. the tensions or suction pressures that may develop in relation to plants and water.

11.1 Energy and water demand.
11.2 Soil water.
11.3 Water tension in plants.

The next three sections cover the main practical issues in managing irrigation.

11.4 Planning for irrigation.
11.5 Irrigation equipment.

11.6 How much water to apply and how often.

In these latter sections, water use is expressed in terms of 'precipitation equivalent', i.e. the amount of rainfall or water that may be applied through irrigation, in terms of depth of water per unit area of land.

11.1 Energy and water demand

11.1.1 Solar energy

Evapotranspiration

Solar energy provides the driving force, directly or indirectly, for all water movement from the earth's surface to the atmosphere. Studies in the early part of this century on crops in arid and semi-arid regions showed a good relationship between crop yield and water transpired by the crop (Vaux and Pruit, 1983); these formed the basis for the first scientific approaches to irrigation practice. However, it was H. L. Penman who established and first developed the concept of 'potential evapotranspiration' and provided a basis in mathematical physics for relating solar energy to water loss by evaporation from the soil and transpiration from plants. His prediction of 'potential evapotranspiration' required estimates of temperature, vapour pressure, wind-run and sunshine-hour data, but also included some assumed constants.

Since his first publication (Penman, 1948) a substantial number of variants or alternatives have been proposed (e.g. Monteith, 1965; Monteith and Unsworth, 1990). Some incorpo-

Plate 18. *Rigipot containers.*

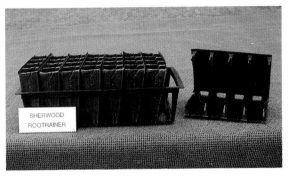

Plate 19. *Rootrainers.*

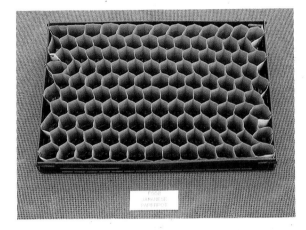

Plate 20. *Japanese paper pots.*

Plate 21. *Oak seedlings growing in containers in a polyhouse.* (R.L. Jinks)

Plate 22. *Rootrainers on carrier frames ready for removal by fork-lift to houses. In background, machinery for filling containers.* (J.R. Aldhous)

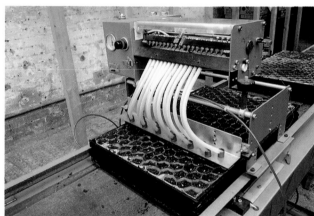

Plate 23. *Trays of Japanese paper pots being automatically sown by vacuum sower.* (E9801)

Plate 24.
Double span polytunnel with benches of rooting Sitka spruce cuttings; fixed overhead mist irrigation pipes. (E8823)

rated refinements to the physics underlying the equation but made the calculation more difficult; others simplified it to make it easier to use in practice, but introduced further assumptions that restricted the general applicability of the simplification.

Penman assumed that all vegetation would behave like a grass sward; however, it is now clear that the structure and in particular, the roughness (aerodynamic resistance) of the crop surface itself affects evapotranspiration so that different constants are required, for example for grass and lucerne, and some quite different assumptions are required for high forest because of the volume of water intercepted by foliage.

Nevertheless, the estimation of crop evapotranspiration, modified to greater or lesser extent for specific conditions, underlies many practical irrigation schedules (Batchelor, 1984; Doorenbos and Pruit, 1977; Penman, 1986; Stewart, 1983).

Percentage ground cover

The first calculations of evapotranspiration assumed a full crop cover; modifications have subsequently been made so that 'reduction factors' can be applied, to take account of incomplete ground cover in the early stages of many crops. Even so, few agricultural or horticultural crops cover the ground as sparsely for so long in the season as young conifers; evaporation from the soil surface is relatively more important in forest nurseries than in crops that cover the ground early in their development.

While the soil surface is moist, evaporation rates from foliage and soil are similar. However, once the soil surface is dry, corresponding to a 'soil moisture deficit' of about 12 mm, soil surface evaporation falls (see p. 151). After sowing and in the early stages of seedling growth, there may be little or no ground cover by vegetation; similarly, after transplanting and sometimes after undercutting, there is nothing like a full ground cover by the crop. Deciding the appropriate allowance for such incomplete cover is central to rational water use. Estimated values for nursery crop types are given in Table 11.3.

Soil surface reflectance

A proportion of solar energy falling on ground and ground cover is reflected. Once the ground is fully covered with uniform vegetation, this factor varies little. However, while exposed, the colour of the soil surface affects the amount of solar energy that is reflected, lighter colours being the better reflectors. In the nursery, the only real choice available to managers is in the colour of the seedbed grit. Lighter colour grits have been shown to be cooler at the soil surface than dark grits in hot weather, the difference often being critical to seedling survival; see Chapter 6, Table 6.4. If irrigation is required to maintain seedbed moisture and reduce surface temperatures during hot weather, lighter colour grit is likely to be advantageous.

11.1.2 Temperature

Air temperature records, mean, maximum and minimum, wet and dry bulb, are essential prerequisites for the calculation of evapotranspiration.

An independent second approach to predicting irrigation needs can be made based solely on temperature and humidity. This follows from the situation that at any given temperature, if the air is fully saturated with water vapour and the leaf temperature is not higher than the air temperature, no further evaporation or transpiration can take place, and that the drier the air, the greater the transpiration from a crop. Transpiration can be estimated from the water vapour pressure potential, or vapour pressure deficit, i.e. the drying power, of the air around plant foliage.

Provided the initial calibration has been done, plants' water requirements at any time can be estimated from the current air temperature and the vapour pressure deficit of the air. These enable an estimate to be made of the foliage temperature for plants well supplied with water; comparison with the actual foliage temperature provides a basis for assessing water need (Idso, 1982, 1983).

11.2 Soil water

A number of systems for assessing and preparing irrigation schedules have been based on the relationship between water in the soil and crop growth.

They work on the assumption that if the soil is always reasonably moist, healthy plants will not suffer from lack of water. Monitored changes in soil moisture provide indirect estimates of the current water balance, i.e.

precipitation – evapotranspiration – drainage – runoff,

and can be used either as an immediate basis for irrigation prescriptions or as a check on water balance sheet calculations from weather data and records of water applied.

Assessment of soil water involves the concepts of:

- Soil water tension/matric potential;
- Soil water content
  - field capacity,
  - permanent wilting point,
  - available water capacity,
  - soil saturation.

11.2.1 Soil water tension/matric potential

Water in a drained soil is held in films enveloping soil particles. Such water is under tension (or 'matric potential' or 'matric suction'). This is the result of the interaction within the soil of:

- gravitation,
- surface tension in water films enveloping soil particles, and
- suction forces, or potentials, arising from evaporation from the soil surface and transpiration from plant foliage.

These forces affect the whole of the soil water and provide the potential for water to move through the soil to replace evapotranspiration losses. Consequently, soil water is under a tension which varies continuously, depending on the scale of water loss through evapotranspiration, the extent this is replaced by incoming water from irrigation or natural rainfall and the rate at which water can move

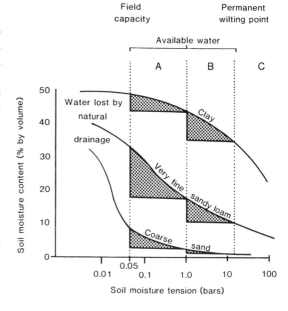

A Readily available water (under low stress)
B Residual available water (under high stress)
C Water too tightly held in soil to be available to plants

Figure 11.1 Relationship between soil moisture content, soil moisture tension (matric potential), availability of soil water and soil texture.

through the soil in response to differences in matric potential.

For any given soil, there is a direct relationship between soil water tension (matric potential) and soil water content (Figure 11.1). However, the relationship will only be the same for soils of very similar soil texture characteristics.

11.2.2 Soil water content/soil moisture content

The amount of water in a soil at any time is most commonly expressed as a volume percentage of the volume of soil (volume/volume or v/v). Less frequently, it is expressed in terms of percentage by weight (w/w).

Field capacity

This is defined as the amount of water remaining in a freely draining soil 48 h after the soil has been saturated, e.g. by prolonged heavy rain. Under these conditions, a 'soil moisture tension' or 'matric potential' of 10.05 bars develops. 'Field capacity' is however not a completely stable constant. On heavier soils, natural gravitational drainage is slow and can continue for several weeks, so that 48 h estimates of field capacity following saturation include some short-term stored water which is absent when the soil is slowly rewetted until the moisture tension equivalent to field capacity is reached (Parkes *et al.*, 1989).

Soil moisture deficit (SMD)

The SMD is the *difference* between the soil water content at 'field capacity' and the soil water content at any given time. It is usually expressed in terms of 'precipitation equivalent' (see last paragraph of the introduction to this chapter).

Permanent wilting point (PWP)

PWP is the condition of the soil where healthy plants can extract no more moisture from the soil; consequently they wilt and do not recover overnight. PWP corresponds to a soil moisture tension/matric potential of approximately 20 bars. As soil moisture tension increases beyond 1 bar, plant growth may slow because of restrictions in water supply. See also section 11.3.1 'Diurnal variation'.

Availability water capacity (AWC)

The water available to plants is the difference in water content between the soil at 'field capacity' and 'permanent wilting point'. Soil texture determines the quantity of water within this range (see Table 11.1 and Fig. 11.1).

At one time it was believed that all the 'available' water in soil was equally available to plants and that plants would grow at a steady rate as long as there was some 'available' water. Re-examination of early data showed that in most cases this was not so and that growth was affected by the extent of water depletion (Stanhill, 1957).

Readily available soil water

For most soils, approximately half the 'avail-

Table 11.1 Typical available water capacities of some common soil textures in approximately increasing order

Available water capacity	Soil texture
Low: not more than 12.5% by volume	Coarse sand Loamy coarse sand Coarse sandy loam
Medium: >12.5 and <20% by volume	Sand Loamy sand Fine sand Loamy fine sand Clay Clay loam Sandy loam Loam
High: >20% by volume	Very fine sand Silt loam Peaty soils

In this list, available water capacities are reduced where there is:

high stone content; appreciable compaction; reduced organic matter.

For full list, see MAFF Reference Book 138 (MAFF, 1981).

able water capacity' of a soil is available at a matric tension of 1 bar or less. While such water continues to be available, plants are under low moisture stress and are not checked in growth. Such water is referred to subsequently in this Bulletin as 'readily available soil water'. As moisture tensions exceed 1 bar, while moisture is available, the stress within the plant increases.

Examples of estimates of *available water* and *readily available water* for different soil depths are given in Table 11.2. It should be noted that for the extreme cases shown here, there are noticeable differences between the amounts of 'readily available water' and the residual available water, the coarsest texture soil having little water left once all the readily available water has been used. See also 'droughtiness' in the immediately following subsection.

Irrigation regimes based on assessment of water depletion are often designed to replenish 'readily available soil water' when the 'available water capacity' is calculated or is found by measurement to have fallen to

Table 11.2 Water availability in surface soil down to 30 cm depth

Soil texture	Available water capacity per 10 cm depth of soil	Readily available soil water (i.e. available at 0.05 – 1 bar matric potential)				Residual available water per 10 cm depth of soil
		per 10 cm depth of soil	In soil-depth			
			10 cm	20 cm	30 cm	
Loamy coarse sand	12	8	8	16	24	4
Sandy loam	16	10	10	20	30	6
Fine sandy loam	20	12	12	24	36	8

Units are mm precipitation equivalent per unit area.

50%, or measurements of 1 bar matric potential are being obtained. Prescriptions for irrigation regimes based on readily available soil water are given in Table 11.3.

Droughtiness

Droughtiness expresses the risk that readily available soil water reserves are used up by the crop or lost by evaporation before they are replaced by precipitation. Droughtiness may arise from:

- small water storage capacity due to soil texture,
- low average rainfall at the time of year water is most needed by crops,
- growth of crops with large water requirements,

or varying combinations of all factors. The concept has been used for agricultural land as the basis for land classification and for assessing the worthwhileness of irrigation.

It will be seen from Table 11.2 that the coarsest texture soil has the least 'readily available soil water' per unit depth, will run out of readily available soil water more quickly and is therefore more 'droughty' than

Table 11.3 Forest nursery crop irrigation prescriptions, reduction factors for incomplete crop cover and accessible soil depths for sandy soils

Crop type	Accessible soil depth (cm)	Ground cover (%)	Reduction factor for partial crop cover	Irrigation prescribed based on calculation of soil moisture deficit (SMD) using reduction factor
Newly sown seedbeds	5	0	0.5	If SMD >6 mm immediately after sowing, apply 6 mm, then 6 mm whenever SMD reaches 6 mm. After end of June, use mid-season regime.
Newly lined out seedlings	10	10–20	0.6	If SMD >10 mm immediately after lining out, apply 10 mm and repeat whenever SMD reaches 10 mm until 8 weeks after lining out, then use mid-season regime.
Newly undercut seedlings	8–10	20–100	0.5–1 depending on density of ground cover	If SMD >10 mm, 10 mm immediately after undercutting, and repeat whenever SMD reaches 10 mm, until late in the season.
Mid-season	30	30–80	0.7 for 1st year 0.9 for 2nd year	15 mm whenever SMD exceeds 15 mm.

soils with greater readily available soil water capacities.

Irrigation regimes on the droughtier soils need to be more frequent and less in quantity, even though the same volume of water is applied in the end. Applying relatively small amounts of irrigation at less than 7 day intervals is sometimes referred to as 'high frequency irrigation' (Hobbs and Krogman, 1978). It requires a mechanised system that can be moved round the nursery efficiently.

Available water capacity and machine access

The disadvantage that is often associated with less droughty soils, is that such soils not only retain more water but are also slower to drain, more easily affected by compaction and may not be so quickly available for machine access after periods of rain, especially in the winter. It should be noted that in Table 11.1 the AWC of very fine sandy soils is higher than for many loams and clays. Consequently, on soils which though sandy, have a high proportion of fine sand, a particularly close watch should be kept for the development of cultivation pans and immediate steps taken to loosen any compaction at the first opportunity.

Soil saturation

Soils are 'saturated' when all the available pore spaces between soil particles are filled with water. As soil water drains under the force of gravity, the emptying pore spaces become filled with air until 'field capacity' is reached.

'Slaking'

While soil surface layers are saturated, and especially if the soil is being bombarded by heavy raindrops or large droplets from an irrigation system, there is a risk that soil particles will be loosened and moved; any soil structure or aggregates left after cultivations may collapse under the impact and 'slake', i.e. particles will slump into the larger air channels and block them. Where this happens, the infiltration rate drops; often when the soil surface subsequently dries, a dense crust forms at the soil surface which slows the rate of water infiltration and, where no seedbed grit has been applied, may also inhibit seedling emergence.

11.2.3 Measurement of soil water

Water in the soil has been measured in terms of:

- weight,
- the tension under which it exists at any given time,
- percentage of the soil volume.

Weighing

Earliest measurements of soil moisture contents were by weighing, drying and reweighing. The technique remains valid, provided the conditions for drying are standardised. The results however may overestimate the water available to plants.

Weighing is of most use when used to assess the change in weight of a sample, with a view to restoring its original weight by watering, e.g. plants grown in special containers (lysimeters), or modules such as trays of seedlings in Japanese paper pots when growing in polytunnels. In this second situation, there is in fact little or no soil in the growing medium and it is the loss from the medium itself which is being monitored (Lane, 1989).

Measurement of soil moisture tension / matric potential

Soil moisture tension can be measured by tensiometers consisting of a porous ceramic container filled with water connected either directly to a water-operated, or indirectly to a piezo-electric, pressure gauge. The most up-to-date designs are less cumbersome than earlier models, with hydraulic circuits which automatically vent any air entering the system. They are used on a small scale in farms in the UK (MAFF, 1981); in the US, they control irrigation schedules in container-grown plants (Burger and Paul, 1987; Lieth and Burger, 1989).

A portable tensiometer has been developed which by careful pushing at a shallow angle into the soil and taking care not to change the angle while doing so, can give an indication of the water status in the surface layers of newly germinating seedbeds and recently lined out transplants.

Electrical resistance blocks made of porous materials have been widely tested as a means of estimating matric potential but have not been sufficiently consistent in operation to come into general use (Duryea and Landis, 1984).

Estimation of soil water content by neutron probe

Soil moisture content can be measured using neutrons from a low grade radioactive source. Aluminium tubes are inserted into the soil wherever soil moisture is to be determined; the neutron source is lowered down each tube when a measurement is required. Neutrons are reflected by hydrogen ions, the amount of neutron reflection recorded being directly proportional to the water content of the soil.

The system has to be calibrated for any particular site and is mostly used as a check on the effectiveness of irrigation regimes based on evapotranspiration, rather than as the primary basis for prescription. It is not suitable for measurements in the top 25 cm of soil.

Proper precautions must be observed when handling the equipment; nevertheless, the technique is utilised commercially in the UK by specialist enterprises offering irrigation prescription services (SAC, 1991).

11.3 Water tension in plants

In the same way as moisture moves in the soil in response to naturally occurring physical forces, water movement in plants is a response to tensions generated at the transpiring surfaces of plant tissue and resistances in the soil and stem water conducting tissues.

In addition, however, in plants, water is able to move in and out of tissues by osmosis, i.e. the property of water to pass through a semipermeable membrane from a solution of low salt concentration to one of higher concentration. Plants may also move water through cell tissues expending energy to do so. Consequently, some plant cells regularly develop positive pressures, e.g. to maintain turgor, while within the main water-conducting tissues, water may be under considerable tension.

High tensions (or potentials) within leaf tissues may lead to closure of stomata on leaf surfaces and reduction of the rate of water loss. One consequence of such closure is that foliage temperature rises to equal or exceed that of the surrounding air. (As long as water is evaporating through transpiration, temperatures should be a few degrees below that of the surrounding air.) A second consequence is that the gas exchange essential for photosynthesis is prevented. Stomatal closure is, however, a very late response to moisture shortage.

11.3.1 Diurnal variation

Plants cannot avoid being exposed to a repeated diurnal cycle of changing atmospheric vapour pressure deficits, reflecting the temperature and humidity of air as it changes through 24 h. On many days, this deficit reaches its maximum for a period from late morning to mid-afternoon and falls to zero overnight.

Water tension in plants follows a similar diurnal pattern, but with a time lag. In hot weather, water may be transpired at a greater rate than can be supplied by the roots so that foliage wilts during warm afternoons. However, as long as there is water available in the soil and plants remain healthy, they will recover unharmed. This temporary wilting is not a sign that the soil is at 'permanent wilting point'.

Currently, schemes for controlling irrigation schedules take no account of diurnal variation except where there is a risk of damage to plants by high temperatures at the soil surface and irrigation is applied for its cooling effect.

11.3.2 Measurement of water tension in plants

Pressure chamber or pressure 'bomb'

Water tension in leaves – normally referred to as 'leaf water potential', may be measured by placing detached leaves in a 'pressure chamber' where pressure is applied up to the point that water is forced out of exposed conducting tissue, counteracting the tension within the leaf (Ritchie and Hinckley, 1975). The technique can be used to test not only the water status of plants in relation to irrigation, but also in relation to storage and handling shortly before despatch from the nursery.

Water tension measurements on NW American conifers have been made in a number of regions, particularly, New Zealand, where the pressure chamber technique is now considered fast, reliable and accurate (Cleary and Zaerr, 1980).

In the UK, pressure bombs have been used to assess effects of undercutting – the results given in Figure 8.1 were obtained by this method. However, it is not in routine use in nurseries.

Relative humidity at plant surfaces

Methods exist for assessing water tension in plants by measuring the relative humidity at the surface of plant leaves, or at the surface of stem tissues from which the epidermis has been removed. Currently, these techniques can be applied to horticultural crops but not yet to forest plants (McBurney and Costigan, 1982).

11.4 Planning for irrigation

When considering the possibility of installing irrigation for open nursery ground, several groups of factors have to be taken into account:

- crop water requirements in dry weather, forecast from plans for the scale of future cropping; these should include forecasts of aggregate and peak seasonal demand, and demands arising from other operations requiring water, e.g. application of fertilisers, frost protection (sections 11.4.1–3);

- long-term rainfall, temperature and wind, etc., for the site, both values (average and range) and distribution during the growing season so as to estimate potential net water loss from the nursery (section 11.4.4);
- availability of water and the scale of provision of sprinklers, pumps, reservoirs/boreholes, pipework, etc. (section 11.4.5);
- soil texture and structure, and the local topography (section 11.4.6);
- the estimated profitability of investment in irrigation (section 11.4.7).

11.4.1 Crop water requirements

Irrigation is currently applied in forest nurseries to prevent or relieve plant moisture stress:

- in germinating seed immediately after sowing, especially where the seed has been treated by moist prechilling;
- when seedlings are transplanted during the growing season;
- when seedlings are undercut during the growing season;
- during the growing season in periods of dry weather.

In each situation, how much water to apply and when to apply is determined by estimating current evapotranspiration rates and soil moisture deficit, and relating these to the particular requirements of the crop and soil at the time, as described in section 11.6.1 below.

Irrigation may also be required:

- to ensure top dressings of fertiliser are washed into the upper layers of the soil;
- to assist the action of herbicides, where appropriate;
- to reduce the risk of damage by unseasonal frost;
- to cool the seedbed surface in periods of very hot weather to prevent heat damage.

For these operations, empirical prescriptions are applied, as described in section 11.4.3.

11.4.2 Irrigation prescriptions, crop cover and soil depth

Table 11.3 (p. 152) gives recommendations for

irrigation for various crop stages, values for the percentage of the ground covered by crops, and associated reduction factors to be used when calculating the daily water balance. It also gives the depth of soil to be considered, when calculating both the size of the water reserves in the soil and the amount of irrigation required for a particular type of crop. Table 11.2 (p. 152) shows the amounts of water readily available to crops for the range of soil textures and rooting depths commonest in forest nurseries.

The recommendations in these tables must be taken as guides only, the nursery manager modifying them according to the actual state of crop and soil as seems necessary. Overwatering must be avoided as any temporary waterlogging could give rise to fungal damage.

The reduction factor for seedbeds is based on assumptions that the surface soil must be kept damp at all times, but that the surface cover of seedbed grit will materially reduce the rate of water loss by surface evaporation from the underlying soil. If seedbeds are shaded, surface evaporation will be further reduced.

It is assumed that netting protection against birds has no effect on moisture loss.

For newly lined out seedlings and for freshly undercut beds, the aim is to ensure that the soil immediately after the operation is well wetted and that for the first 2 weeks afterwards, daily water deficits are kept low. During this period, the soil surface should remain damp. Where a range of reduction factors is given in Table 11.3, a value within the range should be selected based on the estimated ground cover of the crop to be irrigated and the species, checking by the appearance of the crop that the factor chosen is not too low. Particular attention should be paid to soil surface conditions for newly sown pre-treated or stratified seed, especially if this had been well chitted at the time of sowing.

11.4.3 Other uses of irrigation

Washing in fertilisers
Dry granular fertilisers applied as top-dress-

ings can be washed into the soil using irrigation. If the soil surface is damp, a minimum of 7 mm of water should be applied for this purpose; if dry, the minimum should be 15 mm. Fertiliser top-dressings can also be applied just before an irrigation is due, so that the need for extra water is avoided.

Soluble fertilisers may also be applied to crops through the irrigation water. The amount of *additional* irrigation water required is so small as not to affect long-term planning.

Residual herbicides applied over seedbeds or lines
Where herbicides are applied which act through uptake by weed roots in the surface layers of the soil, a light application of irrigation (5–7 mm) will ensure the herbicide is carried down to into the soil sufficiently to become active. Such treatment is not necessary if there has been any significant rainfall since the herbicide was applied. Herbicide should be deferred if a heavy application of irrigation is imminent.

Protection against frost during the growing season
The protection achievable by irrigation against unseasonal frost depends on two effects:

1. the latent heat released when water freezes and
2. the conductivity of the soil as a heat source.

The aim is to keep the foliage of plants wetted, so that even though the air temperature is well below freezing, latent heat from the freezing water will prevent the foliage temperature from falling to a level that plants are physically damaged. If the soil at the same time is well wetted, it will act better as a 'storage heater' and heat conductor than if dry.

The most that a full canopy of foliage can retain before water runs off and soaks into the ground is the equivalent of about 2.5 mm of rain; most crops will be able to hold less than this. Intermittent slow, light applications of irrigation with as fine a droplet as possible are likely to be the most effective in keeping foliage surfaces wet. They should commence when severe radiation frost is expected when ground temperatures are just around freezing point, and continue until temperatures have risen above freezing point again. Plants may become heavily encrusted with ice. Any consequent mechanical damage is likely to be less than frost damage if the plants are at a susceptible stage of growth and the frost is severe.

Temperature reduction

Where seedbed surfaces get so hot in early summer that seedlings are at risk of heat damage, mid-day irrigation can be applied to cool seedbeds as an alternative to shading. Heat damage can be expected when surface temperatures exceed 35–40°C. The effect of irrigation is to reduce temperatures by up to 10°C through the cooling effect of water evaporation (Duryea and Landis, 1984).

Irrigation directly for temperature reduction has not played a large part in irrigation practice in forest nurseries in the UK to date.

Hardening off and irrigation regimes

Growth of several conifer species (e.g. Douglas fir, *Abies concolor,* and *Pinus radiata*) can be prolonged into the autumn by irrigation. In New Zealand and NW United States, regimes have been developed to allow the soil moisture deficit to increase towards the end of the growing season (Rook, 1973; Zaerr *et al.*, 1981). The aim has been to encourage vigorous shoot growth early in the season and gradually to increase moisture deficits in the second half of the growing season.

There is evidence that plants respond to a period of water stress by developing thicker, more waxy foliage cuticle, and that the extent of suberisation (development of a water-resistant layer) in the roots reflects the available soil water (Kramer and Bullock, 1966; Rook, 1973).

In normal seasons, irrigation should not be continued on conventional seedbeds and lines beyond the end of August. For beds on intensive undercutting/wrenching regimes, the need for irrigation has to be determined at the time in relation to crop growth, timing of cutting/wrenching and soil moisture.

11.4.4 Long-term climatic data

The prescriptions given in Table 11.3 are of little use in long-term planning of water need, unless forecasts can be made of how often any given prescription is likely to be necessary. For the United Kingdom, data from long-term records maintained by the Meteorological Office are available, currently for the period 1960–1985. They can be applied to irrigation planning, through the 'Met. Office Rainfall and Evaporation Calculation System' or 'MORECS' (Gardner, 1983).

Estimate of dry year water requirement

The first requirement is an understanding of how much water is likely to be required in 'dry' years. There is no standard 'dry' year; variation in rainfall patterns and amounts can only be viewed on the basis of 'how often over the last 20 years would x, y or z mm of water have been required for crops not to have suffered severe moisture stress/poor germination/poor survival which irrigation could have overcome?'

For agricultural crops, 'model' irrigation plans have been identified and graphs drawn which indicate for given values of rainfall and crop water need, how often over a 10-year period, irrigation would be necessary to avoid crop water stress (Hogg, 1967; MAFF, 1981; 1984 a, c).

For forest nurseries, local calculations have to be made to establish the same principle; these are best done with the assistance of an agrometeorologist able to offer advice. See section 11.6.3 below. Otherwise, calculations must be based on tables of monthly average evapotranspiration such as included in MAFF Booklet 2396, *Daily calculation of irrigation need* (MAFF, 1984b).

Estimate of peak demand

The second requirement is to identify the size

and timing of possible peak water demands, to determine the capacity of the equipment, boreholes, reservoirs, etc., to supply that demand. This does not require additional climatic data; calculations have to be made to show the rate of water use in relation to alternative sources of water supply and methods of application. See also section 11.4.7 'Economic appraisal'.

11.4.5 Availability of water

The availability of a water supply to meet peak short-term demand, which is adequate both quantitatively and qualitatively (especially in dry years) has to be investigated.

Water is likely to come from local boreholes or specially constructed reservoirs. Supplies from mains and from local rivers are often restricted by water authorities, just at the time when plant stresses are building up. Where such supplies are available, the user usually has to provide a reservoir at least capable of holding one day's supply so that it can be recharged overnight. In other circumstances, water may not be available in the dry summer months so that any reservoir has to be large enough to hold several weeks' peak demand.

Water quality

Water used for irrigation should if possible be soft. Hard water used regularly can raise the pH of the soil sufficiently to depress the growth of seedling conifers sensitive to soil reaction; if no other alternative is available, it may be necessary periodically to counter any pH rise by local acidification; see Chapter 3, section 3.2.4 'Soil acidification'.

A water analysis is required, not only to determine pH but also to check for the presence of other dissolved salts, pesticide residues, etc.

Legislation controlling abstraction of water for irrigation

There is separate legislation for Scotland and for England and Wales, regulating abstraction of water for irrigation.

In Scotland, River Purification Boards are responsible for controlling irrigation under the Natural Heritage (Scotland) Act 1991. Control areas may be designated; anyone wishing to abstract water for irrigation within a control area has to obtain a annual licence from the Board.

In England and Wales, applications to obtain water for irrigation have to be made to the National Rivers Authority. The Water Act, 1989, transferred powers to license water abstraction under the 1963 Water Resources Act from River Authorities to the National Rivers Authority. In many areas, the National Rivers Authority operates a regional office from the same address as the previous Water Authority main office.

Licences in England and Wales stay in force unless surrendered or revoked. However, they may be suspended temporarily in times of severe regional drought if a 'General Drought Order' or 'Emergency Drought Order' has been issued. Alternatively, conditions may be included in the licence requiring the maintenance of specified minimum flows of water, or minimum levels in boreholes or reservoirs.

Licences will also specify:

- point of abstraction,
- purpose of use,
- maximum quantity that can be abstracted in a given period,
- means of abstraction,
- basis of assessing the quantity used.

Costs depend on local circumstances but are usually higher in the summer than in the winter.

It may turn out that water is only available during the winter, in which case, construction of a reservoir for summer supplies may have to be considered and a separate licence to impound sought. If granted, a combined licence to impound and extract is normally issued.

11.4.6 Soil factors

Soil factors influencing the scale of irrigation and the type of equipment suitable for the site include:

- available water capacity,

- water infiltration rate,
- soil and site drainage,
- soil bearing capacity.

Available water capacity
(see also section 11.2.2)

The available water capacity of soils encountered in forest nurseries is likely to fall within the range of values shown in Table 11.1. The range is sufficient for it to be worthwhile to have a proper assessment of available water capacity based on soil samples from the nursery site. The *Soil survey field handbook* (Hodgson, 1985) describes how this can be done. Alternatively, ADAS and similar advisory services can undertake this (see section 11.6.3).

Essentially, the assessment measures the size of the water reservoir in the soil; the larger this reservoir, the greater the chances of rainfall replenishing soil water before a critical deficit is reached, and the less the need for irrigation water. This would affect the size of any reservoir necessary, but would not affect the possible maximum rate of daily application.

Water infiltration and soil structure

The maximum rate at which water will enter soil depends on the size and number of stable air spaces at and below the soil surface, soil moisture content at the time, and how long water has been falling on the soil surface.

Infiltration progressively falls with time to reach an 'equilibrium infiltration capacity'; this may take between 20 min and 2 h depending on the soil texture and soil density. Soil compaction can have a particularly marked effect in reducing infiltration capacity.

The infiltration rate can also vary during a season according to whether the soil has a stable surface crumb structure, capable of withstanding the impact of heavy rain and large droplets or has slaked and developed a crust (see section 11.2.2, last paragraph), and whether any cultural operation during the season has compacted the soil. Operations such as undercutting and side-cutting break up any crust and thereby facilitate infiltration.

In practice, many forest nursery soils do develop crusts during the season; in planning, provision should be made using infiltration rates on soils where crusts have developed, so as to have a 'worst situation' figure and avoid the risk of wasteful run-off. Irrigation equipment should be specified that does not generate large droplets, cause capping and reduce infiltration rates.

Soil and site drainage

The consequences have to be considered of excessive wetness caused either by unexpectedly heavy rainfall following shortly after irrigation, or by malfunction of the irrigation system. Normally, a nursery's drainage system will be robust enough to cope with seasonal high intensity downpours and will not need any modification. However, if the soil already shows signs of local soil erosion in such circumstances, serious thought should be given to the consequences of heavy rain, e.g. thunderstorm, on recently irrigated soil.

Soil bearing capacity and cultural operations

Finer textured soils, e.g. loamy fine sands, when fully rewetted may not be able to bear tractors, etc., without damage. If operations such as undercutting or lifting require soil to be under a slight moisture deficit in order to get good traction and avoid soil compaction, this could slightly reduce overall water requirements and necessitate particular attention to good surface drainage.

11.4.7 Economic appraisal

At this point, economic evaluations have to be made as to whether investment in irrigation is justified. Judgements in particular have to be made as to whether to provide for a recurrence of the worst drought that occurred in the last 20 years, so that equipment and facilities will be under-used for most of the time, or whether provision is set at for example, to meet requirements in 7 years out of 10, plants suffering some stress in the other 3 years but much less than if no irrigation were available.

In view of the size of investment if large scale irrigation is in mind, it is important to consider a number of different possible combinations of schedules, equipment and future cropping plans before reaching a decision. 'Sensitivity analysis' should be used to estimate the effects of changing the various judgements and working assumptions incorporated in the initial proposals. While this may appear to involve repetitive calculations, it is the only sure way to reach a clear understanding of the best options.

11.5 Irrigation equipment

There is a very wide range of irrigation equipment available on the market in the United Kingdom, developed for agricultural and horticultural crops. Reference books listed at the end of the chapter provide detailed guidance on principles and practice in operating irrigation equipment. If considering substantial investment in new equipment, professional assistance should be sought for information on currently available equipment, calculations of water need, pipe layout, etc., e.g. from local offices of ADAS in England and Wales, and branches of the Scottish Agricultural College in Scotland. Information on sources of advice, etc., can also be obtained from the Irrigation Association, c/o National College of Agricultural Engineering, Silsoe, Bedfordshire, MK45 4DT.

For open-grown nursery stock in Britain, water has to be applied by some form of sprinkler system. The two methods currently in use are the oscillating sprayline, and the mobile rotating boom.

The oscillating sprayline method works well, involves relatively less capital outlay but requires a lot of manpower whenever the pipes have to be moved.

In recent years, mobile rotating boom sprinklers linked to hose reel and wire reel systems have come increasingly into use because they can be moved and set up by one man and tractor (Plate 29).

11.5.1 Pump, mainline and laterals

Whatever the final means of distributing the water over the crop, the irrigation system must include:

- pump;
- mainline;
- laterals.

Other equipment, such as relief valves, filters, etc., may be required according to local circumstance.

Pump

The pump draws water from a reservoir, borehole or stream and is powered by electric motor or internal combustion engine. The pump must be of a capacity and design to sustain flow of water to meet peak demand, when the water reservoir or borehole levels are at their lowest and the water most likely to be dirty and contaminated with sand.

If it appears that pressure at spraylines is insufficient, because of long pipe runs or other uncontrollable cause, the possibility of installing a supplementary pump near the irrigator should be considered as an alternative to increasing the capacity of the main pump and pipework, or risking inadequate water distribution through low water pressure.

A pressure relief valve and return pipe to the reservoir is desirable in order to maintain even pressure and sustained water flow under all operating conditions.

Filters

Filters may be necessary to reduce the amount of solids flowing through the system, arising from dirty water, borehole sand, corrosion products in pipes and accumulated bacterial slime, etc.

Wherever filters are installed in any system, they must be cleaned out regularly, otherwise they will reduce the flow of water through the system.

Filters are essential to protect any part of

the nursery where trickle irrigation is being used, e.g. container stock.

Mainline pipework

The mainline delivers water from the pump to the lateral distribution system. Often, this line is permanent and is PVC pipe laid below ground so as not to interfere with the passage of machinery. Where the pipe is 50 mm diameter or less it should be at 0.5 m depth or more; if more than 50 mm diameter, the pipe should be 0.75 m deep, both to avoid being damaged by wheeled traffic and to escape the effects of severe frost.

The main pipework layout can all be underground; equally, there may be situations where a smaller permanent layout and one or more portable main spurs is more appropriate, especially where different main sections are likely to need irrigation in different years.

Pressure loss and friction

Pressure is greatest at pipework connections nearest the pump; pipes must be of a grade sufficient to withstand these pressures. The cost of pipes depends on their size and pressure class; in deciding what is an acceptable pressure, the cost of pumping to overcome friction in the distribution system has to be balanced against the cost of increasing pipe size.

- For a given pipe diameter and flow rate, loss of pressure due to friction is proportional to the *length* of the pipe;
- For a given size and type of pipe, the loss of pressure due to friction is approximately proportional to the *square of the flow rate.*
- For a given length of pipe and flow rate, the pressure required is inversely proportional to the *fourth power of the pipe radius.* For example, doubling the pipe radius will reduce the pressure required sixteenfold.

Manufacturers and suppliers can provide graphs and tables showing friction losses for the pipes they supply.

At intervals along main pipe layouts and at the ends, connection points or hydrants are necessary. The number of these should be determined by the cost and time required to move equipment.

Laterals

Laterals deliver water from the main water pipe layout to spraylines; laterals are usually portable, made of lightweight alloy, galvanised steel or plastic, so that they can easily be moved.

They may be replaced by hoses where mobile hose reel systems are in use.

11.5.2 Spraylines and sprinklers

There are two main types of sprayline in use in forest nurseries:

- fixed or oscillating spraylines,
- mobile rotary boom sprayers.

While rotary sprinklers are widely used in agriculture, they normally give too large a droplet size for forest nursery requirements.

Sprayline/sprinkler droplet size is determined by nozzle size and operating pressure.

In forest nurseries, equipment should be selected and operated to avoid:

- production of large droplets which would damage the soil surface;
- surface run-off as a result of too rapid or too prolonged application of water.

See also end of section 11.2.2, 'Soil saturation' and 'Slaking'.

Whenever possible, irrigation spraylines should be laid out as near as possible on a contour, so that pressure at nozzles along the line are affected only by the friction pressure loss in the pipe.

Oscillating and fixed spraylines

Oscillating and fixed spraylines have to be set up by hand. They provide a fine spray applied slowly; oscillating sprayline droplets rarely damage the soil surface.

The advantage of fixed or oscillating spraylines is that they can apply water relatively uniformly to rectangular sections of ground. Any rotary system, whether sprayline or boom-mounted sprinkler does not cover the corners of sections without special provision or waste of water. Where mobile rotary sprinklers are used, corners of sections are only able to be watered if unproductive ground beyond the end of the section is also treated.

Travelling spraylines

Travelling spraylines are mounted on carriages which slowly traverse the area to be sprayed (Plate 30).

The equipment is propelled by a water-powered turbine which turns a drum on to which a guide cable winds. The cable is anchored at the end of the area to be watered, and when the boom gets there, it turns itself off. The supply hose lies in the alley between beds and is dragged along as the machine moves up the section.

There is an appreciable volume of water in the booms and hoses; care has to be taken when draining the equipment before moving it, to avoid local scour or erosion of beds by drainage water.

Self-propelled rotary boom sprayers

Self-propelled rotary boom sprayers have recently been introduced into Forestry Commission nurseries. The spray pattern from this equipment is of acceptably fine droplets, the equipment being set to apply the equivalent of 3–6 mm rainfall per pass. The equipment takes 2 hours to cover 100 m run; the boom is 19.5 m long and covers a swath 35 m wide.

Irrigating in windy conditions

Sprayline performance is distorted even by quite light winds (5 m s^{-1}); in theory, to obtain uniform distribution of water, spraylines and the line of travel of rotary boom sprinklers need to be aligned with the wind direction. In practice, this is not possible as the layout of seedbeds and lines determines the way irrigation equipment can be used.

In windy conditions, especially variable or gusty winds, it is important to set out gauges to monitor the amount of water reaching the ground.

Oscillating spraylines can be adjusted so that the arc of spraying can point into the wind. With rotary boom sprayers, adjustments have to be made according to actual performance, possibly altering the speed of travel and the distance between parallel runs. Trial and error, linked to observations of water distribution in temporary local gauges is the only way to gain experience of how to respond to windy conditions when irrigating.

11.6 How much water to apply and how often

In operation, irrigation water has to be used as effectively as possible, because of the cost of water and its application, and the need to conserve what in dry seasons may be a limited resource.

In the UK, schedules of irrigation in forest nurseries are controlled by water balance sheets. These require records of current rainfall and irrigation applied, and may be based on long-term climatic data alone, or the same data, updated to take account of recent weather.

11.6.1 Rainfall and irrigation records

To control the use of irrigation, it is essential to have a consistent record of rainfall measured using a properly sited standard rain gauge. Information on siting and design can be obtained from the *Observer's handbook* (Anon., 1982).

Additional gauges should be available to be placed wherever irrigation is in progress. The amount of water applied can be estimated from the rated capacity of nozzles, the duration of irrigation and the nominal area treated; however, some gauges should always be set out for every irrigation to check how evenly water is being applied, how equipment is performing in relation to its nominal output, and what allowances should be made, for example, in windy weather.

11.6.2 Balance sheets and irrigation prescriptions based on monthly average data

Irrigation schedules in the UK can be based

on simple water 'balance sheets' using local monthly average climatic data as the basis for estimating water loss. Average daily values are calculated per month and adjusted for crop cover, rainfall and irrigation to estimate soil moisture deficits. Irrigation is applied whenever a threshold soil moisture deficit is exceeded.

The main limitation of this method is that it cannot take into account short-term divergences from the monthly average estimates of water loss. Consequently, in hot weather, plants are subjected to extra moisture stress, while in cold spells, plants could be overwatered, both incurring unnecessary expense and risking leaching soil nutrients.

When to irrigate: calculation using a balance sheet and long-term climatic data

A running daily water balance sheet can be maintained by offsetting the daily estimated water loss against recorded daily rainfall and irrigation.

Values for estimated average monthly water loss by evaporation and transpiration can be obtained from reference books such as MAFF Booklet 2396 *Daily calculation of irrigation need* (MAFF, 1984b). Monthly values for the growing season for the most local reference points to the nursery are taken as the starting point. The monthly figures are converted into an average daily water loss.

The irrigation and rainfall figures are obtained from daily records kept on the nursery.

During the months when natural evapotranspiration is high, i.e. May–August, daily deficits occur frequently and in spite of rainfall, soon lead to a sufficient cumulative deficit to justify irrigation. The amount to be applied should follow the recommendations in Table 11.3 using the balance sheet 'running deficit' multiplied by the appropriate 'reduction factor' from Table 11.3. This allows for incomplete crop cover typical of most forest nursery crops, and is assumed to reduce the soil moisture deficit to zero when the application is completed. Table 11.4 illustrates a typical page maintained by this method.

11.6.3 Prescriptions based on long-term data adjusted for recent weather

Contemporary electronic technology is currently bringing down the cost of instrumentation to measure local weather. It is also providing the software both to enable such measurements to be applied to calculations such as estimating daily evapotranspiration and also to provide irrigation prescriptions

Table 11.4 Example of an irrigation balance sheet (all figures in mm)

Location: South-east Oxfordshire						
Monthly average loss by evapotranspiration: 75						
Daily average loss by evapotranspiration: 2.5						
Date	Daily average loss by evapo-transpiration	Rainfall in previous 24 hours	Irrigation	Running deficit	Reduction factor for current crop	Notes
–	–	–	–	5.7	–	(brought forward)
13.5	2.5	0.0	0.0	8.2	0.5	–
14.5	2.5	0.0	0.0	10.7	0.5	–
15.5	2.5	0.0	6.1	13.2/0.0	0.5	Seedbeds irrigated for 2 hours during day
16.5	2.5	0.0	0.0	2.5	0.5	–
17.5	2.5	1.8	0.0	3.3	0.5	–
18.5	2.5	5.6	0.0	0.0	0.5	–
19.5	2.5	0.0	0.0	2.7	0.5	–
20.5	2.5	1.1	0.0	4.1	0.5	–

which take account of the local recent weather. Consequently, techniques previously restricted to research establishments (Norman and Campbell, 1983; Papadopol, 1984; Phene, 1989), are now commercially available.

Commercially available irrigation prescription services

Commercial services to growers, offering weekly irrigation prescriptions for some agricultural crops, include:

- ADAS 'Irriguide' system. This, though designed for arable farm crops, can be extended to give some guidance to forest nursery managers – for current details apply to the local ADAS office.

- Scottish Agricultural College (SAC);
- Hydro/Agri (fertiliser manufacturers);
- Irrigation Management Services, Silsoe College, Beds.

} these offer services more oriented to farm crops especially potatoes and vegetables.

ADAS also offer a service, 'Irriplan', assessing whether it is worthwhile installing irrigation equipment; this is primarily directed at farmers but can be modified for specified forest nursery irrigation regimes.

Commercial scheduling services require:

- At the start of the season, details of:
  (a) the location (to be able to relate the site to the national meteorological database), and, on a field by field basis, data on soil texture, available water capacity within the profile, and an indication of the slope of the site;

  (b) crops to be grown;

  (c) irrigation regime to be followed for the crops to be treated;

  (d) the time taken to apply a given amount of irrigation with the equipment available.

- Each week:
  (a) rainfall and irrigation each day;

  (b) date of any cultivation or similar operation.

- When appropriate:
  information of crop development and ground cover.

The grower is then regularly given specific advice as to how much water he should apply, when and to which crops. The service may arrange for periodic field visits to check actual soil moisture content against what their predictions show. Any nursery manager using this system should consider following the irrigation regimes given in Table 11.3.

11.6.4 Empirical control

Any balance sheet based on long-term averages can be overridden or adjusted if treatments seem inappropriate, for example because the weather is exceptionally hot or cold or windy.

If a balance sheet cannot be kept at all, for any reason, the following empirical prescription should be followed.

- Germinating seedbeds should be irrigated in dry spells with one 10 mm application of water per week until germination appears complete, or more frequently if the surface of the soil under the grit cover appears to dry out before the next weekly watering is due.

- A similar prescription should be followed for newly lined out and recently undercut seedlings.

- For established seedbeds and lines during dry spells, a weekly application of 15 mm should suffice.

11.6.5 Avoidance of overwatering

Care should be taken never to apply more water than would restore the soil to field capacity.

- There is a risk that a cap of water-saturated soil could allow a sudden temporary depletion of oxygen in the soil, thereby harming actively respiring roots and providing opportunities for attack by fungal pests.

- Irrigating excess water costs money!

- In addition to wasting water, it is probable that some soluble fertilisers will be lost by leaching.

There is also the risk that heavy rainfall

shortly before any fertiliser plus irrigation treatment, will saturate the soil; further water will mainly run off or drain through, taking some of the recently added nutrients away in solution. A local 3-day weather forecast should always be obtained if fertilisers are to be applied in conjunction with irrigation.

REFERENCES AND FURTHER READING

ANON. (1982). *Observer's handbook,* 4th edtn. Meteorological Office, Met.O.933. HMSO, London.

BATCHELOR, C.H. (1984). The accuracy of evapotranspiration estimated with the FAO modified Penman equation. *Irrigation Science* **5,** 1–11.

BURGER, D.W. and PAUL, J.L. (1987). Soil moisture measurements in containers with solid state electronic tensiometers. *Hort-Science* **22** (2), 309–310.

BURMAN, R.D., CUENCA, R.H. and WEISS, A. (1983). Techniques for estimating irrigation water requirements. *Advances in Irrigation* **2,** 335–394.

CLEARY, B.D. and ZAERR, J.D. (1980). Pressure chamber techniques for monitoring and evaluating seedling water status. *New Zealand Journal of Forest Science* **10** (1), 133 *et seq.*, 141.

DOORENBOS, J. and PRUITT, N.O. (1977). Crop water requirements, irrigation and drainage. *Paper* **24** (2nd edtn). FAO, Rome. (144 pp.)

DURYEA, M.L. and LANDIS, T.D. (1984). *Forest nursery manual: production of bare-root seedlings.* Nijhoff/Junk, The Hague.

GARDNER, C.M.K. (1983). Evaluating the success of MORECS, a Meteorological Office model in estimating soil moisture deficit. *Agricultural Meteorology* **29,** 269–284.

HIGGS, K.H. and JONES, H.G. (1988). Water use in strawberries in SE England. *Journal of HortScience* **64** (2), 167–175.

HOBBS, E.H. and KROGMAN, K.K. (1978). Frequent light irrigation scheduling to improve efficiency of water use. *Canadian Journal of Agricultural Engineering* **20** (2), 109–112.

HODGSON, J.M. (1985). *Soil survey field handbook.* Technical Monograph 5. Soil Survey, England & Wales, Harpenden.

HOGG, W.H. (1967). Atlas of long-term irrigation needs for England and Wales. MAFF.

IDSO, S.B. (1982). Non-water-stressed baselines: a key to measuring and interpreting plant water stress. *Agricultural Meteorology* **27,** 59–70.

IDSO, S.B. (1983). Stomatal regulation of evaporation from well-watered plant canopies: a new synthesis. *Agricultural Meteorology* **29,** 213–217.

KAY, M. (1983). *Sprinkler irrigation; equipment and practice.* Batsford, London.

KRAMER, P.J. and BULLOCK, H.C. (1965). Seasonal variations in the proportions of suberized and unsuberized roots of trees in relation to the absorption of water. *American Journal of Botany* **53,** 200–204.

LANE, P.B. (1989). *Thetford nursery gantry for application of liquids to Corsican pine grown in Japanese paper pots.* Eastern Region Work Study Report 129. Forestry Commission, Edinburgh.

LIETH, J.H. and BURGER, D.W. (1989). Growth of chrysanthemum using an irrigation system controlled by soil moisture tension. *Journal of the American Society for Horticultural Science* **114** (3), 387–392.

MAFF (1980). *Methods of short term irrigation planning.* Booklet 2118. HMSO, London.

MAFF (1981). *Irrigation.* Reference Book 138. HMSO, London.

MAFF (1984a). *Irrigation; when and why.* Booklet 2067. MAFF, Alnwick.

MAFF (1984b). *Daily calculation of irrigation need.* Booklet 2396. MAFF, Alnwick.

MAFF (1984c). *Thinking irrigation; farm water supply.* Leaflet 672. MAFF, Alnwick.

MATHIESON, I. (1985). Scheduling by neutron probe. *Horticulture Now,* (Irrigation Review), 16–17.

McBURNEY, T. and COSTIGAN, P.A. (1982). Measuring stem water potential of young plants with a stem hygrometer. *Journal of Experimental Botany* **33** (134), 426–431.

MONTEITH, J.L. (1965). Evaporation and environment. In *The state and movement of water in living organisms,* ed. G. E. Fogg. Academic Press, New York, 205–234.

MONTEITH, J.L. and UNSWORTH, M.H. (1990). *Principles of environmental physics.* 2nd edtn. Edward Arnold, London.

NORMAN, J.M. and CAMPBELL, G. (1983). Application of a plant environment model to irrigation. *Advances in Irrigation* **2,** 155–188. Academic Press.

PAPADOPOL, C. V. (1984). An integrated irrigation system for forest nurseries in Ontario. Paper 84–2619; *Winter Meeting of American Society of Agricultural Engineers, Michigan.*

PARKES, M.E., NAYSMITH, D.B. and McDOWALL, M.A. (1989). Accounting for slow drainage and hysteresis in irrigation scheduling. *Irrigation Science* **10,** 127–140.

PENMAN, H.L. (1948). Natural evaporation from open water, bare soil and grass. *Proceedings of the Royal Society, London (A),* **193,** 120–145.

PENMAN, H.L. (1986). *Scientific aspects of irrigation.* A Royal Society Discussion. The Royal Society, London.

PHENE, C.J. (1989). Techniques for computerised irrigation management. *Computers and Electronics in Agriculture* **3.** Elsevier Science Publishers.

RITCHIE, G.A. and HINCKLEY, T.M. (1975). The pressure chamber as an instrument for ecological research. *Advances in Ecological Research* **9,** 165–254.

ROOK, D.A. (1973). Conditioning *P. radiata* seedlings to transplanting, by restricted watering. *New Zealand Journal of Forest Science* **3,** 54–69.

SAC (1991). *Mechanisation – irrigation scheduling.* Brochure from Scottish Agricultural Colleges, Perth, Scotland.

STANHILL, G. (1957). The effect of differences in soil moisture status on plant growth; a review and analysis of soil moisture regime experiments. *Soil Science* **84,** 205–214.

STEWART, J.B. (1983). A discussion of the relationship between the principal forms of the combination equation for estimating crop evaporation. *Agricultural Meteorology* **30,** 111–127.

VAUX, H.J. and PRUIT, W.O. (1983). Crop-water production functions. *Advances in Irrigation* **2.** Academic Press.

ZAERR, J.B., CLEARY, B.D. and JENKINSON, J.L. (1981). Scheduling irrigation to induce seedling dormancy. Proceedings of Intermountain Nurseryman's Association and Western Forest Nursery Association Combined Meeting, August 12–14, 1980, Bosie, Idaho. USDA Forest Service, Intermountain and Range Experiment Station, *General Technical Report* 109, 74–79.

Chapter 12

Nursery weed control

D. R. Williamson and J. L. Morgan

An effective programme to control weeds in the nursery is essential. Weeds

- compete for water and nutrients
- smother germinating seedlings, and
- their removal may physically disturb seedlings or small transplants.

The great success of crop husbandry in recent years is due to the combination of effective weed control, a balanced supply of nutrients and a soil pH adjusted to suit the crops in production.

The aim is to kill or remove weeds before they are capable of reproducing or competing. While the use of herbicides and pre-sowing partial soil sterilisation has removed much of the tedium of hand-weeding, chemicals are not infallible in their effect, especially where applications are delayed by bad weather or the timing is misjudged. There must always be a place for mechanical weeding and as last resort, hand weeding, where the alternative is a cover of freely seeding weeds.

A clean nursery, more often than not, is one that is well managed and profitable. Nevertheless, hand-weeding is expensive and its effect short-lived; chemical weed control has therefore been generally adopted throughout the forest nursery industry.

The use of herbicides and all other pesticides is governed by legislation under the Control of Pesticides Regulations and the Control of Substances Hazardous to Health Regulations (see Chapter 15, section 15.6.1 *et seq.*).

These regulations must be observed regarding:

- requirements set out on the product label;
- safe application, in terms of competent staff, effective equipment and protection of the environment;
- cleaning of equipment and safe disposal of residues after treatment.

12.1 Weed control over the whole nursery

There is no dormant season for many weed species and some weeds can set fertile seed within a few weeks of germinating, completing four or five generations in a year (Aldhous, 1961). To reduce the weed seed population, managers must be prepared to control weeds at any time of year. The task is made easier if introductions of weed seed with incoming plants or bulky organic manures, and spread of weeds from uncropped land can be prevented.

12.1.1 Sources of weed seeds

Weeds with plants and soil

Unless nursery managers are very familiar with the source of possible plants coming into the nursery, it is impossible to be sure that stock coming in will not bring seeds of several weed species. The same applies to import of soil. In the past, and also very recently, weed-free nurseries established on former heathland or woodland, became weedy through import of stock from weedy nurseries or soil full of weed seed. (There are examples too, of serious nursery pests also being brought in with imported stock.) While herbicides will help minimise the build up of such imported weeds, it is preferable to avoid the risk.

Fence lines and uncultivated land

Fence lines, surrounds of buildings, roads and tracks are best kept bare of vegetation by regular cultivation or by the use of persistent residual weed-killers or by the frequent use of contact and translocated herbicides. If this is impracticable or undesirable, an alternative is to maintain a close cover of perennial vegetation which will exclude other weeds and not give rise to unwanted seed or vegetative parts.

Organic manures and greencrops

Organic supplements are currently used only on a limited scale, usage being related to locally available materials. Whenever such a possibility exists, it is important to consider what weed seeds there may be in the material and to reject potential weed sources.

Where greencrops are grown, herbicides may not be required where the greencrop is to be ploughed in. However, selective herbicides appropriate to the greencrop and weed may need to be considered if there is a heavy weed germination and the greencrop is thin. Alternatively, a non-persistent, non-selective herbicide may be desirable to kill the crop and any weeds, before ploughing in.

12.1.2 Flexibility in control of weeds

The following sections detail alternative methods of weed control. While each is listed separately, it is important to emphasise that no one method is sufficient in itself to give a satisfactory and economical control of weeds. A nursery manager wishing to keep his weeds under control as cheaply and efficiently as possible must be prepared to change from one technique to another when appropriate. Exclusive adherence to any one technique is liable to lead to a rapid build-up of one or more species of weed flora; see also section 12.2.3.

12.2 Chemical control of weeds in nursery stock in open ground

> **Caution**
>
> Some of the materials described here have been subject to small scale research trials and only limited subsequent commercial experience. Any material not previously used on a nursery should be applied on a small scale in carefully observed trials before full scale use.
>
> Recommendations are given as at December, 1993. Checks should be made that these have not been superseded.
>
> All the herbicide 'Products' listed below appear as 'Approved for Agricultural Use' in MAFF Reference Book 500 *Pesticides 1994* (MAFF, 1994). In this context, forest nurseries are grouped with horticultural nurseries as part of 'agriculture'. Nevertheless, listing in the reference book must not be taken to imply that the labels of the products listed there carry full recommendations, covering forest nurseries. In many cases, this is not so and uses recommended are 'off-label'. The use of such products is covered by whatever 'label' arrangements are in force at any time. For 1994, the 'off-label' arrangements current at the start, continue in force until the end of the year. These allow products approved for use on any growing crop to be used on plants grown in forest nurseries. In all cases, those uses of a herbicide which are not specified on the approved product label are at the user's own risk; manufacturers cannot be held responsible for any adverse effect on crops or for any failure to control weeds. Nevertheless, employers and operators must always use the product in accordance with the product label recommendations in respect of safety of nursery staff and visitors to the nursery, and protection of the environment.

12.2.1 Definition of terms

Two sets of terms require definition, relating to the crop and to spray distribution:

Stages of growth

Pre-sowing: Before sowing of the crop has taken place.

Pre-emergence: Before the emergence of seedlings of the crop; this can be before or after the emergence of weed species.

Post-emergence: After seedlings of the sown crop have begun to emerge; this can be before or after the emergence of weed species.

Active: When seedlings are actively growing and have not hardened off, the period of active growth is from when buds begin to swell, through flushing and shoot elongation and ripening, until winter resting buds have formed and shoots are fully lignified and hardened. In addition, for deciduous species, when foliage remaining on plants has not started to senesce.

Dormant: After the shoots of seedlings or transplants have ceased to elongate and have hardened; terminal and side resting buds have formed in late summer/autumn but before buds have started to swell and elongate at the beginning of the following season. For deciduous species, when in addition, the foliage has taken on autumn colouring, or has fallen.

Distribution of sprays in relation to the crop

Overall: The herbicide is applied over the whole weeding site (i.e. crop and weed).

Inter-row: The herbicide is applied to the weeds/ground between the rows of transplants or between drills of seedlings.

Directed: The herbicide is applied so that the spray is directed to hit a target pest or weed but avoid crop trees.

12.2.2 Mode of action of herbicides

Herbicides are often described or loosely grouped according to how they enter and move within plants (Rice, 1986; BCPC, 1990).

Contact and translocated herbicides

These enter through foliage and stem surfaces. Contact herbicides affect only the tissues they touch (and therefore even, overall application is important); translocated herbicides rely on movement within the plant to susceptible parts (e.g. growing points and where cell division is active). Where contact or translocated herbicides have been sprayed on to tall weeds close to growing crops using a shield to protect the crop, it should be remembered that if the treated weeds move in the wind, freshly applied herbicide can be transferred to crop plants.

Most contact and translocated herbicides give better control if the target weed species is actively growing.

Soil-acting (residual) herbicides

Residual herbicides should be applied to soil which has a fine tilth and is free from clods. These herbicides require moisture in the soil to be activated and many (particularly those rapidly degraded by sunlight) need to be incorporated immediately after application by irrigation with 5–10 mm of water, or a similar amount of rainfall if the seedbed surface is not moist. The length of time residual herbicides remain effective varies depending on the chemical in use, soil type and climate, particularly rainfall, sunlight and temperature.

Residual herbicides may achieve selectivity through occupying only the top 2–3 cm of soil, being taken up by roots of germinating weeds in that band of soil. Any crop roots in the same soil may also take up the weedkiller and may be damaged; equally, any well-established weeds with a substantial proportion of roots below the treated soil may resist the effects of weedkiller. Residual herbicides should therefore not be applied to ground with well-established weeds among the crop plants; these weeds should be controlled either by contact herbicide or mechanical means before a residual herbicide is applied.

Care should be taken that the ground is well compacted around the roots of newly lined out stock, otherwise there is a risk of herbicide being carried down by heavy rain into their active rooting zone. Similarly, herbicides should not be applied to freshly undercut or wrenched plants until the soil has settled.

Influence of weather and soil on the use of herbicides

The efficacy of some herbicides may be influenced by weather and soil conditions so that the following precautions should be considered.

- In very hot or dry conditions, the crop is more likely to be under moisture stress and to be more susceptible to damage by the herbicide; if a herbicide must be used, it should be applied towards the end of the day, when it is cooler.
- Avoid applications when the weather is very windy, because of the risk of drift.
- Apply soil-acting herbicides when the soil is moist and rain is expected, or when irrigation can be applied to ensure it is not left on the soil surface where it may be lost through the effects of sunlight.

12.2.3 Herbicide resistance

Nursery managers are strongly advised against using the same herbicide repeatedly over a number of years on the same area of ground, which otherwise may lead to:

- the development and/or spread of herbicide-resistant strains of particular weed species, e.g. groundsel, willowherb and mayweed;
- the development of soil microflora which can rapidly degrade the chemical active ingredient, thus reducing the effectiveness of residual herbicides.

It is therefore recommended that herbicides are used in rotation, e.g. using alternatives regularly.

Identification of herbicide-resistant weeds

Growers with persistent weed species can assess whether these weeds are resistant to specific herbicides used in their nursery. The following test is simple and informative:

1. Fill two seed trays with nursery soil.
2. Sow one tray with seed collected from persistent weeds from the nursery.
3. Sow the remaining tray with seed collected from a wild source of the same weed (i.e. that has never been sprayed). Label trays.
4. Allow seed to germinate and grow to the stage where problems with control are experienced. This may be immediately after sowing.
5. Place trays on the ground and apply the herbicide to be tested as a single pass. The sprayer should be calibrated to match the swathe width and forward speed for the trial.
6. If the wild seed source is killed and the nursery source unaffected then herbicide resistance is likely.
7. If both seed sources are damaged to the same extent then there is a need to examine (a) the choice of herbicides that are used in the nursery and (b) the method of application to explain the lack of efficacy of nursery treatments.

12.3 Recommended herbicides

Table 12.1 gives details of herbicides currently available that should be considered for control of the various weeds commonly found in forest nurseries. This information has to be linked to the type of crop (seedbeds or transplants), and its stage of growth, as outlined in the following sections.

Herbicides are listed and discussed under the name of their active ingredient (a.i.). Where rates of application are given, these refer to the rate of *product* in litres or kilograms *per treated hectare* (1 ha^{-1} or kg ha^{-1}).

N.B. See statement about 'Products named in the Bulletin' in the Preface.

12.3.1 Seed bed pre-sowing treatments

Soil sterilisation

This usually takes place in late summer to

The availability of products always depends on the overall demand in the agricultural and horticultural markets. Products over which there is some doubt as to future availability are marked †. Products no longer manufactured but of which there may be stocks that can legally be used, are listed in Forestry Commission Technical Paper 3 (Williamson et al., 1993).

Products marked with an asterisk (*) in section 12.3 do not have a full 'label' approval; where there is any doubt, enquiries should be made to the Forestry Authority, Research Division, at either the Northern Research Station, Roslin, Midlothian, EH25 9SY, or Alice Holt Lodge, Wrecclesham, Farnham, Surrey, GU10 4LH, for up-to-date information on the status of any product recommended for 'off-label' use.

BEFORE ANY HERBICIDE APPLICATION, READ THE LABEL. IT CARRIES FULL INSTRUCTIONS FOR USE AND THE PROTECTION OF THE OPERATOR AND THE ENVIRONMENT.

early autumn of the year before sowing and controls many soil pests (nematodes, fungi) as well as weeds and weed seed. Sterilants will usually improve the growth of trees as well.

With both soil sterilants, it is important to aerate the soil and release all the sterilant residues prior to sowing. A recommended test for the presence of residues prior to sowing is to grow cress in sealed jars containing samples of sterilised soil. If the cress fails to grow, then further cultivation is required to release the sterilant.

Dazomet

Approved product Basamid; 98–99% a.i.
Rate 380–570 kg ha⁻¹ depending soil type.
The high rate is used only on heavy soils.

Must be incorporated when soil temperature is at least 7°C. Should be incorporated by rotavation and sealed in by rolling or polythene sheeting. Wait at least 4 weeks before cultivating soil to release any residual gas. If dazomet is applied in the autumn it is normal to wait until the spring before releasing residues. See Chapter 6, section 6.1.2.

Methyl bromide

Contains 98% methyl bromide + 2% chloropicrin as a warning odourant tear gas. Rate 300-500 kg ha⁻¹.
Subject to the 1982 Poisons Act and the 1972

Poisons Rules and can only be applied by licensed contractors.

Soil temperature should be at least 8°C at 15–20 cm depth. Treatment period 48–96 hours depending on temperature. Aerate soil for 7–21 days before sowing.

'Stale' seedbeds

Treatment of 'stale' seedbeds is based on the principle that weed seeds buried in the soil only germinate when cultivation brings them very close to the soil surface. Provided there is sufficient time for seedbeds to be prepared and for it to be sufficiently warm for seeds to germinate before sowing, post-sowing competition can be markedly reduced if the early flush of weeds is killed by spraying or very shallow cultivation before sowing.

The technique is invalidated if the beds are deeply cultivated, as this brings up another crop of weed seed.

	Rate per hectare	
	Small weeds	Large or established weeds
Glufosinate-ammonium Approved product: *Challenge;* 180 g l⁻¹ a.i.	3.0 l	5.0 l
Glyphosate Approved product: *Roundup;* 360 g l⁻¹ a.i.	1.5 l	4.0 l

Paraquat: approved product *Gramoxone* is available and has been recommended previously; current products above offer the same efficacy of weed control while providing greater operator safety.

12.3.2 Seedbed pre-emergence

Seeds of small seeded broadleaves and conifers

Table 12.1 Susceptibility of common forest nursery weeds to selective herbicides before weed emergence

Active ingredients

Weeds	Atrazine	Chloridazon + chlorbufam	Chlorthal-dimethyl	Cyanzine	Diphenamid	Diphenamid with chlorthal-dimethyl	Isoxaben	Lenacil	Metamitron	Metazachlor	Napropamide	Napropamide with simazine	Oryzalin	Oxadiazon	Pendimethalin	Propyzamide	Simazine
Annual meadow grass	S	MS	MS	S	S	S	R	S	S	S	S	S	S	S	S	S	S
Bitter cress, hairy					S	S	S					MR	MS	S	S		
Black bindweed	MS	S	MS	S		MS		S	MS	MS	S	S		S	S	S	MS
Black nightshade	S		MS	MS	R	MS		R	MS		R	S	MS	S	S	S	S
Broadleaved dock								S	S							S	
Chamomile spp.	S				MS	MS	S	S	S					S	S		S
Charlock	S	S	MR	S			S	S	S	MR	R	S		S			S
Cleavers	MR	S	R	MR			MS	R		MS	S	S		S	S	S	MR
Common chickweed	S	S	S	S	S	S	S	S	S	S	S	S	S		S	S	S
Common fumitory	MS	MS	R	MS	R	R	S	S	S	R	S	S	S	S	S	MS	MS
Common hemp nettle	S		S			S	S		S	MR	S	S					S
Common poppy	S			S			S	S	S	S	S	S		S			S
Corn buttercup	R			S			S	S						S			
Corn marigold	S		R	S			S	S	S		R	S		S			S
Dead nettle, red	S		MS	S		MS	S	MS	S	S	S	S	S	S	S		S
Fat hen	S	S	S	MS	MS	S	S	S	S	MS	S	S	S	S	S		S
Field pansy	MS	S	S	MS		S	S	R	S	MR	MS	MS	S		S		MS
Field penny cress	S	S	R		S	S	S	S	R		R	S					S
Forget-me-not, field	S	S		S			S	S	S	S			S		S	S	S
Groundsel	S	S	R	S	S	S	S	MS	S	S	S	S	MS	S		R	S
Henbit dead nettle	S	S		S		S	MS	S	S		S	S	S	S	S		S
Knotgrass	MR	S	S	MS	MS	S	S	S	S	R	MS	MS	S	S	S	S	R
Mayweed	S	S	R	S	MS	MS	S	S	S	S	S	S	S	S	S	R	S
Mercury, annual	S		MS			MS											S
Mustard	S		R	S				S									S
Orache, common	MS			S	MS	MS	S	S	S		S	S		S	S		MS
Pale persicaria	MS			S	MS	MS		S	S		S	S					MS
Parsley-piert	S			S			S			S	R	S			S		S
Pineapple weed	S				MS	MS	S	S	S	S				S	S		S
Plantain	S																S
Radish, wild	S	S	R	S			S	S	S		MR	S		S			S
Redshank	MS	S	MR	S	MS	MS	S	S	S	MS	MS	MS		S	S	S	MS
Scarlet pimpernel	S	MS		S			S	S	S		R	R			S	R	S
Shepherd's purse	S	S	R	S	S	S	S	S		S	MR		S	S	S	MS	S
Small nettle	S	S	S	S	S	S	S	MS		MS	S	S	S	S	S		S
Smooth sow thistle	S	S				S		S			S	S	S	S	S		S
Sorrel, sheep's	MR				S	S			S		S	S	MS		S		
Speedwells	MS	S	S	S	S	S	S	MS	S	S	S	S	S	S	S	S	MS
Spurrey, corn	MS				S	S	S	S	S	MS	S	S		S	S		MS
Thale-cress	S						S										
Volunteer cereals	MS																S
Volunteer oil seed rape							S			MR					S		S
Willow herb	MS				S	S					MS	MS	S	S		R	MS

Key:
S   – Susceptible
MS – Moderately susceptible
MR – Moderately resistant
R   – Resistant
    – Not tested

are normally sown on to the surface of raised seedbeds and covered with 2–3 mm depth of grit. Pre-emergence herbicides are then applied after sowing but before crop germination. Large seeded broadleaves such as oak, beech and sweet chestnut are usually drilled into seedbeds and then covered with at least 25 mm of soil. Such species are therefore usually more tolerant of pre-emergence herbicides.

Chlorthal-dimethyl
Approved product: *Dacthal W-75*; 750 g kg^{-1} a.i. Rate 6.0 kg ha^{-1}.
Controls a wide range of grass and broadleaved weeds. Apply immediately after sowing. Tolerated by a large number of tree species but *not* pine. Does not control germinated weeds since it has no foliar activity.

Diphenamid †
Approved product: *Enide 50W*; 500 g kg^{-1} a.i. Rate 8.0 kg ha^{-1}.
Should be applied immediately after sowing. Tolerated by a wide range of tree species; but birch, alder and occasionally larch are damaged by pre-emergence application. Does not control germinated weeds since it has no contact action.

Diphenamid in mixture with chlorthal-dimethyl
Approved products: *Enide 50W**; 500 g kg^{-1} a.i. Rate 8.0 kg ha^{-1}.
Dacthal W-75; 750 g kg^{-1} a.i. Rate 6.0 kg ha^{-1}.

In mixture, these two products control a wider range of weeds and give greater persistence than diphenamid on its own. Apply immediately after sowing.

Glufosinate ammonium
Approved product: *Challenge*; 150 g l^{-1} a.i. Rate 3.0 l ha^{-1}.
This can be used with care to clean up seedbeds post-sowing *provided* crop seed has not started to germinate. Check that no seed radicles are present before deciding to spray.

Napropamide
Approved product: *Devrinol*; 450 g l^{-1} a.i. Rate 2.2 l ha^{-1}.
Controls a wide range of grass and broadleaved weeds. Apply immediately after

sowing. Tolerated by coniferous species. Does not control germinated weeds since it has no foliar activity. This product is rapidly broken down by sunlight and is therefore best applied between November and March unless irrigated into the soil with at least 25 mm of water.

Simazine
Approved product: *Gesatop 50WP*; 500 g kg^{-1} a.i. Rate 4.0 kg ha^{-1}.
Treat only large seeded broadleaves species, i.e. oak, beech, and sweet chestnut which have been drilled into seedbeds. Application should be immediately after drilling. Does not generally control germinated weeds due to lack of contact action.

12.3.3 Seedbed post-emergence

Diphenamid †
Approved product: *Enide 50W*; 500 g kg^{-1} a.i. Rate 8.0 kg ha^{-1}.
Can be applied to all species post-emergence including birch and alder. Apply when first true needles or leaves are fully extended. Stunting can occur if applied earlier. Subsequent applications can be made at 6-weekly intervals.

Propyzamide
Approved products: *Kerb 50W**; 500 g kg^{-1} a.i. Rate 3.0 kg ha^{-1}.
Kerb Flo*; 400 g l^{-1} a.i. Rate 3.75 l ha^{-1}.
Propyzamide is tolerated by all commonly grown forest species and is particularly useful on standover beds when applied at the end of the first growing season. Apply October to December (January north of a line from Aberystwyth to London). For crop safety reasons, propyzamide should not be used within 6 months of an application of simazine or atrazine.

Simazine

Approved product: *Gesatop 50WP*; 500 g kg⁻¹ a.i. Rate 2.0 kg ha⁻¹.

Only apply to second year seedbeds when plants are greater than 5 cm tall. All conifer species except Norway spruce may be treated. Do not treat within 2 weeks of undercutting, i.e. allow soil to settle around the roots of trees before treatment.

12.3.4 Seedbed post-tree emergence: repeat low dose regime

As a result of research, it now appears possible to use a wider spectrum of herbicides at low doses when applied at regular intervals after crop emergence to maintain weed-free conditions.

Apply the following herbicides in a repeat low dose regime after an initial pre-emergence application. The first application should be made as soon as trees have reached the first true leaf/needle stage. Treatments should be repeated at 6-weekly intervals.

These treatments have been successfully screened for three seasons over Sitka spruce, Japanese larch, common alder and birch.

Metamitron

Approved product: *Goltix WG**; 700 g kg⁻¹ a.i. Rate 1.7 kg ha⁻¹.

Limited information on tolerance of crop species.

Metazachlor

Approved product: *Butisan S**; 500 g l⁻¹ a.i. Rate 1.25 l ha⁻¹.

Limited information on tolerance of crop species.

Napropamide

Approved product: *Devrinol**; 450 g l⁻¹ a.i. Rate 1.1 l ha⁻¹.

Limited information on tolerance of crop species.

Propyzamide

Approved products: *Kerb 50W**; 500 g kg⁻¹ a.i. Rate 1.50 kg ha⁻¹.

Kerb Flo*; 400 g l⁻¹ a.i. Rate 1.87 l ha⁻¹.

Limited information on tolerance of crop species.

12.3.5 Transplant lines and second year undercut seedbeds

Soil-acting herbicides with no or limited post-emergence activity on weeds

Residual herbicides are widely used in transplant lines and second year undercut beds. In the case of transplants these are normally applied immediately after lining out to ground which is free from weeds, and repeated as necessary. When a precision sowing and undercutting regime is in operation, residual herbicides should be applied during the first winter dormant period. Many of the residual herbicides listed do not control germinated weeds and therefore if good weed control is to be achieved they must be applied before weeds emerge. It is therefore important to adopt an effective weed control regime on first year precision sown seedbeds to ensure the ground is clean when the second year residual herbicides are applied. Depending on the prevailing conditions, these can be applied any time from when trees become dormant in the autumn to just before bud burst in the spring. When applying soil-acting herbicides to undercut stock application must only take place after soil has settled following undercutting or wrenching. Soil disturbance must be kept to a minimum when these operations are carried out. This is because of the risk of herbicides coming into direct contact with tree roots.

The herbicides listed in this section either have no foliar activity or only control weeds in an early post-emergence stage.

Decision chain when using soil-acting herbicides

1. Where lining out is being considered, cultivate to produce a fine, firm tilth.
2. Identify potential weed problems.
3. Match weed spectrum to a suitable herbicide or mixture of herbicides.
4. Consider the suitability of the herbicide for the crop species and stage of growth.
5. Apply the herbicide to soil which has a firm, fine tilth. Soil should be moist before application; if not, herbicides should be incorpo-

rated with irrigation (5-10 mm of water) immediately after application.

Atrazine

Approved product: *Gesaprim 500SC**; $500\,g\,l^{-1}$ a.i. Rate $4.0\,l\,ha^{-1}$.

Use on conifer transplant lines. Normally applied in spring prior to flushing. Use half rate on sensitive species (e.g. Norway spruce, larch and western hemlock). No control of triazine resistant weeds. Mobile in the soil and can be washed into low lying areas causing local overdosing.

Chlorthal-dimethyl

Approved product: *Dacthal**; $750\,g\,kg^{-1}$ a.i. Rate $6.0\,kg\,ha^{-1}$.

Controls a wide range of grass and broadleaved weeds. Tolerated by a wide range of tree species.

Cyanazine

Approved product: *Fortrol**; $500\,g\,l^{-1}$ a.i. Rate $4.0\,l\,ha^{-1}$.

Controls a wide range of grass and broadleaved weeds. Tolerated by a wide range of tree species, but damage can occur if trees have started to flush or are in active growth.

Diphenamid †

Approved product: *Enide 50W*; $500\,g\,kg^{-1}$ a.i. Rate $10.0–12.0\,kg\,ha^{-1}$.

A wide range of tree species are tolerant. Does not control germinated weeds. Repeat treatments can be applied at 6-weekly intervals.

Isoxaben

Approved product: *Flexidor 125*; $125\,g\,l^{-1}$ a.i. Rate $0.25\,l\,ha^{-1}$.

Controls a wide range of grass and broadleaved weeds but has no activity on grass weeds. Should not be used on areas that will be used for seedbeds next season due to strong residual activity. Land must be mouldboard ploughed at least $20\,cm$ depth before the following crop.

Lenacil

Approved product: *Venzar**; $800\,g\,kg^{-1}$ a.i. Rate $2.2\,kg\,ha^{-1}$.

Controls a wide range of grass and broadleaved weeds. Tolerated by a wide range of tree species.

BEFORE ANY HERBICIDE
APPLICATION, READ THE LABEL.
IT CARRIES FULL INSTRUCTIONS FOR
USE AND THE PROTECTION OF THE
OPERATOR AND THE ENVIRONMENT.

Metamitron

Approved product: *Goltix WG**; $700\,g\,kg^{-1}$ a.i. Rate $5\,kg\,ha^{-1}$.

Controls a wide range of grass and broadleaved weeds. Tolerated by a wide range of tree species.

Metazachlor

Approved product: *Butisan S**; $500\,g\,l^{-1}$ a.i. Rate $2.5\,l\,ha^{-1}$.

Controls a range of grass and broadleaved weeds. Tolerated by a wide range of tree species.

Napropamide

Approved product: *Devrinol*; $450\,g\,kg^{-1}$ a.i. Rate $9.0\,l\,ha^{-1}$.

Broken down by sunlight so best applied November-March unless irrigated into the soil with at least $25\,mm$ of water. Apply immediately after lining out. Has proved satisfactory on most conifers, but only limited information is available for broadleaves.

Napropamide in mixture with simazine

Approved product: *Devrinol*; $450\,g\,l^{-1}$ a.i. Rate $3.5\,l\,ha^{-1}$.

Gesatop 500SC; $500\,g\,l^{-1}$ a.i. Rate $1.0\,l\,ha^{-1}$.

Crop tolerance as napropamide but care is needed on simazine-sensitive tree species.

Oryzalin †

Approved product: *Surflan*; $480\,g\,l^{-1}$ a.i. Rate $4.5–6.0\,l\,ha^{-1}$.

At the time of writing, product temporarily unavailable while the manufacturers gather information to satisfy the Pesticide Safety requirements. Seek manufacturer's advice on approval status before use.

Controls a range of weed species. Tolerated by a wide range of tree species.

Oxadiazon

Approved product: *Ronstar Liquid*; $250\,g\,l^{-1}$ a.i. Rate 4.0 or $8.0\,l\,ha^{-1}$.

Rate depends on the weeds to be controlled. Only apply in late winter before buds start to swell. Contact with young leaves and shoots must be avoided. This herbicide has almost entirely soil activity but will control weeds very early post-emergence before the first true leaf stage. Tolerated by most conifers (e.g. spruces, pines and larches) but there is only limited information on broadleaves. Tree tolerance depends on the above instructions being closely adhered to.

Pendimethalin

Approved product: *Stomp 400 SC**; $400\,g\,l^{-1}$ a.i. Rate $6.0\,l\,ha^{-1}$.

Controls a wider range of grass and broadleaved weeds. Tolerated by a wide range of tree species.

Propyzamide

Approved products: *Kerb 50W**; $500\,g\,kg^{-1}$ a.i. Rate $3.0\,kg\,ha^{-1}$.
Kerb Flo*; $400\,g\,l^{-1}$ a.i. Rate $3.75\,l\,ha^{-1}$.

Apply November to December (January: north of a line from Aberystwyth to London). Treat all common forest tree species. For crop safety reasons propyzamide should not be used within 6 months of an application of simazine or atrazine. In mild autumns application should be delayed until the weather has turned cold and wet.

Simazine

Approved product: *Gesatop 500SC*; $500\,g\,l^{-1}$ a.i. Rate $2.0–4.0\,l\,ha^{-1}$.

All conifer transplant lines may be treated as well as all commonly planted deciduous species except ash. Does not control germinated or triazine-resistant weeds. Higher rate is used on heavier soils. Soils must be moist and sufficiently compacted to prevent herbicide washing down to the rooting zone of trees. Use half rate on sensitive species, e.g. larch.

Herbicides with foliar activity

When the control of weeds after they have emerged is the objective, herbicides with foliar activity are usually required. It is vital to identify correctly the weed problem and select a herbicide which will control the relevant weeds at the appropriate stage of growth. As weeds become larger, the choice of effective herbicides diminishes; it is therefore important to carry out a detailed inspection of the nursery on a regular basis so that surviving weeds can be controlled soon after emergence.

Atrazine

Approved product: *Gesaprim 500SC**; $500\,g\,l^{-1}$ a.i. Rate $4.0\,l\,ha^{-1}$.

Use on conifer transplant lines. Normally applied in spring prior to flushing. Use half rate on sensitive species (i.e. Norway spruce, larch and western hemlock). No control of triazine resistant weeds. Mobile in the soil and can be washed into low lying areas causing local overdosing.

Clopyralid

Approved product: *Dow Shield**; $200\,g\,l^{-1}$ a.i. Rate $0.5\,l\,ha^{-1}$.

Controls a narrow weed spectrum very effectively.

Tolerated by a wide range of tree species when they are dormant. Many tree species have been successfully over sprayed during the growing season once the extremely tender early growth has hardened. Larch can exhibit severe twisting of needles but eventually grows out of this transient damage. Douglas fir shows the same symptom to a lesser extent. Some broadleaved species exhibit transient damage as curling of margins of leaves, particularly alder and beech.

Cyanazine

Approved product: *Fortrol**; $500\,g\,l^{-1}$ a.i. Rate $4.0\,l\,ha^{-1}$.

Controls a wide range of grass and broadleaved weeds early post-emergence. Tolerated by a wide range of tree species, but damage can occur if trees have started to flush or are in active growth.

Fluazifop-P-butyl

Approved product: *Fusilade 5**; $125\,g\,l^{-1}$ a.i. Rate $1.5–3.0\,l\,ha^{-1}$ + Agral 0.1% of final spray volume.

Only effective against grass weeds, but annual meadow grass, fescue spp. and all broadleaved weeds are resistant. When controlling annual grasses (black-grass, barren (sterile) brome), volunteer cereals and wild oats use the 1.5 l ha⁻¹ rate. This will be effective from the 2 true leaf stage (when there is sufficient foliage to take up the herbicide) to the fully tillered stage. Perennial and rhizomatous grasses should be treated at the 4 true leaf stage with 3.0 l ha⁻¹. All forest trees can be treated. This product is not approved for application through hand-held equipment.

Metamitron
Approved product: *Goltix WG**; 700 g kg⁻¹ a.i. Rate 5.0 kg ha⁻¹.
Controls a wide range of grass and broad-leaved weeds but only at the cotyledon stage post-emergence. Tolerated by a wide range of tree species.

Metazachlor
Approved product: *Butisan S*; 500 g l⁻¹ a.i. Rate 2.5 l ha⁻¹.
Controls a limited range of grass and broad-leaved weeds early post-emergence. Tolerated by a wide range of tree species, but pine can be damaged if treated when in active growth before candles have hardened.

Propyzamide
Approved products: *Kerb 50W*; 500 g kg⁻¹ a.i. Rate 3.0 kg ha⁻¹.
Kerb Flo; 400 g l⁻¹ a.i. Rate 3.75 l ha⁻¹.
Apply November to December (January: north of a line from Aberystwyth to London). Controls a range of broadleaved weeds early post-emergence and a wide range of grasses up to an advanced stage of growth. Treat all common forest tree species. For safety reasons propyzamide products should not be used within 6 months of an application of simazine or atrazine.

The two herbicides listed below can be used as a *directed spray* avoiding all contact with the crop to control established weeds in transplant lines.

Glufosinate ammonium
Approved product: *Challenge*; 150 g l⁻¹ a.i. Rate 3.0–5.0 l ha⁻¹.

Glyphosate
Approved product: *Roundup*; 360 g l⁻¹ a.i. Rate 1.5–4.0 l ha⁻¹.

BEFORE ANY HERBICIDE APPLICATION, READ THE LABEL. IT CARRIES FULL INSTRUCTIONS FOR USE AND THE PROTECTION OF THE OPERATOR AND THE ENVIRONMENT.

Paraquat
Approved product *Gramoxone* is available and has been recommended previously; current recommendations offer the same efficacy of weed control while providing greater operator safety.

12.3.6 Fallow
The fallow period in a forest nursery rotation provides an opportunity for controlling deep rooted perennial weeds by a combination of cultivation and chemical control. Repeat applications may be necessary to achieve adequate control.

Glufosinate ammonium
Approved product: *Challenge*; 150 g l⁻¹ a.i. Rate 3.0–5.0 l ha⁻¹.
Only useful against non-rhizomatous weeds. Best used pre-planting to clean up flushes of germinating weeds after cultivation.

Glyphosate
Approved product: *Roundup*; 360 g l⁻¹ a.i. Rate 1.5–4.0 l ha⁻¹.
Repeat applications combined with intervening cultivation can be particularly useful against deep rooting weeds such as *Equisetum* spp.

Sodium chlorate
Approved product: *Atlacide soluble powder*; 580 g kg⁻¹ a.i. Rate 375–500 kg ha⁻¹.
Should only be used in extreme circumstances to control persistent weeds, e.g. *Equisetum* spp. *At least* 6 months should elapse between treatment and sowing or lining out. A 'cress test' should be carried out before any crop is planted on the treated area.

Paraquat
Approved product *Gramoxone* is available and has been recommended previously; current recommendations offer the same efficacy of weed control while providing greater operator safety.

12.4 Mechanical control of weeds

Implements which uproot or sever weeds are mainly used in transplant lines and on fallow ground. They can also be used between drills of drill-sown seedbeds but care must be taken because of the delicate nature of the crop particularly in the early stages of growth. The disturbance of soil through the use of machines will have the effect of reducing the effectiveness of any residual herbicides which have been applied previously.

The various types of implement are normally attached to a tractor-mounted tool bar so that several inter-row strips can be cultivated at one pass. Machines are usually designed to treat one nursery bed at a time but it is essential that the spacing between rows is constant.

Implements for weed control can be grouped into scarifiers, hoes and ploughs or cultivators.

12.4.1 Scarifying implements

This type of implement can be divided up into two main groups. Those which have vertical tines which run in groups of three or more between rows of plants, or those which have wheel like rotating brushes which brush the weeds out of the ground between rows of plants. Both types of implements are most effective when used on light soils at intervals of 2–3 weeks; they are less effective on heavy soils and cannot deal with established weeds.

12.4.2 Hoeing implements

These implements slice the soil just below the surface, severing big weeds and uprooting small ones. In addition to hoes with stationary blades, there are machines where the blades rotate or reciprocate. If carelessly used, mechanical hoes can damage roots and side shoots of plants to a far greater extent than scarifiers. Fixed blade hoes are generally less satisfactory than rotary or reciprocating hoes as they tend to ridge up the soil at the base of plants, smothering lower foliage. Rotary or reciprocating hoe blades move much faster in relation to the soil, and leave the disturbed soil more or less in place.

12.4.3 Ploughing and cultivating implements

These are suitable for controlling weeds only in fallow ground, and act by burying weeds in the case of ploughs or by soil disturbance and uprooting weeds in the case of cultivators. If cultivation using this type of machine is employed on fallow ground, the ground should only be cultivated to a depth of 10 cm, so that any cultivation pan that is formed during the season can be broken by ploughing at the normal depth when the ground is prepared for cropping.

12.4.4 Timing of cultivations

The timing between cultivations will vary depending on the type of weeds to be controlled, the type of cultivator being used and the prevailing climatic conditions. But cultivation must be carried out frequently enough to prevent weeds from seeding.

12.4.5 Control of weeds by hand

The oldest way of controlling weeds is to pull them individually by hand. Although effective, it is generally the most expensive method. Through the use of herbicides and cultivation equipment, the amount of hand weeding has been drastically reduced. Nevertheless, there are circumstances where weeds can only be controlled by hand; in the period soon after the germination of the forest tree seedlings or when the weed is resistant to the herbicide or the crop is unable to tolerate a chemical which is effective against the weed species present.

Hand weeding is a slow job and it is important to start weeding soon after the problem weed species become visible. This allows the weeds to be removed without damaging the crop and the job can be completed before the weeds on the last piece of ground become too large, or shed seed.

12.5 Spraying equipment

The decision on the type of sprayer will depend upon the size of the nursery and the size of the actual spraying operation. Wherever practical, a tractor-mounted hydraulic boom sprayer should be used in preference to knapsack sprayers as it has the advantage of greater output, more even distribution and of isolating the operator from the pesticide.

12.5.1 Tractor-mounted hydraulic boom sprayers

There is a large range of suitable sprayers available. When making a choice, the following points should be considered:

- Tank size. Large enough to spray the maximum area without refill.
- Boom.
  (a) With facilities to adjust height.
  (b) Sufficient length to spray 3 or 5 beds.
  (c) Facility to shut off flow to boom sections to permit spraying of single beds.
  (d) Pressure control system to achieve a constant volume flow to the nozzles.
  (e) Automatic pesticide mixer.

12.5.2 Knapsack sprayers

There are two types of knapsack sprayer, the pressurised which requires pumping up before spraying and the semi-pressurised which requires pumping up while spraying proceeds. There is a wide selection of knapsacks available in the suitable range of 10–15 litres capacity.

The knapsack should be fitted with a pressure control system in order to maintain a constant flow through the nozzle when either the pressure drops in the pressurised knapsack or fluctuates through the pumping action of semi-pressurised knapsack.

The lance should be fitted with a means of interchanging nozzles.

12.5.3 Nozzles

Always read the product label to ascertain if there are any specific recommendations.

As there is a large range of types of nozzle (BCPC, 1988), giving different distribution patterns, spray angles and flow rates, it is recommended that flat fan nozzles are fitted to the tractor-mounted boom sprayer and 'even spray flat fan' or floodjet nozzles fitted to the knapsack.

Flat fan nozzles, which are available in a range of spray angles, produce an elliptical spray pattern. In order to achieve an even deposition over the swathe it is essential that the nozzles are set at an angle on the boom to avoid impact of spray from neighbouring nozzles, and that the boom height is correctly adjusted to take account of the spray angle of the nozzle to give the correct overlapping of the spray.

'Even spray flat fan' or floodjet nozzles produce a rectangular pattern giving an even distribution across the swathe which is necessary for knapsack sprayers being a single nozzle applicator, and for inter-row spraying where the spray from each nozzle must be confined to the soil between crop rows.

The size of the nozzle will depend upon the required swathe width and application rate; the manufacturer's nozzle data literature should be consulted to help select the appropriate nozzle.

12.5.4 Spray pressures

Pressure controls the flow through the nozzle, droplet size and to a limited degree the spray angle and hence the swathe width of single nozzle applicators. Lowering the pressure will reduce flow, increase droplet size and reduce spray angle, increasing the pressure will have the opposite effect.

Generally, larger droplets can be used for soil-acting herbicides than where foliage is to be treated, because it is often critically important to get an even, complete cover of spray on foliage. However, the smaller the droplet size, the greater the risk of drift; for that reason droplets should be no smaller than is necessary to give adequate cover.

The most appropriate operating pressure settings for the nozzles in use and the droplet size required can be obtained from data sheets supplied by the nozzle manufacturers.

12.5.5 Calibration

It is essential, in order to achieve even distribution of the pesticide, that the sprayer is correctly calibrated each time it is used. The calibration procedure is:

- Read label for recommended volume of

application and spray quality (nozzle type and operating pressure).

- Calculate sprayer ground-speed. Measure the time in seconds to cover 100 m and calculate km h^{-1} by the following formula:

$$\text{Speed km h}^{-1} = \frac{360}{\text{Time (seconds)}}$$

- Measure nozzle spacing for boom sprayers or swathe width for knapsacks.
- Calculate nozzle output by the following formula:

Nozzle output =

$$\frac{\frac{\text{Volume of application}}{\text{(litres/hectare)}} \times \frac{\text{Speed}}{\text{(km/h)}} \times \frac{\text{Nozzle spacing*}}{\text{(m)}}}{600}$$

* For knapsack substitute swathe width.

- Select nozzle from manufacturer's data literature.
- Measure the output from at least one nozzle from each boom section. If the nozzle output differs from that calculated, increase or decrease the pressure or change nozzles until the nozzle output equals the calculated nozzle output.

Consult the British Crop Protection Council's *Nozzle selection handbook* (BCPC, 1988) for further information on nozzle selection and calibration.

12.5.6 Cleaning the sprayers

After spraying, the sprayer should be thoroughly washed down and cleaned inside in an approved manner. See Chapter 15, section 15.6.6 'Disposal of pesticide residues'.

12.5.7 General

All operators of spraying equipment should be fully trained and hold the NPTC certificate. They should be supplied with and wear the necessary protective equipment. See Chapter 15, section 15.6.1.

REFERENCES

ALDHOUS, J.R. (1961). Experiments in hand-weeding conifer seedbeds in forest nurseries. *Weed Research* **1,** 59–67.

BCPC (1988). *Nozzle selection handbook.* British Crop Protection Council, London.

BCPC (1990). *Weed control handbook – Principles,* 8th edition. Eds Hance, R. J. and Holly, K., for British Weed Control Council. Blackwell Scientific Publications, Oxford.

MAFF (1994). *Pesticides 1994.* Reference Book 500. HMSO, London.

RICE, R.P. (1986). *Nursery and landscape weed control manual.* Thomson Publications, Fresno, USA.

WILLIAMSON, D.R., MASON, W.L., MORGAN, J.L. and CLAY, D.V. (1993). *Forest nursery herbicides.* Forestry Commission Technical Paper 3. Forestry Commission, Edinburgh.

Chapter 13

Protection against climatic damage, fungal diseases, insects and animal pests

R. G. Strouts, S. C. Gregory and S. G. Heritage

Although insect pests, fungal diseases, extremes of weather and various animals can from time to time cause devastating damage in forest nurseries, few types of damage occur frequently enough to justify the use of chemical or other control measures as a matter of routine. Enough is known about the conditions that encourage certain types of damage, for the nursery manager to be able to avoid them or, where this cannot be done, to reduce their likely severity. Chemical control measures can mitigate the worst effects of some pests and diseases, and guard against consequential secondary outbreaks. It is worth noting however that, serious though pests and diseases can be, the most frequent causes of injury to young plants are cultural malpractices such as the misuse of chemicals, and extremes of weather.

The current legislation governing the use of pesticides is outlined in Chapter 15, section 15.6. Few of the pesticides recommended in this chapter have 'on-label' approval for use on forestry nursery stock; at the time of writing, their use for the purposes described in this chapter is permitted under arrangements that may at any time change. It is incumbent on the user to understand these before using any fungicide or insecticide. The current arrangements may be reviewed at any time, and this may result in the choice of product or active ingredient being restricted (see also Chapter 12, section 12.1). For recommendations on insecticides and fungicides for use on forest nursery stock which take the current legal requirements into account, contact the Forestry Authority Research Stations, addresses in Appendix I.

Descriptions of many pests, diseases and disorders are available in the published literature and are listed in the references at the end of this chapter (e.g. Bevan, 1987; Peace, 1962; Phillips and Burdekin, 1992; Smith *et al.*, 1988).

13.1 Climatic damage

13.1.1 Low temperature

Tree species, provenances and varieties differ greatly in susceptibility to low temperature injury and, since the weather conditions that lead to injury are equally variable, only general guidance can be given here and in the following sections.

Plants may be subjected to damagingly low temperatures at any time of the year. However, other than in exceptionally severe winters, most low temperature injury is caused by autumn and spring frosts. The most damaging frosts are usually those following spells of unseasonably warm weather as this may delay the onset of winter hardening or induce premature breaking of dormancy (dehardening). The risks of frost injury should be borne in mind when selecting nursery sites and when planning the layout of existing nurseries. During the life of a nursery, care must also be taken to ensure that no frost hollows develop as a consequence of growth of adjoining plantations, shelterbelts or hedges. If these do grow up and prevent cold air from draining away, one or more gaps must be cut to let the air escape. These gaps should be about as wide as the barrier is high. See also Chapter 14, section 14.2.5 and 14.3.5.

Shoots and foliage injured by low temperatures are susceptible to secondary fungal invasion. This subject is dealt with in section 13.1.5.

Plants can be protected against low temperature injury by provision of overhead shelter or by spraying with water. In some nurseries and with some very susceptible species, frost protection using overhead shading or netting covers may be justified as a routine measure. Otherwise, because of the variability of the British weather and its influence on hardening and de-hardening processes, the decision to give frost protection has to be taken locally on a daily basis. It is essential, therefore, that the means of protection can be installed at short notice. See Chapter 11, section 11.4.3 for details of the use of irrigation to give local protection against unseasonable overnight frosts.

13.1.2 Spring or 'late' frosts

Most species used in British forestry are liable to be damaged by spring frosts from time to time but Scots pine, lodgepole pine, birch and most poplars are rarely frosted. Germinating conifers are also generally resistant. Newly lined out transplants usually break dormancy later than plants left undisturbed and may also be less at risk from spring frosts.

Autumn sown hardwoods, especially beech and oak, often germinate before the last spring frost and may sustain heavy losses unless protected by plastic shading or netting overhead shelter.

Death of buds, new shoots and leaves is the commonest form of damage: the injured tissues rapidly shrivel and turn brown or black. Affected plants usually recover by producing new shoots from surviving or adventitious buds, though plants which recover are often forked. If singled, the remaining shoot often resumes apical dominance.

Exceptionally, bark on older shoots and stems may be killed. The damage sustained can vary from localised lesions to substantial dieback and occasionally the death of the whole plant.

13.1.3 Autumn or 'early' frosts

By the time the first autumn frosts occur, most forest tree species in the nursery have already acquired a degree of frost hardiness. However, some species and certain provenances of others continue to grow late and there is consequently a high risk of damage to them, especially in northern nurseries. Factors that delay hardening can increase the likelihood of injury in normally frost-resistant plants. A spell of unseasonably warm weather before the first frost is one such factor; others are early defoliation by pests or diseases, and nutritional status.

Autumn frost damage may lead to foliage browning in conifers and death of unhardened buds and shoots. Shoot injury commonly results in forking the following season. Species often damaged are Douglas fir and southerly provenances of Sitka spruce.

13.1.4 Winter cold

Winter cold can cause injury to a number of species, especially if low temperatures alternate with mild spells or are accompanied by strong winds. Western hemlock, western red cedar, Douglas fir and *Abies* species are among those that can be damaged by such conditions. Symptoms are variable but can include foliage discoloration and shoot dieback.

The browning of foliage that may follow strong, dry winds in cold winter and early spring weather is believed to be, in essence, drought damage. Plants may be unable to take up water from frozen or near-frozen soils and hence may be unable to replace rapid moisture loss in very cold weather.

Low winter temperatures on their own can injure less hardy species such as some *Nothofagus* species. Exceptionally cold spells have been known to kill the roots of Lawson cypress in containers.

Although snow cover can insulate buried plants effectively, freezing winds over the snow surface may injure exposed shoot tips.

The exceptionally severe winters that lead to widespread injury are rare events and routine provision of shelters is probably not justified in most situations. However, in northern nurseries, species that regularly suffer slight injury may benefit from winter covers.

13.1.5 Secondary infection following low temperature injury

Tissues killed by frost, or indeed by other abiotic agents, are subject to invasion by a variety of fungi. Some of these are opportunistic pathogens which can subsequently spread into previously undamaged tissues. The most common and probably most damaging such organism is *Botrytis cinerea* (grey mould) which is discussed separately in Section 13.2.2. It is a ubiquitous fungus and can invade frost-damaged tissues extremely rapidly in the cool humid conditions that often prevail in autumn and spring.

Shoots injured by low temperatures may also be infected by *Phacidium (Potebniamyces) coniferarum*, formerly known as *Phomopsis pseudotsugae* and dealt with under that name in older Forestry Commission publications as a cause of dieback in Douglas fir. *P. coniferarum* can invade more substantial woody shoots than is usually the case with *Botrytis*. It is a particular risk on Douglas fir but occasionally occurs on other conifers too.

13.1.6 Frost lift

Freezing in wet, heavy soils causes ice crystals to form just below the soil surface. As freezing continues, these crystals grow, so that the surface of the soil lifts or heaves. The soil surface carries with it shallow or weakly rooted seedlings, forcing them upwards; on thawing, the fine soil particles fall back quickly, leaving the plants partly uprooted. Repeated freezing and thawing can eventually push plants out of the ground altogether. Small stones are brought to the soil surface in the same way.

On heavier soils, frost lift can bring about heavy losses of small 1-year-old seedlings, but it is rare on well drained sandy soils. There is evidence that dense or drill-sown beds are less likely to be damaged because blocks of plants tend to lift and resettle as units. Autumn lined out stock is particularly vulnerable in the months immediately after transplanting.

If frost lift occurs, little can be done except to re-insert the seedlings when ground conditions allow. In severe cases this is, however, often impracticable.

13.1.7 Heat and moisture stress

As noted in Chapter 6, section 6.3.7, the temperature of the soil surface in periods of bright, hot sunlight varies according to the colour and nature of the seedbed surface material and can become high enough to injure the root collar of small, thin-barked seedlings. Such damage has become less common, partly through use of light-coloured grit for seedbed cover, and partly because of the availability in many nurseries of irrigation, the use of which can cool seedbed surfaces in hot weather.

Drought damage, although largely the result of dry soil conditions, can be much worsened by drying winds. Symptoms vary from reversible wilting, through the fading and death of foliage, to the withering and dieback of shoots. Foliage browning usually commences at the margins of leaves or the tips of needles. Irrigation, which will prevent or mitigate drought damage, is discussed in Chapter 11, section 11.4.

In glasshouses and polythene tunnels, where temperatures are more likely to reach damaging levels than in open ground, provision of adequate ventilation is vital.

Cloched seedlings may suffer severe heat and moisture stress from bright sunshine and drying winds should these follow quickly on the removal of the cloches.

13.2 Protection against fungal diseases

Although fungal damage can be locally severe

at times, few diseases warrant the expense and labour of routine preventive treatment. Moreover, repeated use of certain types of fungicide in a limited area can lead to a build-up of resistant strains of pathogens.

If repeated, damaging attacks of a disease occur, check whether there is a local infection source or an inappropriate cultural practice that can be dealt with directly as a first response. Nevertheless, should they be required, effective fungicidal treatments are available against several important nursery diseases.

13.2.1 Damping off and root rot

Serious diseases of seedlings can be caused by several seed- or soil-borne fungi that attack young roots and stem bases. These pathogens are mostly in the genera *Fusarium, Rhizoctonia, Phytophthora* and *Pythium,* the last two being the most commonly identified in British forest nurseries.

Fatal infections that occur in the first 3–4 weeks after germination have traditionally been referred to as 'damping off' but this is a poorly defined term and may cover a variety of symptoms. Germinants may be killed before they emerge from the soil ('pre-emergence damping off') or may brown and wither shortly after emergence, following death of their roots. Sometimes infection occurs at ground level, causing the seedling to fall over while still green and still attached to the (often live) root by the withered base of the hypocotyl (Strouts, 1981).

In nursery beds and lines, root diseases can affect scattered individuals but often, and especially in seed beds, expanding patches of infection develop. The centres of large patches may be devoid of seedlings where pre-emergence deaths occurred.

As plants increase in size, infection by nursery root pathogens is less likely to have a fatal outcome though it may lead to stunting. However, some root disease fungi, particularly *Phytophthora* species, can continue killing nursery stock up to transplant size and beyond. Fungal root diseases of older plants are commonly known as 'root rots'.

Damping off and fungal root rots can be very difficult to diagnose, even with laboratory facilities. In particular, they can be impossible to separate from direct root injury by water-logging, a condition that itself greatly favours attack by the primary and secondary root disease fungi that are often present at low levels in nursery soils.

Several seedling root pathogens can live in water and so, in addition to an association with poor drainage, there is a risk of introducing them into nurseries and greenhouses via contaminated irrigation water. This danger can be avoided by the use of mains water and is unlikely to arise if spring or artesian water is used. Detailed information on the purification of suspect water supplies can be obtained from Ministry of Agriculture's ADAS or, in Scotland, SOAFD advisers or from the the British Effluent and Water Association, 5 Castle Street, High Wycombe, Buckinghamshire HP13 6RZ. Whatever the water source, storage tanks must be kept covered and clean.

Control of seedling root diseases is as difficult a problem as their accurate diagnosis. If they are associated with poorly drained areas, as is often the case, improvement of drainage should be a priority. However, if root disease is a recurrent and serious cause of loss in open seed beds, pre-sowing partial soil sterilisation (Chapter 6, section 6.1.4) probably gives the best chance of control. This treatment will also control nematodes (eelworms) which can cause very similar damage to that caused by fungal root pathogens. Soil sterilisation cannot be guaranteed to provide long-term control of soil-borne disease since the treated beds can be re-invaded from surrounding untreated soil or from infection sources elsewhere in the nursery. Soil sterilisation will not control seed-borne diseases.

In greenhouses, the use of properly sterilised or soil-less compost and clean irrigation water, together with the practice of good greenhouse hygiene, should prevent the occurrence of root diseases. Although the use of suspect rooting medium should be avoided, some soil-borne pathogens can be controlled by incorporating fungicide into the rooting medium before sowing.

It is not possible currently to control established outbreaks of root disease among seedlings; there is no fungicidal treatment of proven efficacy in British forest nurseries against any of this group of pathogens.

13.2.2 Grey mould (*Botrytis cinerea*)

Grey mould is a common colonist of dead organic matter and will also readily invade dead or dying soft tissues on living plants. Under circumstances favourable to the fungus, it can then grow into living tissues and greatly extend the original damage. Infected parts often become invested with a sparse grey web of hyphal threads bearing pinhead-like clusters of spores at their free ends, just visible to the naked eye. As plants become woody with age, the disease becomes less important though occasionally the fungus will kill the main stems of transplant-sized conifers. The humid conditions which often prevail inside dense stands of young plants are conducive to *Botrytis* damage so over-stocking in seedbeds and greenhouses should be avoided wherever possible. In greenhouses raising container stock, good air circulation should be maintained to promote the rapid drying of wet foliage (Anon., 1989).

Plants that do become densely packed should be better ventilated if this is possible, inspected regularly and sprayed with a fungicide at the first sign of the disease. In these circumstances, it is worth taking some trouble to ensure that the particularly susceptible shaded foliage is treated.

Infection can also occur on shoots and foliage damaged by frost or chemicals (including fertilisers). Nursery managers should be prepared to spray crops should such damage occur, especially if this happens late in the season, when wet foliage is very slow to dry.

Fungicidal control of grey mould

Materials

Captan: any 83% w/w wettable powder formulation.

> BEFORE ANY FUNGICIDE APPLICATION, READ THE LABEL. IT CARRIES FULL INSTRUCTIONS FOR USE AND THE PROTECTION OF THE OPERATOR AND THE ENVIRONMENT.

Rate: 3.0 kg product in 1000 litres water applied at high volume (more than $700\,l\,ha^{-1}$).

Thiram: any 80% w/w wettable powder formulation.

Rate: 4.0 kg product in 1000 litres water applied at high volume (more than $700\,l\,ha^{-1}$).

Benomyl: any 50% w/w wettable powder formulation. See note below.

Rate: 1.1 kg product in 1000 litres water applied at high volume (more than $700\,l\,ha^{-1}$).

Timing

Seedbeds: apply immediately damage is seen then every 10 days until no mould is evident. Following autumn frost damage, apply immediately, once only.

Greenhouses: apply immediately damage is seen, again one week later, then every 10–14 days until no mould is evident.

Note

Avoid regular and frequent use of benomyl as this could lead to the development of *Botrytis* strains which are resistant to this fungicide.

13.2.3 *Lophodermium* needle cast of pine (*Lophodermium seditiosum*)

The cause of this disease was formerly thought to be *Lophodermium pinastri* and the disease is dealt with under that name in most older Forestry Commission publications.

Infection usually takes place in late summer or autumn on current needles but sometimes also on older needles. Pale spots appear on them and gradually enlarge and darken. The black transverse bands or 'diaphragms' on needles mentioned in earlier literature are not a useful diagnostic feature. *L. seditiosum* fruit bodies are visible on infected needles but are too much like those of other fungi to be useful in field recognition of the disease. Eventually the needles turn completely brown, often with a characteristic dull, mottled pinkish-brown coloration, and begin to fall. This stage is normally reached in late winter or spring and, in serious outbreaks, whole beds or transplant lines may be almost needle-less by spring.

The additional stress imposed by *Lophodermium* defoliation on plants that are lined out or planted in the forest in the autumn or spring following infection, increases the risk that the affected plants will fail to establish. Severe infection can be fatal to 1-year seedlings, even without transplanting, but older nursery stock usually recovers if carefully lined out or left undisturbed. The current foliage of such plants should be protected with a fungicide during summer and autumn against infection from the old, diseased needles which, by then, will usually have fallen.

Fungicidal control of Lophodermium

Materials

Maneb: any 80% w/w wettable powder formulation.

Rate: 2.8 kg product in 1000 litres water applied at high volume (more than $700\,l\,ha^{-1}$).

Zineb: any 70% w/w wettable powder formulation.

Rate: 4.2 kg product in 1000 litres of water applied at high volume (more than $700\,l\,ha^{-1}$).

Benomyl: any 50% w/w wettable powder formulation. See 'Remarks' below.

Rate: 2.0 kg product in 1000 litres water applied at high volume (more than $700\,l\,ha^{-1}$).

Timing

Once every 4 weeks, the first application in mid July, the last in mid November.

Remarks

- Routine spraying of Scots and Corsican pine may be necessary in nurseries where

the disease is a recurrent problem, such as those near older pine trees, which commonly harbour the fungus.

- Spraying after symptoms appear will not arrest the disease.
- Avoid regular and frequent use of benomyl as this could lead to the development of *Lophodermium* strains resistant to this fungicide.

13.2.4 *Meria* needle cast of larch

Meria occurs on European, hybrid and Japanese larches but is uncommon on Japanese larch. Severe infections may be fatal to 1-year seedlings or other small, weak plants. Normally, however, infected plants recover, though growth may be reduced.

Foliage infection takes place in spring and symptoms may appear as early as May though frequently they do not become evident until later in the summer. Infection generally occurs near the tip or in the middle of the needle and results in a yellow then brown patch. The needle browns and withers from the tip down to the infected zone while the base may remain green.

Typically, symptoms are first seen in the older needles at the base or in the middle of current shoots but they then progress towards the shoot tip during the season. The needles at the very tip of shoots sometimes remain green however – a useful feature which may help distinguish *Meria* from injury caused by frost, where terminal needles are usually the most severely damaged.

The fungus survives over winter on fallen needles and on infected needles that remain attached to the plants. In consequence, severe infections can develop in plants spending a second year in the same beds or lines. Plants that show evidence of infection in one year should be protected by spraying during the following year. Transplanting also reduces the risk of reinfection by distancing plants from old infected foliage.

The disease is only a serious problem in wet seasons or, as mentioned above, in stood-over beds and lines. Although the greatest risk of infection is associated with diseased nursery stock, older larch can probably also act as an infection source. The risk of attacks in nurseries can therefore be further reduced by avoiding siting larch stock near larch plantations.

Fungicidal control of Meria
Materials

Zineb: any 70% w/w wettable powder formulation.
Rate: 4.1 kg product in 1000 litres water applied at high volume (more than 700 l ha^{-1}).

Sulphur: any 80% w/w wettable powder formulation.
Rate: 4.0 kg product in 1000 litres water applied at high volume (more than 700 l ha^{-1}).

Timing

Apply every 2–3 weeks, the first application at flushing, the last in early August. Treatment can be discontinued during settled periods of hot, dry weather but should be resumed if weather changes.

Remarks

As explained above, infected plants which are to be stood over should be sprayed in the following year. Otherwise, treatment is recommended only in nurseries where attacks are regularly experienced.

13.2.5 Oak mildew (*Microsphaera alphitoides*)

Newly emerged leaves are infected in May by spores produced from buds in which the fungus has overwintered. Pale brown spots appear, mostly on the undersides of leaves, and from them the fungus spreads across the leaf as a conspicuous white mycelium covered in a thick powdering of white spores. These are dispersed by air to repeat the process of infection on more leaves and shoots. As summer progresses, the production of spores, and hence infection, can increase enormously. In contrast to many foliage diseases, oak mildew and related 'powdery mildews' (such as that on hawthorn) thrive in dry, warm weather.

BEFORE ANY FUNGICIDE APPLICATION, READ THE LABEL. IT CARRIES FULL INSTRUCTIONS FOR USE AND THE PROTECTION OF THE OPERATOR AND THE ENVIRONMENT.

Badly affected leaves may fail to expand properly and become distorted. They may also exhibit dead, brown patches and fall prematurely. Infected shoots may wither or, if they survive infection, may fail to harden normally in autumn and so become liable to frost injury.

Only young growing tissues are susceptible to infection so that foliage produced late in the season, when spore production is usually at its height, can be heavily mildewed. This is frequently the case with lammas growth and foliage produced on plants reflushing after insect defoliation. Severe attacks of mildew can kill young seedlings and cause stunting and bushy growth in older plants.

Fungicidal control of oak mildew
Materials

Sulphur: any 80% w/w wettable powder formulation. See 'Remarks' below.
Rate: 4.0 kg product in 1000 litres water applied at high volume (more than 700 l ha^{-1}).

Dinocap: any 500 g l^{-1} emulsifiable concentrate.
Rate: 0.5 litres product in 1000 litres water applied at high volume (more than 700 l ha^{-1}).

Benomyl: any 50% w/w wettable powder formulation. See 'Remarks' below.
Rate: 1.1 kg product in 1000 litres water applied at high volume (more than 700 l ha^{-1}).

Timing

Apply at first sign of mildew and every 2 weeks if mildew reappears.

Remarks

- Some sulphur products may not be approved for use in greenhouses.

- Avoid frequent and regular use of benomyl as this could lead to the development of mildew strains resistant to the fungicide.

13.2.6 Keithia disease of western red cedar (*Didymascella* (formerly *Keithia*) *thujina*)

Typically, this disease kills scattered leaves. However, severe infections can lead to shoot dieback or even death of whole plants.

In spring, spores which have overwintered on *Thuja* foliage, germinate and infect scale leaves. Fruit bodies quickly develop on the killed tissue and these, along with others which may have overwintered on tissues killed the previous year, release spores which infect newly developing leaves.

Dead, infected scale leaves may carry up to three of the distinctive *Keithia* fruit bodies. These are easily visible to the naked eye as round or oval, blister-like structures, about 1.0 mm in diameter. They are dark brown or golden brown in colour and covered by a round lid which folds back in moist air to release the spores beneath. Old fruit bodies appear as black cavities.

The disease can cause heavy losses in western red cedar plants from their second year until about their fifth year, when they acquire considerable resistance. *Keithia* can generally be avoided if plants are raised from seed in a nursery at least half a mile from any other western red cedars and if, in addition, each crop is completely cleared and the debris burnt before the next crop is sown. Since this is rarely practicable, plants may require fungicidal protection.

Plants raised from cuttings have the reduced susceptibility of the more mature stock plants.

Fungicidal control of Keithia
(see remarks below)

Materials

Prochloraz: any 50% w/w wettable powder formulation.
Rate: 1.8 kg product in 1000 litres water applied at high volume (more than 700 l ha^{-1}).

Benomyl: any 50% w/w wettable powder formulation.
Rate: 1.0 kg product in 1000 litres water applied at high volume (more than 700 l ha^{-1}).

Timing

Apply at fortnightly intervals from late April until early November.

Remarks

These recommendations are based on French work carried out in the 1980s (Boudier 1983, 1986). We are unaware of any trials or observations made in this country to confirm the efficacy of these treatments.

13.2.7 Moulds on plants in storage

The development of storage mould is generally a reflection of inappropriate storage conditions or faulty practice. By the time the problem is discovered, it is usually too late for control measures to be taken. Cold-store managers should therefore pay strict attention to the guidelines on plant storage given in Chapter 14, section 14.7.3.

13.3 Control of insects

13.3.1 Need for vigilance

To achieve an adequate level of protection from insect and other pests, it is important to examine plants starting from early May, when most insects become active and continuing throughout the summer. Particular attention should be paid to the underside of leaves and needles. When seen, appropriate measures should be taken to reduce infestations before they cause more than local damage.

Few insects cause damage on open-grown stock in the present-day nursery. However, numbers of species may build up and cause appreciable loss in a particular year. Table 13.1 lists those which have from time to time, caused such loss. In the table, moth larvae and beetles which as larvae or adults, damage roots of nursery crops are listed first; spring-tails, a leaf miner and spinning mite follow and then, moths and beetles which feed on foliage. Finally, eight aphids and two sucking insects are listed. Details of the appearance of the insect at the stage it is damaging are given, followed by symptoms of damage, the months of the year when damage is expected and the species damaged.

Most insect outbreaks will require the use of insecticides for their control, although insect-pathogenic nematodes are being developed against some soil-borne pests. Nursery practice can, however, influence the frequency with which certain control measures have to be put into effect. To keep insects down, possible sites where numbers can build up must be eliminated as far as possible. For example, beech should not be used as a hedge within nurseries or as a surround, if beech seedlings are to be raised; (see Chapter 2, section 2.3.5). Weevils and some other species listed are likely to be more prevalent if coniferous plantations immediately surround the nursery.

Cutworm larvae, particularly those of the turnip moth, are susceptible to rainfall and do not thrive and cause extensive damage in very wet summers. Irrigation of nursery soils can also be an effective counter-measure. A pheromone monitoring scheme for *Agrotis segetum* is now operated by MAFF.

Soil insects are generally much more troublesome in bare-root nurseries where crops stand for 2 years than in those where seedlings or transplants are usually lifted after 1 year. However, the warmth provided by growing container stock under polythene can reduce insect generation times considerably and therefore give rise to problems with soil-borne insects during one growing season, both in houses and under cloches in open ground.

13.3.2 Selection of insecticide

The use of insecticides is controlled by The Food and Environment Protection Act 1985 (FEPA), the Control of Pesticides Regulations 1986 (COPR) and the Control of Substances Hazardous to Health Regulations 1988 (COSHH). Approval of individual products

BEFORE ANY INSECTICIDE APPLICATION, READ THE LABEL. IT CARRIES FULL INSTRUCTIONS FOR USE AND THE PROTECTION OF THE OPERATOR AND THE ENVIRONMENT.

marketed by manufacturers is a legal requirement and it is an offence to use non-approved products or to use approved products in a manner that does not comply with the specific conditions of approval. Under these regulations, new arrangements were introduced from January 1990 which allowed any pesticide provisionally or fully approved for use on any growing crop to be used on forest nursery crops before final planting out. There are a number of restrictions attached to these arrangements, the most important, for the forest nursery manager, is that insecticides must not be used on protected crops, i.e. grown in glasshouses, poly-tunnels or under cloches, unless the product label specifically allows such usage. It is essential that the safety precautions, application rate and timing together with any other conditions for use that are described on the pesticide label or accompanying leaflet are strictly observed. (See also Chapter 15, section 15.6.1).

The legislation allows a very wide range of insecticides to be used in forest nurseries to suit the insect species and availability. Agricultural chemical supply merchants should be able to advise on the suitability of an insecticide against specific pests, or more specialist advice should be sought from:

The Entomologist or	The Entomologist
The Forestry	The Forestry
Authority	Authority
Research Division	Northern Research
Alice Holt Lodge	Station
Wrecclesham	Roslin
Farnham Surrey	Midlothian
GU10 4LH	EH25 9SY

13.3.3 Protecting transplants from damage by *Hylobius*

Young trees used for restocking felled conifer sites are liable to be heavily damaged by

Table 13.1 Insect pests found in forest nurseries

Type of pest: Root and stem feeder

Latin name	English name and insect group	Damaging stage	Description of damaging stage and length of insect causing damage	Description of damage, habit of feeding, etc.	Time of damage	Tree species attacked	Remarks
Agrotis segetum	Cutworms – Turnip moth	Larva	Dirty grey-brown or grey-green lined larva; 40 mm.	Feed at night; larvae eat seedlings through at 0–1 cm above ground level and may pull tops down into holes in ground. Small larvae may girdle seedlings.	July–Sept. May	All species	Watch for damage and holes in the ground from mid-July. A pheromone-monitoring scheme for A. segetum is now operated by MAFF.
Agrotis exclamationis	Heart and dart moth		Brownish larva with dark brown pear-shaped back marks. Yellowish stripe on sides; 50 mm.				
Noctua pronuba	Large yellow underwing moth		Dark brownish green larva with small head; eight dark bars on sides; 50 mm.				
Hepialus humuli	Ghost swift moth	Larva	Cream larva with oval orange-brown head. Body with horny brownish dots each with a short stiff hair; 50 mm.	Larvae eat out deep spiral groove or completely sever main root.	May–June	Young transplants of broadleaves	Not uncommon near grassy sites.
Melolontha melolontha	Cockchafer	Larva	Characteristically curved larva with brown head and swollen hind end; 30 mm, 15 mm and 18 mm respectively.	Larvae sever seedlings and young transplants below ground level. Young larvae prune roots. The species with longer life-cycle can cause damage through-out summer. Adults feed on leaves of hardwoods.	Any time during 3–4 year larval life	All species	Formerly a serious pest. Now seldom more than very local. Larvae damaged easily when soil is cultivated mechanically.
Serica brunnea	Brown chafer				2 year larval life		
Phyllopertha horticola	Garden chafer				1 year life July–Nov.		
Barypeithes araneiformis	Strawberry fruit weevil	Adult	Small black weevil; 2–3 mm.	Adults ring bark the stems of young seedlings and cause death. Very similar to young cutworm damage, but earlier in the season.	May–June	All species.	
Barypeithes pellucidus	Short snouted weevil		Similar to above but with long grey hairs; 2–3 mm.				

190

Table 13.1 (continued)

Type of pest: Root, stem and leaf feeder

Latin name	English name and insect group	Damaging stage	Description of damaging stage and length of insect causing damage	Description of damage, habit of feeding, etc.	Time of damage	Tree species attacked	Remarks
Strophosomus melanogrammus	Nut leaf weevil	Adult	Weevil covered in brownish ashy scales, with black line between bases of wing cases; 4 mm.	Adults remove triangular chunks from needles, also patches of bark from young twigs.	April–May and Sept.–Oct.	All species	Pests of new plantings as well as nurseries. Cause some damage in older trees. Most prevalent in nurseries adjoining older plantations.
Otiorhynchus singularis (*picipes*)	Clay-coloured weevil	Adult and larva	Clay-coloured weevil; 5.5–7 mm.	Larvae feed on roots and can sever the root system of young seedlings about 2.5 cm below the soil surface.	April–Oct.		
Otiorhynchus ovatus	Strawberry root weevil	Adult and larva	Black weevil; 5 mm.	Adults damage plants in similar way to *O. singularis* Larvae carry out heavy root-pruning.	May–June peak	All species	

Root feeder

Lycoriella species	Fungus gnats (Sciarids)	Larva	Legless whitish larva with black head; 10 mm.	Feed on and in fine roots, causing death of plants.	April–May	Spruce, Thuja, oak	An occasional pest of seedlings in polyhouses.

Leaf miner

Epinotia tedella	Spruce needle miner (moth)	Larva	Greenish or yellow/brown larva with red brown lines down back. Brown head and neckshield; 9 mm long.	Mined needles turn brown, these are spun to shoot in a 'nest' which contains much silk, frass and needle remains.	Aug.–Oct.	Spruces	

Leaf feeder (sucker)

Oligonychus ununguis	Conifer spinning mite	Adult and juvenile	Very small semi-transparent red and green mite (0.5–1 mm).	All stages feed usually on underside of needles causing wilt and fall. Needles turn dingy yellow and threads of silk are plentiful.	May–Sept.	Spruces	Will also attack other conifers.

191

Table 13.1 *(continued)*

Type of pest: Leaf feeder (biter)

Latin name	English name and insect group	Damaging stage	Description of damaging stage and length of insect causing damage	Description of damage, habit of feeding, etc.	Time of damage	Tree species attacked	Remarks
Cerura vinula	Puss moth	Larva	Large green larva with white-edged saddle-shaped purple band down length; 50 mm.	Larvae eat out chunks of leaf.	July/Aug.	Poplar and other hardwoods	
Leucoma salicis	White satin moth	Larva	Dark grey larva with large pale yellow or white dots down back and 3 pairs of bright red hairy warts on each segment; 40 mm.		April–June	Poplar and other hardwoods	
Operophtera brumata	Winter moth	Larva	Green with dark stripe down back, 2 white lines outside this, and beneath these a pale yellowish line. Head green sometimes marked black; 25 mm.	Small larvae eat out chunks from the bud or mine inside it. Older ones spin leaves together and feed on neighbouring foliage, eating out chunks from the leaves.	April–May	Poplar and other hardwoods	Will also attack conifers.
Operophtera fagata	Northern winter moth	Larva	Green with grey stripe down back, 2 similar coloured stripes on each side, edged above with yellowish white. Head black; 25 mm.		May–June	Poplar and other hardwoods	
Erannis defoliaria	Mottled umber moth	Larva	Colour variable. Reddish brown above and yellowish on sides and below. There is also a black side-line edged with interrupted white. Head brown; 25 mm.	Small larvae eat out chunks from the bud or mine inside it. Older ones spin leaves together and feed on neighbouring foliage, eating out chunks from the leaves.	May–June	Poplar and other hardwoods	Will also attack conifers.
Argyrotaenia pulchellana	Grey red-barred tortrix	Larva	Greenish larva, green head with black-marked prothoracic plate; 8 mm.	Young larvae feed gregariously on shoot tips. Older larvae feed singly in spinnings on needles.	Aug.–Sept.	All conifers	Commonest of several species of tortricids which can transfer from ericaceous host-plants.

192

Table 13.1 (continued)

Type of pest: Leaf feeder (biter) continued

Latin name	English name and insect group	Damaging stage	Description of damaging stage and length of insect causing damage	Description of damage, habit of feeding, etc.	Time of damage	Tree species attacked	Remarks
Phyllodecta vitellinae	Brassy willow beetle	Larva and adult	Dirty grey-brown larvae with black dots; 5 mm.	Leaf skeletonised on under sides	May–Sept.	Poplars	Two generations a year.
Phyllodecta vulgatissima	Blue willow beetle		Adults metallic blue or green; 5 mm.	Larvae feed closely side by side. Adults may gnaw young shoots.			
Chalcoides aurata	Willow flea beetle	Adult	Wing cases green or violet, head copper; 2 mm.	Produce small holes in leaf.	May–Aug.	Poplars	
Trichiocampus viminalis	Poplar sawfly	Larva	Larvae as they develop from pale green, through light yellow and finally to orange with black dots; 20 mm.	They feed side by side and skeletonise under side of leaf.	July–Sept.	Poplars and willows	Two generations a year.
Croesus septentrionalis	Hazel sawfly	Larva	Larva develop from pale green with black dots, through green with black and yellow dots, to greenish yellow with prominent black patches; 25 mm.	Eat out chunks of leaf.	June–Sept.	Hardwoods	Possibly two generations a year.
Nematus salicis	Large willow sawfly	Larva	Larva blue green except for first and last 3 segments which are red brown. The whole dotted with black; head black; length 25 mm.	Eat out chunks of leaf.	May–Oct.	Hardwoods	Two generations a year.

Shoot and leaf suckers

Latin name	English name and insect group	Damaging stage	Description of damaging stage and length of insect causing damage	Description of damage, habit of feeding, etc.	Time of damage	Tree species attacked	Remarks
Cinara pilicornis	Brown spruce aphid	Adult and nymph	Light brown to grey-brown aphid	Slight twist to current years shoots on which it feeds in colonies. Needles sometimes become brown as if frosted.	May–July	Spruces	Produces copious quantities of honeydew on which sooty moulds grow.
Elatobium abietinum	Green spruce aphid	Adult and nymph	Wingless globular bright green aphid; 1 mm.	Feeds in colonies on under-side of needles. Causes yellowing and loss of needles.	July–May	Spruces	More serious in standover crops.
Schizolachnus pineti	Grey pine needle aphid	Adult and nymph	Grey aphid with some wax. May form long dense colonies; 2 mm.	Feeds on needles causing some browning.	June–Aug.	Pine	

193

Table 13.1 (continued)

Type of pest: Shoot and leaf suckers continued

Latin name	English name and insect group	Damaging stage	Description of damaging stage and length of insect causing damage	Description of damage, habit of feeding, etc.	Time of damage	Tree species attacked	Remarks
Stagona pini	Pine root aphid	Adult and nymph	Small white aphid. Bluish waxy wool with globules of honey-dew 1–2 mm.	Feeds on roots, can cause browning and wilt of whole plant.	Through out spring and summer	Pine	
Aphis fabae	Black bean aphid	Adult and nymph	Dark grey aphid; 2 mm.	May cause loss of needles or death of seedlings. Feeds near shoot apices.	Aug.–Oct.	Spruce, larch, pine, hemlock	
Phyllaphis fagi	Beech woolly aphid	Adult and nymph	Yellow to green aphid on under side of beech leaves. Plentiful wax wool; 2 mm.	Aphids feed on underside of leaves causing them to wilt, turn brown and fall. Plentiful honeydew.	May–July	Beech	A heavy infestation can seriously check growth.
Myzus cerasi	Cherry black-fly	Adult and nymph	Blackish aphid forming dense colonies under leaves. Much honeydew. 2 mm.	Aphid sucks new leaves which curl. Shoots may die back.	May–July	Cherry	
Pineus pini	Pine woolly aphid	Adult and nymph	Minute black aphid covered in waxy wool.	Feeds on bark of branches and young stems. Can cause some browning of foliage.	May and throughout summer	Pine	
Adelges cooleyi	Douglas fir woolly aphid	Adult and nymph	Black aphid with waxy wool; 1 mm.	Aphids feeding on under-side of needles cause distortion and sometimes needle yellowing and loss.	June–July peak	Douglas fir	Mainly a forest pest but can occur in the nursery on 2nd year and older plants.
Fagocyba cruenta	Beech leafhopper	Nymph and adult	Yellow/brown, elongate. 3–4 mm.	Adult jumps like a flea. Sucks sap from leaves like an aphid causing them to go chestnut brown.	May–July	Beech	
Lygus rugulipennis	Tarnished plant bug	Adult and nymph	Adults variable in colour, yellow-green to brick red; 8 mm. Moves rapidly.	Feed on apical meristem causing multiple-leader seedlings.	April throughout summer	All conifers	Pest status in UK forest nurseries is uncertain. (Overhulse and Kanaskie, 1989.)

Hylobius abietis (the large pine weevil). These insects feed on the plant stem from the root collar upwards which they can completely girdle and cause plant death. Fifty per cent of plants may be expected to be lost on average, although mortality levels vary unpredictably from site to site and often from year to year within a forest. The most effective method of protecting plants is to treat them before planting with an insecticide.

It is recommended that the application of insecticides to planting stock before planting should be carried out at centralised treatment centres with purpose-built changing and washing facilities. These offer the opportunity for higher standards of safe working practice, including handling of insecticide concentrates and safe disposal of empty containers.

The efficacy of the treatment also benefits from centralised facilities because closer supervision can ensure that the correct concentration of chemical is maintained. Where plants are dipped, the provision of covered heeling in areas enables the insecticide deposit to dry on the plant stem regardless of adverse weather. Such facilities may best be located at nurseries or plant storage and distribution centres.

Dipping the tops and upper root systems of bare-rooted plants in a high concentration of an insecticide product diluted with water provides protection for the growing season for spring planted plants. The main advantage is its simplicity, with no reliance on high technology. Containerised plants such as those grown in Japanese paper pots are best treated by spraying them in their trays. The insecticide may be applied using a knapsack sprayer or using a moving spray-boom system.

As with the control of nursery pests, the use of insecticides against *Hylobius* is controlled by FEPA, COPR and COSHH. Limited 'off-label' approval has been given for the use of permethrin to dip plants before planting and this remains valid until 31 July 1995. Details of the techniques and the necessary protective clothing are contained in the Forestry Commission Research Information Note 185 *Approved methods for insecticidal protection of*

> BEFORE ANY INSECTICIDE APPLICATION, READ THE LABEL. IT CARRIES FULL INSTRUCTIONS FOR USE AND THE PROTECTION OF THE OPERATOR AND THE ENVIRONMENT.

young trees against Hylobius abietis *and* Hylastes *species* and Research Information Note 177 *Application leaflet on the use of 'Permit' and 'Permasect' for pre-planting treatment of young trees against* Hylobius abietis *and* Hylastes *spp.* These publications, and amendments issued at regular intervals, also give the current position regarding approvals for use under COPR and are available from Publications Section, The Forestry Authority, Research Division, Alice Holt Lodge, Wrecclesham, Farnham, Surrey, GU10 4LH.

13.4 Protection of seedbeds against birds

Birds have been known to eat all the seed sown on seedbeds. The loss in one area of almost 40 kg of pine seed due to feeding by small birds has been recorded. Such severe damage is exceptional but in most nurseries there is some feeding, mostly by greenfinches, chaffinches and sparrows. Linnets, skylarks, crossbills and pigeons can also do severe damage. Birds do most harm to sowings of species with large seeds such as Corsican pine, *Pinus strobus* and *P. peuce* and some hardwoods. Species like western hemlock are seldom troubled.

Capercaillie have extensively damaged pine in Scottish nurseries by feeding on young growing shoots.

Pheasants may feed on oak, beech or sweet chestnut seed if sown in the autumn.

The only certain counter-measure to birds feeding on seed is a complete physical barrier of netting over the seedbeds. Bird scarers of flashing metal, strings of cartridges or carbide bangers may be effective for a few days but the birds get used to them and subsequently ignore them. There are no seed dressings that can currently be recommended.

13.4.1 Netting against birds

A suitable physical barrier may be made using 2.0 cm polythene netting laid across seedbeds immediately after sowing and supported on flattened hoops of No. 8 or No. 10 galvanised wire. The hoops should not project more than 15 cm above the seedbed at the highest point, so that a tractor can be used to apply a pre-emergence spray through the netting. Short lengths of wire bent over at one end should be used to pin down the edges of the netting in contact with the soil so that birds do not get under it. The netting must also not be allowed to droop in the middle; otherwise birds will peck through it.

Properly erected, such a barrier should keep birds away completely. The netting must be put over beds as soon as possible after sowing and may have to remain for 6–9 weeks after sowing. It may be taken away once the seedlings have started to produce the first true leaves.

Although polythene netting is relatively easy to put over beds, it is quite expensive, both in capital outlay and in the labour of handling it. Polythene netting is nevertheless both easier to handle and cheaper to buy than light gauge galvanised netting. Also, the zinc used in galvanised netting can render the soil toxic to nursery plants; this risk is serious wherever netting remains in position for several months, especially where air is heavily polluted. On ground where galvanised netting is left rolled up for any length of time, plants may subsequently fail to grow.

13.5 Protection of seedbeds against mice

If mice are thought to be damaging seed, traps should be set. If the damage is too severe to be controlled by trapping or if the seed is particularly valuable, a temporary mouse-proof fence may be erected round the seedbeds concerned. The fence should be of ¼" mesh galvanised netting. It need be no more than 60 cm wide, with 10 cm buried in the ground and the top 8 cm curled over away from the seedbeds to prevent mice from climbing over. Joins in the netting must be made mouse-proof. Traps should be set within the fence to catch any mice already inside.

13.6 Damage by other animals

If freedom from rabbit damage is to be guaranteed, a rabbit fence is virtually essential. See Forestry Commission Bulletin 102, especially Figure 1 (Pepper, 1992).

Hares and deer occasionally get into nurseries. Hares are rarely more than a nuisance, but if deer, present in the locality, are regular visitors, a deer fence should be put up around the nursery. The cheapest form of deer fence is a 1 m width of broad mesh netting erected above a standard rabbit fence, to give a total height of 1.8 m.

Dogs, foxes and badgers occasionally get into a nursery and dig holes but the damage they do is insignificant.

Moles are seldom troublesome in a nursery but where they do occur they should be trapped. A licence is required before strychnine can be used to poison moles.

REFERENCES AND FURTHER READING

ANON. (1989). Breakthrough in grey mould problem. *Information Forestry* **16** (3), 1. Pacific Forest Centre, Victoria BC, Canada.

BCPC (1983). *Pest and disease control handbook,* 4th edtn. BCPC Publication, London.

BEVAN, D. (1987). *Forest insects.* Forestry Commission Handbook 1. HMSO, London.

BOUDIER, B. (1983). *Didymascella thujina,* principal ennemi du *Thuja* dans l'ouest de la France. *Phytoma, Défense des cultures,* November 1983, 51–54.

BOUDIER, B. (1986). *Essai de mise au point de méthode de lutte contre Didymascella thujina.* Internal paper, Ministère de l'Agriculture, 14200 Hérouville Saint-Clair, France. (4 pp.)

COOPER, J.I. (1994). *The viruses diseases of trees and shrubs.* NERC Institute of Virology and Environmental Microbiology. HMSO, London.

CORDELL, C.E., ANDERSON, R.L., HOF-FARD, W.H., LANDIS, T.D., SMITH, R.S. and TOKO, H.V. (1989). *Forest nursery pests*. US Department of Agriculture, Forest Service, Handbook 680.

OVERHULSER, D.L. and KANASKIE, A. (1989). *Lygus* bugs. In *Forest nursery pests*, ed. Cordell, C E. *et al.*, Agricultural Handbook 680. USDA Forest service, Washington DC.

PEACE, T.R. (1962). *Pathology of trees and shrubs with special reference to Great Britain*. Clarendon Press, Oxford.

PEPPER, H.W. (1992). *Forest fencing*. Forestry Commission Bulletin 102. HMSO, London.

PHILLIPS, D.H. and BURDEKIN, D.A. (1992). *Diseases of forest and ornamental trees,* 2nd edtn. Macmillan, Basingstoke.

SMITH, I.M., DUNEZ, J., LELLIOTT, R.A., PHILLIPS, D.H. and ARCHER, S.A. (eds.) (1988). *European handbook of plant diseases*. Blackwell Scientific Publications, Oxford.

STROUTS, R.G. (1981). *Phytophthora diseases of trees and shrubs*. Arboricultural Leaflet 8. HMSO, London.

Chapter 14

Lifting, storage, handling and despatch

H. M. McKay, J. R. Aldhous and W. L. Mason

Introduction

The final and most critical stage in nursery management involves the lifting of plants from a nursery and their delivery to a customer in as good a condition as possible. This stage is made up of a complex chain of operations which can include lifting, storage, grading, insecticide treatment, packing, despatch, receipt, temporary storage and planting. The first part of this chain is the responsibility of the nursery management and the second is that of the customer. Customers will consider a nursery to be successful if the plants are delivered on time, if these conform to previously agreed size specification, and, most importantly, if they find that the plants survive well and grow vigorously after planting. For success to be achieved, the nursery management must always recognise the importance of two concepts:

- there must be careful control of each operation from lifting until delivery and subsequent planting;
- the plants must be in the best physical and physiological condition to withstand the period between lifting and planting.

Foresters have often found that newly planted young trees either fail to survive or grow weakly in the first year. Some of these losses can be due to the conditions at time of or immediately after planting. However, some are the result of plants from the nursery being either of poor physical quality (see standards in Chapter 1, section 1.5.2), or in poor condition as a result of the damage sustained during lifting, storage and handling. The practice of purchasers asking for samples before confirming orders arises out of concern to avoid planting loss and possibly acrimony over the responsibility for such losses. It must be remembered that replacing failed planting stock is expensive and involves additional establishment costs because of slower growth and greater weeding.

14.1 Integrated procedures

It cannot be stressed strongly enough that, if customers are to establish their plants successfully, there must be a close understanding with the nursery manager. The nursery manager must know the customer's needs and the latter must understand the nature of the integrated chain between lifting and delivery of plants. Careful handling of plants at all stages is necessary if plants are to survive and grow. Equally, the best quality plants cannot be expected to survive without good establishment practice.

While individual operations are discussed separately in this chapter, in practice, much thought must be given as to how best to integrate use of machinery, storage facilities, available time and manpower in relation to stock, soils, weather and customers' requirements so that risk of damage to plants is minimised.

The aim is to ensure that plants are in first class physiological condition at the time of planting, and can quickly regenerate roots before seasonal changes in day-length and temperature stimulate plants to break bud and commence shoot growth. It must always be remembered that plants with damaged root systems will struggle to survive after planting.

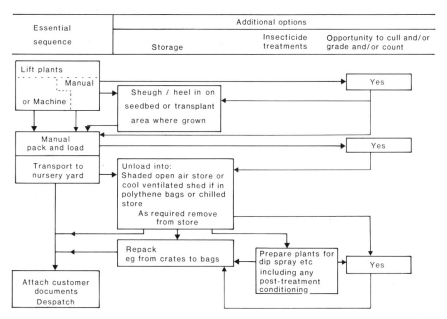

Essential sequence	Additional options		
	Storage	Insecticide treatments	Opportunity to cull and/or grade and/or count
Lift plants — Manual or Machine	Sheugh / heel in on seedbed or transplant area where grown		Yes
Manual pack and load			Yes
Transport to nursery yard	Unload into: Shaded open air store or cool ventilated shed if in polythene bags or chilled store. As required remove from store		
	Repack eg from crates to bags	Prepare plants for dip spray etc including any post-treatment conditioning	Yes
Attach customer documents Despatch			

Figure 14.1 Stages in plant handling and despatch.

Figure 14.1 illustrates in outline, the sequence of operations that has to be followed. The essence of the manager's task is to flesh it out by putting in numbers of plants, dates of delivery, nursery production capacity, rate of work of men and machines, and at the same time decide how much to allow for delays due to severe winter weather and similar contingencies.

14.1.1 Work-study investigations

Two Forestry Commission Work Study teams have studied plant handling in the nursery and methods of despatch from nursery to forest. They showed how effective use can be made of cages for moving plants within the nursery, with pallets and boxes offering reliable physical protection against crushing and mechanical shock while in transit from nursery to forest.

Studies also looked at how the planter needed to carry plants before planting, considering whether anything should be done in the nursery to assist his work, rather than treat nursery work and forest planting as unrelated operations (Dauncey *et al.*, 1988, 1989; Scott, 1987a, b).

14.2 Causes of damage and loss of plant quality

The concept of plant 'quality' expresses its *current ability* to grow well, as soon as seasonal and cultural conditions allow. 'Quality' in this sense, combines 'physiological' and 'physical' condition. The detrimental effect of damage or loss of quality at any stage between lifting and planting is cumulative (Tabbush, 1988); by analogy, plants may be thought of as collecting penalty points at any stage, their final performance reflecting their aggregate penalty point score. See also section 14.4.3 (electrolyte leakage). Unfortunately, there is nothing that can be done to restore quality once plants have deteriorated, other than planting them out as carefully as possible on a well-prepared site in the hope that they may recover and grow. If deterioration has gone too far, then it will be better to start again with good quality plants. Any concern about the quality of plants should be communicated to the nursery *as soon as possible* after receipt.

The aim in lifting, storage, handling and despatch is to ensure that plants are in as good a condition as possible when received for planting. This aim implicitly recognises that plant quality can deteriorate, often very quickly, through poorly timed or executed operations, which can influence quality in a number of ways as described below.

14.2.1 Root loss during lifting, culling and grading

Plants which have grown well in the open nursery and are of suitable size and condition for planting in the forest, can have root systems which are 30 cm or more in depth and with 60 cm or more lateral spread. Inevitably, in lifting such stock, root systems are damaged through breakage of the longer roots, many root tips are lost and symbioses broken between plants and mycorrhiza-forming fungi.

Systematic undercutting and wrenching will reduce the depth of rooting and therefore reduce the worst damage that occurs at lifting. However, it is difficult not to damage roots even when lifting well-conditioned undercut plants. See section 14.5. When plants are being separated and handled during culling and grading, woody roots may be torn off and fine roots detached unless care is taken.

14.2.2 Desiccation

Fine roots of all forest tree species are very sensitive to desiccation so bare root plants in particular must be protected from drying conditions. Hermann (1967), for example, recorded damage to Douglas fir seedlings with washed roots after only one minute's exposure to desiccating conditions in a growth chamber. Desiccation also appears to predispose plants to rough handling damage (Tabbush, 1986). In experiments at Wykeham, Yorkshire, survival of Sitka spruce was significantly reduced by 70 minutes exposure to windy conditions in March, and Douglas fir was even more susceptible (Tabbush, 1987a).

The effect of loss of moisture in fine roots is not reversed by rewetting. Roots which retain a covering of nursery soil dry out more slowly but too much nursery soil can provide a source of fungal infection during storage.

The risk of drying during storage is high unless the store is designed to maintain a very high humidity. Where plants are stored in bags, the bags must be completely sealed to prevent the escape of moist air. Even small slits in bags have resulted in plant deaths through desiccation in directly refrigerated cold stores.

Shoots are unlikely to be damaged by desiccation between lifting and planting. However, exposure to drying winds may lower the plant's water content directly; mild drying conditions may also indirectly induce stomatal closure and hence reduce photosynthesis.

14.2.3 Deterioration during cold and canopy storage

Plants can be damaged by mould growth if they have been stored with wet foliage. In such cases the damage is usually obvious, but in many cases the plants appear to be in good health. Deterioration in cold storage has been inferred in many instances of large-scale planting failure (Mason and McKay, 1989).

Plant survival after cold storage is closely related to the quality of the fine root system as assessed by electrolyte leakage (see 14.4.3) even though the foliage appears in good condition (McKay and Mason, 1991). The following mechanism may explain deterioration of tissue in storage. During autumn and winter, compounds build up in living cells to protect the cell membranes from winter damage. These compounds and the energy required for their transformations cannot be produced in the dark, cold conditions of the cold stores. Adequate levels of protective compounds and energy must therefore be present in the plants at the time of storage to maintain the cells in good condition until they are planted out.

Deterioration of the root system mostly occurs during storage in early winter or late spring when the root system is not fully dormant. It is generally true that nursery stock is best stored between mid-December and mid-January but there are major differences between species, provenances and plant types in the length and timing of safe lifting 'windows' (see Table 14.4). Lifting times must be modified from year to year depending on the condition of the plants and the condition of the nursery.

Deterioration of the root system is also caused if plants are stored for too long (see 14.7). The maximum safe storage period depends on the initial plant quality, the species, the provenance and the plant type.

Desiccation may damage plants in direct cold stores if bags are torn. Desiccation is also a hazard to plants throughout humi-cold stores, if the stores do not operate close to saturation (Sharp and Mason, 1992), and to plants adjacent to doors if vehicles are continuously moving in and out.

Loss of quality during canopy storage is also due to deterioration of the root system rather than the shoot.

14.2.4 Rough handling

Bad handling can adversely affect plant performance. While nursery managers have constantly been exhorted to handle plants with care, it is only during the last decade that figures have been available showing how plant performance can deteriorate if handled badly. For example, Tabbush (1986) subjected Sitka spruce and Douglas fir to a bad handling treatment in which plants were dropped onto a concrete floor (Table 14.1). Bad handling in combination with overheating and drying treatments, which in themselves had detrimental effects, was particularly damaging raising mortality from 2 to 54% for Sitka spruce and from 8 to 35% for Douglas fir. There is some evidence that the reduction in height growth is more closely related to the maximum force experienced by the plants than to the mean or total force (McKay *et al.*, 1993).

There is usually no obvious physical damage visible following rough handling. However there is evidence that physiological changes take place as a result of mechanical damage to roots which may cause the large reduction in root growth observed by Tabbush (1988).

Low levels of physical handling or pressure on the root system can also cause stomatal closure. Water-stressed or mechanically damaged root systems appear to be able to produce

Table 14.1 Root growth potential (number of new roots after 14 days) and percentage loss at the end of the first growing season, following heating, drying and rough handling before planting

Pre-planting treatment	Sitka spruce		Douglas fir	
	Root growth potential	Loss %	Root growth potential	Loss %
No heating	11.5	16	0.25	19
Heating	8.4	22	0.48	17
No drying	19.6	5	0.45	11
Drying	0.3	34	0.28	24
No rough handling	16.8	9	0.68	12
Rough handling	3.1	30	0.05	23
No maltreatment	37.1	2	0.5	8
All maltreatments	0	54	0.01	35

Data from 'factorial design' experiment (Tabbush, 1986).

$$\underset{\text{Heating}}{O} \times \underset{\text{Drying}}{O} \times \underset{\text{Rough handling}}{O}$$

a substance, possibly abscisic acid, that is transported to the leaves causing the stomata to close (Coutts, 1980).

The effects of different forms of rough handling are being investigated; it is possible that small jolts induce stomatal closure, moderate jolts may also rupture cell membranes while severe jolts may break woody roots and fracture the water columns within the plants. The shocks which plants normally receive under operational conditions between lifting and planting are currently being investigated.

14.2.5 Frosting

Roots are much less frost tolerant than shoots (Pellett, 1971) but soil temperatures rarely reach damaging levels. However, frost tolerance of the root system has become increasingly important with the advent of container production where roots do not have the benefit of a massive soil volume to act as a buffer against sudden drops in temperature. Container plants overwintered outside, especially if stored off the ground to maintain air-pruning of the roots, and bare root plants stored in bags in the open may be exposed to damaging temperatures.

14.2.6 Overheating

Temperatures above 40°C can damage both roots and shoots (Levitt, 1980; Tabbush, 1987b). Such temperatures have been recorded inside clear polythene bags left in full sunshine for several hours. The introduction of coextruded black and white bags has reduced this risk of direct damage through overheating. However, temperatures exceeding 20°C have been recorded within black and white bags left in full sunlight in March. These temperatures are unlikely to have any direct damaging effects but may, through hastening bud-break and other growth processes, lower plants' general resistance to stress. Therefore all plants in bags should be stored in shade.

Heating may also result from bacterial and plant respiration in the absence of a good circulation of air. This may happen with densely packed loads of plants in transit late in the planting season or with plants left in uninsulated vehicles for 36 hours or more, especially if the vehicle body is warmed when standing in the sun.

Any buildings used as temporary stores also must be well ventilated.

14.3 Factors affecting the over-winter physiological condition of plants

14.3.1 Dormancy status and stress tolerance

Two physiological measures, bud dormancy and shoot frost hardiness, have been linked to the plants' overwinter condition to the extent that they are often loosely thought to indicate the dormancy status of the plant as a whole.

Bud dormancy

Woody plants have become adapted to the winter environment of their origin and they require a certain amount of chilling over winter. Shoots will not respond to rises in temperature until they have received this chilling requirement. Thus, plants are not normally damaged by short unseasonal warm spells during winter. Temperatures between 0 and +5°C are the most effective in bringing about the physiological changes involved in loss of bud dormancy (van den Driessche, 1975). As the number of chilling hours experienced by plants accumulates, buds take fewer days to burst. When the chilling requirement has been fully satisfied, seedlings take only 10–12 days in a warm glasshouse for their leading bud to open. Plants can be described as 'quiescent' when their chilling requirement has been met, but the environmental conditions are not favourable to growth.

The concept of 'chilling requirement' is relevant to the timing of plant lifting and storage. Ritchie (1986) found that stock of local seed origins deteriorated least when plants were cold stored before their chilling requirements for the winter had been fully met. Storage at temperatures of typical plant cold stores and for the appropriate period enabled any outstanding chilling requirement to be met before the plants left the store. Over a number of years, Ritchie (1984 b) has established for Douglas fir the number of chill hours required in relation to storage practice; chill hours have been used to identify safe lifting windows in Western USA. However, where species (e.g. larches) are raised in climates markedly different from those of the plants' seed origin, bud pre-chill requirements and bud dormancy may not be a reliable guide to plants' overall end-of-winter condition.

Shoot frost hardiness

In typical winters, shoot frost hardiness increases rapidly in November, levelling out during December and January. Dehardening in spring is less predictable and varies from year to year depending on the air temperature. Shoot frost hardiness (Colombo and Hickie, 1987 and Faulconer, 1988) has been used in the USA and Canada to identify times of cold storage. In practice, the decision is based on the degree of damage caused at the selected temperature, e.g. –10°C, rather than the exact temperature causing damage to 50% of the shoots.

Bud dormancy and shoot frost hardiness tests yield information on these particular aspects of the plants' overwinter condition. However, assessments of the ability of plants to withstand the stresses to which they are inevitably exposed between lifting and planting are more useful to the nursery manager. In general, plant tissues are most easily damaged when they are growing rapidly and least sensitive when they are least active (Coutts and Nicoll, 1990; Ritchie, 1986). Since roots are more easily damaged than shoots, the physiological tests most relevant to nursery staff assess the stress tolerance and activity of the root system rather than shoot dormancy status.

14.3.2 Seasonal patterns in plant activity

The time of bud set is dependent on the species and provenance but it can be manipulated by undercutting and nutrition. The periods of shoot extension are obvious but cells in the buds continue to divide for several months after the overwintering buds have formed (McKay and Mason, 1991). During autumn and early winter, the rate of cell division decreases but cells may continue dividing until mid-December before stopping for a few months. The external appearance of shoots changes during this period of decreasing cell division; stem colour darkens and shoots become stiffer. Cell division begins again in April as the buds start to swell.

The cycles of activity are less obvious below ground but the roots too have periods of cell division and cell expansion. The cycles of activity in the root system are not easy to predict for they depend on the amount of energy available, and the environmental conditions, especially soil temperature and moisture. Generally the energy requirement for shoot growth takes precedence over the requirement for root growth, therefore root growth tends to occur between periods of active shoot growth. In general, there is a flush of root cell division and expansion in spring just before bud burst. During the time of greatest shoot growth, root

growth slows. There may be further flushes of growth during summer when temperature and soil moisture allow. In the autumn, active root growth continues well after bud set but slows down gradually during autumn and winter to reach a minimum by mid-December. The length of the following inactive period when roots are neither dividing nor expanding varies with the winter conditions, the species and to a limited extent the plant type. However, since roots are more easily damaged than shoots, it is important to realise that the period of root inactivity is much shorter than the period of shoot inactivity.

14.3.3 Environmental factors influencing plant activity

The conditions inducing shoot dormancy seem to be related to climatic factors operating in the area of plants' natural distributions. In some species which have evolved in areas normally receiving rain throughout the year, the main trigger is day length but in other species most notably Douglas fir, summer droughts are the main factors inducing dormancy.

Shoots develop frost hardiness in two stages (Greer et al., 1989). The first occurs after the day length has shortened to a critical level (Cannell and Sheppard, 1982). In Britain, this is in October for Queen Charlotte Islands Sitka spruce. Hardening is most rapid during November and is in response to low air temperatures. Maximum shoot frost hardiness is reached by mid-December. Later, shoots deharden quickly when air temperatures rise leading to bud break and it is well known that thereafter new foliage is particularly susceptible to frost damage.

The factors influencing activity and frost hardiness of roots are less clearly understood. In autumn and winter when shoot expansion has ceased, undercutting has stopped and soils are moist, temperature and day length are the main controlling factors. Both daylength and temperature affect root elongation but over the range of soil temperatures normally experienced by forest nursery sites, temperature has the greatest effect. Root frost hardiness in some species appears to be

Table 14.2 The relative tolerance of Sitka spruce of Queen Charlotte Islands provenance (QSS), Douglas fir (DF), Japanese larch (JL), Scots pine (SP), Sitka spruce of Oregon provenance (RSS) and Alaskan origin (ASS) to desiccation, cold storage, rough handling and frost

	Desiccation	Cold storage	Rough handling	Frost
QSS	8	8	8	8
DF	1	1	6	1
JL	6	6	8	7
SP	7	6	8	3
RSS	7	5	8	6
ASS	5	9	9	9

0 = very intolerant; 10 = very tolerant.

induced by shortening daylength (Smit-Spinks *et al.*, 1985) but in other species temperature is more important (Lindström and Nyström, 1987; McKay, 1994).

14.3.4 Species and provenance differences in tolerance of stresses

The results of experiments carried out between 1988 and 1991 to study the relative tolerance of some of the main commercial conifers to standard experimental stresses are summarised in Table 14.2. Stock types are ranked on a scale of 0 to 10 according to the electrolyte leakage from the fine roots after stresses applied at intervals from October to April. These results agree with the earlier findings of Tabbush (1986, 1987a and 1988) who compared Queen Charlotte Islands Sitka spruce and Douglas fir on the basis of root growth potential.

Desiccation tolerance

Douglas fir was the most sensitive and Queen Charlotte Islands Sitka spruce the most tolerant to an experimental drying treatment of 5 hours exposure to air circulating at 15°C (unpublished data). There were clear seasonal patterns in these species' tolerance to the standard drying treatment. In general, roots were at their most tolerant from mid-December until March. These results emphasise that, during late autumn planting particularly of Douglas fir, great care must be taken to prevent root drying.

Storage tolerance

Of the species studied, Sitka spruce was the most tolerant to cold storage. For example, the root system showed no deterioration when stored in January of the mild 1988–89 winter for 5 months. Douglas fir (Darrington, Washington origin) was extremely sensitive that year to storage at +1°C. In the more 'typical' winter of 1990–91, Douglas fir could tolerate storage with minimal damage for only one month when stored at the optimal time. Japanese larch resembles Sitka spruce during the early winter but the tolerance of its root system to storage decreases several months earlier in the spring. The tolerance of Sitka spruce provenances increases with increasing latitude (McKay, 1993).

Deterioration during canopy storage has not been studied so intensively but the limited results indicate that Sitka spruce is more tolerant than Douglas fir.

Survival after cold storage was more closely correlated to the condition of the root than the shoot. Shoots of Douglas fir are more tolerant of cold storage than are Sitka spruce yet their roots are less tolerant than those of Sitka spruce. Therefore the appearance of Douglas fir foliage after storage is a poor guide to the plants overall health status (McKay and Mason, 1991).

Rough handling tolerance

Species and provenances did not differ greatly in their ability to withstand a 'moderate' rough handling treatment of five drops from 1 m. However there are clear seasonal patterns in sensitivity to these standard experimental rough handling treatments. In general, all species studied were most tolerant between mid-December and mid-March. Care must therefore be taken when handling freshly lifted plants outwith these months to minimise the physical jolts given to the plants.

Frost hardiness

There are major species differences in the frost hardiness of both shoots and roots.

Overwinter shoots of Japanese larch and Sitka spruce of Queen Charlotte Islands origin are similar in the degree of frost they can tolerate; Douglas fir is much less frost tolerant. For example, even in a mild winter, Sitka spruce and Japanese larch required a temperature of –28°C for 3 hours to kill half of the shoots whereas a temperature of –15°C killed half of the shoots of Douglas fir. The shoot frost hardiness of Sitka spruce provenances increased with latitude.

During the winter of 1990–91, in a series of experiments, Douglas fir roots could tolerate a 3 hour exposure to only –4°C and showed almost no ability to increase frost tolerance between October and March (McKay, 1994). Scots pine roots were slightly more tolerant than those of Douglas fir. Sitka spruce, even of Oregon provenance, and Japanese larch became increasingly tolerant of low root temperatures. By late January, Queen Charlotte Islands Sitka spruce and Japanese larch roots could withstand a 3 hour exposure to –15°C and –11°C respectively. Sitka spruce and Japanese larch became less frost tolerant during mid-January to April when they were tolerant of ~–6°C. These results lead to the recommendation that Douglas fir and Scots pine must be protected from severe or prolonged frosts at all times during winter. During October and from April onwards all stock should be given some protection against frost.

14.3.5 Preconditioning

Plant quality may be altered by 'preconditioning' in the nursery, especially in the second half of the growing season preceding lifting and despatch. Transplanting is the commonest form of physical preconditioning; physical and physiological preconditioning may also be achieved by intensive undercutting and side-cutting regimes.

Undercutting followed by *regular* wrenching causes repeated branching in the upper root system giving a higher proportion of fine root. Undercutting and wrenching also induce physiological changes which usually enable undercut plants to establish themselves more readily where soil or climate factors are unfavourable even though undercut plants, in very dry years, may be smaller.

The nutrient status of planting stock affects many aspects of the physiological quality of stock some of which are important to the plants at the stages from lifting to planting (van den Driessche, 1991). For example, potassium increases drought resistance by improving stomatal function and by increasing the tolerance of the protoplasm to water shortage. The beneficial effect of increasing K on protoplasmic drought tolerance is likely to be of greater relevance to stock between lifting and planting than the effect on stomatal function since the roots will lose water more rapidly than the shoot whenever plants are exposed during the handling chain. The effect of nitrogen depends on the time of its application. Summer and early autumn applications can delay bud set or stimulate lammas growth delaying the development of shoot frost hardiness, whereas late season applications have little effect or a slight beneficial effect on shoot frost hardiness.

Unfortunately there is little information available on the interaction of nutrition and aspects of the physiological condition of the root system which are relevant between lifting and handling. The remainder of this section is therefore informed speculation. Since nutrients, in particular N and P, stimulate root growth, nutrient applications particularly late season applications might be expected to decrease the general tolerance of the root system to stresses such as long-term storage, rough handling and desiccation. N supply is known to affect the root to shoot ratio; high levels have a greater positive effect on shoot growth than root growth resulting in an overall reduction in R:S ratio and might be expected to reduce overall survival. However N applications after bud set should increase root growth and provide adequate N reserves for rapid root growth after outplanting.

14.4 Plant attributes influencing survival

The most important characteristic of plants

immediately after planting is the physiological status of their stomata. If these close, the plant can no longer maintain a high flow of photosynthate to the shoots and roots. Many species, e.g. Douglas fir, are dependent on newly formed photosynthate to produce new roots whereas other species, e.g. Sitka spruce, can use stored energy to produce new roots (Philipson, 1988); even so root growth is greater if newly formed photosynthate is available. Therefore, if the stomata close in response to water deficits or physical shocks, photosynthesis will be curtailed and root growth reduced or inhibited. After planting in the forest, uptake of water from the site to permit photosynthesis will depend on the ability of the existing root system to provide water to the plant.

Ideally nursery stock should have sufficient water to allow photosynthesis immediately after planting (needle water potential should be <20 bars). If not, they should have adequate live fine root in relation to the shoot to quickly overcome water-deficits, thus forming plants with a positive cycle of photosynthesis, new root growth and adequate water uptake. At worst, provided stored carbohydrate can be used for root growth, plants must have adequate stored carbohydrate and a sufficiently large existing root system to support wide-spread new root growth.

14.4.1 Assessing physiological quality

Many methods have been used to measure various aspects of the physiological quality of plants. These were reviewed by Ritchie (1984a). Tests developed between 1984 and 1989 include variable chlorophyll fluorescence, stress-induced volatile emissions, mitotic index, electrolyte leakage from shoots, triphenyl tetrazolium chloride, days to bud break and the phytogram (Hawkins and Binder, 1990). The two tests described in the following section, root growth potential and root electrolyte leakage, have proved useful in recent experiments carried out by Forestry Commission research staff as indices of early survival and growth in forest experiments.

14.4.2 Root growth potential

Early survival after planting in the forest is dependent on the plants' water status and the ability of the root system to supply adequate water. If a plant can produce abundant new roots quickly, it will rapidly establish root contact with the surrounding soil, thereby increasing water and nutrient uptake. There have been many attempts to assess the ability of plants to produce new roots after planting.

Stone (1955) examined the root development of plants after 60 days in favourable greenhouse conditions and then grew them on for a further 120 days. Many subsequent modifications of this type of test are reviewed by Sutton (1990). Generally root growth potential (RGP) is now measured over 2 weeks. The number of new roots produced is a guide to the condition of the plants. If abundant roots are produced by a sample of plants, they are likely to survive and grow well after normal planting (see Burdett, 1979). However, *the opposite is not always true*; some batches of plants showing up poorly in RGP tests do have a low survival potential but others survive well. This reduces the value of the test to the nursery manager.

The standard Forestry Commission Research Division test is to place 15–20 plants per batch individually in root observation boxes – a 45 cm length of plastic roof guttering, filled with moist peat to within 5 cm of one end (the top). The root system of each plant is spread over the peat with the root collar 5 cm below the level of the peat and held firmly in place by a clear acetate sheet taped to the sides and other end of the gutter. If the roots are so muddy that new root growth will not be seen easily, the roots must be washed gently. Air pockets around the root system should be minimised. The root boxes are stood on end in a rack for support and stacked against one another with the clear face angled slightly downwards. This minimises the light striking the roots and encourages the roots to grow against the face.

Plants are grown in controlled environment rooms for 14 days at 20°C, the optimum for root growth of Sitka spruce, a relative humidity of 75%, a light level of 350–450 μmol m^{-2} s^{-1} and a day length of 16 h. Plants are watered twice daily but no nutrients are supplied. After 14 days the number of new white roots >1 cm in length produced by each plant is recorded. For Sitka spruce, the critical value below which survival is unlikely, is ten new white roots per plant (Tabbush, 1988). The results should be evaluated in two ways. Firstly, the mean RGP for the 15–20 replicates is compared with the critical level; secondly, the proportion of plants with a RGP falling above and below the critical value is calculated.

If RGP tests cannot be carried out in a controlled environment room, it is possible to get comparative results in a glasshouse or artificially-lit room. However, since the amounts of root growth vary with temperature, light levels and daylength (Sutton, 1990), *these values can only be used safely to compare plants tested at the same time.*

14.4.3 Fine root electrolyte leakage

All living cells contain charged ions (electrolytes) surrounded by a cell membrane. When healthy tissue is placed in water free of ions a small proportion of the cell contents, including charged ions, will leak out. However, if the cell membranes are damaged the leakage rate is greater. This leakage can be easily measured and used as an expression of root condition. To date, the technique has been used by Forestry Commission research staff mainly to assess damage after cold storage and frosting. Root electrolyte leakage has also been used successfully to measure damage after desiccation, rough handling and overheating. In some cases, such as cold storage damage, root electrolyte leakage was more closely correlated than RGP to survival. While the technique requires further testing, it shows great promise as an indicator of plant quality and has the further advantage that the test can be completed in 2 days. It is hoped that the assessment of electrolyte leakage, could provide a useful guide to the overall deterioration in plants, corresponding to the 'penalty points' concept mentioned in paragraph 14.2 above.

Roots (or shoots) are washed in tap water and rinsed in de-ionized water. Root samples of 100–500 mg fresh weight are taken from the fine roots (<2 mm diameter) approximately 8 cm from the root collar. Shoot samples are taken from the ends of lateral shoots by removing the terminal bud and cutting the next 2 cm length of shoot. The test material is added to distilled or de-ionized water and left for 24 h at room temperature. The concentration of ions in solution is measured with a conductivity probe. The samples are killed by boiling for 10 min. When cool, a second conductivity measurement is made for each sample. The represents the maximum possible leakage. The 24 h reading is expressed as a proportion of the maximum possible value. Normally 10–15 replicates are needed to characterise a batch of plants. Fuller details are given in Forestry Commission Research Information Note 210 (McKay, 1991). A commercial plant quality testing service has been developed using such tests; further details are available from the Forestry Authority's Northern Research Station (address in Appendix I).

14.5 Lifting

When plants are lifted violently, bark may be stripped from roots or stem. Damage during lifting can be minimised if care is taken to ease plants out of the ground as gently as possible, so that as much as possible of the fine fibre and short branched roots plus root tips are retained. This will enhance the chances of good survival in nursery lines or in the forest. Roots exceeding 15–18 cm should normally be trimmed back to that length, or other length selected to suit the following planting operation.

Plants may be lifted by hand or by machine. *As soon as possible after lifting, the plants must be protected from moisture loss.* Exposure even for a few minutes under strongly drying conditions can reduce survival of plants (Tabbush, 1988) and makes them more vulnerable to subsequent damage.

14.5.1 Hand-lifting

When lifting by hand, the beds should always

be worked from an outside edge. A garden fork or spade should be inserted vertically to the full depth of the blade and the handle pressed down until it is at an angle of 45° from the vertical. This movement is repeated until the soil is loose, when the tops of as many plants in the loosened ground as can be grasped comfortably should be lifted, gently shaking the soil from the roots while lifting. The soil should never be removed by swinging roots against a foot since this will reduce RGP (see Deans *et al.*, 1990).

14.5.2 Mechanical lifting

Several types of machines are available which are designed to loosen plants in the soil and lift them. They fall into three groups; the 'line lifters', such as the 'Famo' which can lift stock suitable for forest planting; 'lifting bars' which loosen plants in the bed, but do not lift them, and 'bed harvesters' which lift a whole bed of plants at a single pass. The first type enable large numbers of plants to be lifted completely in a short time but require substantial supporting equipment and organisation. Bed looseners may cover ground even more quickly, but depending on the exact nature of the equipment and the stock being treated, may leave the plants still protected by the nursery soil where they grew, so that lifting can be completed manually at a slower rate. Bed harvesters are expensive machines with conveyor belts to lift plants to a grading table and/or packing line. There were none being used in British nurseries at the end of 1993 although they can be found elsewhere in Europe.

'Famo' lifting

The 'Famo' lifter (Plates 31 and 32) can lift lines of plants at the rate of up to 200 000 plants per day and is suited to the larger nurseries with substantial breaks of single species. It can be adapted to work in rows down to 12 cm apart. There is no restriction of plant spacing in the row as the lifting mechanism is based on two continuous converging belts.

The lifter is attached to the three-point linkage of the tractor, with the lifting shoe offset to the right of the rear tractor wheel.

Plants are loosened by the passage of the shoe under the row, are gripped between two soft-faced endless rubber belts mounted at an angle to the soil surface, which lift them completely from the ground. They then pass over a series of adjustable root shakers to remove soil. When released at the end of the lifting belts, the plants can:

- fall to the ground for subsequent hand-sorting and packing; or
- be collected from the belt and packed into plastic bags held on a carousel – an operator on the machine packs bags and another walking alongside the lifter, removes full bags and replaces them with empty ones; or
- be packed into boxes or pallet-based containers carried on the lifter. Operators fill and remove boxes (Plate 32).

How plants are handled from that point depends on the requirements for grading and storage of the plants.

Where plants are delivered into boxes or bags, these are carried on the forklift or on the trailer of a supporting tractor which follows the lifter. If necessary, lifting can proceed uninterrupted using a second supporting tractor to take the place of the first while that one takes away filled boxes to the grading shed or plant store, and returns with an empty one.

In operation, the 'Famo' lifts plants with very little damage except when the share hits a large stone; the sudden deflection may cause stripped roots on the plants coming out of the ground at that instant. This damage can be excessive on stony sections; on such ground other methods of lifting should be used. There can also be problems when using this type of single-row lifter with undercut plants. Successful operation of the machines depends upon the soil being firm enough to support the plants when the shoe passes through the bed. If the soil has been loosened by intensive undercutting and/or wrenching and has not been reconsolidated by rain, the plants may fall over before being gripped by the rubber belts.

The tractor carrying the 'Famo' and the tractor transporting plants pass over the ground many times, seriously risking soil compaction as a result. The soils must be carefully examined later for signs of compaction; if found, subsoiling must be undertaken as soon as the soil is dry enough and tractors are available.

Lifting bars

Specially designed lifting bars (Plate 34) which loosen soil and so assist lifting continue to be widely used, both for single lines and for beds. The most suitable bars are those on which the angle can be adjusted to lift the soil to a greater or lesser extent; they are set so that the soil is loosened sufficiently to free the roots but not so much that the soil is turned over and the plants buried, or plants are left above the soil with roots exposed. Bars may incorporate an agitator to assist loosening. The setting of the bar may have to be adjusted from time to time in relation to the workability of the soil. Once the soil has been loosened, plants are lifted out by hand. The soil may settle back round the roots if more than a couple of days separate mechanical loosening and lifting, especially if heavy or prolonged rain follows loosening.

If properly supervised, machine lifting is nearly as safe as careful hand-lifting in maintaining root system quality. Table 14.3 gives the results of a RGP test carried out on Sitka spruce transplants of the same age and origin that were lifted in three different ways on one commercial nursery and subjected to different types of handling damage after lifting. Machine lifting using a 'Famo' appears less detrimental than the use of a lifting bar and hand-lifting. The results also show the damaging effects of dropping plants or removing the soil by knocking roots against a boot.

14.6 Culling, grading and counting

On lifting plants, the first priority must be to ensure that, during any subsequent processing, they are handled gently, are kept cool and are not allowed to dry to any extent. Their condition will deteriorate every time they are handled and roots are exposed to the air. Grading should therefore be kept to the essential minimum.

Before despatch or preparation for lining out, plants must be culled, i.e. separated into those of a quality acceptable for use, and rejects, including all diseased plants, together with those that are too small at the root collar, have inadequate roots, or multiple leaders or have been damaged during lifting. Rejects, or culls, should be destroyed. See Chapter 1, section 1.5 for quality standards. The requirements for plants to be described as 'EEC Standard' are given in Appendix IV.

Acceptable plants may be further graded by height into two or more size classes.

In commercial nurseries, plants are usually sold and priced by height grades and careful grading is essential to obtain the best com-

Table 14.3 RGP of Sitka spruce transplants given different lifting or handling treatments [results expressed as a percentage of highest value]

Treatment	Careful hand lifting with fork	Famo lifting	Lifting bar and hand lifting	Careful and knocked against boot	Careful and dropped
RGP	100	80	60	38	28

Results are the average of 10 plants per treatment.
RGP tested over 21 days in a greenhouse.
Plants were in 35–45 cm height category.

mercial advantage. Height grades always cover a range of heights and the average size of a batch of plants should correspond with the middle value of a stated height range.

In estate nurseries raising plants for use on the same estate, grading of stock after culling is necessary only if plants are so variable in size that some will need an additional year's weeding in the forest compared with bigger plants.

The practice of loosening beds and removing plants in the various grades only as required is quite widespread, but the first plants removed are likely to lose more roots in the process than if all the plants are lifted together. Correspondingly the plants which are last to be removed run the risk of being left with roots exposed through the removal of neighbouring plants.

Where hand-lifting and individual working is practised, plants can be counted and graded on the nursery as lifting proceeds.

In nurseries where lifting is mechanised and plants are brought ungraded into store, grading can be done under cover provided there is adequate light and shelter. This has the advantage that work may proceed during wet weather and in the early mornings when the ground is still frosty. Ideally, grading and packing should be done as near as possible to the plant store.

In the many mechanised nurseries, conveyor belts are used either to deliver unsorted plants to staff who remove particular grades, or to remove sorted plants placed on the belt by staff drawing from boxes of unsorted plants.

After grading and counting, plants may be tied in bundles, or if polythene bags or boxes are being used, sufficient plants may be put in a bag or box to fill it comfortably so that plants remain in place without being tied in bundles.

Where it is necessary to apply an insecticide before stock is planted in the forest, and the grower requires this treatment to be applied in the nursery rather than in the forest, plans for counting, grading and storing plants may have to be modified to incorporate

insecticide treatment (p. 189), observing the requirements of current Pesticide Regulations (see Chapter 15, section 15.6).

14.7 Storage

Traditionally, plants should be lifted while dormant, packed, immediately despatched to the forest and planted without any delay at any time. Unfortunately, this is seldom practicable for any but small lots of plants and for some, e.g. larch, there may be benefits in retaining fully dormant plants lifted during November–February in store at 1°C and planting in early spring (McKay and Howes, 1994).

Plants are regularly stored:

- outdoors in the nursery, heeled in;
- in unheated well ventilated sheds;
- in insulated cold stores;
- at the planting site.

Whatever the location, it is essential that conditions are suitable for the plants. Poor storage practice is a major cause of post-planting failure in Britain (Mason and McKay, 1989; Sharpe and Mason, 1992).

14.7.1 Outdoor storage

Outdoor storage in nursery heeling areas or sheughs was formerly widely used for storing plants. Although it has largely been replaced by indoor storage in sheds or cold stores, it still has a place for small numbers of plants for short periods of time (i.e. 7–14 days). Plants are also regularly stored outdoors in co-extruded polythene bags under the shade of plantation canopy or elsewhere out of direct sunlight.

The object of outdoor storage is to have plants readily available for despatch or for lining out while keeping them cool and stopping them from drying out.

Heeling in

Plants may be 'heeled in' or 'sheughed', loose or in counted bundles. A trench with a sloping back is dug and the plants laid in it thinly so that their roots are completely in the trench and most of the tops are out. As soon as the plants are in, loose soil is put back over the roots and lightly firmed down. There must never be so many plants in any part of the trench that the root systems of plants, whether loose or bundled, are in buried air pockets and out of contact with the soil.

If it is anticipated that orders for plants will come in very frosty weather, straw should be spread thickly over the plants to prevent soil being frozen to them. It is important to prevent conifers being frozen in a sheugh in cold, sunny weather when shoots can be severely damaged by 'winter' desiccation. Time must always be allowed for plants to thaw if they have been stored at temperatures below freezing. See also section 14.7.4.

Canopy storage

Plants should not normally be stored in co-extruded bags under a plantation canopy ('canopy storage') for more than 14 days. The risk is that the bags heat up in response to changes in ambient temperature and the carbohydrate reserves within the plants are depleted by respiration. Moulding of foliage can also be a problem under these conditions. While canopy storage may be unavoidable under certain conditions (e.g. if a cold spell occurs at the planting site immediately after plants have been delivered), its use should be kept to an absolute minimum. When plants are stored in bags under canopy storage, the necks of the bags must be turned down to prevent rainwater running down into the bags and flooding the root systems.

14.7.2 Storage under cover

Plants may have to be kept in a cold store or unheated, well ventilated shed, until required where:

- so large a number of orders for plants is expected that they cannot all be met promptly, unless plants can be lifted and stored before the orders arrive, or
- plants are likely to be required at times when the nursery ground is frozen or too wet for lifting to proceed, or

- plants are going to be planted in the forest or lined out in the nursery so late in the growing season that if left *in situ*, they will have started to break bud before they are moved, or
- surplus seedlings are to be stored until mid-summer for lining out, or
- ground has to be cleared and prepared for the coming season's seedbeds and lines.

Cold storage facilities are essential if plants are to be held dormant for any length of time.

Over the last decade, cold stores have come more widely into use and are available in many large and medium-sized nurseries. Their dimensions have caused previous plant storage methods to be reviewed so as to make the best use of the height of stores and the opportunities for efficient mechanical handling of plants. Pallet and stacking box systems are coming into greater use as a consequence (Dauncey *et al.*, 1989). See Plates 35 and 36.

14.7.3 Storage in polythene bags

Polythene bags have been in use for storage and movement of forest plants in the United Kingdom for over 30 years. The reason for storing plants in polythene is to prevent the roots from drying out by loss of moisture to the outside air.

Recent developments

There have been three developments in the last decade affecting their use.

Firstly, transparent bags have been replaced by 'co-extruded' bags where the inner surface is black and the outer surface white opaque polythene (Tabbush, 1987b). They have two advantages over the clear bags; the more important is that co-extruded bags are better able to protect plants from overheating if subject to direct sunlight. Trials in the mid-1980s showed that the foliage of plants exposed to direct sunlight in clear polythene bags reached almost 50°C within 3 h. By contrast, the foliage temperature of plants in co-extruded bags did not exceed 22°C (Tabbush, 1987b). The other advantage is that the white surface can carry printing – e.g. a reminder 'Forest trees – handle gently'.

The second development has been a greater attention to 'storage + handling + transport + planting' as an integrated system, so as to ensure the best performance of every newly planted tree. This is linked with the increase in the number of plants being used for replanting on clear-felled forest sites and the need for insecticide treatment for such plants.

The key point in an integrated handling system is that the protection provided by polythene bags in conserving moisture in plants must be retained. However, it is not clear whether this will be in the form of:

- co-extruded bags transferred in open skeletal crates;
- a light co-extruded liner within a transit box, the liner and contents being transferred to a planting bag on site; or
- whether some other system achieving the same end will evolve.

The third development is a much greater understanding of the consequences of bad handling and storage of plants, and their interaction with dormancy and plant quality.

Storage conditions

Plants may be stored safely for long periods in co-extruded bags provided the recommendations below are strictly observed. Bags should be tightly sealed to ensure there is no loss of moisture through the neck of the bag. The polythene ensures that the roots do not dry out and that plants reach the planting site in as moist condition as when they were lifted.

Plants stored in polythene bags have been found extremely convenient to handle. However, convenience must not lead to carelessness and abuse. *Bags must not be dropped, thrown or otherwise handled roughly.* While deterioration is not obvious, plants' ability to survive and grow after rough handling is markedly reduced. See section 14.2.4 above and Table 14.1.

There have been no cases of *Botrytis* (grey mould) spreading from infected to other plants inside polythene bags. Fungi that are normally saprophytic in the soil have however spread as a white mould starting from the roots or near the root collar. This has developed when plants have been in store for too long, or when they were packed in too wet a condition, or where soil has come into contact with foliage. Plants in bags in which such white mould has started to show itself should be removed from the bag as soon as possible and planted or lined out, or heeled-in in a shady spot.

Where large consignments of plants are to be despatched, counting and checking is simplified if all bags have the same number of plants of a given species in them.

It is essential at all times to know the identity of the contents of bags. They should be marked clearly and unambiguously, for example with permanent felt tip marker pens. With every batch of bags delivered, there should be a form giving the customer a record of the complete history of the plants listing age, when the plants were lifted, how long they were stored, other treatments, etc. See also section 14.9.3 on 'Labelling' at the end of this chapter.

Bag sizes

Bags are readily obtained to order in sizes suited to the stock grown in the nursery. They must be of a large enough size to hold plants without crushing and the shoots should not come out of the top of the bag.

Where bags are to fit inside boxes, gusseted bags may fit more easily; where bags full of plants are to be stored in the open, they should be long enough for the top of the bag to be tied and turned over to prevent rain water collecting in the neck of the bag, seeping into the bag and causing waterlogging of plants.

Summary of recommendations for the use of black and white co-extruded polythene bags for the storage and movement of nursery stock

- Plants should be lifted and placed in polythene bags as quickly as possible. If there is likely to be any delay, roots must be pre-

Plate 25. *Sitka spruce cutting material.* (38037)

Plate 26. *Sitka spruce rooted cuttings.* (E8824)

Plate 27. *Single span polytunnels with netting shading, for production of 1st cycle cutting material of genetically improved strains.* (E8820)

Plate 28. *One-year-old Sitka spruce seedlings in 2-litre pots at wide spacing. These plants are expected to reach 1.5 m or more by the end of their second growing season from sowing.* (E8818)

Plate 29. *Briggs Rotorainer rotating sprayline.* (39383)

Plate 30. *Briggs rainomatic irrigation equipment, showing self-winding hose and reel on carriage.* (A1986)

Plate 31. *Famo lifter.* (40609)

vented from drying out by covering with damp straw.

- The surface of needles or leaves of plants should be dry when being put into polythene bags. Plants lifted and packed with wet foliage are liable to rot. Packing with dry foliage is especially important for Douglas fir, western hemlock, western red cedar and Lawson cypress. Deciduous species should not be stored until the leaves have fallen since dead leaves can act as a source of moulds.

- Plants should be packed with shoots in the same direction.

- Plants must not be packed in layers with the roots of one layer pressing on the tips of shoots of plants in a lower layer. It may be found more convenient to tie plants into bundles before packing, especially where many small plants are being packed in a large bag. Generally, however, it is preferable not to tie into bundles.

- Plants must not be packed too tightly.

- Plants must be fully enclosed inside the bags.

- The thickness of material used for bags should depend on whether they will be reused. Bags intended for the movement of plants freshly treated with insecticide against post-planting beetle/weevil attack should be used only once.

- Check for punctures or tears as these seriously diminish the efficiency of bags. One or two small punctures will have little effect on plants stored for short periods (up to 14 days). However, plants to be stored for more than 3–4 weeks should be put into undamaged bags. All badly punctured or torn bags should be destroyed.

- Bags should be tightly closed at the neck with a string or wire tie. Adhesive or cellulose tape does not stick to damp or dirty bags, while rubber bands quickly perish.

- When tying, bags should be gently squeezed to expel excess air. Tops should be turned over to prevent rainwater entering bags if stored outside.

- Full bags may be stored either in a cold store or, as a short-term measure, in a cool well-ventilated shed or under the canopy of a plantation.

- Where plants in bags have to be stored for any length of time, bags should be packed not more than two layers deep, and preferably in one layer on pallets or shelves. Bags must not be stacked several layers deep for more than a few hours, otherwise heating may occur. Whenever bags are stored, it must be in such a way that air can get to at least one side of each bag.

- When plants are to be stored for more than a week in one place, bags should be arranged so that the plants are more or less upright. For shorter periods, e.g. when in transit, this does not matter.

- Full bags must be kept out of direct sunlight at all times. This is especially important in March and April.

Duration of storage in polythene bags

Table 14.4 gives the maximum recommended safe storage periods and lifting 'windows' for the common forest species, when polythene bags are used. These dates are for guidance and need to be adjusted for season, nursery location and the provenance being used. The key point with broadleaves is to ensure that they are stored after the leaves have fallen and before the buds or roots start to move again in the spring.

Normally, plants should remain fully enclosed in their bags until required, unless the safe storage period has been exceeded, or plants have been damaged in transit, when they must be removed and examined for deterioration. There is no objection to opening bags for a short while to determine the condition or quality of plants. If plants have to be kept towards the end of the recommended safe storage period, regular inspection is well worthwhile, especially if the weather is warm or if there is any doubt that the storage conditions are adequate.

Plants starting to flush while in polythene bags must be removed and heeled-in.

Table 14.4 Lifting dates and storage periods for plants to be cold stored in polythene bags

Species	Lifting window	Optimum lifting time	Normal storage period (months)	Maximum storage period (months)
Sitka spruce (QCI or similar provenances)	late November – mid March	January	Up to 3	5
Sitka spruce (Washington and Oregon provenances)	December – February	January	Up to 3	4
Sitka spruce (Alaskan provenance)	mid November – late March	mid December	Up to 4	5
Larches	December – mid January	mid December	Up to 3	5
Scots and lodgepole pines	December – early March	January	Up to 3	5
Corsican pine	December – February	January	Up to 3	4
Douglas fir	mid December – early February	January	Up to 2	2
Norway spruce	December – early March	January	Up to 3	4
Other conifers (*Abies, Tsuga*, etc.)	December – early March	January	Up to 3	4
Broadleaves	December – February	January	Up to 3	5

The lifting window is defined as the period between the first and last dates for lifting in a *normal winter*. Lifting should be delayed in a mild autumn. In a mild winter, do not exceed the *normal* storage period. The maximum storage period is possible when plants are lifted at the optimum time.

14.7.4 Cold storage of plants

In Britain, cold storage of forest plants came into general practice in the mid 1960s and over the years has found an increasing role in plant handling. It is estimated that 30–40% of plants planted in British forestry each year are cold stored for a short period.

Cold stores* offer nursery and forest managers great flexibility. Once plants have become fully 'storable' in late autumn, they may be lifted when soil conditions are suitable and labour is available. Subsequently plants may be culled and graded and returned to store for despatch to the forest when ordered.

Plants held in store should remain dormant and keep a high RGP well beyond the time in spring when freshly lifted stock has actively developing buds. Trees that have been well stored can be despatched from the cold store against late orders with a higher survival potential than if stock had just been lifted.

Serious deterioration can occur if plants are put into store before they become fully dormant in the autumn or after dormancy has broken in the spring (Plates 35 and 36).

Type of store

Most cold stores are directly refrigerated, i.e. the cooling unit and fan are within the storage chamber. Any water lost from plants or anything else in the store condenses and freezes as ice on the cooling coils, slowly desiccating any unprotected stored material. Plants in such stores must be held in sealed waterproof containers, i.e. polythene bags. The storage

---

* Strictly, plants require 'cool' stores, operating at 0° to +2°C or 'freezer' stores operating at –2° to 0°C. The cold stores used for deep freezing meat and other foodstuffs are not suitable for plants since they operate at temperatures of around –15°C. References to cold stores in this Bulletin refer either to cool or freezer stores unless otherwise specified.

temperature can be just above or just below 0°C. Stores should operate within 1°C of the selected temperature. It is undesirable for the thermostat to be set at 0°C as this causes the coolers to undergo potentially damaging repeated thawing/freezing cycles.

For general storage, stores should be set to operate at 1° to 2°C. However, provided plants are fully storable, long-term storage is probably safer at –2°C in directly refrigerated stores. When operating at that setting, stores should not be used to store seed while it is undergoing moist prechilling. If plants are stored at –2°C, provision must be made for them to thaw out before being handled, otherwise branches and roots may be torn off as frozen plants are separated. This will normally require up to 48 h interim storage in a cool, well ventilated shed.

Two alternative store designs reduce the risk of desiccation, so that plants can safely be left unprotected in them for a period of time. In 'humified' stores, cold air is blown through a water cascade, or fine mist is sprayed regularly, the resultant cold moist air being ducted to all parts of the chamber. However, the storage temperature is always above 0°C. Indirect cold stores may also be built 'jacketed'; i.e. with the cooling air circulating in a wall cavity fully enclosing the store. Jacketed stores are the most expensive of the three types of store.

The main advantage of 'humified' or 'jacketed' cold stores is that plants can be stored bare-rooted without the need for polythene bags. This is an attraction to the nursery manager who can lift plants straight from the nursery to the cold store chamber without needing to bag them first. The plants can then be extracted from the chamber as required, graded and bagged for despatch to the planting sites.

The danger with such stores is that plants will continue to lose moisture from the roots unless >95% relative humidity is maintained (Sharpe and Mason, 1992). Loss of humidity is a particular danger when the doors of the chamber are opened while plants are moved into or out of store. For this reason, humidi-fied stores should have an antechamber with heavy polythene skirts outside the chamber door, to act as a partial airlock between the moist air of the chamber and the drier air of the surrounding building.

Size of store

When planning a cold store, three factors need to be considered when deciding upon the size of storage facility required. These are the size of the unit in which the plants are to be held (bags or pallet), the space necessary for access (e.g. are forklifts being used) and the volume required for good air circulation.

Storage principles and management

Useful discussion of the management of cold stores can be found in Bartsch and Blanpied (1984), Guyer (1991), Hardenburg *et al.* (1986). The following are some principles that should be remembered at all times.

- Successful storage depends upon the maintenance of the desired air humidity and temperature and ensuring good air circulation throughout the store.

- Air humidity should be maintained in all types of stores by hanging a curtain of heavy polythene strips on the inside of the chamber door to act as a seal when the door is open. In humidified stores this should be supplemented by an antechamber as outlined above.

- A stable air temperature is essential, particularly where plants are being stored in polythene bags. Fluctuating temperatures will result in condensation on the inside of the bag and this can result in moulds developing on the plants.

- It should be recognised that there are up to five potential sources of heat in a cold store. These are: the heat generated by outside conditions; the heat of plants that are being brought in fresh from the field at a temperature above that of the store; the heat generated by the respiration of the living plants in the store; the heat that comes in from outside each time the door is opened; and the heat generated by people and equipment in the store (e.g. lights, machinery, forklifts, etc.). The refrigeration system must be designed to cope with these sources of heat. Any material being brought into store should ideally be cooled to the temperature of the store within 24 h of arrival. Checks should be made to see whether the refrigeration equipment can achieve this under the most testing conditions; i.e. on a warm day when a large number of warm plants are being brought in, the door is frequently open, etc.

- There should be adequate air circulation on all sides of the plant material so that there is no danger of heat build-up through respiration.
- The floor should be smooth so that it can be kept clean.
- At the end of the season, the storage chamber and all ancillary equipment (e.g. crates, pallets) should be cleaned and disinfected.

Associated facilities

Provision should be made for a grading shed or working area close to the cold store. Ideally, this should be situated within the same building, so that plants are not exposed to the open air. There must be good access to stores and loading areas for tractors and lorries.

Hire of stores

While most of the bigger nurseries have cold stores, in many parts of the country, it is possible to hire fruit or vegetable stores, the agricultural/horticultural usage complementing the requirements of the forest nursery manager. It is important that these stores should be operated at the temperatures appropriate to forest nursery stock.

Power failure and plants in cold stores

Plants can tolerate several days in store without power if plants have previously been cooled to the normal storage temperature. Access to a store should be minimised to avoid unnecessary warming. The store should have an alarm system to indicate a possible malfunction.

Following a power failure, the refrigerating unit should be switched off and only switched on again when full power has been restored. Electric motors driving compressors in the refrigeration unit can be seriously damaged if run on fluctuating low voltage (e.g. when the room lights flicker and do not deliver full light).

Monitoring cold stores

It is vital that cold stores are properly monitored for both air temperature and relative humidity. Twenty-four hour recording instruments should be used wherever possible in case there is some malfunction out of working hours. Spot checks should also be made in different parts of the store to check that no 'hot-spots' occur.

14.8 Insecticide treatment

Nursery stock planted on forest land where a conifer crop has recently been clear felled, may be in serious risk of attack from the pine weevil (*Hylobius abietis*) or black pine beetles (*Hylastes* spp.); such plants may require treatment with an insecticide before being planted.

Treatments need to be applied after lifting and before planting, to protect stem and root collar tissues that after planting may be up to 2–3 cm below the soil surface. Stems and foliage should also be treated for at least 12–15 cm above the root collar. Plants may remain susceptible to insect attack for 2 years after planting; consequently, insecticide treatments are required which are persistent and which will require the minimum of 'topping up' treatment after planting.

Because even persistent insecticides become less effective with the passage of time, treatments should be applied as shortly before planting as practicable. Some forest managers treat stock on receipt from the nursery; however, the techniques for treatment and the safety precautions for those treating plants have become so demanding that many forest managers prefer plants to have been treated in the nursery shortly before despatch.

14.8.1 Dipping

Dipping is the principal technique for applying insecticides against pine weevil and pine beetles. See Chapter 13, section 13.3.3 for information on approvals for insecticides to be used for this purpose.

Technique for dipping

Currently approved techniques for dipping require plants to be held mechanically while they are being dipped; they should not be held manually.

There are two methods of gripping plants using frames; one where the plants are in bundles, and one where they are spread thinly between two boards (Lane, 1990; Anon., 1990). With both gripping frames, roots can be protected from drying by covering with polythene bags or sheeting.

Plants in frames are held, shoots down, roots up, and immersed gently in the insecticide for a few seconds. The frames are then put on racks where surplus insecticide can drain off; they may be moved to other racking for the insecticide to become thoroughly dry on the foliage and stem. The drainage and drying racks must be so arranged that any insecticide dripping off is collected and stored until it can be safely disposed of.

When the foliage is dry, plants should be put into bags for despatch. The period between treatment and planting in the forest should be minimised; this will require close co-ordination between nursery manager, haulier and customer.

A substantial quantity of contaminated soil sludge will accumulate in dipping tanks and has to be removed periodically. Also, the unused insecticide remaining after all plants have been treated will also have to be disposed of safely. See Chapter 15, section 15.6.6.

14.8.2 Electrodyn spraying

The 'Electrodyn' sprayer system was developed initially to treat tropical crops growing in open ground and using hand-held equipment. Specially formulated oil-based pesticides are passed from nozzles through a high voltage electric field to create numerous small, highly charged droplets in an enclosed treatment chamber. These droplets are attracted to the nearest earthing point and spread themselves evenly across its surfaces, including under surfaces. Nozzles and feedbelts are so arranged that plants carried on the belts into the spraying chamber act as earthing points in such a way that droplets cover plant stem and foliage around and up to 10–15 cm above the root collar.

The Forestry Commission has developed a version of this technique for use on transplants shortly before they are planted in the forest. This is fully described by Scott *et al.* (1990).

Location of Electrodyn units

While the units can be placed anywhere, because they involve an appreciable capital outlay, it is important for them to be fully utilised; location in forest nurseries is the most logical place for them.

Outline of method of operation

Plants are used which are ready for despatch to the forest, i.e. any grading has already been done. They are placed on a conveyor belt consisting of a series of moving support wires, the positioning and correct spacing of plants on the belt being crucial for uniform treatment.

They then pass into an enclosed but ventilated chamber where the plants are sprayed with permethrin at a pre-set rate determined by the insecticide container nozzles. Treated plants should carry a minimum deposit of $0.4. \mu g\,mm^{-2}$ – a similar dosage to that obtained when plants are dipped.

The solvent used as carrier, cyclohexanone, is extremely volatile and vaporises before the plants leave the spraying chamber; consequently, plants are sufficiently dry for them to be packed immediately from the end of the conveyor belt.

The whole set-up is approximately 5 m long and 1 m wide. The main limitation on installation is that the spraying chamber must be connected by an efficient ventilation system to outside air in order to keep operators' exposure to the solvent within acceptable limits.

One advantage of the system over dipping is that there is virtually no waste liquid insecticide and very little contaminated soil and plant material to be disposed of.

Disadvantages are the relatively high cost of the system and the need to observe strict safety procedures over ventilation.

14.9 *Packing and despatch*

The nursery manager having to organise the sending of plants from his nursery to a forest planting site may often find himself in a dilemma. On the one hand, his customers may prefer small deliveries at short intervals; on the other hand, the most economical means of transporting plants is usually a lorry load at a time. Loads of this size normally take a few days to assemble. At the forest, though some plants may be put in immediately after delivery, some may have to wait a couple of weeks before being planted.

The unpredictability of periods of snow and severe frost add to the complexity of management but in this instance provide the basis for favouring early lifting and storage.

The risks to plants in such situations can be reduced to a minimum only by good storage facilities and by close contact between the nursery manager and the forester receiving the plants – adjusting the programmes of lifting and despatch on the one hand and planting on the other.

A nursery manager should encourage his customers to give him 2 months' notice of when plants are required, and a name and telephone number so that any last minute change in arrangements can be agreed. There should also be an agreed delivery point.

14.9.1 **Methods of packing**

Where the planting site is near the nursery and speedy nursery-to-planting site delivery of plants by van can be arranged, no special packing is necessary, other than careful stacking on the vehicle. See 14.9.2 below. However, if the distance is more than a very few miles, and there is *any* risk of drying or

any doubt at all as how long plants will be in transit, plants should be put into bags or lined boxes to reduce the risk of desiccation and travel shock.

Plants should always be packed so that they are unable to move freely within the box or bag. However, they must not be packed in so tightly that force has to be applied to compress the plants to get them in the bag or to close the box.

In the past straw and damp moss were used to reduce moisture loss and to cushion plants from shock while in transit. Use of polythene bags should prevent moisture loss, while bags and boxes can assist in minimising impact shock. Nevertheless, the concept of using these more traditional materials, especially straw, to cushion plants remains valid. Straw should always be remembered as a space filler if a lot of plants do not properly fill the container and a smaller suitable container is not available.

14.9.2 **Methods of despatch**

Virtually all plants are currently despatched by van or lorry. Rail played an important part formerly, but the network is so reduced that it is rare for services such as 'Red Star' to be a relevant choice, and then, only when small numbers of plants are involved.

Refrigerated trailers

Certain larger nurseries are equipped with refrigerated articulated trailers, fitted with shelving. In such trailers, plants can safely be moved long distances within minimum risk. With careful planning and co-ordination between the nursery manager and foresters receiving the plants, large consignments of plants can be delivered in batches over a period rather than in one load.

Box systems

In many nurseries, stacking boxes are used, either by themselves or on pallets, depending on the method employed for loading. These enable articulated trailers to be hired as required from local haulage contractors (Plate 37).

Several systems involving the use of boxes have been under development recently. Details of those in use in Forestry Commission nurseries are given in Table 14.5.

Other methods

Consignments of plants can be moved short distances without specially fitted lorries or trailers. However, greater care has to be taken in ensuring the load can travel safely. Plants should not be despatched in loads more than two layers of bags deep. Single layers are preferable. If necessary, some secure staging or shelving must be installed.

If plants are being sent without protection from boxes or polythene bags, they should be arranged in cones or 'bee-hives', with roots of all plants in the cone to the middle, shoots pointing out, and wet moss in the middle around the roots. The stack should taper upwards with the centre filled with upright

plants. Such arrangements are not recommended if plants have to travel more than a very few miles.

All plants sent without polythene protection must be covered for the whole of the journey with a well tied down tarpaulin, so that the least possible amount of wind gets in and dries the plants. Transparent polythene sheets should not be used in place of tarpaulins. The tarpaulin should be of a light opaque colour so that it does not absorb or transmit excessive sunlight, resulting in the heating-up of the plants.

If the body of the lorry or trailer is fully closed, it must be ventilated to prevent overheating in sunny periods.

14.9.3 Labelling

Consignments of plants must always be labelled so that there is no doubt as to the identity of every part. Where plants within

Table 14.5 Boxes in use for packing and despatch of plants

Box type	'Wykeham' C1471	'Collar pallets'	'Socrates'
Box dimensions			
Length	570	1200	840 (external)
Width	366	1000	400 (external)
Height	328	250 per module*	350
Material	Polypropylene	Wood	White reflective HD polythene
Pallet required for bulk movement	Yes	No (Integral)	Yes 800 × 1000
Boxes per pallet	12 on 800 × 1200 20 on 1000 × 1000		9 (12)
Packing within boxes	Standard bags	Standard bags	Polythene liners
Boxes returnable	Yes	Yes	Yes
Storage when not in use	Nesting (75%)	Collapsible	Nesting (50%)
Maximum stacking height using strapped pallets	12 boxes	5 pallets	16 boxes

* Can be built up to 1250 mm models.
  Data from Dauncey *et al.* (1988).

the Forest Reproductive Material Regulations are included, appropriately coloured labels should be used.

Bags that contain plants treated with insecticide before planting, must also be clearly distinguishable, the marking indicating the chemical used.

Where two or more lots of any species are included in a consignment, e.g. of different ages or of different origins, there must be some positive way of identifying the different lots that is capable of withstanding the hazards of lost or torn tags, etc. This is best achieved by including tags inside packages, and in addition, having some indelible distinguishing mark on the outside of each bag, box, etc., so that they do not need to be opened to establish what they contain.

Accompanying each consignment, there should be duplicate copies of a despatch note, listing all items in the consignment; one to remain with the recipient, the other to return to the sender as proof of delivery. A third copy may be necessary if the carrier has to submit documentary proof of delivery to support his invoice for carriage.

14.10 Handling of plants raised in containers

Containerised plants can be transported one of two ways. The first is for the plants to be delivered to the planting site in the container in which they were grown and to be extracted at the last possible minute. This system is most effective when the container is not returnable (e.g. Japanese paper pots). It can also be used with returnable trays of containers (e.g. Rigipots), but more supervision and care is required to collect up the container sets after use and return them to the nursery. Delivering plants in the containers means that thought needs to be given to methods of handling between nursery and customer which may involve various forms of palletisation and shelving (Stjernberg, 1989).

An alternative approach is to extract the plants from their containers at the nursery

and to group them in bunches of 25 plants or thereabouts. These bunches are wrapped with plastic or polythene film placed round the plugs to prevent moisture loss. The plants are then placed in standard black-and-white bags (see 14.7.3 above) and handled in the same way as bare-root stock. Plants treated in this way have been cold stored for 3–4 months with no effect upon subsequent survival and growth.

Containerised plants should be handled at all times with the same care and attention as bare-root plants. Particular attention should be paid to the moisture content of the plugs. They should not have been allowed to dry out before being brought in for grading and/or despatch. This can be a particular danger if containerised plants are being used to extend the planting season into warm conditions in May and June. Under such circumstances it will be sensible to water the plants before despatch and if they appear dry at any time between delivery and planting.

REFERENCES

ANON. (1990). *Proposed dipping system for bare root transplants.* Departmental report; 17.10.90. Forestry Commission, Wykeham Nursery, Sawdon, Scarborough.

BARTSCH, J.A. and BLANPIED, G.D. (1984). *Refrigeration and controlled atmosphere storage for horticultural crops.* NRAES Bulletin 22, Cornell University, USA.

BURDETT, A.N. (1979). New methods for measuring root growth capacity: their value in assessing lodgepole pine stock quality. *Canadian Journal of Forest Research* **9**, 63–67.

CANNELL, M.G.R. and SHEPPARD, L.J. (1982). Seasonal changes in the frost hardiness of provenances of *Picea sitchensis* in Scotland. *Forestry* **63**, 9–27.

COLOMBO, S.J. and HICKIE, D.F. (1987). A one-day test for determining frost hardiness using the electrical conductivity technique. *Forest Research Note* 45. Ministry of Natural Resources, Ontario.

COUTTS, M.P. (1980). Control of water loss by actively growing Sitka spruce seedlings after transplanting. *Journal of Experimental Botany* **31**, 1587–1597.

COUTTS, M.P. and NICOLL, B.C. (1990). Waterlogging tolerance of roots of Sitka spruce clones and of strands from *Thelephora terrestris* mycorrhizas. *Canadian Journal of Forest Research* **20**, 1894–1899.

DAUNCEY, A.J., SOBOTA, C.M., and JAMES, D.H. (1988). *Packaging and transport of transplants*. Wales Work Study Team, Report 123. Forestry Commission, Edinburgh.

DAUNCEY, A.J., SOBOTA, C.M., and JONES, D. H. (1989). *Integrated handling, packaging and delivery of forest transplants; Delamere nursery*. Wales Work Study Team, Report 131. Forestry Commission, Edinburgh.

DEANS, J.D., LUNDBERG, C., CANNELL, M.G.R., MURRAY, M.B. and SHEPPARD, L.J. (1990a). Root system fibrosity of Sitka spruce transplants: relationship with root growth potential. *Forestry* **63** (1), 1–7.

DEANS, J.D., LUNDBERG, C., TABBUSH, P.M., CANNELL, M.G.R., SHEPPARD, L.J. and MURRAY, M.B. (1990b). The influence of desiccation, rough handling and cold storage on the quality and establishment of Sitka spruce planting stock. *Forestry* **63** (2), 129–141.

FAULCONER, J.R. (1988). Using frost hardiness as an indicator of seedling condition. In *Proceedings, Combined Meeting of the Western Forest Nursery Associations*, Vernon, British Columbia. USDA Forest Service, Rocky Mountain Forest and Range Experiment Station, General Technical Report RM 167, 89–95.

GREER, D.H., STANLEY, G.J., and WARRINGTON, I.J. (1989). Photoperiod control of the initial phase of frost hardiness development in *Pinus contorta*. *Plant Cell and Environment* **12**, 661–668.

GUYER, D.E. (1991). Design basics for bareroot storage. *American Nurseryman* **172** (9), 115–127.

HARDENBURG, R.E., WATADA, A.E. and WANG, C.Y. (1986). *The commercial storage of fruits, vegetables, florist and nursery stocks*. USDA-ARS Agricultural Handbook 66. US Government Printing Office, Washington.

HAWKINS, C.D.B., and BINDER, W.D. (1990). State of the art seedling stock quality tests based on seedling physiology. In *Target Seedling Symposium. Proceedings of the Combined Meeting of the Western Forest Nursery Associations*, Roseburg, Oregon, eds R. Rose, S. J. Campbell and T. D. Landis. 91–121.

HERMANN, R.K. (1967). Seasonal variation in sensitivity of Douglas fir seedlings to exposure of roots. *Forest Science* **13**, 140–149.

LANE, P.B. (1990). *Small scale dipping system for bare root transplants*. Work Study Branch Report (Eastern Region Team) 21/90. Forestry Commission, Edinburgh.

LEVITT, J. (1980). *Responses of plants to environmental stresses*. 2nd edn. Academic Press, London, 347–391.

LINDSTRÖM, A. and NYSTRÖM, C. (1987). Seasonal variation in root hardiness of container-grown Scots pine, Norway spruce, and lodgepole pine seedlings. *Canadian Journal of Forest Research* **17**, 787–793.

MASON, W.L. and McKAY, H.M. (1989). Evaluating the quality of Sitka spruce planting stock before and after cold storage. *Combined Proceedings International Plant Propagators Society* **39**, 234–242.

McKAY, H.M. (1991). *Electrolyte leakage: a rapid index of plant vitality*. Research Information Note 210. Forestry Commission, Edinburgh.

McKAY, H.M. (1993). *Deterioration of fine tree roots during cold storage in two contrasting winters*. Forestry Commission Technical Paper 2. Forestry Commission, Edinburgh.

McKAY, H.M. (1994). Frost hardiness and cold-storage tolerance of the root system of *Picea sitchensis*, *Pseudotsuga menziesii*, *Larix kaempferi* and *Pinus sylvestris* bareroot seedlings. *Scandinavian Journal of Forest Research* (in press).

McKAY, H.M. and HOWES, R.E.J. (1994). *Lifting times for larch establishment.*

Forestry Commission Research Information Note 244. Forestry Commission, Edinburgh.

McKAY, H.M. and MASON, W.L. (1991). Physiological indicators of tolerance to cold storage in Sitka spruce and Douglas fir seedlings. *Canadian Journal of Forest Research* **21,** 890–901.

McKAY, H.M., GARDINER, B.A., MASON, W.L., NELSON, D.G. and HOLLINGSWORTH, M.K. (1993). The gravitational forces generated by dropping plants and the response of Sitka spruce seedlings to dropping. *Canadian Journal of Forest Research* **23,** 2443–2451.

PELLETT, H. (1971). Comparison of cold hardiness levels of root and stem tissue. *Canadian Journal of Plant Science* **51,** 193–195.

PHILIPSON, J. (1988). Root growth in Sitka spruce and Douglas-fir transplants: dependence on the shoot and stored carbohydrates. *Tree Physiology* **4,** 104–108.

RITCHIE, G.A. (1984a). Assessing seedling quality. In *Forest nursery manual: production of bareroot seedlings*, eds M. L. Duryea and D. T. Landis. Martinus Nijhoff/Dr W. Junk, The Hague, 243–259.

RITCHIE, G.A. (1984b). Effect of freezer storage on bud dormancy release in Douglas fir seedlings. *Canadian Journal of Forest Research* **14,** 186–190.

RITCHIE, G.A. (1986). Relationships among bud dormancy status, cold hardiness, and stress resistance in 2+0 Douglas fir. *New Forests* **1,** 29–42.

SCOTT, J.C. (1987a). *Installation of a transplant handling system at Newton nursery*. Northern Work Study Team, Report 104. Forestry Commission, Edinburgh.

SCOTT, J.C. (1987b). *Plant handling*. Northern Work Study Team, Report 105. Forestry Commission, Edinburgh.

SCOTT, J.C., WYATT, F. and LANE, P. (1990). *The 'Electrodyn' sprayer conveyor*. Northern Region Work Study Team, Report 109. Forestry Commission, Edinburgh.

SHARPE, A.L. and MASON, W.L. (1992). Some methods of cold storage can seriously affect root growth potential and root moisture content and subsequent forest performance of Sitka spruce and Douglas fir transplants. *Forestry* **65,** 463–472.

SMIT-SPINKS, B., SWANSON, B.T. and MARKHART, A.H. III. (1985). The effect of photoperiod and thermoperiod on cold acclimatisation and growth of *Pinus sylvestris*. *Canadian Journal of Forest Research* **15,** 453–460.

STJERNBERG, E.I. (1989). *A review of containerised seedling transportation methods*. Forest Engineering Research Institute of Canada, Technical Report TR-05.

STONE, E.C. (1955). Poor survival and the physiological condition of planting stock. *Forest Science* **1,** 90–94.

SUTTON, R.F. (1990). Root growth capacity in coniferous forest trees. *HortScience* **25,** 259–266.

TABBUSH, P.M. (1986). Rough handling, soil temperature and root development in outplanted Sitka spruce and Douglas fir. *Canadian Journal of Forest Research* **16,** 1385–1388.

TABBUSH, P.M. (1987a). Effect of desiccation on water status and forest performance of bare-rooted Sitka spruce and Douglas fir transplants. *Forestry* **60,** 31–43.

TABBUSH, P.M. (1987b). *The use of co-extruded polythene bags for handling bare-rooted planting stock*. Forestry Commission Research Information Note 110/87/SILN. Forestry Commission, Edinburgh.

TABBUSH, P.M. (1988). *Silvicultural principles for upland restocking*. Forestry Commission Bulletin 76. HMSO, London.

VAN DEN DRIESSCHE, R. (1975). *Flushing response of Douglas fir buds to chilling and to different air temperatures after chilling*. British Columbia Forest Service Research Note 71.

VAN DEN DRIESSCHE, R. (1991). Effects of nutrients on stock performance in the forest. In *Mineral nutrition of conifer seedlings*, ed. R. van den Driessche. CRC Press, Florida, 229–260.

Chapter 15

Legislation and the nursery manager

J. R. Aldhous

In contemporary business, forest nursery managers have to work within a continually changing legislative framework.

Sections in this chapter outline current legislation affecting technical operations in the nursery, but not company law, accounting or business taxation, etc. *The guidance that is given must not be regarded as a complete or authoritative statement of the law;* where this is required, a professional legal adviser should be consulted.

Whenever contemplating action in response to any legislation mentioned here, always check whether there have been any more recent amendments to legislation that may affect what you need to do.

In the following sections where current statutes and associated regulations are mentioned, it should be taken for granted that any relatively recent legislation has revoked and largely re-enacted earlier legislation. In the section on the Forest Reproductive Material Regulations, some older, now obsolete, regulations are described; for most other topics, the earlier revoked legislation is not mentioned.

Where appropriate, full references to legislation are given:

- Acts of Parliament are shown giving their title, year of enactment and their chapter number in the statute book for the year, e.g. Plant Varieties and Seeds Act, 1964 (1964, c.14).

- Statutory Instruments or SIs, the subordinate legislation through which powers created in Acts of Parliament are exercised, are given their name, year of making, and reference number, e.g. Forest Reproductive Material Regulations, 1977 (SI 1977/891).

This chapter also includes a section on the OECD 'Scheme for the Control of Forest Reproductive Material in International Trade' (OECD, 1974). While the scheme has no statutory force, it is so similar in operation to the arrangements under the Forest Reproductive Material Regulations that they are most appropriately described in this chapter (section 15.4).

15.1 Forest Reproductive Material Regulations

The Forest Reproductive Material Regulations, 1977 (SI 1977/891; SI 1977/1264) are part of the framework of consumer protection legislation in the UK; they are intended to ensure that anyone establishing a plantation of young trees for *forestry purposes* is supplied with healthy planting stock genuinely of the provenance or origin chosen by the planter.

They are administered by the Forestry Commission as the authority designated under the legislation (Forestry Commission, 1987). 'Forestry purposes' is not defined in the regulations, but in practice is taken as any use of trees that qualifies for a forestry planting grant.

As part of its statutory obligation to ensure compliance with the FRM regulations, the Forestry Commission has appointed staff who inspect the records and growing stock of firms trading in seed and plants falling within the scope of Forest Reproductive Material (FRM) Regulations.

The specific terms of the regulations incorporate the requirements of EEC legislation, and in particular, Council Directive No.

66/404/EEC as amended (EEC, 1966; 1969; 1975), and Council Directive No. 71/161/EEC as amended (EEC, 1971; 1974).

The regulations were enacted first in 1973 and amended in 1974.

The 1977 Forest Reproductive Material Regulations (SI 1977/891) revoke (in Section (20)) and largely re-enact the 1973 and 1974 FRM Regulations. The concepts of 'select' and 'tested' forest reproductive material are introduced, there is a section on seed testing at the Official Seed Testing Station, and minor modifications are made to the previous regulations. The list of species affected is not altered.

The species covered by these Regulations are listed in Table 15.1. Because of their 'European' link, they include species of forest importance in Western Europe as a whole, rather than just the United Kingdom; e.g. species such as *Abies alba* are included and

Pinus contorta omitted. However, the EC directive is currently under revision (1994), and it is possible that the list of species will be extended because of the addition to the community of southern European states subsequent to when the FRM directives were first drawn up.

The forest tree species in the 1961 Seed Regulations were deleted under Section (2) of the 1973 FRM regulations, thereby removing from statutory control all tree species previously in the 1961 Seeds Regulations list not covered by these Regulations.

The revocation in 1977 of the 1973 Regulations does not reactivate that part of the 1961 Seed Regulations from which forest tree species had been removed, because the whole of the 1961 Seeds Regulations were revoked in 1974 under SI 1974/897 (Fodder Plant Seeds Regulations).

Table 15.1 Species to which the Forest Reproductive Material Regulations (1977) apply

Common name	Botanical name	Synonym
Seed or forest reproductive material raised from seed		
Silver fir	*Abies alba* Mill.	*Abies pectinata* DC.
Beech	*Fagus sylvatica* L.	
European larch	*Larix decidua* Mill.	
Japanese larch	*Larix leptolepis* (Sieb. & Zucc.) Gord.	
Norway spruce	*Picea abies* Karst.	*Picea excelsa* Link.
Sitka spruce	*Picea sitchensis* Trautv. & Mey.	*Picea menziesii* Carr.
Austrian and Corsican pine	*Pinus nigra* Arn.	*Pinus laricio* Poir.
Scots pine	*Pinus sylvestris* L.	
Weymouth pine	*Pinus strobus* L.	
Douglas fir	*Pseudotsuga taxifolia* (Poir.) Britt.	*Pseudotsuga douglasii* Carr. *Pseudotsuga menziesii* (Mirb.) Franco.
Red oak	*Quercus borealis* Michx.	*Quercus rubra* Du Roi
Pedunculate oak	*Quercus pedunculata* Ehrh.	*Quercus robur* L.
Sessile oak	*Quercus sessiliflora* Sal.	*Quercus petraea* Liebl.
Forest reproductive material raised from registered clonal stock by vegetative propagation		
Poplar varieties	*Populus* cvs.	

Forest Reproductive Material (Amendment) Regulations, 1973 (SI 1973/1108), and 1974 (SI 1974/877)

These, respectively, set maximum lot sizes from which a sample should be taken for official seed test and made minor changes to the criteria for transplant stock to meet 'EEC Standards'.

15.1.1 Definitions of terms

The Forest Reproductive Material Regulations define certain terms, the more important of these being summarised in Table 15.2.

Table 15.2 Brief definitions of selected terms from the Forest Reproductive Material Regulations, 1977

Basic material
– for seed sources, stands of trees and seed orchards;
– for vegetatively propagated material, clones and mixtures of clones.

Certificate of provenance
– certificate issued by the authority designated by national governments, describing the provenance of seed or plants.

Forest reproductive material (FRM)
– seed, cones and parts of plants intended for the production of plants; also, young plants raised from seed or from parts of plants, natural seedlings and setts.

Indigenous (synonym *native*)
– believed not to have been introduced by human agency.

Origin
– place in which an indigenous stand of trees is growing, or the place from which a non-indigenous stand was originally introduced.

Provenance
– place in which any stand of trees, whether indigenous or non-indigenous, is growing.

Selected reproductive material
– forest reproductive material derived from basic material approved for registration as 'selected' under the FRM Regulations.

Tested reproductive material
– forest reproductive material derived from basic material approved for registration as 'tested' under the FRM Regulations.

Full definitions are set out in Section 2(2) of the Regulations. (FRM Regs, 1977)

15.1.2 Categories of seed or plants under the Forest Reproductive Material (FRM) Regulations

There are two categories of seed or plants of FRM species according to whether they are from reproductive material which is 'Tested' or 'Selected'.

Although not defined formally except through 'derogation' (section 15.1.6), there is also a 'default' category for seed or plants which are neither tested nor selected.

Criteria for 'tested' and 'selected' are fully described in Schedules 2 and 3 of the 1977 FRM Regulations. The essential features are set out below.

15.1.3 Tested forest reproductive material

'Tested' material must be superior to the local standard in characteristics important for the species, both in economic and statistical terms. Normally, volume production is the first criterion; however, stem form, timber quality and disease resistance may each be a supplementary or primary criterion, according to circumstance.

Because of its definition, 'tested' can only be applied to the tested product of a stand or seed orchard, or to vegetatively propagated material.

Tested poplar clones

Poplar has been propagated vegetatively for many decades, many individual clones having been specifically tested for resistance to bacterial canker (Jobling, 1990; Peace, 1962; Phillips and Burdekin, 1992). 'Tested' clones of poplar have shown sufficient resistance for them to be recommended for large scale use on appropriate sites. In 1989, a small number of the more promising, but incompletely tested poplar clones were accepted for use in Great Britain under the FRM Regulations (Potter *et al.*, 1990). A full list of the currently accepted clones of poplar is given in Table 10.2 in Chapter 10, section 10.1.1.

Seed from 'approved' seed orchards

Because of developments resulting from tree

breeding and improvement programmes in many countries, seed is available from seed orchards where the ability of the parent trees to produce superior progeny has been well established, but where the performance of the product of the seed orchard (i.e. from mass collection of open pollinated seed) has not been separately tested. For the immediate future in Great Britain, this superior seed will be available from Forestry Commission seed orchards under the description 'approved' and should be considered at least as the equivalent of 'tested' seed.

Seed orchard seed from orchards for which tests are not yet complete, is described as 'not tested', but is the equivalent at least of 'selected' seed (i.e. seed from registered seed stands).

From 1990, the identity of seed from 'approved' and 'not tested' seed orchards carry the suffix 'A' (*not* 'T'), and 'NT' respectively. See also Chapter 5, section 5.2.1 on identity numbering of seed and plants.

15.1.4 Selected forest reproductive material

Seed

'Selected' seed is collected from registered stands identified as showing good form and above average volume production. The stand must be big enough for there to be adequate interpollination; also, it must be sufficiently separated from other stands to avoid serious risk of cross-pollination with poorer quality trees.

15.1.5 Register of seed and propagating material

Before any source of seed or propagating material can be accepted as 'tested/approved' or 'selected', it has to be scrutinised for its suitability as described in Chapter 5 of the *Seed manual for forest trees* (Gordon, 1992).

Candidate seed stands are inspected and if suitable are entered in the 'National Register of Basic Material'. This register also contains details of seed orchards and of registered stoolbeds of poplar clones.

Forest stands accepted as meeting the criteria for 'selected reproductive material' and entered in the national register are commonly referred to as 'registered seed stands'.

15.1.6 Unregistered seed or plants

Derogation

While preference should always be given to 'selected' or 'tested' stock of preferred origins, seed crop failures and limited production capacity result from time to time in shortages of selected or tested stock of the preferred source. Provision exists, in these circumstances, for authorising the collection of seed 'meeting less stringent requirements than those laid down in the European Commission (EC) Directive'. Such authorisation – often referred to as 'derogation' – is given by the EC in Brussels, following representations from each member state's Forest Authority. The Forestry Commission, as Forest Authority, is responsible for collating forecasts of shortages of seed and plants by seed merchants and forest nursery managers, and making representations to the EC at Brussels on their behalf. 'Derogation' covers the initial collection or import of unregistered seed and the subsequent raising of planting stock from it.

The Forestry Commission makes enquiries annually before submitting a list of requests for 'derogation' for the UK. Currently (1994), this takes place in April to take effect from the following November.

In recent years, the interval of time between forwarding the request and formal EC approval has seldom been less than 2 months.

A procedure also exists, though it has rarely been used, for considering 'out of time' requests for 'derogation', arising out of unforeseen circumstances.

Collection of unregistered seed from small stands

There are no requirements for seed collection from unregistered stands, apart from identifying the source accurately; however, collectors looking at small groups of trees as possible seed sources should be aware that there are dangers of inbreeding if the number of trees is small, especially if it is possible that the parent trees themselves may have originated from a very small number of trees, e.g. a clump of trees in an ornamental landscape.

To maintain the broad genetic base of any seed source, a similar amount of seed should be collected from a minimum of 40 or more seed-bearing trees at any one time.

Further information

All enquiries about any aspect of authorisation to use unregistered seed of species covered by the Forest Reproductive Material Regulations, should be addressed to the Forestry Authority, 231 Corstorphine Road, Edinburgh, EH12 7AT (Tel. 031-334-0303).

15.1.7 European Community standards for seed and plants

In addition to defining the quality of the seed source of plants in terms of origin and potential performance, the EC directive and the associated UK legislation also provides for standards of physical quality.

Seed standards

Seed of the species listed under the FRM regulations has to be marketed as 'EEC Standard'. In practice, the requirements of the standard seed test itself, together with a supplementary test for seed purity, allow any seed with a valid UK or ISTA (International Seed Testing Association) seed test certificate and meeting the EC seed purity requirements, to be categorised as of 'EEC Standard'. See also Chapter 5, section 5.6.

Plant standards

The requirements that plants must meet, if they are to be marketed as 'EEC Standard', are listed in Appendix IV – EEC Plant Standards, and discussed in Chapter 1, section 1.5.2 along with other aspects of plant quality.

15.1.8 Documentation

Nursery managers dealing in species listed in Table 15.1 for forestry purposes, must insist that for *all* the seed or plants of these species which they receive, they get the documents required under the FRM regulations. The documents are summarised in subsection 15.2.1. This includes plants bought in and sold immediately to cover orders which the nursery cannot meet from its own stock. They must also despatch stock to customers with the correct certification.

If a nursery manager collects seed of any species covered by the FRM regulations, or takes cuttings from poplar stoolbeds, there are additional procedures to observe, outlined in section 15.3.

Records must be retained of all certificates and licences received or issued involving basic material covered by the FRM Regulations. The Forestry Commission currently requires these to be kept for a minimum of 7 years.

Field and stock records

Nursery managers must be able to control and record the progress of each lot of stock throughout its life in the nursery. This should include recording the position of stock as it is laid out on the ground, and means to ensure that if any label marking seedbeds, transplant lines or stock in propagating houses is inadvertently dislodged or wantonly vandalised, stock can be correctly identified. This requirement is especially important when a nursery is carrying, for example 'selected' and 'unregistered' stock of the same species, or two or more provenances, for example, of native Scots pine.

Poplars

It is especially important that there are reliable field maps of stoolbeds and plant lines, and that there is a rigorous discipline imposed at the time of taking cuttings, to deal only with one variety at a time and to remove all stray or left-over woody material. Poplar clones are notorious for the difficulty in distinguishing closely related varieties, even when in full leaf; when only setts or cuttings are available, it is often quite impossible. Control procedures should include the rigorous examination during the growing season of poplar rooted cuttings and transplants, any apparent 'rogues' being destroyed.

15.2 Seed and plant sales

15.2.1 Receipt and supply of seed or plants within the United Kingdom

Material received

Nursery managers should receive from any supplier, for all seed lots, and for all lots of plants which will, or may possibly be used for forestry purposes, a 'Supplier's Certificate' containing information shown in Table 15.3.

Table 15.3 Particulars required in a Supplier's Certificate

Part I *Particulars to be furnished in every case*
1. The number of the Master Certificate, if any, or the number, if any, of any certificate of provenance or clonal identity and the name of the country issuing it.
2. Type of material, whether seed, cones, parts of plants or young plants.
3. Quantity of material being marketed.
4. Botanical name: the species and, where applicable, sub-species, variety, clone.
5. In the case of selected reproductive material or tested reproductive material, its category.
6. In the case of selected reproductive material, its region of provenance.
7. In the case of tested reproductive material, its basic material.
8. In the case of forest reproductive material, which, although not derived from officially approved basic material, has been authorised for marketing in accordance with regulation 11(2), its place of provenance and the altitude of that place.
9. Its origin.
10. (a) in the case of seedlings, the length of time the seedlings have been in the seed bed, and also, (b) in the case of transplants, the length of time they have existed as seedlings and as transplants, respectively, and the number of times transplanted.
11. If the forest reproductive material although not derived from officially approved basic material is authorised for marketing in accordance with regulation 11(2), a statement to that effect.
12. If derived from seed orchards a statement that the reproductive material is so derived.
13. Name and address of the supplier.

Part II *Further particulars to be furnished in the case of seed*
1. Number of Test Certificate (if any).
2. The description 'EEC Standard', *or*, where the seed does not comply with the conditions laid down in Part III of Schedule 7, and is authorised for marketing under regulation 11(2), a statement that it does not so comply.
3. Percentage of purity.
4. Percentage of germination.
5. Number per kilogramme of live seeds.
6. Number per kilogramme of seeds capable of germinating.
7. Weight of 1000 pure seeds in grammes.
8. Year in which the seed shall have ripened.
9. If the seed has been kept in cold storage, a statement to that effect.

Part III *Particulars to be furnished in the case of young plants and parts of plants sold or delivered under the description 'EEC Standard'*
1. The description 'EEC Standard'.
2. EEC classification number, in the case of the genus *Populus*.
3. Location of nursery in which the young plants were raised during their last growing season.
4. Age, in the case of parts of plants of the genus *Populus* which have had more than one growing season.
5. The size of the young plants.

The Supplier's Certificate is an important document as it constitutes a legal warranty from the seed supplier to the nursery manager, and from the nursery manager to his customer that the origin and other details given are as described.

The Supplier's Certificate should differ in colour, according to the category of plants or seed:

Category	Certificate colour
'tested',	blue
approved UK seed orchards	pink
'selected'	green
unregistered	usually white

There is no prescribed design for Supplier's Certificates. The certificate format used by the Forestry Commission when supplying seed or plants to the private sector is given in the Forestry Commission booklet describing the regulations (Forestry Commission, 1987). However while these are widely copied, the use of that particular format is not obligatory. Other

Plate 32. *Famo lifter with supporting tractor collecting plants into open-mesh crates before transfer to cold store.* (E8880)

Plate 33. *Grading transplants on a carousel.* (38110)

Plate 34. *Multi-row plant lifter with secondary vibrating tines to loosen soil.* (J.R. Aldhous)

Plate 35. *Open-mesh crates of newly lifted plants being moved in cold store prior to grading and packing.* (E8885)

Plate 36. *Plants in store, showing crates in tiers of four crates strapped to pallets, and stacked three pallets high.* (39390)

Plate 37. *Articulated trailer used for long-distance delivery of plants from nursery to planting site.* (40615)

approaches are acceptable, in particular, certificates linking with invoices or other elements of the essential paperwork arising from sale of seed or plants, or certificates linked in with computer-based stock control and sales documentation. Providing information of the correct coloured paper can be achieved by photocopying computer output on coloured paper, retaining the original as a file copy.

Seed and plants despatched

The seller of seed, cuttings or plants should give the buyer a supplier's certificate within 14 days of the sale or delivery, whichever is later.

Seed which is sold must in addition have a current Seed Test Certificate (Chapter 5, section 5.6.6). However, where seed such as beech and oak have to be despatched for immediate sowing and seed testing may take 3–8 weeks, the supplier's certificate and seed test certificate must be sent to the buyer as soon as available. An interim certificate is often issued, based on a 'quick' test to give the nursery manager some idea of the quality of seed when calculating sowing densities.

15.2.2 Imports of plants and seed

Imports of plants and seed are controlled not only by the Forest Reproductive Material Regulations but also by plant health legislation (see this chapter, section 15.5).

Table 15.4 summarises the documents that a nursery manager should require, when importing any species covered by the FRM regulations.

15.2.3 Exports of plants and seed

Exports to EC member states

Consignments of 'selected' or 'tested' forest reproductive material exported to destinations within the boundaries of member states of the European Community, must be accompanied by:

- An 'Official Certificate of Provenance' – this is obtainable on application to the Forestry

Table 15.4 Documents required when importing plants or seed covered by the Forest Reproductive Material Regulations*

Situation of exporter	Certificate of provenance from exporter†	Import licence from Forestry Commission‡	Licence to market from Forestry Commission	Phytosanitary certificate from exporter	Plant health pass-port‡	Seed test certificate from exporter
Plants imported into the UK						
Based in EC, plants from registered EC source	Yes	No	No	No	Yes	No
Based in EC, plants *not* from registered EC source	Yes	No	Yes	No	Yes	No
Not based in EC	Yes	Yes	Yes	Yes	No	No
Seed imported into the UK						
Based in EC, seed from registered EC source	Yes	No	No	No	No	Yes
Based in EC, seed *not* from registered EC source	Yes	No	Yes	No	No	Yes
Not based in EC	Yes	Yes	Yes	No	No	Yes

* Table based on Fig. 6, Forestry Commission, *Explanatory Booklet, 1987; The Forest Reproductive Material Regulations, 1977.* (Forestry Commission, 1987).
† Or equivalent e.g. under OECD scheme.
‡ A requirement under Plant Health legislation.

Authority, 231 Corstorphine Road, Edinburgh, EH12 7AT.

- A Supplier's Certificate – this should be completed by the nursery manager whose stock is being exported.

- (a) If seed is being exported, a current Seed Test Certificate from an approved official seed testing station.

  (b) If plants are being exported, a plant health passport issued by the nursery manager after a nursery inspection by the Ministry of Agriculture (MAFF) in England and Wales, and the Scottish Office Agriculture and Fisheries Department (SOAFD) in Scotland.

N.B. Plant passports may need to certify that the plants and nursery ground in which they were grown are free from specific harmful pests and diseases. The issue of such certificates therefore depends on the outcome of inspection of plants and soil tests, by a local MAFF or SOAFD inspector. Certain tests may have to have been done in the growing season preceding export; nursery managers should seek plant health inspectors' advice *before* accepting export orders.

Exports to countries not members of the European Community and exports of non-FRM species to EC member states

Regulations vary widely from country to country so that the exact requirements of any country should be found, before any arrangements for export are finalised.

15.2.4 Species not covered by the Forest Reproductive Material Regulations

Nursery managers are not obliged to receive or send 'supplier's certificates', nor to obtain current 'seed test certificates' for plants and seed not covered by Forest Reproductive Material Regulations.

Nevertheless, planters are covered by consumer protection legislation, in respect of the description and quality of seed and plants supplied. See this chapter, section 15.8.2.

Nursery managers and seed suppliers may wish to use the voluntary arrangements under the OECD certification scheme described in section 15.4 of this chapter.

15.3 Seed stand registration and seed collection

Arranging and controlling seed collection has the advantage for the nursery manager that as the collector, he can be in no doubt as to the provenance of the seed gathered. At the same time, he has to be sure that he has the skills and facilities to clean, dry and store the seed safely, so that it is in first class condition when it comes to sowing.

Full details of practical procedures for seed crop forecasting, seed collection and processing are given in Forestry Commission Bulletin 59 *Seed manual for ornamental trees and shrubs* (Gordon and Rowe, 1982) and in Forestry Commission Bulletin 83 *Seed manual for forest trees* (Gordon, 1992).

The following paragraphs summarise, for species covered by the Forest Reproductive Material Regulations, the main points where practice and legislation interact. For species not covered by these regulations, certain steps are not obligatory; nevertheless, anyone organising seed collection is recommended to use the sequence of operation as a check list, especially if an OECD seed certificate (section 15.4) is to be sought.

Commercial seed collectors come within the scope of the Health and Safety at Work etc. Act, 1974, and associated regulations; see section 15.8.1.

15.3.1 Status of stand and access to seed crop

Status of stand

Contact must be made with the owner or his agent, or for Forestry Commission woodland, the local Forest District Manager, firstly, to confirm who is able to give permission for access to a potential seed crop and where appropriate to agree provisional terms for collection, and secondly, to find out whether the stand is registered as a 'selected' seed source. If not registered, the owner, agent or manager should be asked whether any unsuccessful application for registration has been made in the past, whether an application is currently being processed, and whether any 'unregistered' collection has been made in recent years.

Application for registration

If it is necessary to apply, or re-apply for registration, a request for a Form FRP1 'Application for seed stand registration' should be sent to the Forestry Authority, Tree Improvement Branch, Northern Research Station, Roslin, Midlothian, EH25 9SY.

The completed FRP1, giving details of species, approximate age of stand, elevation, variety, origin, total stand area and area in which seed may be collected, as far as these are known, should be returned to the Forestry Commission following instructions with the form. The request should be accompanied by:

- a map on 1:10000 scale showing the location of the stand and access from a public road;

- the name and address of the owner and, if appropriate, the woodland agent or manager; and

- the appropriate non-returnable fee, as advised with the application form. Note that a higher fee is required for inspections after certain dates.

A seed collection organiser may apply for a stand to be registered, if he has the owner's permission. The decision on whether the stand has been accepted for registration will be notified to the owner or the agent responsible for managing the woodland, with a copy to the applicant, if appropriate. Registration, in itself, confers no special rights on the applicant.

Terms of entry

The seed collection organiser should establish with the owner/agent:

- dates and times of access for seed collecting;

- priority and relationship with other contractors in the woods, especially harvesting contractors, pesticide contractors and other seed collectors;

- relationship with shooting tenant and gamekeeping staff;

- third party insurance requirements adequate for collectors in the circumstances of the permission. If appropriate, check terms of current cover under Employers (Compulsory Insurance) legislation

15.3.2 Collection of unregistered seed

If a seed collection organiser wishes to collect from a stand of a species covered by the FRM regulations but the stand is not acceptable for registration, then, *in addition* to the notifications necessary for registered seed, the seed collection organiser must apply for and obtain specific authority to collect unregistered seed from the stand in prospect *before any commercial collection starts*. This may be applied for by the owner, seed collection organiser, nursery manager or seed merchant, from the Forestry Authority, 231 Corstorphine Road, Edinburgh, EH12 7AT.

If the Forestry Authority considers that there are ample supplies of registered 'selected' seed of the same region of provenance/origin, readily available on the market, authorisation to collect unregistered seed may be refused. See also section 15.1.6.

15.3.3 Notification of intention to collect

Seed collection organisers are required to inform the local Forestry Authority office in writing not less than 28 days beforehand of:

- seed source.

- proposed starting and finishing dates of collection.

Addresses of current Forestry Authority offices are given in Appendix I.

During collection, it is essential to ensure that individual collectors stay within the boundaries of the seed stand as notified.

Once the collection has been completed, the collection organiser is required to notify the local Forestry Authority office of the total amount of cones, fruit or seed collected, and if applicable, the amount of seed extracted.

If the Forestry Authority is satisfied with the information given by the collector, together with any reports that may have been made by their inspectors, the collection organiser will receive for the amount of marketable seed or fruit declared:

- if the stand is registered, a *'Master* Certificate of Provenance';
- if the stand is not registered, a 'Certificate of Provenance';
- if seed has been collected under 'derogation', a licence to market.

Without one or other certificate, the seed collected cannot legally be marketed anywhere within the European Community.

15.3.4 Poplars – registration and certification

Stoolbed registration

Procedure for registering poplar stoolbeds is the same as for potential seed stands. A request + local details + fee must be sent to the Forestry Authority who will arrange for the stoolbeds to be inspected (see section 15.3.1).

A valid inspection of poplar stoolbeds can only be made when they are established, and then only after young leaves on developing shoots are fully expanded, as these are the means of checking the identity of the variety. Applications should be made therefore, not later than the beginning of May *preceding* the first proposed marketing season.

15.3.5 Certification of poplar forestry planting stock

Rooted cuttings

Application for a 'Master certificate of provenance' should be made for each year's insertion of cuttings from registered stoolbeds, or of cuttings raised from plants themselves raised from cuttings from registered stoolbeds. Applications should be made to the local

Forestry Authority office not later than the beginning of May of the season the cuttings were inserted.

Unrooted setts; unrooted cuttings

Applications to the Conservator should be made not later than the beginning of May preceding the winter when unrooted setts or cuttings will be taken.

15.4 OECD scheme for the control of reproductive material moving in international trade

This international voluntary scheme run under the auspices of the Organisation for Economic Co-operation and Development (OECD), originated in 1967 and foreshadowed the European Community Forest Reproductive Material Directives. After the latter came into force, the OECD scheme was amended so that definitions and requirements in common were identical, including notification to the national Forest Authorities of proposals to collect seed, and to have records available for inspection (OECD, 1974).

15.4.1 Status in the United Kingdom

The scheme was formally adopted in Great Britain in 1984, the Forestry Commission being the designated authority.

The Forestry Commission in 1982 had previously issued a booklet about the scheme, reproducing details of the Method of Operation, Regions of Provenance, Approved Basic Material, etc., published in 1974 by the OECD (Forestry Commission, 1982).

In practice, the scheme is used principally for seed imports and exports. OECD certificates are accepted where unregistered seed is being imported from outside the European Community. (See Table 15.4 – Documents required when importing seed.)

The Forestry Authority maintains a register of selected stands of species not covered by the Forest Reproductive Material Regulations, but which come within the scope of the OECD scheme. For the UK, the same regions of provenance apply as for the FRM seed collections.

Currently, seed imported from Canada, USA, Hungary, Romania, Japan and the Scandinavian countries are imported under OECD certificates.

The other member countries are: Australia, Austria, Belgium, France, Holland, Ireland and Italy. Germany is an associate member; Spain and Turkey are believed to be applying for membership.

Future developments

The OECD scheme is likely to be revised at some future date, to keep it in step with the EC scheme, taking into account changes in tree breeding practice and the development of vegetative propagation of stock raised in tree improvement programmes (Faulkner, 1987).

For further details about the operation of the OECD scheme in Great Britain, contact the Forestry Authority, 231 Corstorphine Road, Edinburgh, EH12 7AT.

15.4.2 Comparison between the OECD and EEC schemes

The most important differences between the OECD and EEC schemes are:

- While the EEC scheme applies to a restricted list of species when traded between and within EC member states, the OECD scheme is open for any country to apply to join and does not set limits on the species that may be included.

- Within any country which has set up the scheme, observance of the OECD scheme is voluntary. Seed suppliers and nursery managers may apply to enter the scheme when they see the need. *However, neither the OECD nor the EEC scheme operates retrospectively.*

- Under the OECD scheme there are four categories of seed instead of the two under the EEC. The additional categories are:

  (a) 'Source identified'. This applies to unregistered sources of seed of species not covered by the FRM regulations. In the UK, such seed can be collected and sold as 'source identified' seed, provided the Forestry Authority has been given formal and timely notice of the proposal to collect.

  (b) 'Seed from untested seed orchards'. Apart from hybrid larch, this category is of limited relevance to the UK; species for which seed orchards have been established and which might be planted on any scale in Britain are covered by FRM rules.

- There is no requirement in the OECD scheme for seed to be tested prior to marketing.

- In addition to maintaining registers of selected seed stands, the Forestry Authority is obliged to register seed collectors, seed extractories and seed stores where any OECD-certified seed is being stored and nurseries where OECD-certified plants are being raised.

15.5 Plant and seed health

Following the creation of the European Community 'Single Market', previous arrangements for plant health inspections at customs posts at national borders have been withdrawn. In their place, a scheme has been introduced whereby plants for which any health risk of potential significance within the European Community has been identified, are inspected at the nursery where they are being grown (The Plant Health (Great Britain) Order 1993, SI 1993/1320). If no evidence of a relevant pest or disease is found, the nursery manager is authorised to issue a 'plant passport.'

For plants raised in any nursery within the European Community, plant passport requirements relate to specific organisms on named genera. Only where plants are being imported from elsewhere than European Community countries is there any requirement for a phytosanitary certificate of freedom from pests and disease.

Certain parts of the EC have been identified as being free of particular pests and diseases present elsewhere in the EC. These have been designated as 'Protected Zones' in order to maintain that status.

The Plant Health and Seed Inspectorate (PHSI) of the Ministry of Agriculture (MAFF), or the Scottish Office Agriculture and Fisheries Department (SOAFD), is responsible for implementing the new plant health rules in respect of young plants in forest nurseries. More detailed information should be sought from their local offices.

The Forestry Commission, Plant Health Branch, is responsible for plant health matters affecting forests and woodland, wood and wood products. Enquiries should be addressed to: Plant Health Branch, Forestry Commission, 231 Corstorphine Road, Edinburgh, EH12 7AT (Forestry Commission, 1992).

15.5.1 Plant passports

A plant passport is a label or combination of label and delivery note prepared by the nursery manager arranging despatch of plants.

For any plants requiring passports, a label must be attached to the plants or to the plant packaging. This label must state:

i.   the heading 'EEC Plant Passport';

ii. the EEC member state code for the country where the nursery issuing the passport is located, e.g. UK;

iii. a code letter or letters indicating the official body with which the nursery is registered, e.g. EW, S, NI;

iv. the registration number of the nursery issuing the passport;

v.   a serial number, week number, batch number or other number which unambiguously identifies that consignment.

Items ii, iii and iv should run together, ii and iii being separated with a '/', e.g. UK/S1234.

Additional information must either be included on the passport label or must be entered on a document (delivery note) travelling with the plants.

vi. the botanical name of the plants;

vii. the quantity of plants;

viii. if plants were obtained from another nursery, the letters **RP**, and a code number in place of the registration number of the original producer;

ix. if plants were raised outside the EC, the name of the country where they were raised;

x.   if plants can validly be moved into or within a 'protected zone', the letters **ZP**, and the codes for the relevant zones.

If a delivery note is used for this additional information, it must also include items i–v above.

15.5.2 Plant passports for forestry planting stock

A plant passport is needed whenever plants of genera listed as possible carriers of pest or disease are moved, sold or otherwise disposed of to another nursery manager or grower, whether within the UK or the European Community (EC).

Woodland tree and shrub genera requiring a passport whenever plants are moved include:

Crataegus, Malus, Prunus, Sorbus (except *S. intermedia), Pyrus, Cotoneaster, Pyracantha, Chaenomeles, Cydonia,* etc.

These are potential host species for fireblight and/or other pests and diseases of fruit trees and associated ornamental varieties.

Additionally, passports are required for all rooted conifers over 3 m tall, because of possible conifer bark beetle infestation.

Northern Ireland and the Isle of Man have been designated as 'protected zones' within the UK for several potential pests. Consequently, additional requirements have to be met in order to allow plants to be moved into these areas:

i.   plants of species potentially susceptible to fireblight must have been raised in a nursery in a 'fireblight-free zone';

ii   poplars have to be free from *Hypoxylon mammatum;*

iii. conifer genera have to be free from six

specific pests according to genus, as listed in the regulations.

In most circumstances, passports will be required for all movements of plants of:

Abies, Larix, Picea, Pinus, Pseudotsuga, Tsuga, Castanea, Platanus, Populus, Quercus.

However, small producers who are solely supplying local purchasers with stock for woodland planting may be exempted from having to register and issue passports. Nursery managers who consider they fall into this category should check with their local PHSI or SOAFD office.

Plant passports are not required for conventionally raised:

Acer (except *A. saccharum*)*, Aesculus, Betula, Carpinus, Corylus, Fagus, Fraxinus, Juglans, Nothofagus,* etc.

There are no requirements for passports for tree seed or fruits of any genus, except for *Prunus* fruits coming from outside the EC. These may require a phytosanitary certificate in respect of potential fruit crop pests.

15.5.3 Plants imported from outside the European Community

Schedules 3 and 4 of the Plant Health (GB) Order (SI 1993/1320) detail restrictions and some complete bans on all the more important conifer genera and some broadleaved genera, especially *Quercus, Ulmus* and *Castanea.*

For other genera, imported stock from non-EC countries has to meet the same requirements as for stock from EC countries, except that a phytosanitary certificate is required instead of a plant passport.

There are special rules for imported 'bonsai' trees.

15.5.4 Export outside the European Community

Where plants may be exported outside the European Community, the Plant Health and Seed Inspectorate or SOAFD should be approached as soon as the possibility is known, in order to find out what requirements have to be met to enable a 'Phytosanitary Certificate' to be issued.

A fee is charged for issue of a Phytosanitary Certificate.

15.5.5 Registration for plant health

For plant passports to be able to be issued, nurseries must be registered and a 'responsible person' nominated.

New nurseries expecting to be involved in anything more than the most local trade should ensure that they are registered with PHSI or SOAFD. Where the PHSI address is not known, the nearest office of MAFF will be able to give details.

Registered nurseries will be inspected regularly for two aspects of their business. Growing plants of genera requiring passports will be inspected for their health; also the office system of recording stock movements will be reviewed so as to satisfy the inspector that plants can be traced back to their originating nursery should the need arise.

A charge is not made for initial registration; however, for inspections of nursery stock and records, charges are made. In England and Wales, these are (in 1993) on a 'time spent' basis. In Scotland, the charge is related to nursery area.

Details of arrangements for issuing passports and the procedure for passporting plants which are bought in and sold on are supplied to nursery managers, once their nurseries have been registered.

15.5.6 Legislation for plant health

UK legislation is based on the requirements of the amended European Community Council Directive on Plant Health, 77/93/EEC (EEC, 1977), and Commission Directive 92/90/EEC, 92/98/EEC and 92/105/EEC (EEC, 1992 a,b,c).

The principal enabling legislation is the Plant Health (Great Britain) Order, 1993 (SI 1993/1320). SI 1993/256 extends provisions to Northern Ireland, while SI 1993/1641, /1642 and /2344 schedule the fees for inspections for passports and phytosanitary certificates.

15.6 Current pesticide legislation

Current pesticide legislation is directed towards the safe and effective usage of pesticides in the UK, giving particular emphasis on protection of the consumer (where edible crops are being treated), protection of the person applying the pesticide and protection of the environment.

Forest nurseries for the purposes of this legislation are grouped with other parts of the horticultural industry, and not with forestry.

Two sets of 'Regulations' currently define the requirements for the legal use of pesticides in forest tree and other horticultural nurseries, whether stock is raised in open ground or in plastic greenhouses, tunnels, etc., these are:

- The Control of Pesticides Regulations, 1986 (SI 1986/1510), made under the Food and Environment Protection Act, 1985.

  NB: forest and ornamental tree nurseries are included as part of horticulture for the purposes of these regulations.
- The Control of Substances Hazardous to Health Regulations, 1988 (SI 1988/1657), made under the Health and Safety at Work Act, 1974.

These regulations are complex and are supplemented by various codes of practice and guidance notes which amplify the requirements of the legislation. The most important are:

- *Pesticides: Code of practice for the safe use of pesticides on farms and holdings,* prepared jointly by MAFF and HSC and published in 1990 (MAFF/HSC, 1990);

- *Storage of approved pesticides: Guidance for farmers and other professional users.* Guidance Note CS19 (HSE, 1988).

- MAFF Reference Book 500, *'Pesticides 1994'* (MAFF, 1994), or its equivalent for the current year. This lists all the products approved under the Control of Pesticides Regulations.

A copy of each of the above should be available in the nursery office.

Periodically during the year, MAFF issue a *Pesticides register*; this contains details of additions and amendments to the annual issues of MAFF Reference Book 500 (i.e. the current year's issue of *Pesticides 1994*), including 'off-label' approvals and withdrawals. The British Crop Protection Council produce a regularly updated summary of products and their uses (Ivens, 1994); also, the horticultural nursery trade press usually carries editorial comment and feature articles on the more important changes during the year.

Nursery managers should be aware of two other codes:

- *COSHH in fumigation operations: COSHH Regulations, 1988. Approved code of practice* (HSC, 1988), relevant should it be necessary to fumigate greenhouses or polytunnels.

- *The safe use of pesticides for non-agricultural purposes: Approved code of practice* (HSC, 1991a). The coverage of this code includes conventional forestry operations but not forest nursery operations.

For other relevant publications, see the list at the end of the chapter.

15.6.1 Essential operational needs

Four essential legal requirements have to be met:

1. *Pesticides used for any aspect of pest control in forest nurseries MUST be approved for horticultural use on the crop needing treatment. Alternatively, there must be an exemption in force for the crop or species in question.*

   For a period after the introduction of the new regulations, forest tree nursery managers were able, under a temporary exemption for non-edible crops, to use products for which there was not a specific approval, subject to certain conditions. These arrangement are described briefly in Annex C 'Off-Label Arrangements'; pp. xli–xliv of MAFF Reference Book 500 (MAFF, 1994). While it is probable that these arrangements will continue for the short term, it is important to have ready access to the current edition of

MAFF Reference Book 500 and to check, in each new edition as it comes out, that no changes have been introduced which may restrict what has up to that time been good practice.

2. *All staff involved in the use of pesticides must be competent to undertake the work required of them.*

It is the responsibility of employers and self-employed individuals, to organise training, testing and practice to achieve and maintain competence, and to ensure that their employees obtain any necessary certificates.

Initial training can be provided by courses at agricultural or horticultural colleges. Information on what is available locally can be obtained from the Agricultural Training Board or local agricultural advisers (ADAS) in England or Wales, or in branches of the Scottish Agricultural College.

Subsequent up-dating training may be available from colleges; if instruction on new techniques and products is not available within travelling distance, individuals will have to rely on information from manufacturers leaflets, advisory leaflets, visits from advisers, etc.

3. *Certain classes of individuals must have a relevant 'Certificate of Competence' issued or authorised by the 'National Proficiency Test Council' (NPTC) or by the 'Scottish Association of Young Farmers' Clubs' (SAYFC).*

Alternatively, they must work under the direct and personal supervision of a certificate holder.

The classes of individual requiring 'Certificates of Competence' are:

- those born after 31st December 1964;
- anyone applying pesticides as a commercial service, i.e. as a contractor;
- anyone having to supervise any individual who should hold a certificate but does not.

'Personal supervision' should be taken as 'working within sight and sound of the supervisor'.

The 'Certificates of Competence' for pesticide users are issued by or on behalf of the 'National Proficiency Test Council', to those who pass the relevant tests.

Pesticide operations for the purposes of certification of competence are grouped into eleven 'modules'. All operators requiring certification must obtain a certificate for the 'Foundation Module' and, in addition, certificates for those modules directly relevant to their work. Full details are set out in the 'Pesticide Application Test Schedule' available from the National Proficiency Test Council, 10th Street, National Agricultural Centre, Stoneleigh, Kenilworth, Warwickshire, CV8 2IG.

In Scotland, details are also available from: Scottish Association of Young Farmers' Clubs, Young Farmers' Centre, Newbridge, Ingleston, Edinburgh, EH28 8NE.

4. *The 'employer' must make an 'assessment' under the Control of Substances Hazardous to Health (COSHH) Regulations (Reg. 6) and must take all reasonable steps to prevent or to control exposure of employees to hazards from pesticides and other hazardous substances.*

Employees or their representatives should be informed of the results of the assessment, and in particular, they should be provided with details of the assessment relating to any operation which they are required to carry out.

15.6.2 Control of Substances Hazardous to Health (COSHH) assessment

COSHH Regulations 6, 7 and 8 and the associated *Approved code of practice* issued by the Health and Safety Commission (HSC, 1993) amplify requirement (4) above.

The Health and Safety Executive have also issued a guide to COSHH assessments (HSE, 1993); this is in more general terms than the code of practice. Ideally, the two documents should be considered together.

The 'hazardous substances' to be considered include all such materials on the nursery premises, e.g. petroleum based fuel oils, and are not restricted to pesticides.

Nursery managers and others responsible

for the safe use of pesticides in forest nurseries can adequately meet their obligations in respect of COSHH assessments and pesticides, in a four stage procedure, given below. This relies on the substantial programme of testing before any pesticide is marketed, and the care that is paid to the wording of the approved product labels.

- Survey of current and expected future needs; assembly of all relevant information.
- Identification of proper course of action.
- Installation of up-to-date practices, based on the above point.
- Checks just before use, that there have been no material changes in circumstances, requiring corresponding changes in procedures.

Survey

The first stage is to list all the pesticides and other substances hazardous to health, in the current and future production programme of the nursery. This list should include possible pesticides and other substances (e.g. fuels and lubricants) that might reasonably be needed, as well as those for which there is a clear need.

For the materials thus identified, details must be obtained, e.g. from product labels, manufacturer's recommendations, of the best current techniques for applying them.

For some products, there may not be an exactly relevant recommendation on the product label. In these circumstances, other sources of information should be sought – e.g. Forestry Commission recommendations, checking with the body making the recommendation, that such 'off-label' uses are currently permissible.

Proper course of action

Decisions on what operations during the coming 12 months should be provided for, must take into account:

- the existing staff, facilities and practices (trained operators, equipment, store, waste disposal, records, procedures for emergencies, etc);

- the terms of current approvals for the pesticides in mind;
- other hazardous substances listed;
- relevant codes of practice; and
- the particular environment of the nursery.

Installing up-to-date practice

The next stage is to *do* whatever had been shown to be necessary to up-date the capability to use pesticides etc. effectively and safely in the nursery, whether in terms of staff training, improved storage facilities or application procedures, or other action.

Check just before use

The final stage is *always* to check whether any special local circumstance or conditions on the day should cause the previously planned treatments to be modified because of any changed risk. This stage should be repeated before *every* pesticide application.

While the first three stages should normally be carried out as a recorded, formal procedure and should be formally reviewed regularly (e.g. annually), the final stage should be on-going, relating specifically to site, crop, pest and occasion. *It is an essential part of the assessment process.* However, it should involve a modest expenditure of time or work, if the preceding stages have been completed conscientiously. See also section 15.8.1.

15.6.3 Sources of information

The approved label of pesticide product constitutes the principal source of information on which to base the initial assessment of the hazards associated with individual pesticide products.

Government Departments that may be able to provide additional information include:

- The Forestry Commission, 231 Corstorphine Road, Edinburgh, EH12 7AT.
- MAFF, Pesticides Safety Directorate, Rothamsted, Harpenden, Hertfordshire, AL5 2SS or local ADAS offices.

- Health and Safety Executive, Pesticides Registration Section, Health Policy Division, Magdalen House, Bootle, Merseyside, L20 3QZ or local HSE offices.

Manufacturers' data sheets should be available on request, under provisions of the 1987 Consumer Protection Act.

British Crop Protection Council publications include:

- The current *UK pesticide guide* (Ivens, 1994);
- *Weed control handbook* (Holly and Hance, 1990);
- *Pest and disease control handbook* (Scopes and Staples, 1989).

15.6.4 Keeping up-to-date

New products, new uses for existing products and tightening environmental standards result in a continual stream of changes in the list of 'approved products' or 'approved uses' for existing products. Nursery managers must therefore ensure that they have up-to-date information on the status of any pesticide product they intend to use.

The information in this Bulletin was up-to-date at the time of publication. There is no guarantee that limitations may not have been imposed subsequently on any product listed, nor that manufacturers will continue to market products here recommended for use, nor that codes of practice may not have been changed.

15.6.5 Storage of pesticides

As far as possible, the minimum amount of pesticides should be stored.

There are now clear guidelines in the HSE Guidance Note CS19 *Storage of approved pesticides for farmers and other professional users* (HSE, 1988). These distinguish between small scale storage using cabinets or vaults and larger stores. Nursery managers have to set up an effective storage system, meeting the requirements of these guidelines.

15.6.6 Disposal of pesticide wastes

The purchase and use of pesticides inevitably will create some wastes. However, the aim of management should be to keep the wastes to an absolute minimum. For example, when getting to the end of a container of concentrate, it should become a matter of routine to wash out the container and use the washings to dilute the concentrate before making up the spray solution to its final dilution. In this way, you finish up with clean containers without any washing waste.

The MAFF/HSC *Code of practice for the safe use of pesticides on farms and holdings* details alternative acceptable methods of disposing of pesticide wastes. One or other of these methods should always be followed.

Equipment can be installed in a forest nursery for treating insecticide and other residues, so that the bulk of the liquid can safely be returned to the ground and pesticide concentrate in solid form disposed of through an approved waste disposal contractor.

Under the Environment Protection Act, 1990 the Department of the Environment, Scottish Office and Welsh Office have jointly produced a *Code of practice on waste managements* (DoE, 1991). This refers to 'controlled waste'. Waste from agricultural premises is not 'controlled waste'; as long as forest nurseries continue to be considered as a part of agriculture and horticulture, wastes from them are covered under 1985 Food and Environment Act legislation rather than under the 1990 Environment Protection Act.

15.7 Seed and plant breeding

15.7.1 Seeds Act and Seeds Regulations

Plant Varieties and Seeds Act, 1964 (1964, c.14)

This act empowers ministers to regulate seed and plant description, testing and trading, and provides that particulars of seed or plants supplied under this statute, constitute a written warranty from the supplier.

It also introduced the concept of 'plant breeders' rights'; see section 15.7.2.

The Forest Reproductive Material Regulations draw their authority substantively from this Act. It also repealed the 1920 Seeds Act.

European Communities Act, 1972 (1972, c.68)

This Act, in *Schedule 4* D 5, *Seeds and Other Propagating Material,* includes several provisions affecting the 1964 Plant Varieties and Seeds Act:

- para 5(1) adds a new section (16A) to the 1964 Act to cover marketing;
- para 5(4) adds vegetative propagating material and silvicultural planting material;
- para 5(4) also authorises the Forestry Commission to set up and fund an 'Official Seed Testing Station' (where previously, it had been a 'private' seed testing station).

Fodder Plant Seed Regulations, 1974 (SI 1974/897)

Among other provisions, these Regulations revoked the 1961 Seeds Regulations, both for England and Wales, and for Scotland, in their entirety (Section (2) and Schedule 1).

These are the first of several consecutively numbered regulations which cover various groups of agricultural and horticultural seeds. Together and with the FRM Regulations, they replace most of the requirements of the 1961 Seeds Regulations.

Seeds (National List of Plant Varieties) Regulations, 1982 (SI 1982/844; amended, SI 1985/1529; SI 1989/1314)

These regulations provide for:

- a Plant Varieties and Seeds Gazette where additions to the National List of Plant Varieties may be printed;
- establishment of reference collections of plant material;
- conditions for submission of applications and for the results of trials providing supporting evidence.

Marketing of agricultural crop seed is restricted to species and varieties on the National List or which have been in a Common Catalogue for 2 years. These regulations bring the National Lists into line with requirements of EC directives on Common Catalogues.

Seeds (Regulation, Licensing and Enforcement) Regulations, 1985 (SI 1985/980); amended SI 1987/1098)

These prescribe that no person shall carry on a seed business, or sample seed of any sort to which Regulations under the Plant Varieties and Seeds Act, 1964 apply, unless registered. However, 'silvicultural propagating or planting material' is specifically exempted. (Otherwise, seed merchants dealing in forest tree seed would be included, as the FRM regulations are made under that Act.)

Seeds (Fees) Regulations

These set fees for seed testing, etc., for seed categories defined in specific agricultural crop seed regulations, e.g. SI 1985/975, /976, /977, /978, /979. The fees are revised frequently; enquiries have to be made when needed, to find the most up-to-date SI.

15.7.2 Plant breeders' rights

Sections 1–15 of the Plant Varieties and Seeds Act 1964 establish 'plant breeders' rights'. Their definition and the means of establishing them are set out in various regulations which have been subject to frequent amendment and renewal between the commencement of the Act and the present time. Only the most recent versions of the regulations and schemes are listed below.

This Act implements the 1961 'International Convention for the Protection of New Varieties of Plants'. A revision of this Convention was agreed in 1991, the UK having been a signatory both to this and the original Convention (UPOV, 1991); amending legislation will be required but may not emerge until 1994 or later, as the EC is also introducing a 'Regulation' based on the text of the convention. The amendments do not materially alter those parts of the convention relevant to forest trees.

Plant Varieties Act, 1983 (1983, c.17)

This is a short Act; it extends the period of plant breeders' rights by 5 years, and adds into the list of varieties protected under the legislation, 'rootstocks of forest and ornamental trees'.

Plant Breeders' Rights Regulations, 1978 (SI 1978/294, amended by SI 1985/1092)

These revoke and re-enact earlier regulations; they set out procedures for applying for a grant of plant breeders' rights and associated licences, selection of varietal names, register of plant varieties; schedules detail quantities of seed and specification for samples submitted with an application.

Fees, controlled by regulation, are required to cover an initial application, and separately subsequently, for testing and for annual renewal of registration.

15.7.3 Schemes

Under the Regulations, 'schemes' may be promulgated in respect of specified groups of plants, listing the species/varieties covered and the duration of rights. Regulations and schemes currently in force relating to plant breeders' rights cover a vast range of agricultural and horticultural varieties. Two are applicable to forestry genera.

Trees, Climbers and Woody Plants Scheme, 1969 (SI 1969/1024, amended by SI 1971/1093 and SI 1985/1091)

This covers broadleaved ornamental trees and shrubs under the Plant Breeders' Rights Regulations, not only as growing plants but may include varieties grown for blooms, foliage or stems.

Willow and poplar are also included under the scheme. The first registrations of willow biomass varieties were made in 1993. No other varieties of either genus, whether timber producing or ornamental, have been registered (Aldhous, 1992).

Conifers and Taxads Scheme, 1969 (SI 1969/1025)

Similarly, this covers all conifers and taxads, including specifically, varieties of *Cupressus, Thuja, Taxus, Tsuga* and other species, for cut foliage. Varieties registered are currently restricted to ornamentals.

15.8 Other legislation

15.8.1 Health and safety

Health and Safety at Work etc. Act, 1974 (HASAWA)

Legislation to ensure the health and safety of employees has its roots in the 19th century and certain provisions remaining in force are of long standing, e.g. the Employment of Women, Young Persons and Children Act, 1920 (1920, c.65), the Factories Act, 1964 (1964, c.34) and more recently, the Health and Safety at Work etc. Act, 1974 (1974, c.37). Of these, the last is the one having most general effect on nursery operations.

The Health and Safety at Work Act, essentially *added* to the earlier legislation. Its major innovation was to extend the scope of health and safety legislation to all persons at work – employers, self-employed and employees, and to the safety of the general public who may be affected by work activities.

Earlier legislation on health or safety has been amended to enable it to be enforced through Health and Safety regulations.

The Control of Substances Hazardous to Health (COSHH) Regulations, 1988 (SI 1988/1657) described in section 15.6 in the context of use of pesticides, derive their authority from HASAWA, 1974.

The Health and Safety Executive Library and Information Services annually issue a list of currently available Health and Safety Commission and Health and Safety Executive leaflets, booklets, etc. Further information is available from: HSE Information Centre, Broad Lane, Sheffield, S3 7HQ.

Access to information on hazardous substances

As from 1 March 1988, manufacturers and suppliers of 'articles' and 'substances' are obliged under an amendment to the HASAWA introduced through the Consumer Protection Act 1987 (1987, c.43),

- to consider reasonably foreseeable risks during handling, maintenance and storage, as well as use,
- to provide safety information to customers,
- also to take account of non-domestic premises other than work-places to which they supply substances.

Manufacturers consequently now supply on request, 'data sheets' for many of, if not all their products affected by this legislation.

The Reporting of Injuries, Diseases and Dangerous Occurrences Regulations, 1985 (SI 1985/2023) (RIDDOR)

Made under HASAWA, these regulations came into force in 1986 (HSE, 1992). Employers, or anyone who is self-employed or in control of work premises must:

- immediately notify (normally by telephone) their local HSE office or local authority environmental health department, if anyone dies or is seriously injured in an accident in connection with their business or there is a dangerous occurrence (e.g. an overturned tractor);
- report to the appropriate authority within 7 days if anyone is off work for more than 3 days as a result of an accident at work, or if a death, serious injury or dangerous occurrence has been notified by phone, or if a doctor has certified a specific occupational disease (HSE, 1992).

Health and Safety (First Aid) Regulations, 1981 (SI 1981/917)

These regulations are now covered by an *Approved code of practice* issued by the Health and Safety Commission (HSC, 1991b). The regulations place a general responsibility on all employers:

- to make 'adequate and appropriate' provision for first aid treatment of accidents or illness occurring at work;
- to notify employees of these arrangements.

Self-employed people must be able to treat minor injuries themselves.

The regulations supersede the Agriculture (First Aid) Regulations, 1957 (SI 1957/940).

Other legislation affecting health and safety in forest nurseries

Agriculture (Power take-off) Regulations, 1957 (SI 1957/1386).

Agriculture (Field Machinery) Regulations, 1962 (SI 1962/1472).

Classification, Packaging and Labelling of Dangerous Substances Regulations, 1984 (SI 1984/1244, amended by SI 1986/1922 & SI 1988/766).

See also HSE Guidance Note PM15 (HSE, 1978) in relation to stacking of pallets such as in plant stores, and HSE booklet HS(R)4 on offices (HSE, 1989).

15.8.2 Consumer protection

While the following notes are set out in general terms, they are directly applicable to nursery stock bought or sold.

Trades Descriptions Act, 1968 (1968, c.29)

This Act prohibits misdescriptions of goods and services in the course of trade. 'Description' includes: quantity, size, fitness for purpose, physical characteristics, testing and the results thereof. The description must not be misleading, nor must it mislead in respect of price. For there to be an offence under the Act, the description must be false to a 'material degree'.

Descriptions or marks made as a requirement of the 1964 Plant Varieties and Seeds Act are excluded. However, regulations such as the Forest Reproductive Material Regulations under the 1964 Act, themselves require sellers or suppliers to provide certificates giving specified information about seed or plants; in so doing, the suppliers give their warranty that the information in such certificates is correct (Plant Varieties and Seeds Act, Section 17 (1), and FRM Regulations).

Supply of goods

- Supply of Goods (Implied Terms) Act, 1973 (1973, c.13)

- Consumer Credit Act, 1974 (1974, c.39)
- Unfair Contract Terms Act, 1977 (1977, c.50)
- Supply of Goods and Services Act, 1982 (1982, c.29)

These Acts include provisions, covering implied terms of trading for a wide range of transactions. For normal retail sales to customers, the implied terms of trade are set out in statutory form; customers cannot be deprived of them by exclusions clauses. These are that goods must:

- correspond with the description
- be of merchantable quality
- be fit for the purpose.

The first of the above requirements is self-explanatory.

The second, however, involves an element of judgement. 'To be of merchantable quality, goods must be as fit for the purpose as it is reasonable to expect, having regard to any description applied to them, the price and all the other relevant circumstances' (DTI, 1988).

A customer has no right to reject goods on grounds of 'not being of merchantable quality' if the defects complained about were brought to his attention before a sale. Also, if a customer examines goods before buying them, this right does not apply to defects that should have been seen during that examination.

The separate right, 'fitness for purpose' covers the situation when a customer says that goods are wanted for a particular purpose, which may not be one for which the goods are usually supplied. If the trader explicitly supplies goods to meet those requirements, they must be reasonably fit for the purpose specified. If the trader is not confident that the goods will meet the customer's particular requirements, he must make it clear that the customer cannot rely on his skill or judgement in this respect.

Where goods were supplied in breach of these implied terms, customers have a right to a refund. They may also be entitled to compensation if they suffer loss because goods failed to meet the implied terms of trade (DTI, 1988).

In England, Wales and Northern Ireland, these terms are implied in every transfer of goods for private use or consumption. In Scotland, they are for most transactions, but there are no statutory implied terms, for example, where the supply is part of a contract for 'work and materials'. Such transactions are, instead, covered by common law.

15.8.3 Employment

Employment protection

The principal statutory relationships between employer and employee, regarding terms and conditions of employment, are laid down in:

- Employment Protection (Consolidation) Act, 1978, as amended by the Employment Act, 1982.
- Employment Protection Act, 1975 as amended by the Employment Protection (Handling of Redundancies) Variation Order, 1979.
- Transfer of Undertakings (Protection of Employment) Regulations, 1981 (SI 1981/1794) as amended by the Transfer of Undertakings (Protection of Employment) (Amendment) Regulations, 1987 (SI 1987/442).
- Wages Act, 1986.

The Department of Employment has published a series of explanatory leaflets on aspects of this legislation, a full list of which can be obtained from any Job Centre.

Contract of employment

Under current legislation, a contract of employment exists as soon as an employee proves his or her acceptance of an employer's terms and conditions of employment by starting work; both employer and employee are bound by the terms offered and agreed. Often, the contract is not written down.

Under the Employment Protection (Consolidation) Act, 1978, within 13 weeks of an employee starting work, the employer should give the employee a written statement containing certain important terms of employment, with an additional note, mainly on disciplinary and grievance procedures.

The statement can be used as important evidence as to the terms and conditions in an unwritten contract.

A written contract of employment will normally refer to *all* the terms that have been agreed (D.Empl., 1987a).

Wages

Most employees have a statutory right to receive individually, from their employers, a written pay statement when or before they are paid their wage or salary including details of deductions for income tax and National Insurance contributions (D.Empl., 1987b; 1988).

Employment protection – self-employed and part-time workers

The provisions of the Employment Protection Act do not cover independent contractors or freelance agents.

Staff working part-time or on short contracts, especially those who have a fixed term contract for less than 3 months but who have actually worked for more than this period, have to have their entitlements under this legislation determined individually.

REFERENCES AND FURTHER READING

ALDHOUS, J.R. (1992). *Plant breeders' rights. A review of their applicability to poplar and willow.* (Unpublished report.)

D.Empl. (1987a). *Written statement of main terms and conditions of employment (under the Employment Protection (Consolidation) Act, 1982).* Booklet 1, Employment Legislation (PL700), 2nd revision. Department of Employment, London.

D.Empl. (1987b). *Itemized pay statements.* Booklet 8, Employment Legislation (PL704). Department of Employment, London.

D.Empl. (1988). *The law on the payment of wages and deductions: a guide to Part 1 of the Wages Act, 1986.* Booklet PL810. Department of Employment, London.

DoE (1991). *Waste management – The duty of care – A code of practice.* Department of the Environment, Scottish Office, Welsh Office. HMSO, London.

DTI (1988). *A trader's guide. Law relating to the supply of goods and services.* Department of Trade and Industry. DTI/PUB 022.

EEC (1966). Council Directive No. 66/404/EEC on the marketing of forest reproductive material. *Official Journal of the European Communities,* C125, 11.7.1966, p.2326.

EEC (1969). Council Directive No. 69/64/EEC, amending Directive No. 66/404/EEC. *Official Journal of the European Communities,* L 48, 26.2.1969, p.12.

EEC (1971). Council Directive No. 71/161/ EEC on external quality standards for forest reproductive material marketed within the community. *Official Journal of the European Communities,* L 87, 17.4.71, p.14.

EEC (1974). Council Directive No. 74/13/EEC, amending Directive No. 71/161/EEC, on the external quality standards for forest reproductive material marketed within the community. *Official Journal of the European Communities,* L 15, 18.1.74, p.12.

EEC (1975). Council Directive No. 75/445/ EEC, amending Directive No. 66/404/EEC on the marketing of forest reproductive materials. *Official Journal of the European Communities,* L 196, 26.7.75, p.14.

EEC (1977). Council Directive No. 77/93/EEC on regulating plant health in relation to potential threats from imported pests and diseases. *Official Journal of the European Communities,* L 26, 31.1.77, p.20–54.

EEC (1992a). Commission Directive 92/90/ EEC of 3 November, 1992 establishing obligations to which producers and importers of plants, plant products .... details for their registration. *Official Journal of the European Communities,* **L344**, 26.11.92, p.38.

EEC (1992b). Commission Directive 92/98/ EEC of November, 1992. Plants, Plant Products .... which must be subject to a Plant Health Inspection .... *Official Journal of the European Communities,* **L352**, 2.12.92, p.1–5.

EEC (1992c). Commission Directive 92/105/ EEC of 3 December, 1992 establishing a degree of standardisation for plant passports .... and detailing procedures for their replacement. *Official Journal of the European Communities,* **L4**, 8.1.93, p.22.

FAULKNER, R. (1987). *Suggested and required changes to the OECD 'Scheme for Control of Forest Reproductive Material in International Trade'.* Paper to IUFRO Working Group WP S2.02.21. Forestry Commission (Northern Research Station), Edinburgh.

FORESTRY COMMISSION (1982). *Organisation for Economic Development and Co-operation (OECD): Scheme for the Control of Forest Reproductive Material Moving in International Trade.* Forestry Commission, Edinburgh.

FORESTRY COMMISSION (1987). *Explanatory booklet (1987); The Forest Reproductive Material Regulations, 1977.* Forestry Commission, Edinburgh.

FORESTRY COMMISSION (1992). *Plant health and the Single Market.* Explanatory Booklet PH7, 2nd edition. Forestry Commission, Edinburgh.

FRM Regs. (1977). *Forest Reproductive Material Regulations, 1977.* Statutory Instrument 1977, No 891, as amended by Statutory Instrument 1977, No 1264. HMSO, London.

GORDON, A.G. (1992). *Seed manual for forest trees.* Forestry Commission Bulletin 83. HMSO, London.

GORDON, A.G. and ROWE, D.C.F. (1982). *Seed manual for ornamental trees and shrubs.* Forestry Commission Bulletin 59. HMSO, London.

HANCE, R.J. and HOLLY, K. (1990). *Weed control handbook.* 8th edtn. Blackwell, Oxford.

HSC (1988). *Control of substances hazardous to health in fumigation operations: COSHH regulations, 1988. Approved code of practice.* COP 30, Health & Safety Commission. HMSO, London.

HSC (1991a). *The safe use of pesticides for non-agricultural purposes: Approved code of practice.* Health & Safety Commission. HMSO, London.

HSC (1991b). *First aid at work. Health and Safety (First-aid) Regulations, 1981, and*

guidance. Approved code of practice. Revised 1991. HMSO, London.

HSC (1993). *Control of substances hazardous to health (General ACoP) .... Approved codes of practice.* COP 29, 4th edtn., Health & Safety Commission. HMSO, London.

HSE (1978). *Safety in the use of timber pallets.* HSE Guidance Note PM15.

HSE (1988). *Storage of approved pesticides – Guidance for farmers and other professional users.* Health & Safety Executive Guidance Note CS 19. HMSO, London.

HSE (1989). *A guide to the Offices, Shops and Railway Premises Act, 1963.* Health and Safety Executive. Health and Safety series booklet HS(R)4. HMSO, London.

HSE (1992). *Reporting under RIDDOR.* Health & Safety Executive Leaflet, HSE 24. HMSO, London.

HSE (1993). *COSHH assessments. A step-by-step guide to assessment and the skills needed for it.* Health & Safety Executive, HSG 97. HMSO, London.

IVENS, G.W. (1994). *The UK pesticide guide 1994.* CAB International & British Crop Protection Council, Farnham, Surrey.

JOBLING, J. (1990). *Poplars for wood production and amenity.* Forestry Commission Bulletin 92. HMSO, London.

MAFF (1994). *Pesticides 1994: Pesticides approved under the Control of Pesticides Regulations, 1986.* Reference Book 500. HMSO, London.

MAFF/HSC (1990). *Pesticides: code of practice for the safe use of pesticides on farms and holdings.* HMSO, London.

OECD (1974). *OECD scheme for the control of forest reproductive material moving in international trade.* OECD Directorate for Agriculture and Food, Paris.

PEACE, T.R. (1962). Populus. In *Pathology of trees and shrubs.* Oxford University Press, Oxford.

PHILLIPS, D.H. and BURDEKIN, D.A. (1992). *Diseases of forest and ornamental trees,* 2nd edtn. Macmillan Press, London.

POTTER, C.J., NIXON, C.J. and GIBBS, J.N. (1990). *The introduction of improved poplar clones from Belgium.* Forestry Commission

Research Information Note 181. Forestry Commission, Edinburgh.

SCOPES, N. and STAPLES, L. (1989). *Pest and disease control handbook,* 3rd edtn. British Crop Protection Council, Bracknell.

UPOV (1991). International convention for the protection of new varieties of plants of December 2, 1961 as revised .... on March 19, 1991. *Plant Varieties Protection Gazette and Newsletter* 63, 9–28. UPOV 438 (E), Geneva.

WILLIAMSON, D.R., MASON, W.L., MORGAN, J.L. and CLAY, D.V. (1993). *Forest nursery herbicides.* Forestry Commission Technical Paper 3. Forestry Commission, Edinburgh.

Appendix I

(a) The Forestry Authority – list of addresses

England

National office
The Forestry Authority
Great Eastern House
Tenison Road
Cambridge
CB1 2DU

Conservancy offices
Cumbria and Lancashire Conservancy
Peil Wyke
Bassenthwaite Lake
Cockermouth
Cumbria
CA13 9YG

East Anglia Conservancy
Santon Downham
Brandon
Suffolk
IP27 0TJ

East Midlands Conservancy
Willingham Road
Market Rasen
Lincolnshire
LN8 3RQ

Greater Yorkshire Conservancy
Wheldrake Lane
Crockey Hill
York
YO1 4SG

Hampshire and West Downs Conservancy
Alice Holt
Wrecclesham
Farnham
Surrey
GU10 4LF

Kent and East Sussex Conservancy
Furnace Lane
Lamberhurst
Tunbridge Wells
Kent
TN3 8LE

Northumberland and Durham Conservancy
Redford
Hamsterley
Bishop Auckland
Co Durham
DL13 3NL

Thames and Chilterns Conservancy
The Old Barn
Upper Wingbury Farm
Wingrave
Aylesbury
Buckinghamshire
HP22 4RF

West Country Conservancy
The Castle
Mamhead
Exeter
Devon
EX6 8HD

West Midlands Conservancy
Rydal House
Colton Road
Rugeley
Staffordshire
WS15 3HF

Wye and Avon Conservancy
Bank House
Bank Street
Coleford
Gloucestershire
GL16 8BA

Scotland

National office
The Forestry Authority
Portcullis House
21 India Street
Glasgow
G2 4PL

Conservancy offices
Dumfries and Galloway Conservancy
134 High Street
Lockerbie
Dumfriesshire
DG11 2BX

Grampian Conservancy
Ordiquhill
Portsoy Road
Huntly
AB54 4SJ

Highland Conservancy
Hill Street
Dingwall
Ross-shire
IV15 9JP

Lothian and Borders Conservancy
North Wheatlands Mill
Wheatlands Road
Galashiels
TD1 2HQ

Perth Conservancy
10 York Place
Perth
PH2 8EP

Strathclyde Conservancy
21 India Street
Glasgow
G2 4PL

Wales

National office
The Forestry Authority
North Road
Aberystwyth
Dyfed
SY23 2EF

Conservancy offices
Mid Wales Conservancy
The Gwalia
Llandrindod Wells
Powys
LD1 6AA

North Wales Conservancy
Clawdd Newydd
Ruthin
Clwyd
LL15 2NL

South Wales Conservancy
Cantref Court
Brecon Road
Abergavenny
Gwent
NP7 7AX

Forest Research Stations

The Forestry Authority
Research Division
Alice Holt Lodge
Wrecclesham
Farnham
Surrey
GU10 4LH

The Forestry Authority
Research Division
Northern Research Station
Roslin
Midlothian
EH25 9SY

(b) Laboratories undertaking soil analysis

England & Wales

ADAS Laboratories
Woodthorne
Wergs Road
Tettenhall
Wolverhampton
Staffs
WV6 8TQ
(Tel: 01902 754190)

Scotland

Macaulay Land Use Research Institute
Craigiebuckler
Aberdeen
AB9 2QJ
(Tel: 01224 318611)

Appendix II

Glossary

Acid equivalent (a.e.)
The amount of active ingredient of a pesticide in a product, expressed in terms of parent acid.

Active ingredient (a.i.)
That part of a pesticide formulation from which its toxicity to pests is obtained.

Approved product
A pesticide which has been approved for use under the Control of Pesticides Regulations, 1986.

Additive
Of a pesticide, a non-toxic material added to a formulation to improve its performance in any way.

Adjuvant
Of a pesticide, a non-toxic material added to a formulation to enhance its toxicity towards pests.

Basic material (under Forest Reproductive Material Regulations)
In relation to forest reproductive material
(a) produced by sexual means, stands of trees and seed orchards;
(b) produced by vegetative means, clones and mixtures of clones.

Bulked family mixtures
Of vegetatively propagated stock, seed or plants of families mixed in specific proportions.

Certificate of provenance
Certificate issued by the authority appointed by national governments, describing the provenance of seed or plants.

Chlorosis, chlorotic
Loss of green colour in plant foliage.

Clone
A population of genetically identical plants produced vegetatively from one original seedling, (and may include parts of plants), or stock so produced.

Clonal orchard
See 'Seed orchard'

Contact
Of pesticide, having effect by coming into direct contact with pest or target species.

Controlled pollination
The artificial or permitted natural transfer of pollen from a known source to a receptive flower, all other pollen being excluded.

Cultivar
Plant variety, resulting from breeding, and/or selection and/or cultivation; conventionally denoted by species name, followed by 'cv' and cultivar name.

Dominant (trees)
The tallest, largest-crowned trees in closed canopy wood land.

Family
For vegetatively propagated stock, the progeny of a single open-pollinated (f) parent or of a single cross between two individuals.

Flushing
The commencement of growth of a plant above ground in the spring; characterised by swelling and bursting of buds.

Formulation (of pesticide)
The process of preparing a pesticide for commercial sale and use either neat or after dilution. The material resulting from the above process.

Types of formulation include:
Emulsifiable concentrate. A concentrated solution of pesticide and an emulsifier in an organic solvent, forming an emulsion when mixed with water.

Granules. A free-flowing dry preparation of pesticide, ready for use. The diameter size range of the granules is often specified.

Liquid. A concentrated solution of pesticide which mixes readily with water.

Suspension concentrate. A stable suspension of a solid pesticide in a fluid, intended for dilution before use.

Wettable powder. Pesticide in a powder so formulated that it will form a suspension when mixed with water.

Forest reproductive material	Seed, cones and parts of plants intended for the production of plants; young plants raised from seed or from parts of plants.
Frit	Of trace elements (required in very small amounts for healthy plant growth), a very finely ground glassy material containing specified proportions of the named elements.
Genetic qualities	Qualities derived from the inherited characteristics of an individual tree. Cf. *'Phenotypic qualities'.*
Genetically improved	Possessing qualities derived from inherited characteristics, which qualities are superior to the average for a population as a whole.
Indigenous	Of a stand of trees, native to the locality.
Native	Not known to have been introduced by human agency.
Nozzle types	Nozzles for liquid pesticide application are described by the spray patterns produced:

Fan. Spray droplets are emitted in a fan shape. Except for *'Even fan'* jets (see below), the quantity of spray from a fan jet is greatest in the centre of the sprayed swathe; such jets should be spaced so that swathes overlap to obtain an even spray distribution.

Even fan. Spray droplets are emitted so that the whole width of the spray swathe is treated at the same rate.

Hollow cone. Spray droplets from a stationary nozzle form a ring pattern. From a moving nozzle, the edges of the treated swathe receive a higher dose than the centre.

Solid cone. Spray droplets are distributed over the whole of the sprayed area, the centre of a treated swathe usually receiving more than the edges.

Anvil flood. Spray droplets are emitted in a wide fan formed by a stream of pesticide striking a smooth surface (the anvil).

Variable. A nozzle in which the distribution of spray can be adjusted from a narrow jet to a wide cone pattern.

Open pollination	Pollination by natural agencies, e.g. wind, insects, and without man's intervention.
Origin	Place in which an indigenous stand of trees is growing, or the place from which a non-indigenous stand was originally introduced.
Ortet	The original plant from which all members of a clone derive.
Persistence	The length of time a pesticide remains active where applied or where it moves to (e.g. into soil or into plant tissues).
Pest	Any unwanted organism. In the context of pesticide usage, includes species which may have deliberately been cultivated but subsequently are to be killed (e.g. greencrop before ploughing in).
Pesticide	A generic term covering herbicides, insecticides, fungicides, etc. The use of 'pesticide' in the restricted sense of 'insecticide' is not recommended.

Phenotypic qualities	Qualities resulting from the response of trees to the local site and environment.
Polycross	Seed from flowers subject to either supplemental or controlled pollination with a pollen mixture of known composition.
Prill	Of fertiliser, granules formed by cooling in a current of air, such that the granules are more or less spherical in shape and of a relatively small range of diameters.
Product	Of a pesticide, a commercially available formulation of a pesticide. The specific uses of the product set out on the product label have to be approved under Control of Pesticides Regulations.
Provenance	The place in which any stand of trees, whether indigenous or non-indigenous, is growing. Seed collected from such stands.
Ramet	An individual member of a clone derived through one or more cycles of vegetative propagation from the original ortet.
Region of provenance	For a species, sub-species or variety, the area or group of areas subject to similar ecological conditions, in which are found stands showing similar phenotypic or genetic characteristics; for a seed orchard, the region of provenance of the material used for the establishment of that seed orchard.
Registered	Seed, or plants raised from seed, from stands or seed orchards registered under the Forest Reproductive Material Regulations.
Reproductive material	See *'Forest reproductive material'*, *'Selected reproductive material'* and *'Tested reproductive material'*.
Residual pesticide	One which remains active in the soil for a period after it has been applied.
Resistant	In respect of pesticide use, plant or pest unaffected or undamaged by exposure to a pesticide applied at the prescribed rate.
Root pruning	The cutting of roots of plants which have been lifted from the ground. See *'Undercutting'*.
Seed orchards	A plantation of selected clones or progenies which is isolated, or laid out to avoid or reduce pollination from outside sources, and managed so as to produce frequent, abundant and easily harvested seed crops.
Selected (reproductive material)	Forest reproductive material (FRM) derived from basic material approved for registration under the FRM Regulations.
Selective	Of pesticides, killing or damaging pests, leaving the crop plant undamaged, or killing certain groups of pests but not others.
Self	Of plant propagation, a plant or family resulting from the pollination of the female flowers with pollen from male flowers on the same parent. Selfed families usually have poor growth compared with families derived from crosses between different parents.
Shatter	Of plants showing deficiency symptoms, formation of a green tuft of foliage at the end of shoots, with an area of bare branches below due to loss of older foliage.
Sheughing	A synonym for heeling in.
Sibs	Offspring of the same parents, but from separate fertilisations. Full sibs have both parents in common; half-sibs have one parent in common. (Abbreviation for sibling, the unabbreviated word virtually never being used in this context.)
Side-cutting	The severance of roots of plants growing in beds or lines by

	passing a vertical blade or disc between rows of plants. See also 'Undercutting'.
Supplemental	The artificial transfer of pollen from a known source to receptive flowers of a known seed parent, without the complete exclusion of all other pollen.
Systemic	Of pesticides, entering the plant and persisting there. While so remaining, may be taken up by pests feeding on or invading the plant.
Undercut plants	Plants which have been subject to undercutting. Where plants have been undercut as a deliberate cultural operation, 'u' may be incorporated in the abbreviated description of the age, e.g. 1u1 for 2-year-old plants which have been undercut in the seedbed; 1+1u1 for 3-year-old plants which were lined out after 1 year and were undercut in the second year in the tansplant lines.
Undercutting	The severance of tap-roots and other roots of plants in seedbeds or lines, by passing a horizontal sharp blade through the soil at a pre-determined depth. See also 'Root pruning' and 'Wrenching'.
Vegetative propagation	Increase in number of plants by rooting cuttings, grafting, budding, micropropagation from tissue culture, etc.
Wrenching	The disturbance of plants in seedbeds or lines, by raising them a few centimetres and allowing them to drop back. Wrenching may be carried out by horizontal blade drawn by a tractor, or by hand tools, e.g. garden fork.

Appendix III

Common and botanical names of forest trees

Common name	Botanical name	Synonym
Silver fir	**Abies alba** Mill.	**Abies pectinata** D.C.
Grecian fir	Abies cephalonica Loud.	
Colorado white fir	Abies concolor (Gord.) Hildebrand	
Grand fir	Abies grandis Lind.	
Californian red fir	Abies magnifica A. Murray	
Caucasian fir	Abies nordmanniana (Steven) Spach.	
Noble fir	Abies procera Rehder	Abies nobilis Lind.
Sycamore	Acer pseudoplatanus L.	
Norway maple	Acer platanoides L.	
Horse chestnut	Aesculus hippocastanum L.	
Italian alder	Alnus cordifolia Ten	Alnus cordata Desf.
Common alder	Alnus glutinosa Gaertn.	
Grey alder	Alnus incana Moench	
Red alder	Alnus rubra Bong.	Alnus oregona Nuttall
Silver birch	Betula pendula Roth.	Betula verrucosa Ehrh.
White birch	Betula pubescens Ehrh.	
Sweet chestnut	Castanea sativa Mill.	
Lawson cypress	Chamaecyparis lawsoniana (A. Murr.) Parlatore.	
Leyland cypress	×Cupressocyparis leylandii Dallim.	
Monterey cypress	Cupressus macrocarpa Hartw.	
Mediterranean cypress	Cupressus sempervirens L.	
Gums	Eucalyptus spp.	
Beech	**Fagus sylvatica** L.	
Ash	Fraxinus excelsior L.	
European larch	**Larix decidua** Mill.	**Larix europaea** D.C.
Japanese larch	**Larix leptolepis** (Sieb. & Zucc.) Gord.	**Larix kaempferi** Carr.
Hybrid larch	Larix × eurolepis A. Henry	
Southern beech		
Rauli	Nothofagus obliqua Bl.	
Roble	Nothofagus procera Oerst.	Nothofagus nervosa (Phil.) Dim. & Mil.
Norway spruce	**Picea abies** Karst.	**Picea excelsa** Link.
Serbian spruce	Picea omorica Purkyne	
Oriental spruce	Picea orientalis Link.	
Sitka spruce	**Picea sitchensis** (Bong.) Carr.	**Picea menziesii** Carr.
Arrola pine	Pinus cembra L.	

Common name	Botanical name	Synonym
Lodgepole pine	*Pinus contorta* Dougl.	
Aleppo pine	*Pinus halepensis* Mill.	
Bosnian pine	*Pinus leucodermis* Ant.	*Pinus heldreichei* v. *leucodermis* Ant.
Mountain pine	*Pinus mugo* v. *uncinata* Ramond	
Austrian and Corsican pine	*Pinus nigra* Arn.	***Pinus laricio*** Poir.
Monterey pine	*Pinus radiata* D. Don	*Pinus insignis* Dougl.
Maritime pine	*Pinus pinaster* Aiton	*Pinus maritima* Poiret
Stone or umbrella pine	*Pinus pinea* L.	
Weymouth pine	***Pinus strobus*** L.	
Scots pine	***Pinus sylvestris*** L.	
Poplar varieties	***Populus*** cvs (See Table 15.1).	
Wild cherry, gean	*Prunus avium* L.	
Bird cherry	*Prunus padus* L.	
Douglas fir	***Pseudotsuga taxifolia*** (Lamb.) Britt.	***Pseudotsuga douglasii*** Carr.
		Pseudotsuga menziesii (Mirb.) Franco.
Red oak	***Quercus borealis*** Michx.	***Quercus rubra*** Du Roi
Turkey oak	*Quercus cerris* L.	
Pedunculate oak	***Quercus pedunculata*** Ehrh.	***Quercus robur*** L.
Sessile oak	***Quercus sessiliflora*** Sal.	***Quercus petraea*** Liebl.
Western red cedar	*Thuja plicata* D. Don	
Small-leaved lime	*Tilia cordata* Mill.	*Tilia parvifolia* Ehrh.
Common lime	*Tilia* × *europea* L.	*Tilia vulgaris* Hayne
Broad-leaved lime	*Tilia platyphyllos* Scop.	*Tilia grandifolia* Ehrh.
Western hemlock	*Tsuga heterophylla* (Raf.) Sargent	
Wych elm	*Ulmus glabra* Huds.	

Species ***shown in bold italic*** are included in the Forest Reproductive Material Regulations.

Appendix IV

EEC Standards for nursery stock

Standards are set for stock to be described as of 'EEC Standard', both in respect of 'parts of plants' i.e. setts and cuttings, and rooted plants.

These standards are reproduced in schedules 5 and 6 of the Forest Reproductive Material (Amendment) Regulations, 1977 (SI 1977/1264).

Conditions which parts of plants must satisfy

1. Lots shall include at least 95% of parts of plants of fair marketable quality.

2. Fair marketable quality shall be determined by reference to the criteria relating to general characteristics, health and, where appropriate, size, set out in the two following paragraphs.

3. *Populus* species:
   (1) General characteristics and health
   Parts of plants shall not be considered to be of fair marketable quality if:
   (*a*) the wood is unripe;
   (*b*) the wood is more than two seasons old;
   (*c*) they have abnormalities of form, such as forking, branching or excessive bending;
   (*d*) they have less than two well-formed buds;
   (*e*) they have not been severed with a clean cut;
   (*f*) they are partly or totally dried out, injured or have the bark detached from the wood;
   (*g*) they are affected by necroses or damage caused by harmful organisms;
   (*h*) they have any other defects which reduce their value for reproductive purposes;
   except that paragraphs (*a*), (*b*), (*c*) and (*d*) shall not apply to root cuttings and soft wood cuttings.
   (2) Minimum dimensions of parts of the plants of the *Aigeiros* section, other than root cuttings and soft wood cuttings:
   (*a*) – minimum length: 20 cm;
   (*b*) – minimum top diameter:
   8 mm for those described as Class 1/EEC
   10 mm for those described as Class 2/EEC.

4. Forest species other than *Populus:*
   General characteristics and health
   Part of plants shall not be considered to be of fair marketable quality if:
   (*a*) they have abnormalities of form or insufficient vigour;
   (*b*) they have not been severed by a clean cut;
   (*c*) their age or size makes them unsuitable for propagation purposes;
   (*d*) they are partially or totally dried out or show injury other than wounds incurred in the taking of cuttings;
   (*e*) they are affected by necroses or are damaged by harmful organisms;
   (*f*) they have any other defects which reduce their value for reproductive purposes.

   NOTE: All these criteria shall be considered in relation to the species or clones in question.

Conditions which young plants must satisfy

1. Lots shall include at least 95% of young plants of fair marketable quality.

2. Fair marketable quality shall be determined by reference to the criteria relating to general characteristics, health, age and size, set out in paragraphs 3 and 4 below.

3. General characteristics and health.

   An asterisk in the following table shows for each genus and species in question the defects which prevent young plants from being classified as of fair marketable quality. All these criteria shall be considered in relation to the species or clone in question and to the suitability of the reproductive material for forestry purposes.

Defects which prevent young plants from being classed as of fair marketable quality	Abies alba, Picea	Larix	Pinus	Pseudotsuga taxifolia	Fagus sylvatica, Quercus	Populus sp.
(a) young plants with unhealed wounds						
– except cutting wounds where excess leaders have been removed	*	*	*	*	*	*
– except other such wounds incurred in the taking of cuttings	*	*	*	*		*
– except branch wounds	*	*	*	*	*	*
(b) young plants partially or totally dried out	*	*	*	*	*	*
(c) stem showing considerable bending	*			*		*
(d) multiple stem	*	*	*	*	*	*
(e) stem with several leaders	*	*	*			*
(f) stem and branches incompletely ripened	*(1)		*(1)			*(2)
(g) stem without a healthy terminal bud...	*(1)	*(1)	*(1)	*(1)		
(h) branching either absent or clearly insufficient	*			*		
(i) youngest needles so seriously damaged as to endanger the survival of the plant	*		*	*		
(k) damaged root collar (4)	*	*	*	*	*	*(3)
(l) main roots seriously entwined or twisted (4)	*	*	*	*	*	
(m) secondary roots either absent or severely cut	*	*	*	*	*(5)	
(n) young plants showing serious damage caused by harmful organisms	*	*	*	*	*	*
(o) young plants showng signs of heating, fermentation or mould following storage in the nursery	*	*	*	*	*	*

(1) Except where the young plants were taken from the nursery during the first growing season.
(2) Not applicable to clones of *Populus deltoides angulata*.
(3) Not applicable to *Populus* plants butt trimmed in the nursery.
(4) Not applicable to sets.
(5) Not applicable to *Quercus borealis*.

4. Age and size

A. *Species other than Populus*

   (*a*) Criteria of age and size of young plants shall not apply to young plants which have not been transplanted.

   (*b*) Minimum standards for age and size are listed in the table below:

	Normal young plants			Stocky young plants		
	Maximum age [1] (years)	Height [2] (cm)	Minimum diameter of root collar (mm)	Maximum age [1] (years)	Height [2] (cm)	Minimum diameter of root collar (mm)
Abies alba	4	10–15	4	4	10–15	4
	5	15–25	5	4	15–20	5
	5	25–35	5	5	20–25	6
	5	35–45	6	5	25–35	7
	5	45–60	8	5	35–40	8
	–	60 and over	10	–	40 and over	10
Larix	2	20–35	4			
	3	35–50	5			
	4	50–65	6			

Species	Normal young plants			Stocky young plants		
	Maximum age [1] (years)	Height [2] (cm)	Minimum diameter of root collar (mm)	Maximum age [1] (years)	Height [2] (cm)	Minimum diameter of root collar (mm)
	4	65–80	7			
	5	80–90	8			
	5	90 and over	10			
Picea abies	3	15–25	4	4	15–20	4
	4	25–40	5	5	20–30	5
	5	40–55	6	5	30–40	6
	5	55–65	7	5	40–50	8
	5	65–80	9	5	50–60	9
	–	80 and over	10	–	60 and over	10
Picea sitchensis	3	20–30	4			
	4	30–50	5			
	4	50–65	6			
	5	65–75	8			
	5	75–85	9			
	–	85 and over	10			
Pinus sylvestris	2	6–15	3	2	6–10	3
	3	15–25	4	3	10–20	4
	3	25–35	5	3	20–30	5
	3	35–45	6	3	30–40	6
	4	45–55	7	4	40–50	7
				–	50 and over	8
Pinus nigra (forma *austriaca*)	2	6–15	3	2	6–10	3
	3	15–25	4	3	10–20	4
	4	25–35	5	4	20–30	5
	4	35–45	6	4	30–40	6
	4	45–55	7	4	40–50	7
				–	50 and over	8
Pinus nigra (other than forma *austriaca*)	2	5–10	3	3	10–15	4
	3	10–20	4	4	15–30	5
	3	20–30	5	4	30–40	6
	4	30–40	6	4	40–50	7
	4	40–50	7	4	50 and over	8
	–	50 and over	8	–		
Pinus strobus	2	6–10	3			
	3	10–20	4			
	4	20–30	5			
	4	30–40	6			
	5	40–50	7			
	5	50–60	8			
	5	60 and over	10			
Pseudotsuga taxifolia	2	20–25	3	3	20–25	4
	3	25–30	4	4	25–35	5
	3	30–40	5	4	35–40	6
	4	40–50	6	4	40–45	6
	4	50–60	7	4	45–55	7

	Normal young plants			Stocky young plants		
	Maximum age [1] (years)	Height [2] (cm)	Minimum diameter of root collar (mm)	Maximum age [1] (years)	Height [2] (cm)	Minimum diameter of root collar (mm)
	4	60–70	8	4	55–65	8
	4	70–80	9	4	65–70	9
	4	80–100	12	–	70 and over	12
	–	100 and over	14			
Fagus sylvatica, Quercus	2	15–25	4			
	3	25–40	5			
	4	40–55	6			
	4	55–70	7			
	5	70–85	9			
	–	85 and over	11			

Notes:

[1] Age: Age is expressed in complete years. Each growing season or part thereof shall count as a complete year. The growing season shall be considered as having begun:
- in the case of plants with a terminal shoot not yet containing a dormant terminal bud, when this shoot is not less than one quarter of the length of the previous year's shoot.
- in the case of young plants with a shorter terminal shoot, when this shoot contains a dormant bud.

[2] Height: Height shall be measured to within plus or minus 1 cm in the case of young plants not exceeding 30 cm in height, and to within plus or minus 2.5 cm in the case of young plants exceeding 30 cm in height.

B. *Populus*

(*a*) Age of young plants.

The maximum age shall be four years for the stem and, where appropriate, five years for the root.

(b) Size standards shall apply only to *Populus* plants of the *Aigeiros* section, and shall be as set out in the following table:

Age	Point of diameter measurement	EEC Classification Number	Diameter (mm)	Height (m)	
				minimum	maximum
0 + 1	0.50 m	N1a	6 to 8	1.00	1.50
		N1b	more than 8 but not more than 10	1.00	1.75
		N1c	more than 10 but not more than 12	1.00	2.00
		N1d	more than 12 but not more than 15	1.00	2.25
		N1e	more than 15 but not more than 20	1.00	2.50
		N1f	20	1.00	–
more than 1 year	1 m	N2	more than 8 but not more than 10	1.75	2.50
		N3	more than 10 but not more than 15	1.75	3.00
		N4	more than 15 but not more than 20	1.75	3.50
		N5	more than 20 but not more than 25	2.25	4.00
		N6	more than 25 but not more than 30	2.25	4.75
		N7	more than 30 but not more than 40	2.75	5.75
		N8	more than 40 but not more than 50	2.75	6.75
		N9	50	4.00	–

Appendix V

Conversion factors

Length

1 centimetre	= 0.3937 inches
1 foot	= 0.3048 metres
1 inch	= 2.540 centimetres
1 metre	= 3.281 feet
	= 1.094 yards
1 yard	= 0.9144 metres

Area

1 acre (4840 sq. yards)	= 0.4047 hectares
1 hectare	= 2.471 acres
1 square foot	= 0.0929 sq. metres
1 square metre	= 10.76 sq. feet
	= 1.196 sq. yards
1 square yard	= 0.8361 sq. metres

Weight

1 gram	= 0.03527 ounces
1 hundredweight (cwt)	= 50.80 kilograms
1 kilogram	= 2.205 lb
1 ounce	= 28.35 grams
1 pound (lb)	= 0.4536 kg
1 ton (long) (2240 lbs)	= 1.016 metric tonnes
1 metric tonne	= 0.9842 (long) tons

Volume

1 litre	= 0.2200 gallons
1 gallon (Imperial)	= 4.546 litres

Weight per unit area

1 cwt per acre	= 125.5 kg per hectare
1 kg per hectare	= 0.8922 lb per acre
1 pound (lb) per acre	= 1.121 kg per hectare
1 metric tonne per hectare	= 0.3983 tons per acre
	= 7.966 cwt per acre
1 ton (long) per acre	= 2.511 metric tonnes per hectare

Volume per unit area

1 gallon per acre	= 11.23 litres per hectare
1 litre per hectare	= 0.08902 gallons per acre

Index